THE BISHOP'S GRAMMAR

The Bishop's Grammar

*Robert Lowth and the rise of
prescriptivism in English*

INGRID TIEKEN-BOON VAN OSTADE

OXFORD
UNIVERSITY PRESS

OXFORD

UNIVERSITY PRESS

Great Clarendon Street, Oxford OX2 6DP

Oxford University Press is a department of the University of Oxford.
It furthers the University's objective of excellence in research, scholarship,
and education by publishing worldwide in

Oxford New York

Auckland Cape Town Dar es Salaam Hong Kong Karachi
Kuala Lumpur Madrid Melbourne Mexico City Nairobi
New Delhi Shanghai Taipei Toronto

With offices in

Argentina Austria Brazil Chile Czech Republic France Greece
Guatemala Hungary Italy Japan Poland Portugal Singapore
South Korea Switzerland Thailand Turkey Ukraine Vietnam

Oxford is a registered trade mark of Oxford University Press
in the UK and in certain other countries

Published in the United States
by Oxford University Press Inc., New York

British Library Cataloguing in Publication Data

Data available

Library of Congress Cataloging in Publication Data

Library of Congress Control Number: 2010935048

Typeset by SPI Publisher Services, Pondicherry, India
Printed in Great Britain
on acid-free paper by
MPG Books Group, Bodmin and King's Lynn

ISBN 978–0–19–957927–3

1 3 5 7 9 10 8 6 4 2

Contents

Abbreviations

ECCO   Eighteenth Century Collections Online
ODNB   *Oxford Dictionary of National Biography*
OED   *Oxford English Dictionary*
PDE   Present-day English

LIST OF FIGURES

List of Tables

Acknowledgements

Robert Lowth and his grammar have been of interest to me throughout my academic life. I first became acquainted with the *Short Introduction to English Grammar* (1762) when, for my master's thesis supervised by Noel Osselton, I searched the Topical Glossary of S. A. Leonard's *Doctrine of Correctness* (1929). Intrigued by the topic 'Double negatives', I tried to find the grammar which Leonard had marked with a double asterisk to indicate that it 'possibly influenced a change in usage'. At the time, the library of the University of Leiden had just acquired R. C. Alston's microfiche series *English Linguistics 1500–1800*, which, uniquely within English linguistic historiography, allowed for a systematic analysis of a large collection of first editions of eighteenth-century grammars and other works. Lowth's grammar, however, did not deal with double negation, and this remained a puzzle until I discovered that the library possessed a copy of the grammar's second edition, which did discuss double negation. It was not until the University Library acquired the database Eighteenth Century Collections Online (ECCO) that it became possible to study systematically any further changes made by Lowth to later editions and reprints of his grammar, or to analyse the impact of this important and highly authoritative grammar on later grammar writers. Having access to ECCO thus allowed for a similarly revolutionary change in research as Alston's microfiche series: ECCO enables researchers to ask questions of a scope undreamt of before and to find answers of incredible detail and degree of information – not to mention the retrieval speed. The acquisition of ECCO was made possible with the help of my VICI research project 'The Codifiers and the English Language: Tracing the Norms of Standard English', which was funded by NWO, the Netherlands Organisation for Scientific Research. This project started in July 2005 and it ran until the year of the three hundredth anniversary of Lowth's birth, 2010. The present book is one of the results of the Codifiers project.

My interest in Lowth's language dates from the time when I discovered that Robert Dodsley had published the grammar. Having been advised by my colleague Paul Hoftijzer to read Tierney's edition of Dodsley's correspondence for information on eighteenth-century book production, I was surprised to discover Lowth's letters to Dodsley, as many as seventeen of them, as well as the only letter by Dodsley to Lowth that has come down to us. Reading the letters showed that Dodsley had had an important hand in the publication process of the grammar: he seemed at first to have been the instigator of the grammar, as in the case of Dr Johnson's dictionary. He had caused a draft version of the grammar to be read by another author of his, William Melmoth, whose comments were included in the final version of the grammar. My subsequent discovery of more letters by Lowth, addressed to his friend and fellow scholar James Merrick, showed, however, that the grammar had originally been written by Lowth for his son Thomas Henry. This confirmed the suggestion for the grammar's origin made by Ian Michael in his entry on Lowth in the *Lexicon Grammaticorum* (Stammerjohann 1996), though Michael informed me that he had never been able to find any evidence for this. How could I have doubted him?

Meanwhile, I began to reconstruct Lowth's social network on the basis of his letters. Reading them had already shown the importance of viewing the writing and publication history of such an important – but today generally misinterpreted – work as Lowth's English grammar within its own context, but the letters also demonstrated that Lowth's spelling and grammar was far from uniform, variation in usage depending on who his letter was addressed to. I first reported on this at the 11th International Conference on English Historical Linguistics in Santiago de Compostela in 2000. Later work, notably Beal (2003), showed that such an approach yielded equally fruitful results when applied to eighteenth-century lexico-graphers, and so does the work carried out within the Codifiers project by Lyda Fens-de Zeeuw, Karlijn Navest, and Robin Straaijer.

The present book reflects my work on Lowth, his grammar, and his language since I first began to collect his letters about ten years ago, but in particular that which I carried out subsequently within the Codifiers project. Enjoying, in this project, large amounts of research time is what was needed to undertake the present study. In particular I was able to place my research on Lowth into the wider perspective of the standardization process, a topic I have long been interested in as well. Lowth's grammar plays a pivotal role in the final stages of this process, particularly in the change from codification to the prescription stage. This helps explain the peculiar nature of the proscriptive footnotes in Lowth's grammar in relation to the rest of the work, as well as the phenomenon of his linguistic strictures as anticipating the formation of what developed into a canon of prescriptivism. The usage guide, a well-known example of which is Fowler's *Modern English Usage* (1926), is a typical product of the prescription stage, but it hails back to the critical approach Lowth adopted in these footnotes, where he illustrated grammatical mistakes by authors of the highest reputation. It also helps explain how and why Lowth acquired negative prestige in the eyes of modern linguists.

At the start of the Codifiers project, in July 2005, I was contacted by Anthony Lowth, the great-great-great-great-grandson (if my calculations are correct) of the Bishop. Reconstructing his family history, Anthony was curious about my research on his ancestor. Since then, we have exchanged information about Robert Lowth's life and that of his family, and I'm extremely grateful to Anthony for his interest in my work, the findings he generously shared with me, and his comments on various chapters. Anthony's parents Mark and Gillian kindly invited me to a Sunday lunch in their home, supervised by Robert Lowth's life-sized portrait. This took me one generation further back in the direction of the object of my research.

There are many other people who, in one way or another, encouraged me in my research. First and foremost there is Carol Percy, who herself has published on Lowth's grammar. Her encouragement during my studies on Lowth has been extremely valuable, and I am very grateful for her readiness to provide me with information from her database of eighteenth-century reviews as well as from the wonderful store of knowledge in her head. Then there are the members of the Codifiers project, in particular Anita Auer, Lyda Fens-de Zeeuw, Froukje Henstra, Karlijn Navest, and Robin Straaijer, but also Anni Sairio, who all contributed to the continuing development of my insights into Lowth and his grammar. It has been an unusual and extremely fruitful experience to have so many people in my immediate context with whom I could exchange ideas. The project assistants, Marjolein Meindersma, Patricia Chaudron, and Matthijs Smits, have had to carry out many a chore for the preparation of this book: I am grateful for their labours as well.

One of the features of the Codifiers project was to have workshops related to our particular topic of research. There have been several of them, but the one that was most special was the very first, called 'Grammars, grammarians and grammar writing', held on 9 December 2005. It was also attended by various guest speakers: Astrid Buschmann-Göbels, Victorina González-Díaz, Jane Hodson, Richard Watts, and Nuria Yáñez-Bouza. Supplemented by papers from Randy Bax, Karen Cajka, Don Chapman, Carol Percy, and María Rodríguez-Gil, it led to the first major publication of the Codifiers project, *Grammars, Grammarians and Grammar Writing in Eighteenth-Century England*, published in 2008. It is, I believe, currently the most comprehensive account of the subject, and it has led to further important developments in the field, such as the database of eighteenth-century English grammars prepared by María Rodríguez-Gil and Nuria Yáñez-Bouza.

For the present book, I have relied on large amounts of manuscript material, letters but also other documents. Many archivists and librarians have been helpful to me in providing access to this material, sometimes even supplying me with free copies or documents the existence of which I wasn't aware of. Before having a budget for doing this kind of research, as in the Codifiers project, collecting eighteenth-century letters was a very expensive hobby. I should therefore like to express my acknowledgements to Tricia Buckingham and Clare Brown (Bodleian Library), Simon Coleman, Jaap Haarskamp, and Joe Maldonado (British Library), Rachel Cosgrave and Sarah Wickham (Lambeth Palace Library), Caroline Dalton (New College, Oxford), Geoffrey Day (Fellows' Library, Winchester College), Suzanne Foster (Winchester College Archives), Steven Hobbs (Wiltshire and Swindon Archives), Naomi van Loo (New College Library, Oxford), Lucy McCan (archivist, Bodleian Library of Commonwealth and African Studies), Andrew Peppitt (Chatsworth House), Miranda Poliakoff (Fulham Palace), and Sandra Stelts (Pennsylvania State University Library). Mirthe Luteijn did research on the life of Lowth's wife Mary Jackson for her master's thesis, while Carlene Tromp transcribed Dean Cheyney's Will for her bachelor's thesis. Thanks to Chris Heesakkers for the translations of the Latin epitaph on Molly's grave and the inscription in the Bible commemorating Thomas Henry's death. In addition, I'd like to thank various colleagues abroad and at home for their interest and advice on many different matters: Nadine Akkerman, Charlotte Brewer, Trinidad Guzmán-González, Kari Haugland, David Reibel, and Eunice Smith. To Noel Osselton I owe thanks, among very many other things, for presenting me with his spare copy of Alston's bibliography, without which much of my work on Lowth would have been impossible. My book proposal, when submitted to Oxford University Press, was met with enthusiasm, and I'd like to thank in particular John Davey for his encouragement throughout the writing process as well as the referees themselves, Geoffrey Pullum, David Cram, and a third anonymous one. Their comments for improvement have been extremely helpful. Adrian Stenton tirelessly checked—and corrected—all internal references in the book, substituted all my -*ise*'s into -*ize*'s, and saved me from making several foolish mistakes, for which I am truly grateful; thanks also to Lesley Rhodes for carefully proofreading the text and to Elmandi du Toit for seeing the book through its final stages. Finally, after many years of living with an eighteenth-century grammarian who later became a bishop, my warmest thanks and acknowledgements for having put up with Lowth for so long go to the three real men in my life, my husband Herman and my sons Christiaan and Casper. It is to them that I dedicate this book.

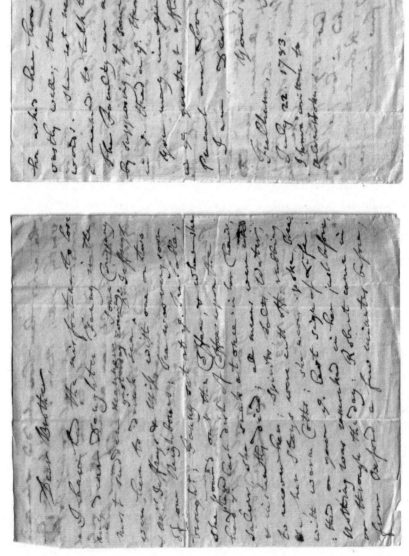

LETTER BY ROBERT LOWTH TO HIS BROTHER WILLIAM, ANNOUNCING THE DEATH OF HIS DAUGHTER FRANCES.
REPRODUCED WITH THE PERMISSION OF THE LOWTH FAMILY.

1

PREJUDICE AND MISCONCEPTIONS

1.1 THE GRAMMAR AND ITS STATUS

TO the majority of those who are familiar with his name, Robert Lowth (1710–87) has the status of an icon of prescriptivism. This is how he is depicted to the public at large, as in Bill Bryson's book *Mother Tongue* (1990), Melvyn Bragg's *The Adventure of English* (2003), and David Crystal's *Encyclopedia of the English Language* (1995). He owes this dubious reputation to the publication of *A Short Introduction to English Grammar* in 1762. This grammar was frequently reprinted during Lowth's own lifetime and well beyond, and it was pirated, pilfered, and plagiarized. It was, moreover, the first English grammar that was marketed in a way that reminds us of modern publishing practices, and this resulted in what was then an unprecedented numbers of copies printed – for an English grammar, that is. Lowth's name consequently acquired almost mythical status, as the bishop who single-handedly reduced the English language to rule, and to whom we still owe many linguistic strictures, which are generally experienced as unnecessarily constraining. This is also how he is viewed by modern linguists, who believe that any approach to language should have an empirical basis, though this is at odds with the normative purpose of Lowth's grammar. A plea for a re-evaluation of Lowth's grammar had already been made by Geoffrey Pullum in 1974, though it seems to have largely gone unnoticed, possibly due to a lack of interest in its subject.

It is widely assumed that Lowth wrote his grammar as Bishop of London, and that this influenced both his linguistic choices for the grammar and its popularity. Having been made Bishop of Oxford in 1766, he didn't obtain the

London post until 1777, but the misconception is due to the fact that the *Oxford Dictionary of National Biography* (*ODNB*) characterizes people by their position at the end of their lives. One example of the misconception out of very many may be found in a section called 'The makers of 18th-century English' in Görlach's *Eighteenth-Century English* (2001), which reads:

> Most important, perhaps, is the prescriptive tradition in grammars and diction-aries. Among these the works of **Bishop Lowth (1762)** and Samuel Johnson (1755) represent highlights in a trend that was to last well into the 19th century and which provided clear guidance to linguistic right and wrong for the increasing number of Britons who wanted to write correct English (2001: 37; here, as throughout, emphasis added in bold type).

Lowth's achievements are placed in a very different light when it is realized that his grammar was already popular well before he obtained his first major post within the Church of England as Bishop of Oxford and that the popularity of the grammar was due to a carefully planned publisher's campaign rather than to his own high status in the church, the latter suggested by Jean Aitchison in her popular book *Language Change, Progress or Decay?* (1981).

Lowth based his grammar on linguistic errors committed by what were then considered to be the best authors. Such an approach to English grammar had never been previously attempted, and it was the cause of the grammar's immediate popularity among the general public. As for subsequent writings on grammar, the *Short Introduction*, according to Percy (2008: 126), soon developed into a standard by which new grammars were measured if they were to be considered successful. But the approach taken by Lowth at the same time came to be the reason for the grammar's negative perception by present-day linguists. It is the wagging finger of the prescriptivist that readers identify in the grammar – though primarily in the footnotes to the section on syntax only – that is, Hussey (1995: 154) argues, the cause of considerable irritation today. Not so, however, in his own time. It is usually overlooked that the grammar served an important function for its readers who, in their desire to climb the social ladder at a time when the early effects of the Industrial Revolution were making themselves felt, needed guidance as to the norm of linguistic correctness – 'polite' usage – that accompanied the new status they aspired to. Lowth's grammar had not originally been written for this purpose, but this was the function it came to have in the eyes of the general public.

Due to its normative nature, Lowth's grammar also provided a basis for what subsequently developed into a canon of prescriptivism – a collection of usage problems identified by normative grammarians in their attempts to codify the English language. An early overview of these may be found in the appendix to S. A. Leonard's *Doctrine of Correctness* (1929; see also Vorlat 1996). Often, the origin of these strictures is attributed to Lowth, while in actual fact he adopted them from other sources, such as the works of Dryden or James Harris's *Hermes* (1751). Because Lowth's grammar was enormously influential, many of his strictures were adopted – and adapted – by his successors in the field, particularly Lindley Murray (1745–1826) (Vorlat 1959). Murray's grammar, first published in 1795, was phenomenally successful, with nearly two million copies printed during the nineteenth century (Tieken-Boon van Ostade 1996a: 9), and it is through this grammar that many of Lowth's strictures gained widespread currency, thus shaping the popular notion, even today, of what Standard English entails. For all that, it is Lowth who is generally blamed for having first formulated the rule against preposition stranding, for causing the disappearance from Standard English of the double negative, and for inventing the rule against the split infinitive. This last stricture was in fact first formulated only in the course of the nineteenth century, but the attribution to Lowth is due to his iconic status as a prescriptivist.

Close analysis of Lowth's strictures shows that they were often not formulated prescriptively but that they represent a descriptive approach to language, in the process of which he would carefully distinguish between different levels of usage, such as 'common conversation' and 'the familiar style in writing' as against 'the solemn and elevated Style' (1762: 127–8). Thus, while normative grammarians such as Lowth are usually blamed for taking a prescriptive rather than a descriptive outlook on language, in reality the situation is much more complicated. In Lowth's case, it is often in the process of being copied by other grammarians that his strictures were made prescriptive, as when Murray added to Lowth's description of double negation that '**it is better to** express an affirmation by a regular affirmative than by two negatives' (1795: 121). One of the aims of my analysis of Lowth's grammar is to show that he owes his status as a prescriptivist to the use that was made of his grammar by others.

Lowth's *Short Introduction* is a product of the codification process which was applied to the English language, whereby the rules of the language were laid down in grammars and dictionaries. This codification was part of the larger standardization process which the language underwent, representing one of its final stages. The next stage, according to James and Lesley Milroy in *Authority in Language* (1991: 27), is the prescription stage, when we see the rise of the usage guide as a new type of text to assist readers in search of a model of linguistic correctness. In my introduction to *Grammars, Grammarians and Grammar Writing in Eighteenth-Century England* (2008) I argue that this last – unfinished – stage in the standardization process of the English language has its beginning in the course of the second half of the eighteenth century.

The first usage guide, according to Leonard (1929), was Robert Baker's *Reflections on the English Language* (1770), a strange and unique collection of usage problems (Vorlat 2001). Despite Baker's professed ignorance of English grammar writing, his approach is remarkably similar to that of Lowth in his exposure of grammatical errors. Many of the items he deals with had also been treated by Lowth. If, therefore, the publication of Baker's *Reflections* heralds the birth of the usage guide, Lowth's grammar, and particularly its syntax section, represents the usage guide in embryonic form. Lowth's grammar represents the formal beginning of a tradition which reached full maturity with the publication of Fowler's *Modern English Usage*, of which the third edition, edited by R. W. Burchfield, was published in 1996, and which was reissued with an introduction by David Crystal in the Oxford World Classics series in 2009. Many of the usage items dealt with by Lowth in his grammar can still be found in 'Fowler' today: the *Short Introduction* thus represents an early stage in the rise of prescriptivism.

1.2 LOWTH'S REPUTATION TODAY

Lowth is usually cited, often along with Murray, as a representative of the prescriptive tradition in grammar writing. Baugh and Cable (2002: 274), for instance, call him 'a typical representative of the normative and prescriptive school of grammarians', noting that his grammar was so popular that 'at least twenty-two editions appeared during the eighteenth century, and its influence was spread by numerous imitators, including the well-known Lindley Murray'. Though a fifth edition, Baugh and Cable (2002) still largely represents the text of the first edition, published in 1951.

Since then, Alston's bibliography of eighteenth-century grammars (1965) has been published, and this presents a much longer list of editions and reprints of Lowth's grammar. The *Oxford Companion to the English Language* (McArthur 1992) also notes that Lowth's 'name has become synonymous with prescriptive grammar'. His entry opens with the curious comment that Lowth was 'a philologist "more inclined to melancholy than to mirth"'. A philologist he certainly was, and this, as his entry in the *ODNB* confirms, is still primarily his reputation today. In his own day, Lowth became widely known, at home as well as on the Continent, as a result of his other publications, *De Sacra Poesi Hebraeorum Praelectiones* (1753), *The Life of William of Wykeham* (1758), and *Isaiah, A New Translation* (1778). I will argue below that his philological interests served him as inspiration for his grammar and that they gained him his status as an expert on grammar at a time when linguistics was not as yet a discipline on its own. Lowth's characterization as being 'more inclined to melancholy than to mirth', however, is not supported by any evidence from my own research on Lowth and his grammar. It derives from the entry on Lowth in the first edition of the *Dictionary of National Biography*, and it is emblematic of Lowth's treatment generally, and by linguists in particular: much is attributed to him, including normative strictures that were not even an issue during his time, as well as, it seems, details about his character that prove to be unfounded.

Lowth's poor reputation among modern linguists may perhaps be best illustrated by Aitchison's discussion of his grammar in *Language Change, Progress or Decay?* (1981). In this book, Aitchison observes that 'the most notable' eighteenth-century purist

was Robert Lowth, Bishop of London [sic]. A prominent Hebraist and theologian, with fixed and eccentric opinions about language, he wrote *A Short Introduction to English Grammar* (1762) which had a surprising influence, perhaps because of his own high status...His grammar is bespattered with pompous notes in which he deplores the lamentable English of great writers. He set out to put matters right by laying down 'rules', which were often based on currently fashionable or even personal stylistic preferences (1981: 23–4).

This account presents a far from objective description of Lowth and his grammar, as is evident from Aitchison's use of modifiers like 'fixed and eccentric' and 'surprising', of her use of derogatory words like 'bespattered', 'pompous', 'deplores', and 'lamentable', and of her marking of the word 'rules' with quotation marks. Aitchison makes assumptions about

Lowth and his grammar without providing any evidence for them, saying that his grammar was so influential 'perhaps because of his own high status' and, more confidently, that his rules were 'often based on currently fashionable or even personal stylistic preferences'. At the time she wrote this, no studies were available on the relationship between Lowth's grammatical rules and actual usage of the period, nor had his own language ever been the subject of analysis, so that it is unlikely that Aitchison was familiar with his language use, let alone with what his 'personal stylistic preferences' were. In her belief that Lowth wrote his grammar as a bishop, Aitchison even suggests that in doing so he must have been 'divinely inspired':

In brief, Lowth's influence was profound and pernicious because so many of his strictures were based on his own preconceived notions. In retrospect, it is quite astonishing that he should have felt so confident about his prescriptions. Did he believe that, as a bishop, he was divinely inspired? It is also curious that his dogmatic statements were so widely accepted among educated Englishmen. It seems that, as a prominent religious leader, no one questioned his authority (1981: 25).

In writing about Lowth's grammar, Aitchison, and many scholars like her, probably never got much beyond the first line in the *(O)DNB* entry.

Lowth embarked on his grammar in or around the year 1757, when he was still busy making a career for himself in the Church: as a prebendary of Durham and rector of Sedgefield, he was hardly, as Aitchison writes, a 'prominent religious leader'. The grammar was indeed extremely popular immediately upon its publication, but this had nothing to do with Lowth's position in the Church. Far from it: the grammar was in fact very much a publisher's product, having been marketed in ways which today seem remarkably modern. It was published at a time when there was potentially a demand for precisely the kind of approach Lowth had taken in the grammar, and it became popular not because of 'his own high status' but because it happened to be published by a man, Robert Dodsley (1704–64), who had an exceptionally keen eye for the demands of the market (Solomon 1996). In the early days of the Industrial Revolution, there was a steadily growing group of socially ambitious readers in need of instruction as to the correct ways to speak and write: as a grammar, Lowth's *Short Introduction* was simply there at the right time.

Aitchison's discussion of Lowth and his grammar, which remained unchanged in the second and third editions of her book (1991, 2001), is characterized by a lack of interest in the grammar as such and in particular in the man behind it. In this, it is quite typical of the approach generally taken: Aitchison is far from alone in assuming, for instance, that Lowth wrote his grammar in his status as a bishop (cf. Poldauf 1948; Michael 1970; Fitzmaurice 1998, 2000a; Honey 1997: index; and many others). An exception is Percy (1997), who discusses Lowth's approach to language and grammar from the perspective of his being 'a critic of Hebrew poetry' (1997: 129); Lowth had after all published *De Sacra Poesi Hebraeorum Praelectiones* in 1753, well before the grammar came out. This biased treatment of Lowth had already been noted by Pullum in 1974, who wrote that Lowth 'is more mentioned than read by the majority of grammarians today' (1974: 63). Lowth's grammar is rarely studied in any serious detail, and references to it usually serve to show that he caused the disappearance of multiple negation or to illustrate the kind of normative strictures – against preposition stranding or the use of *it is me* – that were drawn up in the course of the eighteenth century as part of the effort to provide a standard of grammatical correctness.

The widespread lack of scholarly interest in Lowth's grammar has led to much prejudice and misunderstanding about his motivations for undertaking to write the grammar, about the reasons for his approach to grammar, and even about the approach itself. Aitchison calls Lowth's rules 'pseudo-rules' on account of their 'artificial and constraining effect' (1981: 27). His rules, she asserts, are prescriptive instead of descriptive, as linguistic rules ought to be. As rules, however, they were nevertheless very real to Lowth's readers, who memorized them in order to be able to use them to the best possible effect. The most famous example of such a reader is William Cobbett (1763–1835), author of *A Grammar of the English Language* (1818), who, according to Aarts (1986: 609), bought a copy of Lowth's grammar in 1784, 'copied the book and learned it by heart'. What is more, in the form in which Lowth's rules were later adopted by Murray in his grammar of 1795, they can be found to have been repeated verbatim in numerous nineteenth-century novels. One example, identified by Sørensen (1984: 238), is the following quotation from Dickens's *Dombey and Son* (1846–8):

1. It then appeared that she had used the word [*party*], not in its legal or business acceptation, when it merely expresses an individual, but as **a noun of multitude, or signifying many** (Chapter 2).

The phrase identifying the grammatical category to which the word *party* belongs was lifted straight from Murray, who in his turn had borrowed the passage from Lowth (though from a second or later edition of the grammar, not the first):

MURRAY

A noun of multitude, or signifying many, may have a verb or pronoun agreeing with it, either of the singular or plural number; yet not without regard to the import of the word, as conveying unity or plurality of idea (1795: 94).

LOWTH

A Noun of Multitude; or signifying many, may have the Verb and Pronoun agreeing with it either in the Singular or Plural Number; yet not without regard to the import of the word, as conveying unity or plurality of idea (2nd edn., 1763: 111–12).

That the quotation is indeed from Murray, not Lowth, is confirmed by the fact that Murray also plays a role in another novel by Dickens, *Nicholas Nickleby* (1838–9; Jones 1983: 34):

Nicholas sighed, and hurried in. Mr Squeers, having bolted the door to keep it shut, ushered him into a small parlour scantily furnished with a few chairs, a yellow map hung against the wall, and a couple of tables; one of which bore some preparations for supper; while, on the other, a tutor's assistant, a **Murray's grammar**, half-a-dozen cards of terms, and a worn letter directed to Wackford Squeers, Esquire, were arranged in picturesque confusion (Chapter 7).

Many other novelists from the period, such as George Eliot, William Makepeace Thackeray, Herman Melville, and James Joyce (Tieken-Boon van Ostade 1996a: 18), must have spent long hours in their youths memorizing Murray's grammar, much of which, as has been shown by Vorlat (1959), had been derived from Lowth. Consequently, it is only through Murray that Lowth's influence in shaping the rules of Standard English much as we know it today came about.

Lowth is depicted by Aitchison as someone who was unaware of what grammar was really about. By modern standards, he would lack all qualifications as a linguist, having obtained his degree as Doctor of Divinity at the University of Oxford in 1754 after lecturing there as Professor of Poetry between 1741 and 1751 (Hepworth 1978). But at a time when English was not part of the school curriculum, and when linguistics as a discipline did not exist, other qualifications should be considered in order to understand his status as a grammarian, and perhaps as a linguist as well. Chapman (2008: 23) proposes a writer's 'education, university degrees, occupation, publications and membership of professional societies' as factors that need to be taken into account when assessing the expertise of an eighteenth-century grammarian. With the exception of the last qualification – Lowth only became a member of the Royal Societies of London and Göttingen in 1765, well after his grammar was first published – he scores extremely well on all of these points, certainly in comparison with someone like Dr Johnson (1709–84), whose main qualifications for writing the famous *Dictionary of the English Language* (1755), according to Chapman, had been 'his learning, ability and "encyclopedic temperament" for excelling at large projects and his need of another such large project' (2008: 27, citing Reddick 1996). Chapman consequently calls Lowth 'a language expert par excellence', and in his own time Lowth carried enough status as a grammarian to be invited to write the preface to the sixth edition of John Wallis's *Grammatica Linguae Anglicanae* (1765; 1st edn., 1653) – an invitation he allegedly refused (Kemp 1972: 72). (Perhaps he did write the preface after all, for the anonymous author shows too thorough a familiarity with Lowth's authorship of the *Short Introduction*, which, as I will discuss in more detail in Chapter 3, was also published anonymously, and his academic and scholarly status at the time for this to be merely a matter of coincidence.) From a present-day perspective the qualifications identified by Chapman would be unthinkable for linguists. But a major qualification for would-be grammarians at the time was a skill in Latin, which would be possessed by anyone who had been trained as a clergyman, as Lowth had been. Many clergymen from the period undertook tutorships to supplement what was frequently a meagre income, and during the eighteenth century many authors of English grammars were clergymen. An example is John Kirkby (c.1705–54), author of *A New English Grammar* (1746), who had briefly been tutor to Edward Gibbon (Tieken-Boon van Ostade 1992). Most eighteenth-century English grammars, including Lowth's, were consequently based on the model of Latin grammars (Michael 1970), a fact which is often cited as one of their major shortcomings (Pullum 1974: 66) – unjustly, for what other model would have been available to them? This was also something Lowth was criticized for by several writers coming after him, such as Noah Webster and John Horne Tooke (Percy 1997: 132). Percy, however, argues that although Lowth did use Latin terminology in the grammar, this 'did not imply that he felt that English should be described in terms of Latin' (1997: 133). As I will argue below, Lowth wrote his grammar for his eldest son, Thomas Henry, as a means of facilitating his learning of Latin by the time he would be old enough to enter grammar school. Familiarity with the appropriate terminology, even when acquired by a study of his mother tongue, would prove a considerable advantage in this.

1.3 NORMATIVE GRAMMARS

Lowth's *Short Introduction* is thus firmly rooted in the Latin tradition; indeed, its title, as Percy (2008: 142) notes, must have been inspired by the Latin grammar that every eighteenth-century schoolboy had been acquainted with: Lily's *Short Introduction to Grammar*. Thus, Lowth's grammar customarily dealt with spelling, morphology, and syntax, though not with prosody as other grammars did (Vorlat 2007: 504); instead, there is a section on punctuation. Furthermore, the division into nine parts of speech – substantive, adjective, pronoun, article, verb (including the participle), adverb, conjunction, preposition, and interjection – is characteristic of Michael's Latin System 10 (Michael 1970: 225). The Latin context in which the grammar was written is also evident from the way in which definitions are phrased. The term 'preposition', for instance, reflects the Latin etymology of the word:

PREPOSITIONS, so called because they are commonly **put before** the words to which they are applied, serve to connect words with one another, and to shew the relation between them (1762: 91).

But Lowth also had an eye for the specific characteristics of English, as well as for differences in usage between speech and writing, and between different levels of style. A good illustration of this is his discussion of the phenomenon now known as 'preposition stranding':

The Preposition is often separated from the Relative which it governs, and joined to the Verb at the end of the Sentence, or of some member of it: as, 'Horace is an author, *whom* I am much delighted *with*.' ... This is an Idiom which our language is strongly inclined to; **it prevails in common conversation, and suits very well with the familiar style in writing**; but the placing of the Preposition before the Relative is more graceful, as well as more perspicuous; and **agrees much better with the solemn and elevated Style** (1762: 127–8).

'An almost exclusive concentration on written language to the exclusion of spoken' is another of the alleged shortcomings of eighteenth-century normative grammars listed by Pullum (1974: 66), but this illustration shows that such criticism is unfounded when Lowth's grammar is looked at more closely.

Another shortcoming discussed by Pullum is that normative grammars are widely believed to have 'a prescriptive, as opposed to descriptive, bias' (1974: 66). I have already referred to this in the light of Aitchison's criticism of Lowth's grammar. Straaijer (2009) notes that Trudgill, in his *Glossary of Sociolinguistics* (2003), goes so far as to equate the terms 'normative' and 'prescriptive', arguing that 'proponents of this point of view believe that norms of "correct" usage should be adhered to' (2003: 107). In reality, however, the situation is not quite as simple as that, and Lowth's grammar, and particularly his treatment of double negation, may serve as a good illustration of this. It is often claimed that double negation disappeared from Standard English grammar due to the influence of the strictures against its use in the normative grammars of the eighteenth century (e.g. van Kemenade 2000: 11; Beal 2004: 88). Baugh and Cable (2002: 279) refer to Lowth in this context, noting that he 'stated the rule that we are now bound by'. Aitchison (1981: 24) does likewise, while earlier Leonard (1929: 286) had marked Lowth as having 'possibly... influenced a change in usage' in this respect. But if we look at the history of the stricture against double negation in eighteenth-century English grammars, we see that Lowth was not the first English grammarian to deal with the phenomenon by a long way. Double negation was first discussed in Greenwood (1711), and subsequently in six other grammars before Lowth took up the subject: Jones (1724), Duncan (1731), Kirkby (1746), Martin (1748), Fisher (2nd edn., 1750), and Gough (1754). What is more, the stricture first appeared only in the second edition of Lowth's grammar, which suggests that one of his readers pointed out an oversight to him with regard to this phenomenon. But as for his alleged influence on usage, my analysis of eighteenth-century usage, as presented in Tieken-Boon van Ostade (1982), shows that double negation was far from common in the language of educated speakers at the time. This is confirmed by Nevalainen and Raumolin-Brunberg (2003: 71–2), who demonstrate on the basis of data obtained from their Corpus of Early English Correspondence that double negation was already in the process of disappearing at the end of the seventeenth century. Beal (2004: 113–14) similarly claims that the disappearance of double comparatives and superlatives was due to the eighteenth-century grammarians, though here, too, according to González-Díaz (2008), the process was already in evidence a century before. The real point of interest is therefore why these strictures played such an important role in normative grammars produced during the eighteenth century.

But before looking into this question, an analysis of Lowth's stricture on double negation shows that it is not phrased as a *prescriptive* rule to begin with (1763: 139–40):

Two Negatives in English destroy one another, or are equivalent to an Affirmative: as,

> 'Nor did they *not* perceive the evil plight
> In which they were, or the fierce pains *not* feel.'
>
> Milton, P.L. i. 335.

In a footnote, Lowth gives two examples from Shakespeare's *Much Ado about Nothing* and one from Chaucer to show that in the past double negation was used differently from his own day:

> 'Give not me counsel,
> Nor let *no* comforter delight mine ear.'
>
> Shakespear, Much ado.
>
> 'She cannot love,
> Nor take *no* shape *nor* project of affection.' Ibid.

Shakespear uses this construction frequently. It is a relique of the antient style abounding with the Negatives, which is now grown wholly obsolete:

> 'And of his port as meke as is a maid,
> He *never* yet *no* villany *ne* said
> In all his life unto *no* manner wight;
> He was a very parfit gentil knight.' Chaucer.

Lowth here merely *describes* the effect of the use of two negatives, following what was by then already a common maxim, that two negatives cancel each other out, noting at the same time, in the footnote, that usage had been different in the past. It is only when Lowth's rule is copied by Murray that the stricture actually becomes prescriptive, by the addition of the advice to avoid the use of two negatives, even if they serve to express a positive statement:

RULE XVI.

Two negatives, in English, destroy one another, or are equivalent to an affirmative; as, 'Nor did they not perceive him;' that is, 'they did perceive him.' 'Never shall I not confess;' that is, 'I shall never avoid confessing;' or, 'I shall always confess.' **But it is better to express an affirmation by a regular affirmative than by two negatives** (1795: 121).

Why double negation should be avoided is not made explicit; however, as a sentence with two negatives that are intended to cancel each other out is usually harder to process than a simple positive one, this might explain the advice against their use. More relevant at the time, though, was that double negation was common in the language of the classes from which the upwardly mobile were aiming to escape, and against which they had to guard themselves if they did not want to run the risk of having themselves and their children associated with the servant class (see Tieken-Boon van Ostade 2008a). This would even apply today, as Standard English is the only variety of English in which double negation no longer occurs (Hughes and Trudgill 2005: 24).

Today, grammars are required to be descriptive and to be based on an empirical analysis of usage (see, for instance, Aitchison 1981: 27). To expect a similar approach to language from English grammarians writing at a time when linguistics was not an academic discipline does little justice to their aims and achievements. In a sense, moreover, even Lowth's grammar has an empirical basis. The grammar in fact consists of two parts, the text proper and the running footnotes, which are particularly elaborate in his section on syntax, called 'Sentences'. Here, we find what Aitchison refers to as the 'pompous notes in which he deplores the lamentable English of great writers' (1981: 23–4). An example of such a footnote is the one following the observation that 'in English [prepositions] always require the Objective Case after them' (Lowth 1762: 127):

'We are still much at a loss, *who* civil power belongs *to*.' Locke. It ought to be *whom*.

But, as I will argue in Chapter 3, Lowth used such examples of grammatical mistakes as a basis for his chapter on syntax. He had collected them, intentionally as it transpired, in a way comparable to that in which modern corpora are set up, for in his preface he wrote:

But perhaps the Notes subjoined in the following pages will furnish a more convincing argument, than any thing that can be said here, both of the truth of the charge of inaccuracy brought against our Language as it subsists in practice, and of the necessity of investigating the Principles of it, and studying it Grammatically, if we would attain to a due degree of skill in it (1762: viii).

In other words, the function of the notes was to illustrate the need for his audience to study grammar systematically, for even the best writers 'for want of some rudiments of this kind have sometimes fallen into mistakes, and been guilty of palpable errors in point of Grammar' (1762: ix). Lowth, moreover, believed that his collection of grammatical errors was to some extent representative of usage generally – an important requirement of corpus linguistics (see, e.g., Biber et al. 1998) – for he wrote in the preface that he had collected his examples 'such as [they] occurred in reading, without any very curious or methodical examination: and they might easily have been much increased in number by any one, who had leisure or phlegm enough to have gone through a regular course of reading with this particular view' (1762: ix). As a collection of illustrations of usage, the notes are not very different from those gathered by Jespersen for his *Modern English Grammar on Historical Principles* (1949–54) or by Visser for his *Historical Syntax of the English Language* (1963–73). These studies are very typical of the kind of approach taken before the days of corpus linguistics.

Lowth's discussion of double negation, in contrast to Murray's adaptation of it, also provides evidence of the fact that, in his case at least, the fourth allegation against the normative grammarians' shortcomings listed by Pullum (1974: 66), 'a tendency to confuse the synchronic and the diachronic and to mistakenly offer historical explanations instead of descriptions of the facts', does not apply. Again, strictly separating the synchronic from the diachronic is an important criterion in modern linguistics, which may be dated back to de Saussure (see, e.g., Lyons 1968: 45). But it is hardly relevant to provide such a strict criterion with hindsight to the eighteenth-century grammarians. Lowth's aim in providing examples from Shakespeare and Chaucer was to show that the use of double negation in the past was quite frequent and that it was a mere 'relique of the antient style abounding with the Negatives, which is now grown wholly obsolete'. His use of an example from Milton to illustrate what was then present-day usage is comparable to what we find in Visser (1963–73, Vol. III, first half: 1649), when he refers, for instance, to Thackeray (1846) and Trollope (1864) for evidence of modern English. An historical approach, moreover, is not unusual, even today, in works that deal with usage. As Burchfield explains in his introduction to Fowler's *Modern English Usage* (1996: xi), 'Judgements based on the distribution of competing constructions or pronunciations are intrinsically fragile and diminished in value if the constructions are not also examined historically'. Fowler's *Modern English Usage*, in its different editions, is nothing if not normative, and there are interesting similarities between Fowler and Lowth in their approach to language.

Inevitably, Lowth's concerns with grammar were different from those of modern linguists. His focus was on *usage* rather than on the *system* of the language – the latter is, again, an important requirement of modern linguistics (cf. Lyons 1968: 51–2) – and he was well aware of this, for he shows in the preface that he knew perfectly well how to distinguish between the two: 'It is not owing then to any peculiar irregularity or difficulty of our Language, that the general practice both of speaking and writing it is chargeable with inaccuracy. It is not the **Language**, but the **practice**, that is in fault' (1762: v–vi). By thus opposing 'Language' (the system) with 'practice' (usage) he indicates that his approach had been the result of deliberate choice. And, he added, those of his readers who might be less interested in usage, and 'who would enter more deeply into this Subject, will find it fully and accurately handled, with the greatest acuteness of investigation, perspicuity of explication, and elegance of method, in a Treatise intitled HERMES, by JAMES HARRIS Esq; the most beautiful and perfect example of Analysis that has been exhibited since the days of *Aristotle*' (1762: xiv–xv). Harris's *Hermes* was a philosophical grammar, which dealt with precisely the kind of questions that were of less interest to a readership consisting of people in need of practical advice on how to acquire a norm of correct usage.

1.4 'CUSTOM' VERSUS 'PROPRIETY'

The same awareness is evident from an exchange of letters between Lowth and James Merrick (1720–69), a friend and fellow scholar, who had asked him to comment upon his translation of the Psalms. The correspondence took place between December 1761 and October 1764, the period when the grammar first came out and when its popularity was already in evidence (a third edition was published in 1764). Lowth had asked Dodsley, his publisher, to send Merrick a presentation copy of the grammar, and pointed out that he hoped to receive comments from his readers that would contribute to an improved version of it. Upon receiving the grammar on 25 February, Merrick must have started to read it at once, for he informed Lowth two months later, on 29 April: 'And the Remarks which You, Sir, have offered to the Public on errors of that kind may greatly contribute to the improvement of our Language in point of accuracy'. (For an overview of the sources of Lowth's correspondence, see Appendix 1.) Merrick here refers to Lowth's criticism of the grammatical errors committed by well-known authors, and his comment suggests that, contrary to the reception of Lowth's grammar today, this was a feature which his readers found particularly appealing.

Lowth's comments on Merrick's translation of the Psalms have survived in the form of a manuscript which consists of more than a hundred sheets (Bodleian Library MS Eng. Lett. C. 573, ff. 5–117). They primarily deal with matters of translation and interpretation, but also with language. While Lowth criticized Merrick for his use of *thou wert* in the indicative, of *thy* instead of *thine* before words beginning with a vowel, of *fly* instead of *flee*, and of *sate* instead of *sitten* as a past participle (occasionally presenting fairly forceful arguments to prove his point), Merrick in turn expressed criticism of certain issues Lowth had raised in his grammar; he had, after all, been invited to do so. One topic he raised relates to the fact that Lowth regarded the adjectival use of *heavenly* 'improper, and not agreeable to the Genius of the English Language' (1762: 125n), while he himself was quite happy to use it. Though the letter in question has not come down to us, Merrick also sent Lowth a number of illustrations of grammatical errors from 'D^r. Birch's Life of Tillotson, 2^d Edition', which had been published in 1753. Unfortunately, Lowth replied, 'I c^d. not meet with y^t. Edition time enough, nor find y^e. place referred to, in y^e. first Edition [1752]. The 2 Editions of y^e. Grammar $^{now\ published}$ have been finished at the Press some months ago; so that y^e. opportunity of Correction is past' (Lowth to Merrick, 25 October 1764). The excuse looks real enough, as Lowth does not seem to have possessed the relevant edition, but I believe that there was possibly a different reason why he decided not to adopt Merrick's additions for his grammar, particularly as this was not the first time Merrick had drawn his attention to Birch's edition. I will return to this in Chapter 3.

Lowth's linguistic criticism of Merrick's translation was not accepted without comment. In fact, a lively discussion ensued between the two men, which primarily revolved around the question of whether 'custom [should] prevail over Propriety' (Merrick to Lowth, 29 April 1762). These opposite perspectives, with Merrick favouring 'custom' or usage and Lowth grammatical 'propriety' or correctness as a decisive principle in matters of disputed usage, represent different approaches in the codification attempts adopted by eighteenth-century grammarians (see Baugh and Cable 2002: 282–5). Azad (1989) deals with this question in detail, showing that, in line with the ideas of Locke as expressed in *An Essay concerning Human Understanding* (1689), 'the best writers' were frequently invoked as providing a standard of correctness. This idea is behind Johnson's decision to use quotations as a basis for his dictionary. Lowth, however, only allowed for 'the authority of y^e. best Writers...in a <u>dead</u> language; not so, in a <u>living</u>', as he explained in a letter to Merrick dated 28 October 1782. His position in the debate helps explain why, as I will argue in Chapter 4, his grammar may be interpreted as a rather fundamental reaction against Johnson's notions with regard to linguistic correctness. From a modern perspective, the different views might be interpreted as reflecting the question of whether in codifying a language a descriptive approach should be taken by letting 'custom' decide on what is to be considered grammatically correct, or a prescriptive and proscriptive one, imposing a norm of linguistic propriety on the user. In this light, as advocating a descriptive approach, Merrick would qualify as the more modern linguist of the two. In actual fact, however, the situation is a little more complicated for, in their debate, Lowth distinguished between dead languages, like Latin, and living ones, like English. It had been his intention to produce a normative grammar of English, and as he had tried to explain to Merrick a few months earlier, he felt determined '**in my capacity of grammarian**...to repell the invasions of y^e. enemy to the utmost of my power, & to give no quarter to any of their straglers that shall fall into my hands. I look upon myself, as in Duty bound to abide by these Principles' (Lowth to Merrick, 4 May 1762).

1.5 THE GRAMMAR IN CONTEXT

Lowth and his grammar have been the subject of much undue criticism, largely due to the fact that his efforts as a grammarian have been seriously underestimated and because his original aims with the grammar were never properly recognized. Lowth tends to be viewed as an authoritarian bishop, whose intention it was to impose a norm – allegedly his private norm – of correctness on the language, and at the same time as an exponent of an approach to language which is unacceptable within the discipline of linguistics. Lowth has been condemned for taking a prescriptive attitude to language, while if his grammar had been viewed in its proper light, as a private attempt at writing a grammar of English for his son Thomas Henry on the basis of a method not previously attempted, but also in the context of the time in which it was written, a more subtle and certainly more accurate picture would have emerged of the achievements of the man and his work. Like Pullum (1974), Azad (1989: 148) has shown that 'Lowth's *Grammar* has been distorted by those attempting to interpret it within a polarized "prescriptive–descriptive" framework', but neither study had much immediate effect.

The focus of my study of Lowth and his grammar is on their own context, that is, the age in which Lowth lived and the purpose for which he originally designed the grammar. By analysing the publication history of the grammar in detail I will be able to show that, once it was accepted for publication, it developed into a publisher's project, in which respect it became very similar to Johnson's dictionary, which had also been published by Dodsley and which it was supposed to complement. The main tools for my analysis will be the large variety of personal documents relating to Lowth that I have been able to lay my hands on: his correspondence, of which I have collected well over three hundred pieces altogether, in letters included: a brief Memoir he wrote towards the end of his life, possibly to serve as a basis for an obituary to be written after his death; two lists of presentation copies for his book *Isaiah* (1778), which provide important information both on his social network membership and on his social aspirations; and his Will, which allows us to estimate the extent of his social success at the end of his life (National Archives, Ref. PROB 11/1160). As the Will also includes a list of books to be disposed of after Lowth's death, it offers insight into what books he read during his lifetime, and which may have provided input for his grammar. Lowth's letters allow us to reconstruct the social networks he belonged to at different stages in his life, but they also provide evidence of his own language use. As they are addressed to many different people, and consequently vary in style accordingly, an analysis of the language of the letters enables us to study Lowth's language as an idiolect, and thus his communicative competence, in as much detail as could be expected. His language is consequently of considerable interest from a sociolinguistic perspective, despite the fact that we are dealing with someone who is no longer alive and whose language use cannot be monitored in order to gain access to his different styles of writing – let alone speech. Lowth proves to have been first and foremost a language user, though obviously a highly educated one, and, like all language users, he was able to vary his style depending on such features as context, topic, and the nature of his relationship with the addressee (cf. Traugott and Romaine 1985). His letters are expected to provide evidence of this at all levels of language (spelling, lexis, grammar), as well as of his social ambitions, which, as will be shown in Chapter 2, were considerable. Comparison with the strictures in his grammar will demonstrate, among other things, that Lowth's own language often differed considerably from that of the norm presented by his grammar, and this will help us identify where he found the norm he advocated.

The most conspicuous feature of Lowth's grammar, now as well as in its own day, are the footnotes in which he deals with the grammatical errors of well-known writers, 'our best Authors' as he called them. Introducing such comments in a grammar of a living language was an important innovation at the time and, as I will demonstrate in Chapter 3, this feature about the grammar particularly appealed to its readers. From the perspective of the grammar, however, they are an anomaly: they do not form part of the grammar proper, and instead of providing additional information on a particular stricture, they usually take the form of quotations from authors offending against the stricture in question and that are subsequently corrected. In other words, they illustrate by negative rather than by positive example. Nothing like it had ever been encountered in an English grammar before. As far as both their content and approach are concerned, however, the notes show considerable similarity with what is found in usage guides or popular collections of grammatical problems published in our day, such as Robert Burchfield's *The Spoken Word* (1981) or John Simon's *Paradigms Lost. Reflections on Literacy and its Decline* (1980). Even Lynne Truss's more recent *Eats, Shoots and Leaves* (2003) is written in the same tradition. Usage guides are a typical feature of the prescription stage in the standardization process of a language, as following upon the codification stage, when grammars and dictionaries are composed to take an inventory of the rules and characteristics of the language. As the first usage guide proper, Robert Baker's *Reflections on the English Language* (1770) enjoyed some popularity during the final decades of the eighteenth century (Vorlat 2001). Baker claims that he was not influenced by any grammar or dictionary in the writing of his book – 'Such as my Work is, it is entirely my own . . . Not being acquainted with any Man of Letters, I have consulted Nobody' (Baker 1770: iv). For all that, there is a surprising similarity between the type of grammatical problems he deals with and the errors discussed by Lowth. What is more, many of the usage problems discussed by Lowth and Baker can still be found in Fowler's *Modern English Usage* (1926) and in books like Simon (1980). In the items these works dealt with, in the approach taken, but also in the way the works and their authors are treated by linguists today, there is a striking similarity. There is, therefore, a direct continuity between the strictures discussed by Lowth in his grammar, and illustrated by negative examples in his footnotes, and the modern usage guide. Lowth's syntactical footnotes can therefore in my view be looked upon as a kind of Fowler *avant-la-lettre*.

This was one of the reasons for the grammar's immense popularity, from the first moment of its publication, and lasting well beyond Lowth's lifetime. In 1784, John Fell paid tribute to Lowth in his *Essay towards an English Grammar* by noting on the subject of the use of the modals *may, might, would, could,* and *should* in the indicative mood that 'it is not probable that another English grammarian should arise, in our times, equally qualified with himself, all things considered, to illustrate and determine the nature and use of these hypothetical verbs' (1784: 26). Analysing its reception in the public press, Percy (2008) discovered not only that Lowth's grammar was very well received, but also that it was spoken highly of in reviews of grammars published after it, especially in reviews of 'less impressive texts'. She consequently argues that the grammar soon came to be seen as a kind of benchmark for subsequent publications, often enough to the disadvantage of such works. As late as 1798, well after Lowth's death, Ellenor Fenn (1743–1813), author of *The Mother's Grammar*, still spoke highly of the grammar, though expressing the need for an introduction to it, in the form of her own *Child's Grammar* (1799), for very young learners (Navest 2008). Even Lowth himself, towards the end of his life, was surprised by the popularity of his grammar, which he originally appears to have treated as a mere incidental publication, a small book that was not to be taken too seriously. His surprise is evident from the reference in his Memoirs to the number of copies of the grammar that were printed, considerably more than the print runs of his more important works, but it is also evident from his own references to the grammar in the Preface, as a 'little' or 'short System' (1762: xiii, xv). Lowth's influence on other grammars is evident from the number of times his work is quoted – not always with acknowledgement – and particularly by Murray thirty years later. It is striking how, in the process of being quoted, his strictures were made increasingly prescriptive, as has been shown by Yáñez-Bouza (2008) in her analysis of preposition stranding in eighteenth-century grammars. Lowth, as I will demonstrate in the present book, doesn't deserve his iconic status. He owes his reputation as a prescriptivist not so much to his own grammar as to the way in which the *Short Introduction* was received, in his own time as well as today, and to the use that was made of it by successive grammarians after him.

1.6 THE GRAMMAR'S 'DISTRESSINGLY INFLUENTIAL LIFE'

Eventually, Lowth's popularity began to wane. Perhaps an early indication of this is the following sentence, found in Richard Postlethwaite's *Grammatical Art Improved: In which the Errors of Grammarians and Lexicographers are Exposed* (1795):

Dr. Lowth, than *who* no better English Grammarian has existed, was an excellent Poet, a great Latinist, a famous Grecian, and a good Hebrician (1795: 218).

The sentence is an example of bad English, provided as part of a lesson with which Postlethwaite tested a rule that had originated with Lowth: 'When a Relative has a Reference to its Antecedent only,... *than* must govern it in the Objective Case' (1795: 172). By linking Lowth's name and reputation with the kind of grammatical mistake Lowth himself would have condemned, Postlethwaite is, I think, mocking him. Postlethwaite's grammar includes several references to the fact that Lowth's grammar may be of a high standard but that it nevertheless contains a number of imperfections; hence the reason for his own, as indeed the title suggests. Eventually, the number of reprints of Lowth's grammar decreased. Figure 1.1 below suggests that this may well have had to do with the publication of Murray's grammar, first in 1795 and soon followed by the even more popular abridgement of 1797. I will show in Chapter 3 that there even appear to have been deliberate attempts on the part of the publishers of Murray's grammar to take grammars like Lowth's off the market.

Lowth is looked upon with disdain by modern linguists like Aitchison and others. But he is also popularly blamed for burdening the English language with prescriptive strictures such as that against the use of preposition stranding. An example is the best-selling writer Bill Bryson, who discusses Lowth in his book *Mother Tongue* (1990) in terms similar to Aitchison:

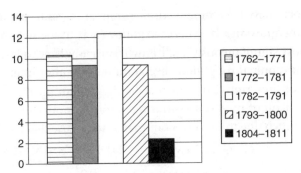

FIG. 1.1. Number of reprints and editions of Lowth's grammar (1762), based on Alston (1965) (Tieken-Boon van Ostade 2006a: 540)

Consider the curiously persistent notion that sentences should not end with a preposition. The source of this stricture, and several other equally **dubious** ones, was one Robert Lowth, an eighteenth-century clergyman and **amateur grammarian** whose *A Short Introduction to English Grammar*, published in 1762, enjoyed a long and **distressingly influential life** both in his native England and abroad. **It is to Lowth we can trace many a pedant's most treasured notions**: the belief that you must say *different from* rather than *different to* or *different than*, the idea that two negatives make a positive, the rule that you must not say 'the heaviest of the two objects', but rather 'the heavier', the distinction between *shall* and *will*, and the clearly nonsensical belief that *between* can apply only to two things and *among* to more than two... Perhaps the most remarkable and curiously enduring of **Lowth's many beliefs** was the conviction that sentences ought not to end with a preposition.... He suggested only that he thought it generally better and more graceful, not crucial, to place the preposition before its relative 'in solemn and elevated' writing.... Until the eighteenth century it was correct to say 'you was' if you were referring to one person.... *Was* is a singular verb and *were* a plural one. Why should you take a plural verb when the sense is clearly singular? **The answer – surprise, surprise – is that Robert Lowth didn't like it** (Bryson 1990: 132–5).

Many (though by no means all) of the strictures popularly attributed to Lowth can indeed first be found in his grammar, and it is due to his influence on later grammarians, particularly Lindley Murray, that the strictures came to be in widespread use, but Lowth rarely made them up himself. His rule for the use of different forms for the preterite and past participles of strong verbs, for instance, he adopted from Harris's *Hermes*, while he appears to have found the one against preposition stranding in the works of Dryden, of which he owned a copy. His proscription of *you was* appears to have been more widely current at the time, because we also find it in the grammar by Joseph Priestley (1733–1804), which was published almost simultaneously with Lowth, in 1761. These are not isolated instances. It is only through Lowth that these strictures came to be part of the canon of prescriptivism, not that he drew them up himself. Lowth's status as an icon of prescriptivism is a dubious honour, but it is one that was not so much due to his own grammar as to the use that has been made of it since.

LIFE AND CAREER

2.1 LOWTH'S MEMOIRS

TOWARDS the end of his life, some time around 1783, Lowth sat down to review his life's achievements. He was in his early seventies at the time, and he possibly felt inspired for this act of contemplation by the recent death of his daughter Frances (1757–83), at the age of twenty-six. His Will dates from around the same time. Frances was the fifth of his children to die well before their time: only two of the Lowths' seven children outlived their parents. Comprising only about 500 words, the document, which is in the Bodleian Library (MS Eng. Misc. C. 816, ff. 126–7), is not very long, but it informs us of a number of details that are important in reconstructing Lowth's life, from his own perspective at least. It deals with a number of topics, starting with his birth 'in his Father's Prebendal house in the Close Winchester, Novr. 27.1710' and the names of his parents, 'William Lowth B.D. Prebendary of Winchester, & Margaret Daughter of Robert Pitt of Blandford Esqr.'; next, it mentions his education at Winchester College, and at St John's College and New College in Oxford, where he also obtained his degree as Doctor of Divinity in 1754. The doctorate was awarded for his *De Sacra Poesie Hebraeorum Praelectiones*, which had been published in 1753. Summarizing his subsequent career, Lowth mentions his professorship of Poetry in Oxford, to which he was elected in 1741 and which he retained until 1751. If the annual stipend for one of his immediate predecessors in this chair continued similarly, Lowth would have received an income of £180 a year from this (Wright 1950: 34). As for his career within the Church of England, Lowth was first appointed rector of Ovington, Hants, in 1744, two years after his ordination as a priest, and he became archdeacon of Winchester in 1750, rector of East Woodhay in 1753, and prebendary of Durham and rector of Sedgefield in 1755. In 1766, he was appointed Bishop of St David's and, later that year, of Oxford, and he became Bishop of London eleven years later in 1777. He had already been offered the bishopric of Limerick before he was made Bishop of St David's, during the time he had been 'First Chaplain to the Marquis of Hartington L^d. Lieutenant of Ireland May 1755'. He had, however, declined the offer, for reasons I will go into below. Two years later, he was made 'Chaplain to the King, appointed by y^e. Marquis of Hartington L^d. Steward of y^e. Household'.

This overview, based as it is on Lowth's own record, shows his steady progression through the ranks of the church, though it doesn't mention the fact that, around the time that he wrote his brief Memoirs, he had been offered the archbishopric of Canterbury, upon the death of Frederick Cornwallis (1713–83). Lowth declined the offer for reasons of ill health, and suggested John Moore (bap.1730, d.1805), the Bishop of Bangor, instead. All this we can conclude from a letter of sympathy addressed to him by Sir Alexander Dick (1703–85) on 9 April 1783, who asked '[i]f it be true what the Newspapers say, of Your Lordship's being offered Canterbury, and declined to His Majesty, but he upon that, asking who should be prefered; your being pleased to recommend D^r. Moore of Bangor, whom the King has wisely adopted'. Sir Alexander Dick was a physician, though no longer active as such, and in the same letter he offered Lowth medical advice on 'the Painful and wasting complaint of the Stone which afflicts you'. Dick also suggested that Lowth should invoke the help of his children in writing his letters: 'as I see your Lordship does not make use of an Amanuensis as I do – I entreat you not to write me any Letter with your own hand, but if your Son [Robert], or any of the young Ladies [Frances or Martha] will do me that honour, to inform me now & then how you are, it will be great consolation to me and all this Family'. Lowth, fortunately from the perspective of the present study, invariably wrote his letters himself, though the unsteady nature of his handwriting in several of his letters suggests that that letter writing was at times very painful.

Another topic of the Memoirs is that of Lowth's Continental travels. From 1748 to 1749 he had 'Accompanied the Honble. Henry Bilson Legge Envoy Extraordinary' on a visit to Berlin. Bilson Legge (1708–64) later became Chancellor of the Exchequer, and he was one of Lowth's powerful friends whose acquaintance helped advance his career. Lowth had accompanied

Legge on his mission to Berlin as his chaplain (Hepworth 1978: 33), and he continued to be in touch with Legge afterwards. Their amicable relationship is evident from the fact that during Lowth's stay in London in the spring of 1755, Mrs Legge offered her services to his wife: 'M^rs. Legge bid me tell you, that if ^you have any business about Silks, Caps, or the like, you may employ her' (Lowth to his wife, 6 March 1755). Legge was also instrumental in the publication of Lowth's grammar: upon hearing about it, as Lowth explained to his friend James Merrick in February 1762, 'M^r. Legge desired ^to have it for his Son; wch. purpose it could not very well serve without being printed'.

Lowth's second trip to the Continent took place shortly afterwards, when he 'Travelled with the Lords George & Frederic Cavendish Sons of the Duke of Devonshire, to Italy through France, & returned the same way 1749 & 1750' (Memoirs). The elder brother of Lowth's charges was William Cavendish (bap.1720, d.1764), Marquess of Hartington and, after his father's death in 1755, Duke of Devonshire. The three young men's father was, according to Hepworth (1978: 34), 'one of the greatest landowners in the country and a leader of the ruling Whig party'; he was also an intimate friend and fellow party member of Henry Bilson Legge, Lowth's other patron. Lowth thus 'had at his fingertips', according to Hepworth, 'almost unlimited patronage'. He would eventually profit from this, for when Hartington was appointed Lord Lieutenant of Ireland in 1755, he chose Lowth as his chaplain to accompany him. Lowth reported the honourable offer in a letter to his wife on 8 March 1755, explaining, however, that he was not readily inclined to accept. He asked for time to consult with his friends, 'M^r. Legge & the Dean', i.e. Thomas Cheyney (c.1694–1760), but also his wife, for he wrote to her, 'You are as much concern'd as I, & I can't do it without your concurrence'. In his next letter, written three days later, he referred to his wife 'being scared with y^e. thoughts of Banishment into Ireland'. What lay behind her fear was the possibility that Lowth might be promoted to an Irish bishopric, a not very desirable prospect in those days. Lowth tried to put her mind at rest: 'I have nothing more at present to add to what I have said already as to that affair: matters stand just as they did; L^d. H. has been out of Town for two or three days. You may depend upon it I shall persist in my resolution; but possibly something may be made of it in another way.' What he meant by these last words becomes clear in a letter written about a week later:

But you may imagine I have turn'd it much in my mind; & I have likewise talk'd it over fully with M^r. Legge. By what I can find upon the whole I see no light at all in my prospects, my affairs seem to be at a dead stand, without we can turn this offer to some advantage. Suppose then (if the Duke [of Newcastle] & L^{d}. H. should be desirous of my going, as they seem to be,) I could go with a full declaration $^{on\ my}$ ^{side} of accepting nothing in Ireland, & an explicit promise on theirs of my being pay'd in English Preferment! (Lowth to his wife, 15 March 1755).[1]

Lowth did go to Ireland as part of the Lord Lieutenant's train, and he did receive 'English Preferment' eventually, but it did not go as smoothly as he and Bilson Legge in their deliberations might have expected: he had to refuse the bishopric of Limerick first, preferring to wait, as Hepworth puts it, 'in a less important status in a strategically sounder location' (1978: 35), as prebendary of Durham and rector of Sedgefield. It would take more than ten years before a bishopric would come his way again, but it would eventually be one that brought him the desired opportunity.

Hartington continued to play an important role in Lowth's life. His patronage brought Lowth a chaplainship to the King, as the Memoirs record, while it also brought him in contact with the Duke of Newcastle, Lord Pelham-Holles (1693–1768), another Whig and at that time Prime Minister:

L^{d}. Hartington has order'd me to wait upon y^{e}. Duke of Newcastle, to thank him, & likewise to satisfy him about some particulars relating to Irish affairs. I represented to him what difficultys I s^{d}. have in accomplishing this visit: he answer'd this objection, by saying, he w^{d}. write to the Duke, & refer him to me, upon wch. he w^{d}. see me immediately (Lowth to his wife, 28 October 1755).

Pelham-Holles was to be instrumental in realizing Lowth's 'English Preferment' for, on 2 December 1765, Lowth wrote to Pelham-Holles, who was then Lord of the Privy Seal, as follows:

I have the honour of Your Grace's Message, transmitted to me by Lord George Cavendish; who has explained to me at large the infinite obligation which I have to Your Grace, for intending of your own motion & good will to recommend me to His Majesty for a Promotion of the highest rank. I beg Your Grace to be assured, that Your kind remembrance of me **unsolicited & unasked**, Your testimony & approbation, gives me more real pleasure, than any Promotion which may be the consequence of it can do (Lowth to Pelham-Holles, 2 December 1765).

---

[1] In transcribing the letters, I have tried to render the original as closely as possible, including insertions above the line and words or phrases that were struck through in the process of revising the text. These changes may provide important evidence of Lowth's attitudes to linguistic correctness or what he felt was otherwise stylistically more appropriate to the context in question.

But another promotion lay in store for Lowth, who again wrote to Pelham-Holles, about seven months later, as follows:

I have received a Letter from My Lord Archbishop of Canterbury, acquainting me, that it is His Majesty's pleasure, that I should remove from the See of S^t. Davids to that of Oxford. I immediatly expressed my ready Obedience to his Majesty's Commands. . . .

I cannot omit therefore renewing upon this occasion my most sincere Thanks, & warmest acknowledgements, for all Your Grace's favours to me, **unsolicited & unasked**; & for this last honour in particular now conferred upon me, which I know is to be placed to the same account (Lowth to Pelham-Holles, 31 July 1766).

The repetition of the words 'unsolicited & unasked' here is striking: it may have been true at the time, but the machinery of ecclesiastical preferment had been set in motion well over ten years previously. Neither Legge nor Hartington were alive any longer – both had died in 1764 – but their patronage of Lowth had a long-term effect. In a document included in a letter of 12 April 1770 addressed to Thomas Warton (1728–90) concerning a correction of a page in Warton's edition of Theocritus, Lowth's successful career is attributed to his appointment as First Chaplain to the Lord Lieutenant of Ireland in 1755, but his ascendancy had actually started nearly ten years earlier, when he accompanied Henry Bilson Legge on a diplomatic mission to Berlin. The same document reads that 'all the preferment which he . . . received . . . was but the due reward of his talents and services', but it is unlikely that Lowth managed all this solely by merit of his own talents; the account of his career is a good example of how the system of advancement worked in those days.

Lowth's Memoirs deal with two more topics: his wife and children, and his publications. On 26 December 1752, in the Cathedral Church of the Holy Trinity, Winchester, Lowth married 'Mary Daughter & Heiress of Lawrence Jackson of Christchurch Hants Esqr'. Though he was already in his early forties when he got married, this was not unusual at the time. According to Stone (1990), men from middle-class families needed time to establish themselves in life so that they could start a family in a style similar to that which they had been accustomed to themselves when they were young. In Lowth's case, this time had come after his return from Italy in 1750, when he had secured for himself the favourable attention of his two patrons, Henry Bilson Legge and the future Duke of Devonshire.

According to the records of Christchurch Priory, Mary Jackson was baptized on 8 April 1734, but the Lowth family possesses a silver rattle with the inscription 'M[ary] I[ackson' and the date 1730, which appears to be the year of her birth. She was therefore twenty-two when she got married. There is a portrait of Molly, as Lowth called her in his letters to her, as a young girl, still in the possession of the Lowth family today, which looks as if it was taken upon the occasion of her 'coming out'. Molly was the ward (official or otherwise) of Thomas Cheyney, already referred to above, who was Dean of Winchester from 1748 until his death in 1760. Cheyney was Molly's father's cousin; this becomes clear from a kind of family tree which Lowth drew up as an aid to administer Cheyney's highly complex Will (National Archives, Ref. PROB 11/866). After Lawrence Jackson's death, some time before May 1749 according to one of the versions of the Will, Cheyney kept a close watch over Molly until she was married and financially provided for. After that, she no longer benefited personally from any legacies in his Will. The relationship with Cheyney continued to be a close one after the marriage, as appears from the correspondence between Lowth and his wife during his long absence from home in 1755. Lowth frequently referred to letters Cheyney had written to him: 'Thanks to the Dean for his kind Letter: I will write to him as soon as I have any thing material to communicate' (12 June 1755). Occasionally, he sent an enquiry to Cheyney concerning his own career through his wife, as in 'Pray ask the Dean, if he knows any thing of the Bp. of Winchester's designs with regard to my Arch-Deaconry' (19 October 1755). Cheyney lived in the Deanery House in the Cathedral Close, evidently near to where the Lowths lived, for messages passed back and forth directly, and Lowth frequently sent greetings 'to Miss Stevens [possibly Molly's cousin], & the Dean, & all friends in the Close'. Upon Cheyney's death in 1760, the final version of his Will specified that '3 thousand pounds be vested in the hands of D^{r}. Robert Lowth and his Brother Willm. Lowth, for the sole use and benefit of [his kinswoman Mary Lowth's] Son Thomas-Henry Lowth, and in case of his Death under Age, to be equally divided for the use of his two Sisters now living' (Frances and Mary). The reason for this substantial legacy may have been that Cheyney, who never married and appears to have had no children of his own, was Thomas Henry's godfather. One of the three principal beneficiaries of Cheyney's Will was a Mrs Ann Preston, who, when she died in 1771 or so, according to a document in the Bodleian Library headed 'M^{rs}. Preston's Bequests' (MS Eng. Misc. C. 816, ff. 129–30), left a hundred pounds 'To M^{rs}. Lowth & her Heirs', along with 'all her other Plate engraved with the Arms of the late Dean Cheyney' and 'Dean Cheyneys Picture & the Glass under it'.

In the few records I have been able to find about her, Molly is referred to as 'heiress', and according to Scott Mandlebrote, in his entry on Lowth in the *ODNB*, the marriage was financially advantageous to Lowth, bringing him 'substantial property and a considerable fortune'. Precisely what this property consisted of, or the amount of money Molly brought into the marriage, I have been unable to ascertain, as I have not managed to trace her father's Will. From Lowth's Will it appears that he settled £3,000 on Molly through Henry Bilson Legge and Thomas Cheyney as part of the marriage articles, drawn up three days before the couple were married. Whether or not the marriage was a so-called arranged one, as would have been common enough in those days, it seems to have been full of affection. This is amply illustrated by Lowth's correspondence during his absence in Ireland in 1755. Though only Lowth's end of it has come down us, it appears from references in his letters that Molly must have written as many letters as her husband while they were apart: well over sixty. The letters suggest that she must have been as well educated as would be possible for any girl of her social standing in those days. Lowth compliments her on the style of the first letter he received from her while he was away, writing 'acknowledgements for [your] exceedingly well wrote Letter' (6 March 1755). In the same letter he informs her that 'M^r. Dodsley [his bookseller] tells me he has sent me y^e. 4th. Volume of his Miscellany: open y^e. packet and entertain yourself'. Molly must have enjoyed reading, and in his Will dated 11 September 1783 Lowth specified that she might like to keep some of his books after his death:

In the little Dressing Room at ffulham there are some small Books which may be worth keeping chiefly those on the two Upper shelves. If the Books written in Y^s. paper shall be thought too many to keep some of them may be sold. And M^{rs}. Lowth may take to herself whatever she pleases of them. R.L.

There are, furthermore, several references in their correspondence that suggest that Molly took it upon herself to teach their son Thomas Henry to read and write. The above quotations concerning Lowth's career prospects suggest that Molly played a central role in his life. His question 'Would you choose to be a Bishopess in the Kingdom of Ireland?' (6 March 1755) in one of his first letters to her, and their subsequent deliberations about what decisions to take relating to his career, indicate that he took her opinion seriously. In many of his letters he passed on her greetings to his friends, and he appointed her as the 'sole Executrix' of his Will.

Following the reference to his wife in his Memoirs, Lowth lists his children along with their dates of birth as well as, sadly, some of their deaths:

> Thomas Henry Lowth born Dec[r]. 16.1753:
> he died (Fellow of New Coll. Oxf[d]. Rector of
> Thorley Hants), June 7. 1778: a most excellent Youth!
> Mary Lowth b. June 11. 1755. died July 5. 1768.
> Frances Lowth b. Sep[r]. 28. 1757. died July 21. 1783.
> Martha Lowth, b. Sep[r]. 19. 1760.
> Robert Lowth, [b.] Mar. 5. 1762.
> Margaret Lowth b. June 6. 1763. d. Mar. 10. 1769.
> Charlotte Lowth b. June 9. 1765. d. May 29 1768.

A family of six to seven children was an average size for an eighteenth-century middle-class family (Vickery 1998: 97); similarly, the high number of pre-teen deaths, Margaret at the age of five and Charlotte at nearly three, was not unusual at the time. Lowth reports Margaret's death to his friend Glocester Ridley (1702–74) on 22 March 1769: 'Since I heard f[m]. You I have gone through the melancholy Scene of the sickness & death of another of my Children, my youngest Daughter'. By this time, Charlotte was also dead, having died some ten months previously. Margaret's god-mother had been Anne Covey (d.1780), a cousin of Thomas Cheyney and one of the beneficiaries of his Will after the death of her sister Barbara. Her own Will specified that her principal heirs were Lowth and his wife, but that all was to go to Margaret after her parents' deaths (National Archives, Ref. PROB 11/1072). Sadly, Margaret didn't live that long, and Anne Covey never seems to have got round to changing her Will.

The children were born at fairly regular two-year intervals, influenced by pregnancy and lactation (Stone 1990); it was not unusual for eigh-teenth-century middle-class women to breastfeed themselves rather than employ wet nurses, and there are several references to Molly's breastfeed-ing in Lowth's letters from Ireland. Thomas Henry and Mary, called Molly, like her mother, feature large in Lowth's Irish correspondence in 1755. Tom was not yet fifteen months old when his father left home on 1 March 1755, and little Molly was born during his absence, an event which, as is amply shown in his letters home, filled Lowth with concern: it was not uncom-mon in those days for either mother or child to die in the process. George

Cavendish appears to have been her godfather, for Lowth immediately informed him of Molly's birth: 'I wrote to L^d. George Cavendish, as soon as I heard the Good News; I suppose you will have heard from him as you expected'. Cavendish was unable to attend the baby's baptism on 13 July, asking someone else to represent him instead, as Lowth informed Molly on 11 July, but he did take his responsibility seriously, as appears from a message Lowth passed on to Molly: 'So now the little Molly is a Christian: her God-Papa says he will refresh her memory in the Catechism, that he may instruct ^{her} as his duty requires' (13 July 1755). In later letters to his friends Robert Dodsley and Joseph Spence (1699–1768), Lowth reported the birth of two of his other children, Robert and Charlotte, as follows:

I have the pleasure of informing You, that my Wife has just now brought a little Boy into the world. (Lowth to Robert Dodsley, 5 March 1762).

In the first place I have the pleasure of informing You that my wife was yesterday Morning happily & safely delivered of a Daughter & that Thank y^e. Lord are both as well as can be (Lowth to Spence, 10 June 1765).

Lowth and Dodsley had known each other since at least the early months of 1753. Lowth's first book, the *Praelectiones*, had been published in Oxford, and Dodsley acted as his London bookseller. He subsequently also became his publisher and, as is evident from their correspondence, they soon developed a close friendship. Joseph Spence was a lifelong friend of Lowth's and a fellow Wyckhamite, both having been educated at institutions which had been founded by William of Wykeham (1324–1404), Winchester College and New College, Oxford. Spence had, moreover, been one of Lowth's predecessors as professor of Poetry in Oxford, from 1728 to 1738. According to Wright (1950: 175), Spence was Martha Lowth's godfather, and upon his death he left her a legacy of £100, which is referred to in a letter Lowth wrote on 15 August 1769 to Glocester Ridley, with whom, along with a certain Edward Rolle, he was co-executor of Spence's Will. There is a letter from Lowth to Spence dated 5 August 1765 which he concludes with: 'Your little Friend gives a sharp look out & thinks of nothing but of being within reach of Tommy'. The reference must be to Martha, who was at that time nearly five years old. She already seems to have been able to write, for the letter contains the words '& You M^r. Spence' in a different hand, which, given the context, can only be that of little Martha. Teaching children to read and write was begun early in those days (Navest 2009), and in middle-class families this was usually the mother's responsibility, as with the Lowths. On 13 August 1755, Lowth ended his letter to Molly with the words 'My Love to all in the Close & at home to y^e. little Mollykin, & y^e. Dear Boy Tom, with thanks for his fine Letter'. This may be no more than a reference to a drawing by the little boy, but it might equally be a reference to Tom practising his letters, for a month later Lowth commented 'I am very glad to hear that the dear Tom learns his book so well' (26 September 1755). Teaching one's children at home at a very young age became regular practice during the second half of the eighteenth century, and the Lowths seem to have been pioneers in this new develop-ment (Tieken-Boon van Ostade forthcoming).

Molly was the third of the Lowth children to die, at the age of only thirteen. Unlike in the case of Frances, who died unexpectedly when she was twenty-five, I have not come across any record of Molly's death in Lowth's correspondence, but Lowth must have been deeply distressed by the event. This is clear from the epitaph on her grave:

> Cara, vale, ingenio praestans, pietate pudore,
> Et plusquam natae nomine, care, vale!
> Cara Maria, vale! at veniet felicius aevum,
> Quando iterum tecum (sim modo dignus) ero;
> Cara, redi, laeta tum dicam voce, paternos
> Eja age in amplexus, cara Maria, redi.
>
> (Cook 1879: 15n)[2]

This elegy was set to music by the composer John Wall Callcott (1766–1821). Molly was buried in Cuddesdon (the home of the Bishop of Ox-ford), where the family lived at the time of her death. Her grave is still there. It is unclear what Molly died of; nor is the cause of Thomas Henry's death, almost exactly ten years later, known. In the only letter addressed to him by his father I have been able to find, written some five months before he died, there is a reference to his health:

I saw D^r. Addington yesterday & told him of Your complaints: he says, he is very clear as to y^e. nature & cause of them; that [they] are owing to some bad matter in your health, perhaps y^e. remains of some former illness, wch. must be thrown off; he speaks with great assurance of success from y^e. method he has put you into: thinks it hazardous to try experiments; & is sure that no skill in surgery will be of

---

[2] 'Beloved girl, farewell, excellent in intelligence, piety and modesty/ And even more beloved than merely as a daughter, farewell!/ Beloved Mary, farewell! But may a happier time arrive,/ When I will once more be with you (if only I am worthy of it)/ Beloved girl, come back, I will then say with joyful voice,/ Throw yourself into your father's arms, beloved Mary, come back.'

y^e. least service to You. He looks upon y^e. new complaint in your other finger rather as a good than a bad Symptom; as if Nature was making an effort ^{to} throw off the bad matter. He speaks with more assurance upon all this than I ever heard him do on any subject. But he says, You must have patience (Lowth to Thomas Henry Lowth, 24 December 1777).

In his Memoirs, Lowth referred to him as 'a most excellent Youth!', who, at the age of twenty-four, was 'Fellow of New Coll. Oxf^d. Rector of Thorley Hants'. A promising young man, he followed in his father's footsteps, and would have had a great future ahead of him. In the letter referred to above, Lowth congratulates his son upon his ordination as a priest. 'My dear Tom,' he began, 'I heartily congratulate You on Your being a Priest; on wch. I shall give You no other advice at present, than that You would always remember, that You are so'. Some time after Tom's death, Lowth wrote a letter to the Librarian of New College Library, though only part of the draft version has come down to us:

I have taken the liberty to send by [no name filled in] a Box directed to You. It contains Basket's Great Bible in 2 Vols. As I am informed, that you have nothing of y^t. kind upon y^e. Communion Table in N.C. Chapel, I thought it might be no improper ornament for y^t. place. If you sh^d. think it ~~such~~ so, I sh^d. be ~~happy~~ glad if y^e. Coll. w^d. do me y^e. favor to accept ~~it I~~ it as a small Memorial of my late dear Son: ~~& with that~~ to explain wch. design have ~~xxx~~ written his Name in it. I desire to refer this matter intirely to Your judgem^t.

The Bible is still there, and it is inscribed with the following words: 'ΜΝΗΜΟΣΥΝΟΝ Thomae Henrici Lowth, Novi Collegii socii, juristae; juvensis eximii, ingenio, doctrina, moribus, probatissimis; qui abiit VIImo die junii, AD. MDCCLXXVIIIvo, AET. XXVto'.[3] The gift of the Bible was accompanied by the sum of £100 (New College Archive 928).

Tom was buried in Fulham, in the family tomb in All Saints Church cemetery, to which the remains of Charlotte and Margaret, who had died before him, were subsequently transferred, and where Frances, Martha, and their parents as well as a grandson, George Thomas Lowth (1807–93), one of Robert Junior's thirteen children, were to be buried afterwards (Guille and Buxton 2003: 125–6). Robert Junior, who, like his father, became a clergyman, was buried there as well after he died in 1822.

---

[3] 'A token of remembrance of Thomas Henry Lowth, fellow of New College, student of law, an excellent young man, of approved talent, scholarship and character; who departed on the seventh day of June, in the year 1778, in his 25th year'.

A later edition of a poem Robert Junior wrote on fox-hunting, called 'Billesdon Coplow' and originally published in 1800, contains a brief memorial from the hand of a friend who visited the grave shortly after Robert's death. The tomb still exists today, and is in good condition. Apart from a letter to his brother William, in which Lowth announced the death of Frances, there is also a letter in which he mentions the death of Margaret: 'Since I heard f^m. You [i.e. Glocester Ridley] I have gone through the melancholy Scene of the sickness & death of another of my Children, my youngest Daughter. And my Wife, myself, & Children, have been ill since, of the same disorder, a low Fever, but slight in comparison' (22 March 1769). Here, he gives the cause of her death, a fever which affected the rest of the family as well. The cause of Frances's death appears to have been 'y^t. some Vessel was broken in y^e. Head or y^e. Heart' (Lowth to William Lowth, 22 July 1783; see letter facing page 1).

Throughout Lowth's correspondence, we get occasional glimpses of his family life. I have already referred to Martha looking over her father's shoulder when he wrote to her godfather Joseph Spence, adding a few words herself. Another example is a family outing to London, either purely for pleasure or to combine a business trip for Lowth with an opportunity to take his wife and their two eldest children, Tom and Molly, to see the sights. On 21 March 1764, Lowth asked James Dodsley (1724–97), brother and successor to his publisher Robert Dodsley, to make the following arrangements:

I beg the favour of You to take the trouble of hiring me Lodgings against I come to Town, where I propose to be by the 10th. of next Month: any where in Your Neighbourhood, between S^t. James's Street & the lower part of the Haymarket, the busier or in either of them; or Pall Mall, Berry Street, Duke Street, Kings Street, or the better part of Jermyn Street: I shall want a Dining Room, Bed-Chamber for my Wife & Me, another for a Maid Servant & a little Girl, & a Camp Bed in either of them for my little Boy; & a Bed for two Men Servants (Lowth to James Dodsley, 21 March 1764).

The other children – by this time Frances, Martha, Robert, and Margaret had been born as well – were left behind in Sedgefield, presumably in the care of a servant.

The Memoirs, finally, mention Lowth's publications, as follows:

Published,
De Sacra Poesi Hebræorum Prælectiones Oxonij habitæ, 1753. 4to.
Second Edition 8vo. 1763

Third Edition 8vo. 1775.

An Edition at Leipsic with Notes by Professor Michaelis in 2 vols. 12mo. 1758. 2^{d}. Edition of y^{e}. same 1768.

Life of W^{m}. of Wykeham 8vo. 1758. 2^{d}. Edition 1759. 3^{d}. Edition 1777.

Short Introduction to English Grammar 8vo. 1762. Many Editions since in 12mo. $^{all\ corrected}$ with some alterations, additions, &c by y^{e}. Author. The number of Copies printed in the whole including the Edition of 1780 $^{(or\ 1781)}$ amounted to about 34.000.

Isaiah. A new Translation with Notes. 4to. 1778. 2^{d}. Edition 4to. 1779. Translated into German by Professor Koppe Goettingen. 4 vols 8vo. 1780.

   Controversial.

Answer to an Anonymous Letter, concerning the Election of Warden of Winchester College, 1759.

Letter to Bp. Warburton 1766, $^{8vo.}$, 4 Editions.

Confutation of Bp. Hare's System of Hebrew meter in a Letter to D^{r}. Edwards, 1766.

Lowth thus published four books: his lectures on the sacred poetry of the Hebrews (1753), for which he was awarded a doctorate, his *Life of William of Wykeham* (1758), his *Short Introduction to English Grammar* (1762), and *Isaiah, A New Translation* (1778). These publications show him to have been a scholar of Hebrew, a writer on Hebrew literature and Church history, and a grammarian of English. All his books lived through more editions than one, his most popular book being, perhaps to his own surprise, the grammar. The lectures on Hebrew Poetry were translated into English in 1787, by George Gregory (*ODNB*, 'George Gregory'). All books except for the *Life of William of Wykeham* were, moreover, brought out in Germany as well: *De Sacra Poesi Hebræorum Prælectiones* was annotated by Johann David Michaelis (1717–91) from Göttingen and published in Leipzig between 1758 and 1761 (Hepworth 1978: 39), and *Isaiah*, as Lowth notes, was translated into German by Johann Benjamin Koppe (1750–91), also published in Leipzig (1779–81) (*Biographisch-Bibliographisches Kirchenlexikon*, 'Johann Benjamin Koppe'). Lowth was not uncritical of Michaelis's translation, as becomes clear from a letter addressed to James Merrick some time in the spring of 1762:

I have received from Prof^{r}. Michaelis his Edition of my Lectures. He has made large additions of Prefaces, Notes, & Epimetra; (or addit[ions from the Di] ssertations.) He is a learned, ingenious, [...] free, & indeed very bold Critic. His [text w]^{ch}. is intermixed with mine, makes about [a] third of the whole: there are a great many things in wch. I do not agree with him, & much wch. I cannot judge of as depending on a knowledge of Arabic; but upon the whole,

I think, his performance very well deserves to be examined & considered: & at present I have it in my thoughts, to republish his part together with my new Edition; but intirely detached from my Volume, & leaving the Purchasers of mine quite at liberty to take or leave his as they please. This method will give my Readers the satisfaction of being able to see, (wch. otherwise they w^d. not, without procuring the whole German Edition,) what he has done by way of correcting what is wrong, & supplying what is defective in my work; for this is his design: & it will save me the trouble of entering into a Critical Dispute with my Editor about matters in wch. we are not agreed (Lowth to Merrick, 4 May 1762?).

A lengthy correspondence between the two men ensued, largely, from Lowth's end at least, in English. The German edition earned Lowth his election as a Fellow of the Royal Society of Göttingen in 1765, the same year in which he was elected Fellow of the Royal Society in London (Hepworth 1978: 42). Lowth's grammar was also translated into German, in 1790, and again in Leipzig, but he did not live to witness this.

Lowth's correspondence with his publishers Robert and James Dodsley suggests that the grammar was not a major concern of his scholarly life, but the Memoirs indicate otherwise; in retrospect, that is. The fact that this work, with its 34,000 copies, became the most popular of his published books must have filled Lowth with pride. He seems to have felt quite differently about the remaining titles mentioned in the Memoirs – 'Answer to an Anonymous Letter, concerning the Election of Warden of Winchester College, 1759; Letter to Bp. Warburton 1766, ^8vo., 4 Editions; Confutation of Bp. Hare's System of Hebrew meter in a Letter to D^r. Edwards, 1766' – for he labelled them 'Controversial'. Lowth's decision to write a public letter to William Warburton (1698–1779), who became Bishop of Gloucester in 1760, is characterized by Hepworth (1978: 104) as the 'greatest literary battle of the century'. There are various letters in Lowth's correspondence that deal with the Warburton affair, including one in which Lowth is reprimanded, however mildly, for his role in it by the Archbishop of Canterbury, Thomas Secker (1693–1768). The battle, which started after the publication of the lectures on Hebrew poetry in 1753, was ostensibly about the dating of the Book of Job but in reality concerned the rivalry between the two men for Church preferment. As Hepworth (1978: 101) puts it, in 1755, when the controversy was in full swing, 'both were heading for a bishopric; but Warburton was fifty-seven; Lowth, forty-five'. Lowth's friends and fellow prebendaries of Durham, Joseph Spence and Thomas Chapman (1717–60), had been summoned by Warburton to mediate between him and Lowth. A draft has survived of the letter which Lowth subsequently wrote to Warburton:

Our good Friends D^r. C. & M^r. S. have agreably to your desire communicated to me some particulars of y^e. conversation wch. you have lately had with them relating to me: f^m. wch. I collect that you think you have reason to be offended with me on acc^t. of some things wch. I have said in my Prolections on y^e. subject of the book of Job, wch. you look upon as aimed against you; & y^t. you expect y^t. I sh^d. explain myself on this head (Lowth to Warburton, 9 September 1756).

The affair was temporarily patched up, with Lowth concluding his last letter to Warburton in 1756 as follows:

I write this in a very great hurry, as you may well imagine, when I tell you, I am preparing to remove with my Family to Durham the beginning of next week. I hope I shall there have frequent opportunitys of improving the friendship wch. you so generously offer me, & wch. I shall highly esteem; & of demonstrating in every way wch. lies in my power the sincerity wth. wch. I am, Dear S^r. Your most faithful & Affectionate humble Servt. R.L. (Lowth to Warburton, 14 October 1756).

But it was revived again upon the publication of the second edition of the *Praelectiones* in 1763, in which Lowth demonstrated that he would not bow to Warburton's point of view. This induced Warburton to publish an attack upon Lowth in an appendix to the fourth edition of his *Divine Legation of Moses* in 1765. Lowth retaliated that same year by publishing *A Letter to the Right Reverend Author of the Divine Legation of Moses*, which was so popular that it ran through four editions in eighteen months (Hepworth 1978: 102). Both men were now furious, and their outrage is clear from the language adopted in the letters they subsequently exchanged. This second correspondence consists of eight letters, written between 21 November 1765 and 31 January the following year, but the immediacy of the conflict becomes clear from the fact that five of the letters were written on five consecutive days: with Lowth staying in Bath at the time, and Warburton writing from Prior Park, a few miles south-east of Bath, communication could take place much faster than usual. The letters are full of insults and strong language from both sides ('I am grossly insulted', 'in abusing me infamously & actrociously', 'the charge is absolutely false', 'your very extraordinary Letter', 'I will answer no more Such Letters', 'your last insolent Letter', 'to teach you a little common civility') and biting sarcasm on the part of Warburton ('Your System of morals seems to be very uncommon').

One indication of the serious nature of the quarrel is the way in which the rules of politeness were broken. While it was common practice at the time to repeat the form of the opening formula in the closure of the letter, Warburton refrained from doing so. Thus, 'Rever^d Sir' becomes plain 'Sir' in the closing formula to the first letter, while the opening 'Sir' in later letters is not repeated in the conclusions. Lowth, however, sticks to 'My Lord' throughout, though even in his case we can detect his anger from the closing formulas. While his most neutral epistolary conclusion is 'Your most obedient humble Servant', his last letter to Warburton closes with 'Your humble Servant Robt. Lowth': in leaving out the customary 'most obedient', this must be interpreted as downright and deliberate rudeness. Lowth's label 'Controversial' of the publication of his letters to Warburton in the Memoirs suggests that he was not proud of the affair, and this is confirmed by his reply to the Archbishop of Canterbury's critical letter, of 5 December 1765, referred to above:

I am moreover in a very particular manner obliged to YG. for your most kind & gentle reproof on a late occasion: a reproof wch. I acknowledge w^d. have been much too gentle, had I had any other person for my Adversary. I beg YG. to be assured, y^t. y^s. sort of employm^t. is most hateful to me: but withal to consider, what my situation was. That my moral character was attacked in a very ~~sensible~~ ^{tender} part; & y^t. I owed it, not only to myself, but also to y^e. Univ^{ty}. of Ox^d., to wch. I have singular obligations, & wch. was ~~attack:~~ ^{woun}ded through me, to repel the insult (Lowth to Secker, 9 December 1765).

The date of this letter shows that his stay at Bath that year had been far from quiet. The affair, according to Hepworth (1978), even came to the attention of the King, and in her analysis of the correspondence of Elizabeth Montagu (1718–1800), the well-known bluestocking hostess, Anni Sairio discusses a letter that testifies to the popularity of the published letters. In this letter Montagu informed her husband that the book had been discussed at a social gathering at the house of the Archbishop of York, Robert Hay-Drummond (1711–76),

where we had a great deal of mirth about Dr. Lowth's book and I find his Grace is as much pleased with it as you and I are. I hear Warburton like all bullies is frightened at a brisk attack, and the menace to attack the divine legion has made him shrink in his shell (as quoted by Sairio 2008: 142).

Though the affair had supporters on both sides, the letter suggests that public opinion sided with Lowth. According to the entry on Warburton in the *ODNB*, the affair with Lowth was believed to have contributed to 'Warburton's decline' (*ODNB*, 'William Warburton').

The Memoirs, to conclude this section, do not mention any of the verse Lowth wrote, or the book of fables published by Dodsley, to which he contributed. While still a schoolboy, Lowth had written a poem called *Katherine Hill*, which was published a few years later in *The London Magazine* (Hepworth 1978: 63). Another poem he wrote around the same time was called *The Genealogy of Christ as it is represented on the East Window in Winchester Chapel* (1729), and he is also the author of a long poem called *The Judgment of Hercules*, published, according to information provided in ECCO, in Glasgow in 1743 as written 'By a STUDENT of Oxford'. The poem was later used as a libretto by Handel. I have, moreover, come across a letter to Spence, dated 29 September 1761, that suggests that he was working on another poem around that time, but the poem itself I've been unable to identify. Wright (1950: 91) characterizes Lowth as 'a theologian, a Hebrew scholar, a literary critic, and a minor poet'. Hepworth calls *Katherine Hill* 'an authentic work of art' and *The Genealogy of Christ* 'an accomplished poem' (1978: 65, 68), while his *Judgment of Hercules* drew the attention of a well-known composer like Handel. Lowth possibly produced more poetry besides, for, in the *Berlinische Monatsschrift* in 1795, a translation was published from Lowth's hand of a poem by the German poet Karl Wilhelm Ramler (1725–98). Published well after his death, this translation is evidence of Lowth's familiarity with German, a language which he studied, though with some difficulty – 'the German is, I think, a very difficult language,' he wrote to Michaelis on 28 May 1770, complaining three years later of weakness of memory as an impediment to these efforts – so that he would be able to read Michaelis's translation of the Bible. In a draft letter addressed to the writer William Duncombe (1690–1769), Lowth referred to a Latin ode he had written in honour of a lady identified in a note to the letter as 'Miss Molineux of Winchester' (18 May 1758). The passage in question, however, was subsequently struck out. Two Misses Molyneux are referred to in Cheyney's Will and, as Lowth is referred to in the same Will, it appears that they were all part of Cheyney's social network around this time. Precisely what Lowth's relationship with them was, however, remains unclear, but it is interesting to see that twenty years later he presented a 'M[rs]. Molyneux' with a copy of *Isaiah*.

Dodsley's *Select Fables of Esop and Other Fabulists* came out in 1761. The work consisted of three volumes, the first containing the fables of Aesop, the second fables of modern writers, and the third fables written by Dodsley and a number of his friends. Besides listing Lowth as one of the contributors, Tierney (1988: 16) mentions Richard Graves, William Melmoth, Thomas Percy, Joseph Spence, and Dodsley's brother James. Tierney even suggests that the idea for the fables came from Lowth (1988: 147n); as Lowth's grammar came out a year later, which was likewise a project in which both men were involved, the two works may have been intended as a kind of set of educational works. Fables were popularly used to teach children to read in those days. There are two references to Dodsley's project in Lowth's correspondence. The first,

I am glad to hear the Fables are in such forwardness. As to the form & the decorations I do not presume to say any thing; well knowing that You are the best Judge of what will please the public (Lowth to Robert Dodsley, 19 June 1760),

confirms Lowth's hand in the project: he is consulted on the book's 'form & the decorations', which he, however, considered to be Dodsley's responsibility. The second shows that Lowth had the fables in mind for his son Thomas Henry:

I am very glad to hear that Your Fables are pretty near re[ady] to make their appearance: My li[ttle] man is impatient for them; he presents his Compts., & desires you to make haste. Be pleas'd, as soon as they are ready, to send one very ha[nd]somely bound, with a Note in <u>my Name</u> To the Honble. Master Legge; to M^r. Legge's House at the Treasury: & one neatly bound, in my Name likewise, To M^{rs}. Galand at the Boarding School at Newington Butts: and also to send to me here Six neatly bound (Lowth to Robert Dodsley, 9 January 1761).

He evidently also ordered a number of copies for children of friends, including the son of his former patron, Henry Bilson Legge; Lowth's relationship with 'M^{rs}. Galand at the Boarding School at Newington Butts' is unclear, but he wished her to use the book in her school. The book came out six weeks later, on 23 February, and its publication was very well received (Tierney 1988: 15).

Lowth's Memoirs do not mention any of the sermons he delivered that were subsequently published either; ECCO includes ten of them, published in 1757, 1758, 1764 (2), 1765, 1767, 1771 (2), 1773, and 1779.[4] Though he may not have considered them worth mentioning in the Memoirs, they are

---

[4] The figures from ECCO include those editions and reprints of Lowth's work that became available to me when ECCO Part II was published.

included in the list of books in his Will, along with his published letters, which he did include among his 'Controversial' publications in the Memoirs.

2.2 LOWTH'S WILL

The second major document that is important in reconstructing Lowth's life and career is his Will. It consists of two parts, the Will proper, drawn up on 11 September 1783, and a Codicil of 10 November 1785. The first document bears the names of Lowth's brother William, someone called Stephen Eaton, and Richard Burn, who was Lowth's secretary when he was Bishop of London; the second those of Thomas Foster, Lowth's steward at that time, a certain John Warne, and, again, Richard Burn. These men acted as Lowth's witnesses to the Will and its Codicil respectively. Neither document is in Lowth's own hand. On 13 December 1787, nearly six weeks after Lowth's death, Burn and Foster had to make a deposition to testify to the veracity of the Will and its Codicil, declaring that 'they have often seen him write and thereby became well acquainted with his manner and Character of hand writing'. The original version of the Will was thus in Lowth's own hand, and its language, though highly formulaic, can there-fore largely be considered his own. Only the spelling must be attributed to the scribe. Next, the deposition states that 'these Deponents having now carefully viewed and perused the paper writing hereunto annexed being or purporting to be a List or Catalogue of Books . . . they do depose that they verily and in their Consciences believe the whole of the said list or Catalogue as well as the several Notes made thereon to be all of the proper hand writing of him the said Robert late Lord Bishop of London deceased'. The list of books is of particular interest, informing us of what books Lowth read and how well read a man he was, but it also helps us in identifying some of the sources which he used in writing his grammar.

The Will allows us to determine how much Lowth was 'worth' at the time of his death. In the Will proper he bequeathed as much as £16,100 to his heirs, and in the Codicil £5,000 more. This is a considerable amount of money – compared, for instance, to the estate of Joseph Spence referred to above, which at the time of his death amounted to some £1,800 (Wright 1950: 175). Using the concordancing program WordSmith Tools (for further details, see §6.2), I discovered that there is also linguistic evidence for the fact that Lowth died a very wealthy man. In the Will, the word *pounds* occurs seventeen times, in thirteen instances of which it collocates with *thousand* and three times with the word *hundred*. Most of the money for the legacies, which had to be raised out of Lowth's personal estate, i.e. his movable goods and possessions and, failing that, his real estate or immovable property, went to his wife and his children: the £3,000 he had settled on his wife as part of the marriage articles (see above), increased by £4,000 in the Will proper, and £2,000 according to the Codicil; to his daughter Martha he left £4,000, increased by £3,000 by way of a 'further legacy' upon the death of his wife, and an additional £3,000 as specified in the Codicil; he wished to provide well for his daughter, who never married and thus would have been left without any financial resources upon her father's death. To his son Robert he bequeathed £4,000 as well as, after his wife's death, all his real estate and 'the rest and residue of my said Personal Estate'.

There were three more legacies: £500 to his sister Martha Eden and another £500 to her daughter Mary Blackwell. This raises the question of why he didn't leave any money to his other sister, Margaret Sturges, as both women were widows at the time. Possibly John Sturges, who was Prebendary of Winchester and Rector of Alderstoke (Guille and Buxton 2003: 123), had left his widow better off when he died in 1740 than his brother-in-law Robert Eden, who died in 1759. Lowth's niece Mary was also a widow at the time Lowth drew up his Will: her husband, Ebenezer Blackwell, had died the year before in 1782 (see *ODNB*, 'Blackwell, Ebenezer'), leaving her with six children, all below the age of ten. She must have been able to make good use of this legacy. The third legacy was intended for 'the incorporated Society for the Propagation of the Gospel in fforeign parts ... to be applied to the pious designs of the said Society'. As this is the only legacy to an outside institution, it is clear that Lowth wished his accumulated wealth to remain within the family.

Lowth appointed his 'Dear Wife Mary Lowth sole Executrix of this my last Will and Testament'. There is a note dated 14 February 1837 in the margin of the record book into which Lowth's Will was copied which states that 'the Goods Chattels & Credits of The Right Reverend Robert Lowth Lord Bishop of London dec[d]. left unadminister[d] by Mary Lowth Widow', and that Robert Lowth Junior, to whom they reverted upon his mother's death in 1803 by the Will of his father, but who had died in 1822, had similarly left his inheritance unadministered. What this entailed is unclear: the Society for the Propagation of the Gospel did receive its legacy, as its receipt is recorded in its annual report for the year 1789 and in a Benefactions Book (USPG X788) under the date November 1788, both of which mention a 'legacy of Dr Lowth, late Bishop of London, 100 pounds'. After Robert Junior's death, Lowth's inheritance passed on to his eldest grandson, Robert Henry Lowth (1801–70). What the real estate Lowth referred to in his Will consisted of is unclear; as the Lowth family has informed me, it appears to have included an estate in Somerset, called Litton Manor, which was still in their possession a generation after Robert Henry's death (see also Hampshire Archives 111M94W/P60). Further research will have to bear out what happened to it subsequently.

As far as can be made out, the list of books in the Will contains over two hundred different titles. The hand in which the copy of the Will is written is often hard to read, which seriously impeded identification of each individual title, all of which, moreover, occur in abbreviated form. Another difficulty in identifying the number of books Lowth possessed is the fact that occasionally different books were bound together into a single volume. An example is Burton's Greek tragedies, of which he ordered a copy from Robert Dodsley on 9 June 1758 as follows: 'be pleas'd to send ... Tragædiarum Græcarum Delectus by D^r. Burton, wth. De Græc. Litt. Institutione Dissertatio by the same, **bound together**'. Only the tragedies are listed in the Will. Some of the titles consist of different volumes, so altogether Lowth's library, consisting of some 440 books, in folio, quarto, and octavo format, was therefore considerable. In addition, there were books 'in the little Dressing Room at ffulham ... which may be worth keeping – chiefly those on the two Upper shelves', while there were 'Many Copies of *Praelectiones*', of Michaelis's annotated edition, and the third edition of *The Life of William of Wykeham* with his booksellers Daniel Prince (d. 1796) in Oxford, 'with whom there is a running Acc^t.', and Thomas Cadell. But at some stage in his life Lowth owned more books. Searching the frontmatter of books in ECCO gives access to information provided by subscription lists, a common way by which books were published at the time (Gaskell 1972: 185). Though the results from such searches are not always fully reliable, due to incomplete and at times careless tagging of words, I came across as many as twenty-six books not listed in the Will, such as Sheridan's *Pronouncing Dictionary* (1780) and Ann Yearsley's *Poems on Several Occasions* (1785). The former title testifies to Lowth's continued interest in linguistic matters – Sheridan's main aim in publishing the pronouncing dictionary was to offer equal opportunities for social advancement by presenting a uniform pronunciation, an issue which was new at the time (Mugglestone 2003) – and the latter suggests that Lowth was acquainted with the bluestocking Hannah More (1745–1833), who had been the main driving force behind the discovery of the poetic qualities of the milkmaid Ann Yearsley (bap.1753, d.1806) (Clarke 2000). In addition, Lowth's correspondence shows that he received presentation copies of books from fellow writers; I have come across some ten such references, none of which appear in the Will. Examples are Thomas Warton's *Life and Literary Remains of R. Bathurst* (1761), the receipt of which he acknowledged as follows: 'Accept of my best thanks for your kind present of your Life of Bathurst', 28 June 1761); Thomas Percy's 'very elegant & ingenious Work on the Song of Solomon' (Lowth to Percy, 3 July 1765); John Rotherham's 'kind Present of the Essay on y^e. Distinction between the Soul & Body of Man' (Lowth to Rotherham, 9 February 1781); and Sir David Dalrymple's 'Presents of Lactantius De Iustitia; & of Christian Antiquities' (Lowth to Dalrymple, 7 June 1779). The Will doesn't mention Dodsley's *Select Fables of Esop* either, though Lowth had contributed to it himself, but perhaps it simply went the way of most other popular children's books. Nor do we find the two books he ordered from Dodsley when he had just started on the grammar, the 'Four Essays upon the English Language, by Professor Ward; An Introduction to Languages &c, by M^r. Bailey' (Lowth to Robert Dodsley, 9 June 1758). What happened to the books not listed in the Will can only be a matter of speculation.

Among the titles in the Will there are, obviously, many works relating to Lowth's theological background: various editions of the Bible, including a 'Hebrew Bible with my ffather's Notes 8 Vol^s. (not to be sold)', a Book of Common Prayer, various collections of sermons (including his own), theological studies, such as Clarke's *A Discourse concerning the Being and Attributes of God* and Pilkington's *Evangelical History and Harmony*, as well as a copy of the Koran. Lowth's philological interests are evident from the list as well, which contains standard writers such as Plato, Thucydides, Pindar, Plautus, Xenophon, Terence, Horace, Cicero, and Homer, to name but a few. Lowth was also interested in English literature: he possessed the works of Milton, Addison, Shakespeare, and Dryden, as well as *The Spectator* (eight volumes) and *The Guardian* (two volumes). A particularly prized item in his library must have been 'Pope 5 Vol^s. his own Edit.'; it is not clear how Lowth acquired this work; possibly it was part of the estate of Joseph Spence, who had been a particular friend of Pope's (*ODNB*, 'Joseph Spence'), which Lowth had administered after his death. To know which works of English literature Lowth read is important from the point of view of his grammar, in which he criticized many grammatical errors he encountered in works of modern literature. What is also of interest here is the fact that Lowth possessed a copy of James Harris's works and of Johnson's *Dictionary*. Both were important to him in the writing of the grammar. The *Dictionary* he seems to have had in his possession at least from the year 1757 onwards, as he refers to it on a matter of spelling in a letter to Robert Dodsley of November that year. Lowth was evidently presented with a copy of Merrick's *Annotations on the Psalms* (1768), which he had been asked to comment on before it went to press. The book opens with an acknowledgement to Lowth's contribution:

OF the following Annotations, those which have the name of Dr. LOWTH (now the Right Reverend the Lord Bishop of OXFORD) subjoined to them were in a great measure communicated to me in the course of a correspondence, relating to a Translation or Paraphrase of the Psalms, in English Verse, which has been twice published (Merrick 1768: iii).

A full-text search for his name in the copy of the book in ECCO produced 180 hits, which testifies to the extent of this.[5] Other books worth mentioning are the sermons and works of Archbishop Secker, Spence's *Polymetis*, and Newton's edition of Milton and Thomas Warton's edition of Virgil, which Lowth had ordered from Robert Dodsley in 1753. The list also includes several copies of his own books: his sermons, the published letters to Warburton (see §2.1), his 'Life of Wickham 2^d. & 3^d. Ed.', and Michaelis's edition of his *De Sacra Poesi Hebraeorum Praelectiones* as well as his own 1753 edition of the book – both listed twice – and his grammar. It is somewhat surprising that the list mentions only a single copy of the grammar, while many editions and reprints of it were published during his lifetime. Perhaps he never received any copies of them.

Lowth specified in his Will that the majority of his books were intended for his wife and children:

---

[5] It is important to note here that full-text searches in ECCO are never wholly reliable. Searching Lowth's grammar, for instance, for the verb *understand* showed that the verb in question as it appears on page 128 of the 1762 edition was not produced. This is possibly due to the fact that the word *understand* has been hyphenated at the end of the line. Other hyphenated words, however, such as *barbarous* on page 43 do show up. Often, words have not been tagged at all and are consequently impossible to retrieve. Searching for the word *custom*, for instance, does produce a hit for page 90 of the grammar but not for the previous page. Important though ECCO is as a research tool, this is a major shortcoming (cf. Brewer 2007: 252).

I also give to my Dear Wife such of my Books as she shall choose for her own use so likewise I give to my Daughter Martha such of my ffrench and English Books as may be useful and she shall choose for herself and I give to my Son Robert such Books as will be most useful to him.

I have already referred to the fact that Lowth's wife Molly enjoyed reading, and that Thomas Henry was looking forward to his copy of Dodsley's fables. Martha, the Lowths' only surviving daughter, evidently read English as well as French literature, like her father, as his library contained several French books (e.g. a 'Dictionaire Historique'). Which books his son Robert found useful or even interesting we don't know; unlike his elder brother Thomas Henry, or, indeed, his father, he does not appear to have had the makings of a scholar. Some books were to go to Lowth's brother William, i.e. the 'Duke of Marlborough's Gems', while Lowth noted that 'Sydenham's Plato, 3 Vol^s. 4to [had been] sent to him' already; others, including Pilkington's *Evangelical History and Harmony* and a two-volume 'English Bible', were intended for his nephew John Sturges, also a clergyman. Five more theological books were destined for his former college in Winchester. Of these, Castell's *Lexicon Heptaglotton* (1669) is still in the library today.

2.3 AN UPWARDLY MOBILE PHILOLOGIST

According to the entry in the *ODNB*, Lowth 'died at Fulham Palace, London, between 2 p.m. and 3 p.m. on 3 November 1787, probably following a stroke'. He had been unwell for some time, suffering from 'the Stone', due to which he was no longer fit enough to be able to accept the archbishopric of Canterbury, which had been offered to him in the spring of 1783, when he was 72 years old. He referred to his illness in a letter to Michaelis, dated 8 January 1782: 'but I have been much out of order with a complaint, which has frequently afflicted me for about two years past, Gravel, or perhaps Stone; which increases upon me, & renders me almost incapable of all application of body or mind: a disease, which, I am afraid, admits of no remedy, but patience & resignation.' He may, moreover, have been greatly affected by the death of his daughter Frances a year later: he wrote his Memoirs around that time, and his Will is dated 11 September 1783, less than two months after she died. Apart from two brief notes addressed to Richard Burn, his secretary when he was Bishop of

London, dating from April and July 1785, I have not come across any personal letters written after the one to his brother in which he announced Frances's death. He lived for a few more years, but he must have felt that his end was near.

Lowth was given a place in the *ODNB*: not surprisingly, as Bishop of London and as someone who left his mark in the field of Hebrew scholarship. It is not, however, so much as an author of a grammar that he became widely known, even though within linguistics it is this achievement that has made him both famous and an object of criticism. In the *ODNB* entry, he is identified as Bishop of London, the highest office he reached during his career as a clergyman, in which capacity he is consequently often believed to have accomplished the achievements that have made him famous in the eyes of posterity. A full-text search of the *ODNB* shows that as a bishop he ordained men such as Charles Daubeny (bap.1745, d.1827) and John Eyre (1754–1803) as deacons, and Thomas Maurice (1754–1824) as a priest, and that he encouraged Sir Herbert Croft (1751–1816) to take orders, while he also conferred various church positions upon men such as Samuel Horsley (1733–1806), Benjamin Kennicott (1718–83), William Julius Mickle (1734/5–88), Thomas Twining (bap.1734, d.1804), and Joseph Warton (bap.1722, d.1800). All these men became so well known that, like Lowth, they were felt to merit a place in the *ODNB*. Lowth is occasionally described as their patron, so, like the patrons who assisted him in his own career, he in turn was, as Bishop of London, in a position to do the same for others. As for his political persuasion, Lowth was a Whig, and was well acquainted with some of the most influential and important men of his day. He was not, however, a man of politics. For all that, I will show in Chapter 5 that, in seeking alliances after he became Bishop of London, he did not limit himself to men of his own political persuasion. My analysis of Lowth's Will has demonstrated that his prime interest was in other things: his library was that of a scholar, a philologist, rather than that of a clergyman or a politician, and this is confirmed by his correspondence. In this light it is interesting to quote from a letter of 18 December 1778 by Shute Barrington (1734–1826), the Bishop of Llandaff, which is filled with praise for Lowth's *Isaiah*:

Interrupted much more than I either wished or expected, I did not finish your Lordship's Isaiah till yesterday. If you wanted literary immortality this work would bestowe it in the amplest form. Indeed, My Good Lord, it is impossible for me to express what I feel for the honour you have done yourself, or the benefits which will result from your various & extensive abilities to the cause of scriptural Knowlege, & sacred criticism . . . Allow me only to lament that the scene of business in which you are involved forbids the world's forming any expectations of your being more extensively useful in the same line, by continuing your labours on some of the other Prophets, & rendering them, what you alone of all mankind can do, equally worthy with Isaiah, of their inspired origin (Barrington to Lowth, 18 December 1778).

Barrington clearly recognized where Lowth's real strengths lay.

The documents I have analysed in this chapter confirm Hepworth's description of Lowth's career as showing a certain amount of 'upward mobility' (1978: 15), and I have argued that his social mobility was assisted by the personal contacts he made in the course of his life. Lowth's upward mobility also caused him to move about geographically: born in Winchester, he travelled on the Continent in his late thirties as well as to Ireland several years later, then moved to Durham for about ten years, and subsequently to Oxford and London, where he remained until his death. It is not unreasonable to characterize Lowth as having been socially and geographically mobile, even though, as the son of a clergyman, he already moved in relatively well-to-do middle-class circles. But his aspirations went further than that, and we learn from his correspondence that he wished to associate with the more highly stationed in society – in which ambition he proved successful. His social ambitions also made him write his grammar in the first place: it was originally meant as a tool for his elder son to facilitate linguistic access to the social classes above those in which the Lowth family customarily moved around the time when he and his wife started a family. The Will demonstrates how successful Lowth had been during his life: he managed to amass a large fortune, which he intended to keep within his family. It is, however, striking to notice that it was only Lowth himself who reached such a high rung on the social ladder: as Lord Bishop of London, he was entitled to a seat in the House of Lords, and there are one or two references that show that he occasionally attended parliamentary sessions. Lowth's only remaining daughter never married, and his son Robert did not exactly follow in his father's footsteps. It wouldn't have been easy for a clergyman to be the Bishop of London's son.

Lowth's social and geographical mobility make him of particular interest from a historical sociolinguistic perspective. As Milroy (1987) argues, socially and geographically mobile people abound in weak ties with other members of their social networks, as a consequence of which their own language is subject to linguistic change, while at the same time they may act as bridges along which linguistic change travels from one social network to another. Lowth's social aspirations would have made him – consciously or unconsciously – aware of the existence of different linguistic norms, to which he had to adapt himself if he wished to participate in the networks concerned. From the perspective of Milroy's social network model, Lowth may well have been a linguistic innovator. To investigate whether he actually was lies outside the scope of the present study, as this would also require a large-scale analysis of the language of his social peers, to which I do not have access to the same extent as in the case of Lowth. What will be addressed here is the question of to what extent his *grammar* served the role of being, metaphorically speaking, a linguistic innovator. In one respect it was – in presenting linguistic criticism of what were considered the best authors in the footnotes in his grammar, which was an innovation within the current grammatical tradition. In another respect, the popularity of the grammar caused it to serve as a model of linguistic correctness to those who used it. This had been the reason why Lowth wrote the grammar to begin with, though he would never have been able to guess at the extent of its eventual influence. In taking a normative approach to grammar, and in dealing, particularly in the syntax section, with grammatical features that were at the time issues of divided usage, Lowth's grammar came to constitute a canon of prescriptivism. This was how it was perceived, and how it was frequently resorted to by grammarians coming after him, in the process of which the items adopted from Lowth's grammar were phrased in increasingly prescriptive terms. Murray's grammar in particular is a good example of how the strictures from Lowth's grammar were adopted and adapted. The popularity of Murray's grammar caused Lowth's strictures to spread further and to shape a model of linguistic correctness. Much of it lives on to the present day in the form of usage guides like Fowler's third edition (Burchfield 1996).

Lowth's strictures often clashed with his own usage, particularly that of his most informal letters. He must therefore have taken the norm of correctness that he presented in his grammar not so much from his own, private usage as from elsewhere. Given his social ambitions, I believe that he looked for it in the language of the aristocracy, or at any rate such as he perceived it to be, having access to it through his patrons and through members belonging to the higher ranks in the Church hierarchy with whom he communicated. Consequently, as a publication taking a new kind of approach, and due to its popularity as well as to the fact that it developed into a standard of English grammar writing, the grammar brought a new norm within reach of an audience of socially mobile speakers and writers of English wider than the social class to which he himself belonged. In the next two chapters I will describe how this important grammar came into being, how it was set up, and what its subsequent publication history was.

THE GRAMMAR: ORIGIN AND PUBLICATION HISTORY

3.1 ORIGIN

'THE history of [the grammar] is this,' Lowth wrote to Merrick some time in early February 1762:

I drew it up for the use of my little Boy, for the reasons mentioned in the Preface. M^r. Legge desired to have ^{it} for his Son; wch. purpose it could not well serve without being printed. I therefore finish'd it, as well as I could for the present; & have printed an Edition of no great number, in order to have the judgement of the Learned upon it. It is capable of considerable improvements, if it shall be thought worth the while. You in particular are desired to comply with y^e. Request at y^e. end of the Preface (Lowth to Merrick, February 1762).

Lowth's 'little Boy' was Thomas Henry, who had just turned eight a few months before. Tom had, however, been much younger when Lowth embarked upon the grammar. There is evidence in Lowth's correspondence with Robert Dodsley that he was working on the grammar in June 1758, when, along with several other books, he ordered two works on grammar from him:

I must [beg] of You to send two more of W^m. of [Wk]^m. to Winchester directed to D^r. Eden, [&] one to M^r. Prince at Oxford, for [P]resents. To me also two more: & with them be pleas'd to send, *Four Essays upon the English Language, by Professor Ward*; *An Introduction to Languages &c, by M^r. Bailey*; Tragædiarum Græcarum

Delectus by D[r]. Burton, wth. De Græc. Litt. Institutione Dissertatio by the same, bound together: Voltaire's Histoire Universelle, the best Edition in French. All bound & Letter'd. The first Volume of Duncombe's Horace, w[ch]. M[r]. Duncombe says he order'd for me, as a Present; & pra[y] enter my name as a Subscriber for [the] same. Pray send me lik[ewis]e [a] Specimen of different sorts [of] your best Letter Writing Paper. And add likewise to the Books above order'd, Theatre des Grecs, par l[e] Pere Brumoy, the very best Edition [(in 8vo or 12[mo])] handsomely bound (Lowth to Robert Dodsley, 9 June 1758).

Both books had just come out, and Lowth must have read about them in the public press. Ward's *Four Essays upon the English Language* was reviewed in the *Monthly Review* (Alston 1965: 32), and we know from Lowth's correspondence that this is a periodical which he read. But an earlier letter in my collection suggests that he was already engaged on the grammar in November of the year before. Upon returning a sheet of proofs for *William of Wykeham*, Lowth first referred to a spelling issue in his own text on which he disagreed with Dodsley and then took Dodsley to task for having confused the verbs *to fly* and *to flee* in his ode *Melpomene* (1757):

Be pleas'd to consider, whether to *fly [away]* & to *fly*, or to [go] swiftly away, are not two [distinct] words; whether *flew*, the past time of y[e]. for[mer] expresses more than *was upon the wing*, with[out] any intimation of *to* or *from*, coming or *going*; & whether to express what you mean, you should n[ot] have said, *fled*, or *flew away*. I mention this, because I am willing to suppose y[t]. y[e]. Public have taste enough to call for a new Edition of Melpomene soon; when, if you approve of my remark, you may easily alter it: and I expect that you repay me my Criticism in kind & with interest (Lowth to Robert Dodsley, 3 November 1757; Tierney 1988: 305).

Usage problems like this were typical of the kind of features which Lowth would deal with in his grammar, and we find this particular issue discussed in a footnote to the verb *to fly* on page 77 as follows:

[1] That is, as a bird, *volare*; whereas *to flee* signifies *fugere*, as from an enemy. This seems to be the proper distinction between *to fly*, and *to flee*; which in the Present Time are very often confounded. Our Translation of the Bible is not quite free from this mistake. It hath *flee* for *volare* in perhaps seven or eight places out of a great number; but never *fly* for *fugere* (1762: 77).

The addition of the final sentence in the above letter – 'I expect that you repay me ... in kind & with interest' – is significant, I think, as it suggests that the topic of the grammar had been discussed by the two men. What is also significant here is that in the same letter to Dodsley, on the subject of a disputed spelling (*Bull* or *Bulle*), Lowth referred to Johnson, saying 'You will tell me [that prac]tice & custom are against me, & [make an app]eal to Johnsons Dictionary, &c. Ne[vertheless,] I think I am right...'. Johnson's dictionary had been published two years before in 1755 by a group of publishers that included Robert Dodsley. It had been Dodsley who had suggested the idea for the dictionary to Johnson (Reddick 1996: 17). Though we have no written evidence that the possibility of writing a grammar was ever mentioned between them, the letters indicate that Lowth and Dodsley would occasionally meet in person, either in London where Dodsley had his bookshop, in Sedgefield, where Lowth lived at the time, or in Durham, where Lowth was a prebendary between 1755 and 1766, and through which Dodsley would occasionally pass on his way to Scotland (see Tierney 1988: 125n, 362n). By the time of the above letter, the unspoken message behind it suggests that the grammar was a project for the fairly immediate future.

In November 1757 Thomas Henry was not yet four, but earlier that same year Mary Hill (1726–80), wife of Lowth's patron Henry Bilson Legge, had given birth to their son Henry, and the above quotation from the letter to Merrick shows that the two men had been discussing the education of their children. Grammar schools in those days, according to Fairman (2006), only accepted pupils who were already able to spell, and from the correspondence between Lowth and his wife during his absence from home in 1755 it appears that Molly was engaged in teaching their son Tom to read and write. Perhaps Tom was a precocious child, but it also seems that his parents were ambitious for their eldest, wishing him to have the best possible educational opportunities. If Molly took care of the practical side of Tom's education, Lowth must have taken responsibility for his academic schooling by deciding to write a grammar of English for this purpose. Teaching English as a preparation for the learning of Latin, which occupied the major part in any grammar school curriculum, had been a matter of pedagogical interest for some time (see, e.g., Vorlat 2007: 502–3). The English grammar published by John Kirkby in 1746 illustrates this. As the title page announces, it includes 'A Brief LATIN GRAMMAR Upon the same Foundation'. The reference to the Latin grammar stresses the importance of a comparative approach by the advice to the teacher to 'let [the Learner] learn the Agreement between the English and Latin Tongues in all those Rules, which are marked, as common to both, in the foregoing English Grammar' (Kirkby 1746: 155). Lowth believed he could prepare his son for his lessons in Latin by teaching him the rudiments of English grammar before sending him to school; he even said as much in the preface to his grammar:

If this method were adopted in our Schools; if children were first taught the common principles of Grammar by some short and clear System of *English* Grammar,...they would have some notion of what they were going about, when they shoud enter into the *Latin* Grammar (1762: xii–xiii).

The Lowths were not alone in taking the early education of their children into their own hands; this was increasingly felt to be the responsibility of middle-class parents in the course of the second half of the eighteenth century (Navest 2009). Bilson Legge was evidently of the same opinion, and, upon hearing of Lowth's activities in relation to his son's education just after the birth of his own son on 22 February 1757, he asked Lowth for a copy of the grammar. This, however, could only be done, as Lowth explained to Merrick, if the grammar was printed, and for this he approached his publisher Dodsley, who was at that time about to publish the *Life of William of Wykeham*.

Dodsley had published Johnson's *Dictionary of the English Language* only two years before. The dictionary had been an ambitious project (Reddick 1996), and it was to include not only a dictionary but also a grammar. Thus, Dodsley hoped, he would be able to produce both an authoritative dictionary and a grammar of the English language at the same time, something for which he expected – correctly, as it happens – that there would be considerable interest among the general public at the time. The dictionary was indeed an immediate success (Reddick 1996: 84), but the grammar prefixed to it was severely criticized. Writing the dictionary had taken much longer than expected, and when the book was finally about to go to press, little time remained for the grammar. Much of the grammar is a straightforward translation from John Wallis's *Grammatica Linguae Anglicanae*, published in 1653, and one of the most important grammars published thus far (Subbiondo 1992). Wallis's grammar had also been one of the main sources of Greenwood's *Essay towards a Practical English Grammar* (1711) (Lehnert 1937–8: 193–6). One of the major shortcomings of Johnson's grammar was that it barely dealt with syntax (Sledd and Kolb 1955: 179). Older grammars of English, and Wallis's grammar is a good example of this, primarily dealt with etymology, that is, with the parts of speech and their declension. This is due to their origin in the Latin tradition, in which syntax barely played a role. Since the mid-1740s, however, English grammarians became interested in actual usage (Tieken-Boon van Ostade 2000*a*), and thus began to develop an eye for the peculiarities of the syntax of English, and in particular for matters of 'government, concord and word order' (Vorlat 2007: 504). Such features had played only a minor role in the earlier Latin-derived grammars. Johnson's grammar did not reflect this new development, by which, according to Sledd and Kolb (1955: 179–80), he had let an important opportunity slip by. Lowth, in the preface to his own grammar, commented on this, though without mentioning Johnson by name:

The last *English* Grammar that hath been presented to the public, and by the Person best qualified to have given us a perfect one, comprises the whole Syntax in ten lines. The reason, which he assigns for being so very concise in this part, is, 'because our Language has so little inflection . . . that its Construction neither requires nor admits many rules' (1762: v).

The reference is, however, unmistakable, and the sentence quoted is indeed from Johnson, from the first edition of the *Dictionary* (sig. c2^{r}). The passage in Johnson's grammar continues with the comment that 'Wallis therefore has totally omitted it [i.e. syntax]; and Johnson [i.e. Ben Jonson], whose desire of following the writers upon the learned languages made him think a syntax indispensably necessary, has published such petty observations as were better omitted'. It is, however, not true that Johnson paid no regard to syntax in his dictionary as such, for, according to Nagashima (1968: 223n), 'it should be remembered that in the body of the *Dictionary* there are interspersed a large amount of grammatical and critical comments, which, when gathered together, will easily fill up a fairly large volume'. Johnson had, however, run out of time (Tieken-Boon van Ostade 1988: 23), and he resorted to Wallis (1653) and Ben Jonson (1640) as earlier authorities to justify his failure in this respect.

When, therefore, Lowth raised the possibility of printing the grammar he had written, Dodsley must have jumped at the opportunity, for an authoritative grammar of the English language was what he had hoped to bring out all along. This, however, required a change of approach in the sense that the grammar in its original version had to be adapted so that it would appeal to a more general reading public. Percy (1997: 131), quoting a review of Lowth's grammar in the *Critical Review*, writes that the grammar in the form in which it was published contains sections that suggest that it had originally been intended as a grammar for children. Traces of the fact that the grammar had been written for his elder son may indeed be found in the following example sentences:[1]

'*Thomas's book*:' that is, '*Thomasis* book;' not '*Thomas his* book,' as it is commonly supposed (1762: 26).

A Verb Active expresses an Action, and necessarily implies an agent, and an object acted upon: as, *to love*; 'I love Thomas.'
    A Verb Passive expresses a Passion, or Suffering, or the receiving of an Action; and necessarily implies an Object acted upon, and an Agent by which it is acted upon: as, *to be loved*; 'Thomas is loved by me' (1762: 44).

The Substantive before a Verb Active, Passive, or Neuter; when it is said what thing *is*, *does*, or *is done*: as, 'I am;' 'Thou writest;' 'Thomas is loved:' where *I*, *Thou*, *Thomas*, are the Nominative Cases, and answer to the question *who*, or *what*?, as, 'Who is loved? Thomas' (1762: 96–7).

Participles have the nature of Adjectives; as, 'a learned man;' 'a loving father' (1762: 101).

The Participle frequently becomes altogether an Adjective;...and as such it admits of the degrees of Comparison: as, 'a learned, a more learned, a most learned, man; a loving, more loving, most loving, father' (1762: 114–15).

In its final form, the *Short Introduction* was no longer a grammar for children. When published, it became a grammar for scholars, though, due to its innovative feature of the footnotes which exposed grammatical errors of the greatest writers in English literature, it also came to serve the needs of an audience seeking linguistic guidance. It is for these two aspects that the grammar was praised by contemporaries, and for the latter that it is spurned by modern linguists.

3.2 THE FIRST EDITION

By November 1759, a first draft of the grammar was finished. We know this because Robert Dodsley's collected correspondence (Tierney 1988) contains a letter by William Melmoth (bap.1710, d.1799) which reads:

I hoped to have returned these M.S.S. to you in person, but being prevented, I must in this manner desire you to make my acknowledgements to D[r]. Lowth for y[e]. pleasure & advantage I have received from his fables & grammar. His

---

[1] These references were first identified by Karlijn Navest.

observations on the structure of our language, wch. he has ranged under the article of *sentences*, are <?> particularly judicious & useful (Melmoth to Dodsley, 20 November 1759; Tierney 1988: 429).

Melmoth is described in the *ODNB* as a writer and translator of Latin verse and, like Lowth, he had his major works published by Dodsley (Tierney 1988: 106n), such as Pliny's letters (1746) and those by Cicero (1753). For the latter translation Dodsley paid him the enormous sum of £600, so Melmoth must have been an author of considerable standing. Melmoth also contributed to Dodsley's *Select Fables of Esop*, which would be published in 1761, but he was not personally acquainted with Lowth. Dodsley sent him the manuscript of the grammar for comments, and Melmoth returned it to Lowth through Dodsley. Lowth acknowledged the comments in a letter to Dodsley written seven months later:

I ought to have thank'd You long ago for the Papers you sent me from M^r. Melmoth, & to have desired You to present my Comp^{ts}. & Thanks to him for being so kind as to communicate them. The remarks are all very proper, & many of them have been of use to me in my design; ot[hers are] **above the rank of Grammatical [use]**. If M^r. Melmoth desires to have his papers back again, I will take care to return them to You. I am very sorry to find you speak of him, as in ^a bad state of health (Lowth to Dodsley, 19 June 1760).

Melmoth's papers, as far as I know, have not come down to us, so we will perhaps never know what Lowth meant by saying that several of Melmoth's remarks were 'above the rank of Grammatical use', but it is striking that in the above letter to Dodsley, Melmoth particularly praised Lowth's critical footnotes. Lowth subsequently revised the grammar, announcing to Dodsley on 9 January the following year:

I shall be in Town probably about the latter end of March: I [brin]g up the Grammar with me, **a [goo]d deal improved**. I am not re[sol]ved whether to print a few Copies [to] give about to friends & critics, to [ge]t their remarks; or to publish an [ed]ition of a small number, with y^e. [s]ame design, & to feel the pulse [of] the public (Lowth to Dodsley, 9 January [1761]).

Lowth's intention to print 'an edition of a small number' only was in line with the original idea of providing his patron Bilson Legge with the requested copy. With the grammar's changed purpose, however, a proper print run was to be produced, though one, as he explained to Merrick in the quotation at the beginning of this chapter, 'of no great number, in order to have the judgement of the Learned upon it'. Exactly how large this print run was I don't know. Dodsley, according to Tierney (1988: 29), published books in print runs of various sizes, depending on the expected popularity of the book. As at this stage they were only 'feel[ing] the pulse of the public' as Lowth put it, a small print run might have been decided on, consisting of no more than 250 copies, but since over twenty copies of the first edition were traced by Alston (1965: 42), a larger print run of 500 copies seems more likely. After all, the grammar was read widely as soon as it came out, which does not contribute to its chances of survival (cf. Suarez 2000: 141). A larger print run of 1,000 copies was, according to Suarez (2000: 136), the usual size of a print run at the time, and, as I will argue in Section 3.3, this was the number decided on for subsequent editions and reprints.

The publication of the grammar was announced in the *Public Advertiser* of 8 February 1762 (Tierney 1988: 461n), nearly ten months after Lowth had delivered the manuscript to Dodsley. As is still the case today, such a period of time for the grammar to be finally published would have been quite normal for a book of its size, 186 pages (Suarez 2000: 136). The first edition was printed in octavo; later editions were also published in duo-decimo format, while one sextodecimo edition is listed in Alston (1965). The imprint on the title page says that the grammar was 'Printed by J. HUGHS; For A. MILLAR in the Strand; And R. and J. DODSLEY in Pall-mall'. As in the case of Johnson's *Dictionary* (1755), Dodsley had teamed up with other booksellers or, in modern terms, publishers (see Suarez, 2000: 132, on this distinction), in order to share the financial risks involved in the publication of the grammar. To do so was accepted practice at the time (Gaskell 1972: 180). Dodsley's brother James and Andrew Millar (1705–68) had similarly been partners in the dictionary project, along with John and Paul Knapton, Thomas and Thomas Longman, and C. Hitch and L. Hawes. The Dodsleys and Millar had also published *William of Wykeham*. James Dodsley took over his brother Robert's publishing business in 1759 (Tierney 1988: 405n) but, as Lowth's correspondence shows, Robert continued to be involved with Lowth's grammar until his death in 1764. After that date, only the names of James Dodsley and Andrew Millar appear on the title page of the grammar until 1767, when it is joined by Millar's former partner Thomas Cadell (1742–1802), while Millar died in 1768 and thus disappeared from the title page when the grammar was reprinted; all negotiations about later editions and reprints of the grammar were, however, conducted between Lowth and James Dodsley.

Lowth's grammar was published anonymously: none of the regular editions and reprints, that is, those published by the Dodsleys, came out with Lowth's name on the title page. For all that, the book was known as 'Lowth's grammar' from the start: this is how it was talked about by those who had read it, how it was advertised and reviewed in the public press, and how it became known abroad. The copy of the grammar's first edition in ECCO has Lowth's name written on the title page in the hand of its original owner, as do those of the second edition (1763) and of the one published in 1778, so people clearly wished to link his name to the grammar. But Lowth was, strictly speaking, no longer technically the owner of the grammar, for he had sold its copyright to his publishers. Tierney (1988: 507) notes that James Dodsley paid £50 for half the copyright of the grammar and, as after Robert Dodsley's death Andrew Millar was the only other name on the imprint of the grammar's title page, Tierney assumes that Millar owned the other half of the copyright (1988: 508). Lowth therefore received £100 for the copyright of his grammar, much less than Melmoth was given for his translation of Cicero's *Ad familiares* but still a considerable sum of money for something which in his own eyes and in comparison with his other books probably seemed no more than a fairly incidental publication. Lowth's great expectations of *William of Wykeham* are voiced in the following discussion of the book in a letter to Robert Dodsley (9 August 1757), which also informs us that he kept the copyright of this book himself:

The Life of William of Wykeham is fin[is]h'd; & ready for the Press. I beg you [to] confer with M^r. Millar about the Pub[lic]ation of it, & give me your joint advice [up]on y^e. matter. As far as I can guess, it [wi]ll make a pretty large Octavo, without [sw]elling it in the printing; tho' I would have [it] printed well & decently. It will not be [a] Book for Common Readers; it will not have [mu]ch either in the matter or the manner [th]at will be entertaining to the generality: [it] is chiefly calculated for those that have [so]me relation to the Subject of it, & may [m]erit the attention of a few others that [see] something more curious than ordinary in... Antiquities & History. So that it [may?] not safely admit of a large Impression. [The] Title is to be The Life of W of W... And when I have told you, that I wo[uld] not part with the property of y^e. Copy & shall want a number (about 60 or [70?]) for Presents, you may easily determine upon your Proposals, & I shall as easily agree to them. – If you choose to print now, ~~to be~~ ready to publish early [in] y^e. winter, I can send it as soon as you please. I have nothing to add but a Pr[e]face, giving an account of my Material[s] for wch. the Book itself need not wait[.]

Little could he have guessed that the grammar was to become his most controversial publication, among linguists at least, nor could he have foreseen that it was to be by far the best selling of all his books.

After Millar's death in 1768, all copyrights owned by him were sold on 13 June 1769 at the Queen's Arms Tavern (Tierney 1988: 511). James Dodsley and Thomas Cadell made a successful bid for seven 1/20 shares of the copyright of Lowth's grammar. They paid £315 for these shares, which amounts to a total of £900 for the full copyright to the grammar. The grammar's market value had thus gone up considerably since Lowth had sold its copyright: from its first moment of publication, the grammar had been immensely popular.

3.3 THE SECOND EDITION

Four weeks after the grammar had come out, Lowth replied to a letter by which Dodsley had informed him how well the *Short Introduction* was selling:

I am very glad to find the Public has so good an Appetite for Grammar: but hope, that what we have already treated them with, will stay their stomachs for some time. For I shall certainly wait for the opinions of the Critics; & when I have leisure, will endeavour to give it all the improvements I can. So that possibly by about this time two years we may be able to give them another Edition (Lowth to Dodsley, 5 March 1762).

As he had explained to Merrick, he had only wished to print 'an Edition of no great number, in order to have the judgement of the Learned upon it'. He himself believed that the grammar was 'capable of considerable improvements, if it shall be thought worth the while'. To this purpose, he had ended his preface with a request to his readers to supply him with comments and additions for improvement:

The following short System is proposed only as an Essay, upon a Subject, tho' of little esteem, yet of no small importance; and in which the want of something better adapted to real use and practice, than what we have at present, seems to be generally acknowledged. If those, who are qualified to judge of such matters, and do not look upon them as beneath their notice, shall so far approve of it, as to think it worth a revisal, and capable of being approved into something really useful; their remarks and assistance, communicated through the hands of the

Bookseller, shall be received with all proper deference and acknowledgement (1762: xv).

In order to make sure that comments would be sent to him, Lowth had distributed presentation copies among his friends: 'I shall desire M^r. Dodsley to send to You A Short Introduction to English Grammar', he told Merrick just after the grammar had come out, adding 'You in particular are desired to comply with y^e. Request at y^e. end of the Preface'. And he wrote similarly when replying to his friend Joseph Spence's letter of acknowledgement in receipt of the grammar,[2] in which Spence had evidently congratulated him upon his achievement: 'I am very glad You approve of Tom's Grammar, on its appearance in y^e. world: You do very well in laying in materials for the improvement of it' (Lowth to Spence, 2 March 1762).

Lowth informed Dodsley that he preferred to wait at least two years before publishing a second edition of the grammar, but Dodsley didn't want to wait that long. The grammar was selling well, and he wished to keep up the momentum of its sales. As the second edition came out in April 1763 (Tierney 1988: 461n), revision of the first edition must already have started very soon after its appearance. The appeal in the preface had produced so many comments that an entirely new text had to be produced. The second edition, published in duodecimo, is longer than the first (196 pages). It not only contains many additional quotations for the critical footnotes, as is shown by a comparison between the index of names quoted in the first edition which I compiled in 1997 and the one of the second and 1764 editions compiled by Navest in 2006, but a number of strictures were added as well. These were evidently felt to be indispensable to any English grammar that took its subject seriously. One example is the discussion of double negation, which first appeared in the second edition, and it is interesting to realize that whereas its disappearance from Standard English is frequently associated – wrongly, as it happens – with Lowth, it is very likely only because one of his critical readers pointed out this oversight that it was included in his grammar at all. A second example is the stricture against another double feature, the use of double comparatives and superlatives, which similarly only made its appearance in the second edition. In the first edition, Lowth had merely observed that 'The Double Superlative *most highest* is a Phrase peculiar to the Old Vulgar Translation

---

[2] The copy listed in the catalogue of the libraries of Joseph Spence and William Duncombe to be sold after their deaths (White 1769: 182) is probably this very copy.

of the Psalms' (1762: 42n), while the second edition actually condemns the double forms in so many words: 'Double Comparatives and Superlatives are **improper**' (1763: 41n). There are many other differences between the two editions of the grammar, and I will discuss several more instances below. To Lowth, the second edition in its fuller form represented his grammar proper, and Reibel was therefore right in reproducing this edition rather than the first in his facsimile edition of Lowth's published work (Reibel 1995). All of this testifies to the significance of being specific as to which edition is referred to in any study involving Lowth's grammar: as he noted in his Memoirs, he continued to improve upon his grammar, as comments kept coming in. An example of the kind of comments received may be found in a letter to Robert Dodsley, from the hand of a certain Richard Burn, dated 16 September 1764, a week before Dodsley's death:

Observing in the papers, that a new edition is intended, of Dr Lowth's Grammar; I beg leave, by your means, to communicate an observation that occurs to me, con-cerning the article a. ...

These are little matters: but to a work so exceeding useful, every one ought to contribute his mite. The public is highly indebted to Dr Lowth, for a piece of excellent criticism, clear & convincing, & which carries its own evidence along with it, & is the more agreeable perhaps, as it is found where one would not readily have expected it (in an introduction to English Grammar) (Burn to Robert Dodsley, 16 September 1764).

Burn may have responded to the following advertisement, which appeared in the *Public Advertiser* on 6 September 1764 (*The 17th–18th Century Burney Collection Newspapers*):

> *Speedily will be published,*
> Two new Editions, of
> A Short Introduction to ENG-
> LISH GRAMMAR, with Critical Notes.
> 1. On a large new Letter and a fine Writing Fools
> Cap Paper, for Gentlemen, bound in Calf, Price 3s.
> 2. On a smaller Letter, and worse Paper, for the
> Use of Schools, bound in Sheep, Price 1s. 6d.
> Printed for A. Millar in the Strand; and R. and J.
> Dodsley in Pall-Mall.
> **Of whom may be had,**
> Dr. Lowth's Life of William of Wyckham, Bishop
> of Winchester. The Second Edition, with Cuts,
> Price 6s.

– De Sacra Poesi Hebræorum, 8vo. 7s.
Johannis Davidis Michaelis Notæ ad Lowth de Sacra
Poesi Hebræorum, Price 4s. bound.

Other newspapers that announced the grammar around this time were the
London Chronicle and the *St. James's Chronicle*. The advertisement shows
how Lowth's name was linked in the press with the anonymously published grammar. The *London Chronicle* of 7 October 1764, in advertising
the publication of one of Lowth's sermons, even referred to the grammar
as 'Dr. Lowth's Introduction to English Grammar':

> *This Day was published*, Price 6d.
> A SERMON preached before the Hon.
> and Right Rev. Richard Lord Bishop of Dur-
> ham, the Hon. Henry Bathurst, one of the Justices
> of the Court of Common Pleas, and the Hon. Sir
> Joseph Yates, one of the Justices of the Court of
> King's Bench; at the Assizes holden at Durham,
> August 15, 1764.
> By ROBERT LOWTH, D.D.
> Prebendary of Durham, and Chaplain in Ordinary
> to his Majesty.
> Published at the Request of their Lordships, and of
> the Gentlemen of the Grand Jury.
> Printed for A. Millar in the Strand, and J. Dodsley
> in Pall Mall, London; and R. Manistry, in Durham.
> Of whom may be had,
> Two Editions of **Dr. Lowth's Introduction to**
> **English Grammar**; one printed on a fine Paper,
> Price 3 s. bound, and another on coarse, Price 1 s. 6 d.
> in Sheep.

In the subsequent editions of his grammar, Lowth acknowledged the
comments he received merely in general terms:

The Author is greatly obliged to several Learned Gentlemen, who have favoured
him with their remarks upon the former Edition; which was indeed principally
designed to procure their assistance, and to try the judgement of the public. He
hath endeavoured to weigh their observations without prejudice or partiality,
and to make the best use of the lights which they have afforded him. He hath
been enabled to correct several mistakes, and encouraged carefully to revise
the whole, and to give it all the improvement which his present materials can

furnish. He hopes for the continuance of their favour, as he is sensible there will be abundant occasion for it (1763: xviii).

But he did not include all comments that reached him. In Chapter 1, I mentioned that Merrick had sent him additional examples for his footnotes from the second edition of Thomas Birch's *Life of the Most Reverend Dr. John Tillotson, Lord Archbishop of Canterbury*, published in 1753. The instances had been collected by Merrick himself and some of his friends, including John Loveday (1711–89), who was an old friend of theirs from Oxford (Markham 1984: 23). Lowth acknowledges the comments as follows:

I am much obliged to You & Your Friends for the Remarks. In the Paper inclosed I acknowledge the hand of M^r. Loveday, to whom I beg my best Respects & Thanks. On Grammar p. 117, 118. You sent me something, to the same purpose I believe, before, referring to D^r. Birch's Life of Tillotson, 2^d Edition; but I c^d. not meet with y^t. Edition time enough, nor find y^e. place referred to, in y^e. first Edition. The 2 Editions of y^e. Grammar $^{now\ published}$ have been finished at the Press some months ago; so that y^e. opportunity of Correction is past (Lowth to Merrick, 25 October 1764).

As said, the excuse for not incorporating the quotations at first sight looks real enough. At the same time, however, the elaborateness of the excuse raises suspicions: Lowth claims he could not get hold of the book referred to by Merrick, that he was unable find the relevant pages in the first edition, while moreover the new edition of the grammar had already been published, 'so that y^e. opportunity of Correction is past'. In reality, I think he did not want to include the grammatical errors Merrick had found in Birch's *Life of Tillotson* because Thomas Birch (1705–66) was still alive. Percy (1997: 134) observes that all authors treated critically by Lowth in his grammar were dead. He must have had good reasons for not including the grammatical mistakes of living authors: running the risk of offending 'our best Authors' would have been tricky, and it was one that Lowth clearly did not wish to take. Being dependent on the favours of those in a position of power, as Lowth had been all his life, one couldn't be too careful. The subject of Tillotson's book, moreover, was the life of a former Archbishop of Canterbury. Lowth, as discussed in Chapter 2, had high expectations of his own career in the Church. Birch was a well-known historian and biographer of his own generation, and Lowth may have hoped one day to be the subject of one of his books as well. Though this highest position within the Church of England was indeed offered to him, Lowth never did become Archbishop of Canterbury, nor did Birch live long enough to witness his ecclesiastical ascendancy: he died from a fall off his horse at the age of sixty. All this shows that the grammar, as it continued to grow – in his Memoirs he had noted that its different editions had been 'all corrected with some alterations, additions, &c by y^e. Author' – can be looked upon as the result of considerable interaction between the author and his reading public, an unusual thing for its time.

3.4 SUBSEQUENT EDITIONS AND REPRINTS

When Lowth noted in his Memoirs that for the grammar 'The number of Copies printed in the whole including the Edition of 1780 $^{(or\ 1781)}$ amounted to about 34.000', he appears surprised at the evident success of what had seemed to him his least significant publication. The figure he mentions, 34,000 copies, suggests 34 editions of reprints of 1,000 copies each. In comparison with his other publications, this was indeed phenomenal: ECCO, the contents of which are primarily based on the holdings of the British Library, contains copies of three editions of Lowth's *De Sacra Poesi Hebraeorum Praelectiones*, published in 1753, 1763, and 1775, as well as a copy of the Oxford edition of the work by Johann David Michaelis of 1763 and of a two-volume English translation by G. Gregory from 1787. There are also copies of three editions of the *Life of William of Wykeham*, published in 1758, 1759, and 1793, as well as a separately published twenty-one-page supplement to the first edition with the corrections to the second. *Isaiah, a New Translation* is recorded in an eleventh edition from 1835 in the British Library catalogue, and ECCO contains copies of the editions published in 1778, 1779, 1791, and 1793. The above figure was also very high from the perspective of the publication of grammars at the time: it is only at the end of the century, with the publication of Murray (1795) and Fenn (1798?; 1799), that grammars begin to appear in print runs of really high numbers (Tieken-Boon van Ostade 1996*a*; Navest in preparation).

The figure of 34,000 obviously may be no more than an estimate. By the time of his death, Lowth's private library, according to the information in his Will, contained only a single copy of the grammar, which is surprising in view of what looks like a fairly simple calculation of the number of editions or reprints published between the first edition of 1762 and the time when he wrote the Memoir, around 1783. It is quite possible that the figure is based on a general understanding between Lowth and the Dodsleys that two editions or reprints of the grammar would be published each year. I have not found any written evidence for this in their correspondence (though the possibility exists that they discussed the matter in person), but I have found another letter which confirms this. On 25 October 1764, Lowth informed Merrick: 'The 2 Editions of y^e. Grammar $^{\text{now published}}$ have been finished at the Press some months ago'. The advertisements quoted in Section 3.3 confirm that two editions were published simultaneously, an ordinary version, 'On a smaller Letter, and worse Paper, for the Use of Schools, bound in Sheep', and what might be called a de luxe version, 'On a large new Letter and a fine Writing Fools Cap Paper, for Gentlemen, bound in Calf'. The prices differed accordingly, 1s. 6d. and 3s. respectively. Alston (1965: 43) lists two different editions that were published that year, a third and a so-called 'new edition', both of them in octavo, but no other details are given. The above advertisements appeared in September and October 1764, respectively, but the *Lloyd's Evening Post* of 29 June of that year also announced the publication of an edition of Lowth's grammar. The dates of these advertisements are so far apart that it is likely that, indeed, two different editions were published in 1764, each, as usual, in two formats. For 1765 I have found advertisements for the grammar in July and in November, and for 1766 for January, May/June and November. Could this refer to three editions for 1766, or would the January 1766 edition be the same as the one advertised for November the year before? The problem is that the announcement 'This day is published' rarely refers to the day on which the advertisement itself appeared as being the actual publication date of the grammar.

In his bibliography, Alston (1965: 42–8) lists 48 editions and reprints altogether, including pirated editions (see §3.5), as well as two German translations. Of these, 23 were regular editions and reprints in that they were published by the Dodsleys, Millar, and Cadell, who possessed the copyright of the grammar. Two more bear the imprint 'for the Booksellers', but whether this referred to Lowth's regular publishers is unclear. The editions listed in Alston that bear the imprint of other publishers on the title page I consider to be pirated copies, that were published without authority either from Lowth or his publishers. The grammar was published interchangeably in different formats, in octavo (8°), as with the first and third editions, and in duodecimo (12°), as with the second and the 1767 editions. There was also a sextodecimo (16°) edition, likewise published in 1767 but never again. Different formats might appeal to different readers, with the octavo edition being perhaps more suitable for use in schools, and it is clear that the publishers had a keen eye for the market. Lowth, it seems, had a say in the matter as well, for in a letter addressed to James Dodsley dated 18 October 1773 he wrote:

For the New Edition of the Grammar **in yᵉ. smaller size** [duodecimo], You will give the Printer directions from any of the Editions **of small size** in regard to the Letter, yᵉ. Form of the Page &c; but be pleased to observe, that he must print from yᵉ. last Edition of 1772, (of **yᵉ. larger size** [octavo], & better paper,) as yᵗ. differs by some Corrections fᵐ. yᵉ. rest. Be pleas[ed] to give him orders to send the Sheets to me, after one Correction, by the Post; & I will return them regularly (Lowth to James Dodsley, 18 October 1773).

For 1773, no editions are listed by Alston, but the inventory does include a 'New Edition' that was published in 1774, listed as octavo. The duodecimo edition of that year may not have survived. There was, however, a pirated edition in duodecimo published in Dublin that year, which may have been based on a regular duodecimo edition (the same is true for the 1769 edition). Only for the year 1767 does Alston list two editions in different sizes (12° and 16°). No editions or reprints are recorded either for the years 1765, 1766, 1768, 1770, 1777, 1779, and 1780, the final year covered by Lowth's comment in the Memoir.

All of this suggests that Alston's inventory does not tell the whole story: it is far from complete, due to the wear and tear that grammar books are usually subject to. All copies of the grammar I have seen during my research for this study, including my own, showed very little sign of use. This obviously contributed greatly to their chances of survival (Suarez 2000: 141). Using Lowth's figure of 34,000 copies printed down to the edition of 1781 as a starting point, as well as the number of copies listed in Alston (1965) for this period, I calculated that only about 0.5 per cent of the copies that were once in circulation have come down to us (Tieken-Boon van Ostade 2008*a*). Alston's inventory, moreover, dates from the mid-1960s, and new copies and even some editions have come to light since. ECCO II, for instance, which became available to me in February 2010, now includes two editions and reprints not recorded

FIG. 3.1. Loveday's inventory of grammars used as a source of collation of his own copy of the first edition (Pennsylvania State University Library, PE1109.L85 1762)

by Alston: a sixth edition published in Belfast in 1785 and another Belfast edition (1795) labelled 'SEVENTH EDITION, CORRECTED'. What is more, it doesn't list copies of the grammar that are privately owned; my own is an obvious case in point. Two examples are the octavo editions ('New Editions, Corrected') published in 1767 and 1772 listed by Loveday opposite the title page of his own copy of the first edition of the grammar, which is held by Pennsylvania State University Library (see Figure 3.1).

I mentioned above that Loveday sent Lowth comments on the grammar; Lowth had probably given him a presentation copy for this very purpose. Loveday's copy is filled with annotations in his hand, so he subsequently updated the grammar whenever a new edition or reprint appeared. Doing so was common practice at the time: two of the copies of the grammar held by Winchester College Library similarly contain manuscript annotations, and one of these Navest (2007) attributed to William Warburton. Loveday died two years after Lowth, in 1789, so he kept up this practice all his life (no edition is recorded in Alston for the year 1788). Alston only lists duodecimo editions for the years 1767 and 1772, along with the sextodecimo one for 1767 already referred to. Could its unusual size be the result of a one-off experimental third edition that year? In addition to the ones already listed, ECCO contains another edition not in Alston, dated 1790, published in London, 'for E. Wenman', and the

National Library of Australia contains an additional London edition for 1791, 'printed for William Osborne'.

Alston's survey includes a regular third edition of the grammar published in 1764, and after that only 'new editions'. A fifth, sixth, seventh and eighth edition, published in Belfast in 1765, 1785, and 1795, and in Dublin in 1787, are pirated editions, for which the publishers very likely made use of copies of the regular editions, none of which have come down to us. (Nor have any copies of a fourth edition.) The question is whether we have to do with proper editions here or with mere reprints of earlier editions. The difference between an edition and a reprint, according to Gaskell (1972: 313), is that, by way of 'a simple rule of thumb... there is a new edition when more than half the type has been reset'. Gaskell also writes that from the second half of the eighteenth century, 'books of medium length... of marked popularity might be kept in type... for several impressions after the first, which were often described on their title-pages as new editions' (1972: 117). This does not apply to Lowth's grammar: as said, the grammar's second edition was a considerably enlarged version of the first, while Lowth also made a number of additions to the new edition of 1764. There are several references in his letters that suggest that Lowth indeed continued to do so, such as the one quoted above (1773), but also an earlier letter from 1764:

I sent the Corrections for the Third Edition of the Grammar ab^t. a fortnight ago to M^r. Millar wch. I suppose he has received (Lowth to James Dodsley, 21 March 1764).

Also in the Memoir he noted that the editions that had come out since the first had all been 'corrected with some alterations, additions, &c by y^e. Author'. Whether for each new edition of the grammar Lowth altered the text to such an extent that more than half the type would need to be reset and that we would thus be dealing with new editions proper is hard to say. A comparison of the layout of the first pages of all the regular editions included in ECCO, those published in London by the Dodsleys, Millar, and Cadell (fourteen in all), does suggest that each issue of the grammar was newly set up in type. The differences are often minute, as when the first word on the page is variously printed GRAMMAR (1763), GRAMMAR (1764, new edition) or GRAMMAR (1769). Not even the two 1764 editions are identical in layout. The 1772, 1775, 1783, and 1793 editions are identical except for the fact that the second word in the second paragraph, *Grammar*, is capitalized in all but the 1772 edition. The grammar was evidently never reprinted from 'standing type' (cf. Gaskell 1972: 117). Possibly, different printers were employed for the production of reprints; who these printers were is hard to ascertain, as only the first edition of the grammars in ECCO mentions a printer, J. Hughs.

The publishers stopped numbering the editions after the eighth, though the evidence for this, coming from a pirated edition, is circumstantial; none of the regular editions after the third are numbered. According to Suarez (2000: 141) so-called 'edition statements' on the title page of an eighteenth-century book should not be taken at face value, as a high edition number on the title page might be used as a selling device, informing the would-be buyer of the alleged popularity of the book in question. In the case of Lowth's grammar, this method was not resorted to by the publishers, nor did they need to do so: the grammar was selling well as it was. The case of the pirated editions which do show higher edition statements may be a different matter, and this may obviously apply to the pirated eighth edition, too.

The question of whether we have to do with editions or reprints with every new issue of the grammar is difficult to answer. When Richard Burn enquired with Robert Dodsley in September 1764 about the 'new edition . . . of Dr Lowth's Grammar' that had been announced in the papers, this may have been a reference either to the third edition, which is indeed numbered as such on the title page, or to the 'New Edition' so-called. Lowth himself claims that he continued to correct his grammar every time a new edition was to be published; Percy (1997), indeed, found differences in successive editions down to the time he made this comment. This may be why Lowth didn't keep any earlier copies of his grammar, as he may have used them for making annotations for subsequent reprintings, sending them to the publisher for this purpose. But whether the number of changes he made would have been so many that half the type would have to be reset, according to Gaskell's definition of the difference between editions and reprints, seems unlikely to me. I believe that in the modern sense of the word only the first three editions of the grammar can be considered as proper editions; in the case of later issues of the grammar we seem to have to do with reprints. But in the eyes of Lowth himself, as well as his publishers, each newly published version of the grammar would have been a new edition: this was how the grammar was advertised, on the title page ('A New Edition, Corrected') and in the public press. This represented a sound selling device, even when, as for the 1793 edition, Lowth was no longer alive.

3.5 PIRATED EDITIONS

Alston's inventory contains many more editions and reprints of the grammar than those already discussed. These, however, were not published by the Dodsleys, Millar, or Cadell, nor did they come out (with two exceptions) in London. Instead, they were all published abroad. Such editions are known as 'pirated' editions. Copyright in England came to be protected after the introduction of the Statute of Anne in 1710. According to this law, copyright lasted for twenty-one years after original publication, after which two further extensions of fourteen years each could be applied for (Feather 1988: 74). But this copyright law applied to England only, and though Gaskell (1972: 185) notes that as a result 'local piracy was virtually eliminated...there was still damaging competition from piratical publishers overseas (especially in Ireland and Holland)'. In the case of the *Short Introduction*, none of the pirated editions listed in Alston were

Table 3.1 **Pirated (and other) editions of Lowth's grammar down to 1800 (Alston 1965)**

Year	Numbered		Size Comment
1763	second		12° Dublin: H. Saunders
1765	fifth		12° Belfast: J. Hay and H. & R. Joy
1769		new edition	12° Dublin: James Williams
1774		new edition	12° Dublin: Thomas Ewing
1775			12° Waterford: Hugh and James Ramsey
1775			12° Philadelphia: R. Aitken
1780		new edition	12° Hartford (America): [no publisher]
1783		new edition	12° Hartford: Nathaniel Patten
1783			8° Newbury-port: John Mycall
1785	sixth		12° Belfast: John Hay, and Henry Jay, Senr. and Junr.
1785		new edition	12° Dublin: R. Jackson and T. White (Cork)
1786	eighth		12° Dublin: R. Jackson
1794			8° Basil: J. J. Tourneisen
1794		new edition	12° Leeds: J. Binns
1795	seventh		12° Belfast: W. Magee
1795		new edition	12° Cork: Thomas White
1795		new edition	12° New York: Rogers and Berry
1799		new edition	12° London: J. Johnson, G. G. & J. Robinson, J. Waler [et al.]
1799			12° Philadelphia: R. Aitken
1800		new edition	12° [no place] Wilmington, Bonsel and Niles

published in Holland, but, as Table 3.1. shows, as many as ten of them came out in Ireland (Belfast, Dublin, Waterford, and Cork). Six were published in America (in Philadelphia, Hartford, Newbury-port, and New York), one in Basle, Switzerland, and two in England (Leeds and London). One more grammar was published in London, by A. Millar, W. Law, R. Cater, and Wilson, Spence & Mawman. This one, as I will argue in Section 3.7, as well as the reprints made after this date, were not pirated copies proper, because by then the grammar had fallen into the public domain.

The first time Lowth's grammar came out in unauthorized form was in 1763, in Dublin. The version pirated was the second edition, to which the publisher, H. Saunders, had added Joseph Priestley's 'Observations on Style'. These observations derived from Priestley's *Rudiments of English Grammar*, which had been published in 1761, allegedly about a month before Lowth's grammar came out (Priestley 1768: xxiii). By adding this twenty-page section from Priestley's grammar, Saunders in fact adapted Lowth's grammar to current notions of what a grammar should be like. According to Vorlat (2007: 504), grammars traditionally 'consisted of four parts, usually called orthography, etymology, syntax and prosody'. The sections on orthography and syntax are largely self-evident, but, she continues, etymology (morphology in modern terms) 'deals with the parts of speech or word classes, sometimes also with inflexion and derivation', while 'prosody deals with stress placement, figures of speech, style, and more than once also with homonymy and synonymy'. Lowth's grammar did not include a section on style but did have one on punctuation, as well as a section called 'A PRAXIS, or Example of Grammatical Resolution' (1762: 173–86), in which sample sentences were parsed by way of illustration of the uses to which the grammar could be put. Both sections were kept in by Saunders but, by adding Priestley's section on style, he aimed to improve upon the set-up of the grammar. He had thus – in his own eyes – produced a better grammar, and announced it as such on the title page. There, he supplied both authors' names, thus making the most of this new edition for publicity purposes.

Whether Saunders was very successful in his attempt at jumping, as he clearly did, on the bandwagon of Lowth's immediate popularity, is unlikely: Alston (1965) only mentions this single edition, which has come down to us in no more than two copies. Other Irish publishers similarly tried their hand at publishing the grammar: J. Hay and H. & R. Joy jointly from Belfast; James Williams, Thomas Ewing, and R. Jackson from Dublin; and

Thomas White from Cork. In all these instances the number of surviving copies is very small, which may suggest that the print runs had not
been very large. By contrast, many more copies of the American editions have come down to us, particularly of the ones published by
R. Aitken in Philadelphia and Rogers and Berry in New York, and the
Wilmington edition of 1800, perhaps because the grammar had been
printed in larger numbers. Possibly there was a greater interest in the
grammar in America than in Ireland. Lowth's grammar was also published in Basle, in 1794, by J. J. Tourneisen. ECCO contains as many as
127 items published by Tourneisen, ranging from Hugh Blair's *Lectures
on Rhetoric and Belles Lettres* (1788), David Hume's *History of England*
(1789–90), and Edward Gibbon's *Miscellaneous Works* (1796–7) to a 23-
volume edition of Shakespeare's plays (1800–02) (Barber 1960). Lowth's
grammar was also translated into German. It is interesting to see from
this, as well as from the pirated editions, how Lowth's grammar foreshadows the later popularity of Lindley Murray's *English Grammar*,
which was popular not only in America and England, but which was
reprinted throughout the world (Tieken-Boon van Ostade 1996a: 10).
An interest in English as a foreign language was clearly already budding
around that time, but from the perspective of the present study it is
important to note that Lowth's name on the title page served as a major
selling device.

3.6 RECEPTION OF THE GRAMMAR

The first proof of the immediate popularity of Lowth's grammar dates
from within about a month of its publication. On 26 February 1762, a
certain Thomas Fitzmaurice enquired from Adam Smith (1723–90), who
was later to write *An Inquiry into the Nature and Causes of the Wealth of
Nations* (1776):

Pray have you seen Dr Louths English Grammar which is just come out? It is talk'd
of much. Some of the *ingenious men* with whom this University overflows, are
picking faults and finding Errors in it at present. Pray what do you think of it? I am
going to read Harris's Hermes now, having read this Grammar. I heard lately an
objection to an Expression in your Book, which I think has some foundation. It is
in the Beginning of the 1st Section upon Custom: the Expression is a *Haunch*

Button, which is not, I imagine exactly English (Fitzmaurice to Smith, 26 February 1762; Mossner and Ross 1987, letter 64).

Fitzmaurice must have ordered a copy of the grammar as soon as he had seen it announced in the press. This may well have been in the *London Chronicle*, a newspaper which was jointly owned by Robert Dodsley and the printer William Strahan (1715–85) (Sher 2006: 363). The paper first came out on 1 January 1757 and, according to Sher, it 'was a prime vehicle for book advertisement'. Fitzmaurice read the grammar at once. The book, he noted, had already become the talk of the University of Oxford, inspiring its readers to 'pick faults and find Errors in it', evidently in response to the challenge in the preface to supply Lowth with suggestions for improvement. Fitzmaurice next criticized Smith's use of the expression *Haunch Button*, whatever it may mean, which suggests that he felt similarly inspired by Lowth's critical comments to hunt for linguistic errors in Smith's book, *Theory of Moral Sentiments* (1759). The source in question, 'a meanness and aukwardness in the absence even of a **haunch button**' (Smith 1759: 372), occurs in all editions of the book in ECCO, but nowhere else: not 'exactly English', indeed. If, however, Fitzmaurice considered sending the instance to Lowth, the grammar would not have been the place to expose this kind of lexical error. Besides, Lowth would not have included it as evidence of a linguistic mistake, as it was from a living author. Linguistic criticism like this, according to Percy (2008), was also commonly found in book reviews of the time, published in the *Monthly Review* and the *Critical Review*. Percy, moreover, believes that particular instances of grammatical errors 'may even have been cited in reviews before they appeared in grammar books' (2008: 137–9; 2009). This is where Lowth, who read the *Monthly Review*, as his correspondence shows, may have picked up the idea to discuss errors by 'our best Authors' in the footnotes of his grammar. The canon of prescriptivism may indeed have originated with Lowth's grammar, but in many instances the book merely formalized what was already being frowned upon elsewhere.

In announcing in the above letter to Adam Smith that he was 'going to read Harris's Hermes now, having read this Grammar', Fitzmaurice again referred to the preface of the *Short Introduction*, where Lowth referred those 'who would enter more deeply into this Subject' (1762: xiv–xv) to James Harris's *Hermes* (1751). The grammar had not only inspired Fitzmaurice to pick faults and find errors, but it had also awakened an interest in English grammar proper. I have come across another letter that refers to the grammar soon after its publication, written on 20 May 1762 by the author William Shenstone (1714–63) to his friend Richard Graves (1715–1804), reading: 'What think you of Dr. Lowth's Grammar? – Livie met him at Mr. Dodsley's, and says, he is well pleased with *our* frontispiece, &c. to Horace' (Shenstone 1769: 379). Though the grammar is not praised in so many words, the enquiry confirms its immediate popularity, as in Fitzmaurice's letter. By this time, Lowth had acquired the status of an authority, whose opinion on a matter such as a frontispiece was worth quoting. The quotation also presents Dodsley's bookshop as a meeting place for writers and publishers.

Alston (1965: 42) notes that the grammar was reviewed in the *Monthly Review*, the *Dublin Magazine* (twice, already in March and July 1762), and in the *Critical Review*. The piece in the *Monthly Review*, dating from July 1762, indicates that the author, William Rose (1719–86), knew about Lowth's authorship of the grammar, for it opens with the sentence 'THE public is indebted for this judicious performance to the ingenious and learned Dr. Lowth' (Carol Percy's 'Database of Linguistic and Stylistic Criticism in Eighteenth-Century Periodical Reviews'). Rose had also reviewed Lowth's *Life of William of Wykeham* (Nangle 1934: 150, 198). The author of the review in the *Critical Review* remains anonymous. Unlike in the case of Rose, he seems to have been unfamiliar with the name of the author of the book he reviewed. He praises Lowth, hailing him as a 'complete philologist', but also expresses a certain amount of criticism:

It must be allowed that the author of this introduction to grammar, is extremely well qualified to write upon the subject. He seems to be a complete philologist, well acquainted with the antient dead languages, and particularly versed in the Saxon, which gave birth to the English. His rules are just, concise, and explicit: his examples well chosen and satisfactory: yet his method of arrangement, is, to our apprehension, a little embarrassed, so as **not to be easily comprehended, or retained by young beginners** (*Critical Review* 14, 1762: 504–5; Percy's 'Database of Linguistic and Stylistic Criticism in Eighteenth-Century Periodical Reviews').

As discussed in Section 3.1, Lowth's grammar was, indeed, not a grammar for children. The reason the reviewer took him to task here is Lowth's claim, made in the preface to the grammar, that his 'little System, [was] intended merely for a private and domestic use. The chief end of it was to explain the general principles of Grammar as clearly and intelligibly as possible', to which he added that 'it was calculated for the use of the Learner even of the lowest class' (1762: xiii–xiv).

The same point was made well over thirty years later by Lady Ellenor Fenn in the preface to *The Child's Grammar* (1799):[3]

Dr. *Lowth* speaks of his Introduction to English Grammar as being calculated for the Use of the Learner, even of the lowest Class: but a Perusal of it will convince any Person conversant with *such Learners*, that the Doctor was much mistaken in his Calculation. It is a delightful Work! highly entertaining to a young Person of Taste and Abilities, who is already initiated: and perhaps in the *private* and *domestic* Use for which it was designed; his Lordship's Commentary might render it intelligible to those of his own family; but for general and public Use there is certainly Need of an Introduction to it: – There must be a DAME to prepare a Scholar for the Lessons of such a Master: And should I be gratified in my Wish to supply that Office, I shall think myself highly honoured (Fenn 1799: vi).

The immediacy of the reference to Lowth's family is striking, because Lowth had already been dead for more than ten years, and his children, those who were still alive, would long have outgrown any need for their father's commentary. Fenn, however, is referring to Lowth's comment in his preface about the intended readership of the grammar. She makes her point about the unsuitability of the grammar as a teaching instrument for children in order to advertise her own grammar as a suitable introduction to the one by Lowth. Her little grammar – its format is so small that it fits into the palm of one's hand – was intended for very young children, who were to be prepared for formal schooling by their mothers at home. Fenn rightly spotted a market for herself here, as the grammar became enormously popular (Navest 2008), including its companion volume for mothers.

The Methodist John Wesley (1703–91) is another grammarian who believed that his own grammar would serve as an introduction to Lowth's. Wesley's *Short English Grammar* first came out in 1748, and had been written as one of a series of textbooks for Kingswood School (Vallins 1957: 9–10), a school for Methodist children which had been founded by Wesley in that same year. The grammar, according to Vallins (1957: 25), 'bristles with inconsistencies, inaccuracies, and obvious errors'; yet it was considered suitable enough as a school grammar to merit a third edition in 1778. Wesley thought highly of Lowth's grammar, for in a letter of 12 February 1767 to his brother Charles (Telford 1931) he called it 'the best English

---

[3] The grammar is undated; for its date of publication see Percy (2006) and Navest (in preparation). The quotation below was taken from my own copy of the book.

Grammar that is extant'. But like Fenn many years later, he considered it too difficult for absolute beginners, and like Fenn he believed that his own grammar would suit this purpose better. Evidence for this may be found in letters of advice which he wrote to two women, a certain Margaret Lewen (c.1742–66) and his niece Sarah Wesley (1759–1828) (Telford 1931), in which he made a number of suggestions as to how they might proceed to educate themselves. In one of the points in his list Wesley refers the women to Lowth's grammar, but not until they had read his own:

The first thing you should understand a little of is Grammar; in order to which it will suffice to read first the Kingswood English Grammar (which is exceeding short), and then Bishop Lowth's Introduction (Wesley to Lewen, June 1764; Telford 1931).

His advice to Sarah Wesley is phrased in almost the same words (8 September 1781). As Wesley refers to 'Bishop Lowth's Introduction' in the letters, the original version of the letter to Margaret Lewen must date from the year 1766 (when she died), not 1764 as the editor suggests. Both women were in their early twenties when they received Wesley's advice. As women, they may not have had much formal education, and they appear to have sought advice from Wesley to remedy this. Wesley likewise recommended Lowth's grammar in his lesson plan for Kingswood school (1768), for pupils who were enrolled in the first year of a 'Course of Academic Learning' (1768: 10). Presumably, this was a more advanced course of studies, which lasted four years, than the one presented in the regular lesson plan. By way of preparation, the pupils first learnt English grammar from Wesley's own grammar in their second year at school (1768: 4).

Apart from the grammars by Fenn and Wesley, a third grammar that was similarly believed to provide a suitable preparation for Lowth's more advanced *Short Introduction* was Ellin Devis's *The Accidence, or First Rudiments of English Grammar* (1775). Devis (1746–1820) was one of a new group of 'teacher-grammarians' who operated during the second half of the eighteenth century, all of whom were female and all of whom owned their own schools (Cajka 2008). Eight regular editions of the grammar are recorded by Alston (1965: 60–1) down to 1800, and several more after the turn of the century, as well as a pirated edition (Dublin, 1798), which suggests that her grammar was similarly popular to Lowth's. In 1797, Erasmus Darwin (1731–1802) wrote in his *Plan for the Conduct of Female Education, in Boarding Schools*: 'Mrs. Devis has publish'd a small and useful rudiment of grammar purposely for the use of young ladies; which may be taught **as an introduction to Lowth's grammar**' (1797: 16). The teacher and educationist Vicesimus Knox (1752–1821) also specifically recommended Lowth's grammar as suitable material for girls: 'As soon as they can read with fluency, **let them begin to learn Lowth's Grammar**, and to read at the same time some very easy and elegant author, with a view to exemplify the rules' (Knox 1781: 233). Studying Lowth's grammar was thus not considered a male prerogative.

Lowth may not have thought highly of Johnson as a grammarian, but the reverse was true for Johnson with respect to Lowth, both for his general learning and for his grammar. Johnson is claimed to have said that 'Lowth is another bishop who has risen by his learning' (Pottle and Bennett 1963: 56), and that 'all Scotland could not muster learning enough' for his *Praelectiones* (Wimsatt and Pottle 1960: 112n). With respect to the grammar, Percy (1997: 131), basing herself on Boswell's journal, writes that Johnson had recommended Lowth's grammar to a certain Mr Astle, a clergyman from Ashbourne in Derbyshire. The grammar is part of a fairly lengthy list of books which Johnson proposed to Astle for his studies. Johnson and Lowth, however, never appear to have met in person, despite the fact that they shared a publisher with whom they were both on more than friendly terms. Nagashima (1968) identified a certain amount of mutual influence between the two, but Lowth never referred to Johnson in his grammar more than a couple of times.

A grammarian who profited from the criticism of Lowth's grammar in the public press was John Ash (1724–79). Ash had published a grammar called *Grammatical Institutes: or Grammar, Adapted to the Genius of the English Tongue* in 1760, which he 'had written originally for his five-year-old daughter, and had printed ... for the use of schoolmaster friends' (Michael 1970: 278). In this, we see an interesting parallel with the origin of Lowth's grammar. Both grammars, moreover, were equally popular, for Alston (1965: 32–8) lists as many as forty editions and reprints for Ash's grammar and, as in Lowth's case, pirated editions appeared abroad, in New York, Dublin, and Philadelphia, and they were both translated into German. After 1763, the grammar appeared with a new subtitle, 'an easy introduction to Dr. Lowth's English grammar', and occasionally even as 'the easiest introduction to Dr. Lowth's English grammar', though Navest (in preparation) argues that the latter were unauthorized publications, even though they were brought out by Ash's regular publishers, E. & C. Dilly. Adding this new subtitle reflects an effort comparable to those later

made by Fenn in her own grammar, and by Wesley in his private com-
munications as well as his lesson plan for Kingswood school, to profit
from the popularity of Lowth's grammar, and it is significant that it
happened as soon as Lowth's second edition came out. This shows that
Robert Dodsley was right in not giving in to Lowth's request to wait two
years before publishing a second edition (§3.3): the 1760s were busy years
for publishers of grammars, particularly the first few years of the decade,
when as many as six new English grammars saw the light of day: Ash
(1760), Wells (1760), Henson (1760?), Priestley (1761), Buchanan (1762),
and Lowth (1762) (Tieken-Boon van Ostade 2008a).

That Ash's grammar was used according to the suggestion made in its
subtitle is clear from a quotation from *Letters on Education* (1790) by
Catherine Macaulay (1731–91), cited by Sairio (2008: 143):

If any of my pupils should shew any marks of a more than ordinary vigor or
intellect ... I would at the age of ten years enter him into a course of reading,
which should commence with the most celebrated fables in the English, Latin,
and French languages. At the age of twelve, and not before, his studies may be
extended to a proper selection of Plutarch's Lives ... ; and Addison's Spectators
ought to be written as exercises ... During this period, the English grammar
ought to make part of the pupil's study, **beginning with Ash's introduction to
Lowth, and then with Lowth's introduction** (Macaulay 1790: 128–9; see further
Navest in preparation).

It thus acquired a similar function to the grammars by Wesley, Devis, and
Fenn. The teacher-grammarian Mrs Eves (fl.1800–1809) similarly advised
her readers to proceed to Lowth's grammar or, interestingly, Devis's, after
they had reached a certain stage of proficiency in learning grammar (Cajka
2008: 206).

Ash's grammar was translated into German twice, first in 1775 and again
in 1789, both published in Berlin. Alston (1965: 34) notes that the identity of
the translator is not certain, but that in both cases it was probably Christian
Heinrich Reichel (1734–1807). According to the online catalogue of the
Herzogin Anna Amalia Bibliothek, Weimar, Reichel was a teacher of
French, Swedish, and Danish, as well as a translator; another book he
translated into German was John Entick's *Speculum Latinum: or, Latin
Made Easy to Scholars, by an English Grammar Only* (1728) (Klippel 1994).
Reichel's second translation of Ash's grammar, which is based on one of the
later editions, is subtitled 'oder eine leichte Einleitung in D. Lowth's
Englische Sprachlehre für Schule', and it must have given him the idea of

translating Lowth's grammar itself as well. This translation came out only a year later, in 1790 (Leipzig). The same thing may have happened when Lowth's grammar entered the American market in 1775: Ash's grammar had been reprinted in New York the year before (Alston 1965: 34; see further Navest in preparation). The publication of a grammar in 1784 by Heinrich Christoph Albrecht, called *Versuch einer critischen englischen Sprachlehre. Vorzüglich nach dem Englischen des Dr. Lowth, Bischofs zu London* (Halle),[4] suggests that Lowth's grammar was already known in Germany before Reichel's translation came out. The Herzogin Anna Amalia Bibliothek also contains a copy of a grammar by the Irishman Thomas Connelly, called *Gramátia que contiene reglas faciles para pronunciar, y aprender metódicamente la lengua inglesa, con muchas observaciones, y notas criticas de los mas célebres autores puramente ingleses, especialmente de Lowth, Priestley y Trinder*. The grammar was published in Madrid in 1784, and it was the second English–Spanish grammar published on the Iberian peninsula (Viña Rouco 2005: 186; see also Guzmán-González 1989: 77). Connelly's grammar thus introduced Lowth's grammar into Spain; according to Wilhelm (2005: 244, 297), the grammar was also known in the Netherlands, though not until the early nineteenth century.

In the preface to the second edition of his grammar, Priestley wrote:

I must, also, acknowledge my obligation to *Dr. Lowth*, whose *short introduction to English grammar* was first published about a month after the former edition of mine. Though our plans, definitions of terms, and opinions, differ very considerably, I have taken a few of his examples (though generally for a purpose different from his) to make my own more complete. He, or any person, is welcome to make the same use of those which I have collected. It is from an amicable union of labours, together with a generous emulation in all the friends of science, that we may most reasonably expect the extension of all kinds of knowledge (Priestley 1768: xxiii).

If what Priestley says here is true, his grammar would have been published around December 1761. His reason for making this point has been interpreted as suggesting the possibility of plagiarism (Smith 1998: 438), particularly as he had referred to the notion himself in the preface to the first edition:

It is not denied that use hath been made of other Grammars, and particularly of Mr. *Johnson's*, in compiling this: But it is apprehended, that there is so much that is properly original, both in the materials and the disposition of them in this, as is more

---

[4] A reference to this book occurs in Jansohn and Mehl (2007: 52).

than sufficient to clear a work of such a nature from the charge of plagiarism (Priestley 1761: iv).

I believe that there is a different reason for Priestley's reference to the order in which the two grammars were published: he wished to assert that his grammar had been there before Lowth's.

His reason for this is that, as Hodson (2008) argues, Priestley appears to have been so intimidated by the immediate success of Lowth's *Short Introduction* that he decided not to use his own grammar in Warrington Academy, where he had been appointed as a teacher in 1761. Hodson cites a letter from 18 May 1766 addressed to his friend Caleb Rotheram, in which Priestley expressed his admiration for Lowth's grammar:

My *English Grammar* was not ready time enough [while at Nantwich, his previous teaching post] for me to make trial of it. It has been out of print two or three years, and I shall not consent to its being reprinted. *Lowth's* is much better, but I question whether it will signify much to teach any English grammar (Schofeld 1997: 98; as cited by Hodson 2008: 179).

In this light, it is interesting to read the entry Wesley made in his diary in June 1770: 'looked over Dr. Priestley's English Grammar. I wonder he would publish it after Bishop Lowth's' (as quoted by Telford 1931, 12 February 1767, note). But, as the quotation above shows all too clearly, a second edition did come out, so Priestley must have changed his mind shortly after he wrote to Rotheram. His discussion of the differences between the two grammars in the quotation from the 1768 preface, Hodson argues, illustrates that Priestley had come to realize how different Lowth's grammar was from his, and that 'Lowth [had not] offered the last word on the subject' (2008: 185). Though he made considerable changes to the text of his first edition for the purpose of the second (Hodson 2006), the above quotation indicates that, in retrospect, Priestley did not think his original work was such a poor grammar after all. By claiming that it had been there before Lowth he asserts the independence of his own approach, which may be interpreted as an attempt to show that there was room in the market for his own grammar alongside the one by Lowth, despite the fact that the latter had already been reprinted several times. Percy (1997: 132) writes that though 'Priestley and Lowth often concur', the differences between the two grammars have never yet been analysed in detail. The points of agreement between the two noted by Percy have to do with their 'disappointment with Dr Johnson's grammatical endeavours' and their 'condemnation of some grammatical constructions'. Percy, however, refers to Priestley's second edition while pointing this out, and a search in ECCO shows that Priestley, in his later editions, refers to Lowth in his grammar, while the reverse is not the case. The agreement is, however, also evident in Priestley's first edition where, like Lowth, he deliberately uses an instance of preposition stranding when dealing with the phenomenon in a context in which the construction was less appropriate (cf. Lowth's 'This is an Idiom which our language **is strongly inclined to**' (1762: 127), with Priestley's 'though that be a situation **they naturally incline to**' (1761: 50)). Priestley, as the above quotation shows, would have welcomed collaboration with Lowth, but Lowth's apparent lack of interest in Priestley's grammar may have been inspired by the fact that Priestley was a Dissenter: with Lowth being a member of the established Church, he may simply have regarded the grammar as being beneath his notice.

Lowth's reputation as a grammarian was thus established almost as soon his grammar came out, and it was to last throughout the century at least. The grammar was widely praised in the public press, according to Percy (2008: 127), but also in grammars published after him. One example is John Fell's *Essay towards an English grammar* of 1784, which reads:

This Dr. Lowth clearly saw, and gives examples of *may, might, would, could,* and *should*, in which he acknowledges all these terms to be verbs of the indicative mode. It is a pity that, with this view of the matter, he should ever consider them as mere signs of tenses, in what is called the subjunctive mode; and the rather, since **it is not probable that another English grammarian should arise, in our times, equally qualified with himself**, all things considered, to illustrate and determine the nature and use of these hypothetical verbs (1784: 25–6).

Searching ECCO for 'Lowth's grammar' produced a variety of texts that refer the reader to the *Short Introduction*. Apart from other grammars, such as those by Ash and Devis, and catalogues of booksellers which advertised the book (see Auer 2008), the grammar is referred to in Jeremy Bentham's pamphlet *A View of the Hard-Labour Bill* (1778), Thomas Warton's second edition of Milton's poetry (1791), and Joseph Warton's edition of the works of Pope (1797). The Wartons belonged to Lowth's social network – Lowth was even acquainted with their mother Elizabeth, as appears from a reference to her in a letter to his wife: 'Tell **M^rs. Warton** that I luckily met with **her son Jo** today, & had a great deal of discourse with him' (Lowth to his wife, 22 March 1755) – so they may have been favourably disposed to him, but an instance of a reference to the grammar from an unrelated source is John Lawrence's *Philosophical and Practical Treatise on Horses* (1796–8), which criticized a particular book by saying: 'It had however been better, had this author consulted **Lowth's Grammar**, as well as the veterinary writers, previous to adventuring abroad; since he has invited his reader "to think a tedious hour in the serious task of criticism!"' (1796–8: 47). This kind of criticism shows that by this time Lowth's grammar was looked upon as a kind of usage guide, which anticipates similar use much later of works like Fowler's *Modern English Usage* (1926).

One interesting search result is a reference to Lowth's grammar in the second volume to *The Scientifical Magazine*, published in 1797, which contains 'The Life and Adventures of Peter Porcupine'. The first page includes the following passage:

Being totally ignorant of grammar, I made many mistakes in copying. The Colonel saw my deficiency, and strongly recommended study, and promised reward in case of success. I accordingly procured **a Lowth's Grammar**, and applied myself to the study of it with such attention, that at length I could write without falling into very gross errors. The pains I took cannot be described: I wrote the whole grammar out two or three times – I got it by heart – I repeated it every morning and evening, and when on guard I said it all over once every time I stood sentinel. By this study I was kept out of mischief... (1797: 455).

The passage, which suggests by the presence of the article that 'Lowth's grammar' had by this time acquired the status of an actual entity, produced a reply from a certain Mathew Carey (1760–1839), called *A Plumb Pudding for the Humane, Chaste, Valiant, Enlightened Peter Porcupine* (second edition 1799), in which the author enumerates a number of grammatical mistakes made by Peter Porcupine, such as the use of *learn* for *teach* and *had went* instead of *had gone*, adding: 'And yet this poor creature pretends he learnt **Lowth's grammar** by rote' (1799: 38). 'Peter Porcupine' was the pseudonym of William Cobbett, who is often referred to precisely for the reason that he had 'learned English grammar from Lowth's work' (Görlach 1999: 10; see also Aarts 1986: 609), and the writer and publisher Carey was one of his noted adversaries (*ODNB*, 'Mathew Carey'). Cobbett is described by Aarts as a teacher, translator, publisher, and bookseller but also as a reformer and political journalist (1986: 603, 606). Cobbett was a prolific writer, and among a number of other works on the English language he also wrote a grammar, called *A Grammar of the English Language* (1818). Aarts (1994: 324) writes that Cobbett rarely lacked confidence in himself and his achievements, 'believing that his grammar was superior even to the grammars that enjoyed the greatest prestige at the time', Lowth and Murray. For all that, he thought more highly of Lowth, considering Murray's grammar a mere compilation (as, indeed, Murray had conceded in his preface), though he considered even the *Short Introduction* to be 'wholly deficient in *definitions*'. Nevertheless, Aarts notes, Cobbett was influenced by these grammars in writing his own grammar, especially by Lowth, which is perhaps not surprising since he could recite the book by heart. Carey's criticism of Cobbett's language is characteristic of later attitudes to usage problems, and as such it anticipates the nineteenth century, during which prescriptivism was at its height.

The significance of Lowth's grammar is finally evident from references to it in the titles of other works. The reprints of Ash's grammar are a case in point, and so are the grammars by Albrecht (1784) and Connelly (1784), but Navest (2008: 234) also mentions Egelsham's *Short Sketch of English Grammar... Abstracted chiefly from* JOHNSON, LOWTH, ASH, *etc.* (1780), Scott's *Short System of English Grammar; with Examples of Improper and Inelegant Construction, and Scotticisms: Selected Chiefly from* **Lowth's** *Introduction to English Grammar* (1793), and Miller's *Concise Grammar of the English Language. With an Appendix Chiefly Extracted from Dr.* **Lowth's** *Critical Notes* (1795). The grammar by Scott confirms the continued interest in Lowth's critical footnotes at this time.

3.7 A PUBLISHERS' PROJECT

What started out as a mere grammar for his son developed into the most authoritative English grammar published during the eighteenth century. (Murray's grammar was, of course, published in far greater numbers than Lowth's, but its impact really belongs to the nineteenth century, when it superseded both Lowth's popularity and his influence.) Together with Samuel Johnson and John Walker, author of the *Critical Pronouncing Dictionary* (1791), Lowth formed, according to Beal (2003: 84), 'the great triumvirate of eighteenth-century guides to usage'. Between them, these men were largely responsible for codifying the English language, its lexis

(Johnson), its grammar (Lowth), and its pronunciation (Walker). But, as in the case of Johnson's *Dictionary* (cf. Reddick 1996: 16–17), Lowth owes the popularity of his grammar to the fact that the book was, despite its homely origins, largely a publishers' project: the grammar was published anonymously (apart from the pirated editions), Robert Dodsley had it refereed (to use an anachronistic expression) by Melmoth, upon which the grammar was revised, its copyright was in the hands of the publishers, and it was marketed very carefully – and successfully – indeed. Rather than producing print runs of 1,500 or even 2,000 copies, as would be done 'for those authors or works that had already proven themselves with the public and for which there continued a high demand' (Tierney 1988: 29), the Dodsleys chose to bring the grammar out 1,000 copies at a time, advertising it on each occasion as 'A New Edition, Corrected'. This was a successful strategy, as it ensured continued interest among the buying public.

Even Lowth considered the grammar to be primarily the responsibility of his publishers. When asked by James Dodsley in July 1778 whether he would agree to an 'index', or rather a table of contents (see *OED Online*, *index*, n., 5), being added to the grammar, he replied:

I have just looked over M^r. Holmes's Index to the Grammar; very cursorily: if I had had time to do it carefully, I could not have examined it without great trouble, not having at hand the Edition of 1774, upon wch. it is formed. I have no objection to make to y^e. Performance, except that it seems to me to be unnecessary. An Index to a Grammar, especially so short a one, is for that reason a very uncommon thing. A Grammar always is, or ought to be, ranged so exactly under its proper heads in so clear a method, y^t. no one can be at a loss to find y^e. part on wch. it is to be consulted (Lowth to James Dodsley, 21 July 1778).

So, despite the fact that a table of contents had already been prepared, he advised against adopting it. But he added: 'You may consult M^r. Cadell upon it; it is Your affair. And I leave You to do, as You shall agree together, & shall think it will answer, if added, in promoting the Sale'. Lowth, not in favour of the suggestion, thus left the final decision to his publishers. The grammar was indeed published without an 'index', although, as I will argue in Chapter 4, to have added a table of contents would not have been a bad idea.

Due to the publishers' efforts, and somewhat to Lowth's own surprise, the grammar became a huge success. Its market value, if reckoned by the trade in shares in its copyright, increased nine times in a period of only seven years. Reprinting the grammar must have remained a relatively lucrative affair even after Lowth's death in 1787, for editions – or rather reprints – continued to appear until at least 1795. Even the Leeds schoolmaster and bookseller John Binns (fl. 1789–97) (Michael 1970: 552) issued a reprint of the grammar in 1794, of which, significantly, the title page reads 'A NEW EDITION, Corrected'. James Dodsley died in 1797, for which year Alston (1965: 48) records another reprint, published – anonymously – by 'A. Millar, W. Law, R. Cater, and Wilson, Spence & Mawman (York)'. This is peculiar, for by this time Millar had been dead for almost thirty years. I myself possess a copy of Ann Fisher's grammar, originally published in 1745, that was reprinted in 1789, again for Millar, Law, and Cater, and for Wilson and Spence (the grammar is not listed in Alston). Ash's *Grammatical Institutes* was also reprinted, in 1791, by several of these publishers: A. Millar, W. Law, and R. Cater (Alston 1965: 36). Fisher had died in 1778 and Ash a year later. As explained in Section 3.5, copyright lasted for twenty-one years with two additional options of fourteen years each for renewal. If we apply these terms to the three grammars discussed here, which were the three most frequently reprinted grammars of the eighteenth century, we may reconstruct a possible explanation of what happened and why (Table 3.2).

Only in the case of Ash does the copyright extension not seem to have been applied for, presumably because he had died before it expired. Both Fisher and Lowth died during the period of the copyright extension; in neither case does a second extension appear to have been applied for. All three grammars could thus be reprinted by others, Binns as well as the conger variously comprising Millar, Law, and Cater (Ash), with Wilson & Spence (Fisher) & Mawman (Lowth), because they had fallen into the public domain. Despite the copyright expiration of Ash's grammar in 1781,

Table 3.2 **Terms of copyright and copyright extensions for Fisher (1745), Ash (1760), and Lowth (1762)**

Date of publication	Copyright (21 years)	Extension (14 years)	Death of author	Binns	Millar, Law, & Cater
Fisher (1745)	+ 21 = 1766	+ 14 = 1780	died 1779	reprint 1780	& Wilson & Spence reprint 1789
Ash (1760)	+ 21 = 1781		died 1779		reprint 1791
Lowth (1762)	+ 21 = 1783	+ 14 = 1797	died 1787	reprint 1794	& Wilson, Spence, & Mawman reprint 1797

Charles Dilly, one of the grammar's original publishers from 1763 according to Alston (1965: 37), continued to bring out the grammar at least eight
more times down to 1799, while in the meantime pirated copies appeared
as well, in England and abroad (for further details, see Navest in preparation). The copyright of Lowth's grammar ran out in 1797, the same year
that James Dodsley, the copyright owner, died. Wilson, Spence, and Mawman, who had published Lindley Murray's grammar two years previously,
in 1795, immediately published a reprint of Lowth's grammar that same
year, along with the *Abridgement* of Murray's grammar (1797). As shown in
Table 3.2., Binns not only reissued Lowth's grammar but also the one by
Fisher, the latter immediately upon the expiry of its copyright. In 1788, he
also published a grammar written by himself (Alston 1965: 83).

All of this illustrates what a lucrative business the publishing of grammars of English had become by the final decades of the eighteenth century,
as well as the power of groups of publishers. Teaming up with Law and
Cater, and Millar – could this be Cadell, using the name of his long-dead
former partner Millar as a pseudonym to avoid possible damage to his
reputation? – Wilson, Spence, and Mawman may have wished to test the
market value of formerly popular grammars that were in the public
domain, upon which they abandoned their efforts once Murray's grammar, which was after all their own enterprise, entered the scene. Compared
to Murray's grammar, of which altogether some two million copies were
printed down to 1850 (Tieken-Boon van Ostade 1996a: 9), Lowth's 34,000
copies seem insignificant. But while Lowth's grammar had been the first to
be published in substantial numbers of copies, Murray was to set a pattern
for the years to come, for Fenn's grammars were similarly published in
print runs of 10,000 rather than Lowth's 1,000 copies (Navest 2008: 225),
while Cobbett's grammar also came out in much larger print runs: according to Aarts (1994), the grammar was so popular that, within a fortnight,
the first edition of 5,000 copies had run out. By 1836, as Cobbett himself
claimed, 'more than 100,000 copies had been sold' (as cited by Aarts 1994:
321). Indeed, as Michael (1991, 1997) has shown, this was the start of a new
era in the production of practical grammars of English, though without
actually producing any significant new developments in the analysis of
English grammar. However, in terms of sheer numbers, both of new titles
and of actual copies, the market came to be flooded with them, even to the
point, as Michael argues, of overflowing.

The part of Lowth's grammar that enjoyed greatest popularity was its
syntax section. This is evident from Melmoth's comment to Dodsley upon

having seen the draft version of the first edition ('His observations on the structure of our language, wch. he has ranged under the article of *sentences*, are particularly judicious & useful'; Lowth to Dodsley, 20 November 1759). It is also clear from the response by Thomas Fitzmaurice, who subjected his addressee Adam Smith's language to the same kind of linguistic criticism as Lowth had done with other established writers. Navest (2006) has shown that many additions came in for the 1763 and 1764 editions of the grammar. A tally of these additions shows that about 55 per cent new quotations were added to the second edition of the grammar, mostly from Shakespeare (38 instances), the Bible (25), Milton (14), Addison (11), and Pope (8), and that a further 21 quotations (5%) were added to the 1764 edition, most of them from Swift (6), Addison (5), the Bible (2), Dryden (2), and Pope (1). Even quotations from authors who did not appear in the first edition were added to the 1764 edition, such as Wentworth Dillon, Earl of Roscommon (1637–1685), and Thomas Sprat (bap.1635, d.1713), but, in accordance with Lowth's practice in the earlier editions, all these writers were dead (Tieken-Boon van Ostade and Navest 2006; Percy 1997: 134). Lowth's grammar had clearly served as inspiration for his critical readers here, but other sections of the grammar were read with interest as well. On 5 April 1778 James Boswell (1740–95) noted in his journal that John Wilkes (1725–97) '[s]howed me some very good notes on Lowth, one on *ghost* that *it* and *he* both applied properly, as ghost a dubious being' (Weis and Pottle 1971: 242). This is possibly a reference to the 1778 edition which had appeared that same year, which provides both *it* and *he* as alternative pronouns for *ghost*, though the point was made in the first edition as well, if somewhat less clearly. It is interesting to see here a glimpse of Lowth's readership: even a politician in his early fifties and a lawyer of nearly forty showed an interest in the grammar, though whether Boswell actually ever read the grammar remains uncertain.

When telling his friend Melmoth about the grammar's origin, Lowth wrote that he 'drew it up for the use of my little Boy, for the reasons mentioned in the Preface'. In the preface Lowth had written that his 'little System [was] intended merely for a private and domestic use', but the preface also expresses Lowth's expectations for the grammar if put to use outside the 'private and domestic' sphere:

If this method were adopted in our Schools; if children were first taught the common principles of Grammar by some short and clear System of *English* Grammar, which happily by its simplicity and facility is perhaps of all others the fittest for such a purpose, they would have some notion of what they were going about, when they should enter into the *Latin* Grammar; and would hardly be engaged so many years, as they now are, in that most irksome and difficult part of literature, with so much labour of the memory, and with so little assistance of the understanding (1762: xii–xiii).

We have already seen that Wesley included the grammar in the reading list for the more advanced pupils of Kingswood school. Use of the grammar was also recommended in the fifth edition of George Chapman's *Treatise on Education* (1792: 13), though it recommends 'An English Grammar, such as Fisher's or Ash's Introduction to Dr. Lowth's Grammar' in his list of 'Books proper for Boys while they read the Classics at School' (1792: 173). If Lowth's grammar was used in schools at all, it was on a much smaller scale than Lowth had hoped for. In its published form, it was, after all, more a grammar for scholars than for children.

4

THE GRAMMAR: CONTENTS AND APPROACH

4.1 STARTING A GRAMMAR

L OWTH'S decision to write a grammar of English can be traced back to the early years of his son Thomas Henry, whom he wanted to prepare for the time when he would be old enough to go to school and embark on the grammar of Latin. By the end of the year 1757, as we can conclude from Lowth's correspondence with Robert Dodsley, Lowth was definitely engaged on the grammar. But how did he go about this? Vorlat (2007: 506), though referring to English grammarians from an earlier age, writes that 'prior to writing a grammar, an author must decide on the criteria by which to establish grammatical categories'; she adds that 'on these criteria it depends how many word classes he will distinguish and how he will define them'. Lowth's situation must have been very similar to that of the seventeenth-century grammarians referred to by Vorlat, and he, too, must have deliberated with himself over the question of how to set up his grammar, what sections it would have, and how many parts of speech there would be to deal with. As a classical philologist he would have known very well how a grammar of Latin, Greek, or Hebrew was structured, but he must have felt himself faced with the question of whether the same set-up would be suitable for a modern language like English. On a level of greater detail, he must have asked himself questions like the ones listed by Lass (1994) in his discussion of the normative grammarians' treatment of the strong verb: 'How many grades should a strong verb have? ... Should the past participle end in -*(e)n* or not?' (1994: 88).

Various options would have been open to Lowth: he could have copied an existing grammar or translated a grammar of Latin into English and adapted it to the requirements of a living language. Plagiarism as we call it today was very common among the early grammarians, but it was not regarded as a true offence until the end of the eighteenth century (Tieken-Boon van Ostade 1996*b*). Alternatively, he could write his own, starting from scratch and setting it up along his own principles to produce a grammar that would deal with the characteristics that were typical of English in, perhaps, a unique and innovative way. As for the first option, unlike in the case of Murray some thirty years later, who decided to make only 'a careful selection of the most useful matter' from various English grammars already published, not so many grammars were available to Lowth for this purpose, and as for grammars of any reputation, such as those by Wallis (1653), Brightland and Gildon (1711), or Greenwood (1711), I have not come across any evidence suggesting that he made use of them, apart from Wallis. He certainly knew about Wallis's *Grammatica Linguae Anglicanae* by 1765, when Millar asked him to write the preface to the sixth edition (Kemp 1972: 72), but, as I will show below, he may have been familiar with the fourth edition of 1664 as well, though he doesn't refer to Wallis until the 1769 edition of his grammar. In the preface to the first edition Lowth does refer – albeit obliquely – to Johnson's grammar prefixed to the *Dictionary* (1755) as 'the last *English* Grammar that hath been presented to the public' (1762: v), which suggests that he was not aware of the fact that Benjamin Martin's grammar, first published in 1754, had been reissued in 1756. But not much else had come out since Johnson's *Dictionary*, for Alston (1965) only lists an eighth edition of Loughton (1734) and a third edition of Newbery (1745), both published in 1755 in London, and a fifth edition of Fisher (1745) which, however, came out in Newcastle in 1757.

Though Lowth's comment was thus not wide of the mark, he may merely have relied upon what he had read in the *Monthly Review* in 1758, in which two reviews had appeared 'claiming that a good English grammar was "wanting"' (Percy 2008: 128). The reviews were of Anselm Bayly's *Introduction to Languages* (1758) and John Ward's *Four Essays upon the English Language* (1758), and Lowth immediately ordered copies of them from Dodsley (Lowth to Robert Dodsley, 9 June 1758). Neither of these books, however, were grammars as such. The former work is basically a comparative grammar of Latin, Greek, and Hebrew, while the latter, as its title suggests, consisted of four separate essays, on spelling, syllable division, articles and verbs, and of a list of irregular verbs (Michael 1970: 174). By the time his own grammar was finished, Lowth had found no occasion to refer to these works other than in a single footnote, where he mentions Ward only as a source for his somewhat remarkable observation that 'The whole number of Verbs in the English language, Regular and Irregular, Simple and Compounded, taken together, is about 4300. See Dr. Ward's Essays on the English Language; the Catalogue of English Verbs' (1762: 83n). The books thus don't seem to have been of much use to him. By the time Lowth's grammar was about to be published, the situation was completely different, and a veritable competition had arisen among publishers trying to obtain a market share for a grammar of English (Tieken-Boon van Ostade 2008*a*).

The second option open to Lowth would have been to base himself on an existing grammar of Latin. Percy (2008: 142) notes that the title of Lowth's grammar is almost identical to William Lily's *Short Introduction of Grammar*. The grammar that is usually attributed to Lily had been officially authorized as a grammar of Latin by Henry VIII in 1540, and it 'held that powerful position', according to Vorlat (1975: 7), 'for three centuries'. Various editions of Lily's grammar are included in ECCO that would have been available to Lowth in his youth, published in 1702, 1707, 1709, 1712, 1714, 1715, 1716, 1720, and 1723, and it seems more than likely that he learnt Latin from this grammar when attending Winchester College as a boy. Even during the eighteenth century, Michael (1987: 320) writes, 'most pupils...were expected to learn the grammar by heart'. As with the nineteenth-century novelists cited in Chapter 1, who reproduced grammatical rules memorized in their schooldays, this would almost inevitably leave a trace in any newly produced grammar. An example of this can be seen in Lowth's contemporary Joseph Priestley, whose own grammar shows the effect of having learnt by heart the grammar of his former teacher John Kirkby. Priestley, according to Michael (1970: 231), was the first to adopt a particular system of parts of speech, but the same system had been used before him by Kirkby, whose school Priestley had attended from 1746, when Kirkby's grammar was published, until 1749 (*ODNB*, 'Joseph Priestley'; Tieken-Boon van Ostade 1992: 168). But apart from the title of Lily's grammar there are few other correspondences with the one by

Lowth.[1] This is most evident from their different systems of parts of speech, eight in Lily's grammar: Noun (substantives and adjectives), Pronoun, Verb, Participle, Adverb, Conjunction, Preposition, and Interjection (Vorlat 1975: 46), and nine in Lowth's: Substantive, Adjective, Pronoun, Article, Verb (including the participle), Adverb, Conjunction, Preposition, and Interjection (Michael 1970: 225). Lowth's system thus not only differs in the number of parts of speech dealt with but also in his treatment of the noun, which he subdivided into substantives and adjectives, and of the verb, in which category he included the participle. The article is a different matter, as it did not exist as a Latin category; according to Vorlat (2007: 509), this was one of the problems English grammarians were confronted with when deciding upon the question of the number of parts of speech to be distinguished.

But Lowth did not entirely start from scratch either, for he possessed a copy of Johnson's *Dictionary* (1755): he had referred to it in a letter to Dodsley from 3 November 1757, and the book was still listed in his Will some twenty-five years later. The letter to Dodsley suggests that he regularly used the dictionary as a source of reference, so he may already have possessed a copy at this time. Johnson's *Dictionary* also included a grammar, though it had not been so well received. In the preface to his own grammar, Lowth refers to Johnson several times, taking care – in his usual circumspect way – to keep his references anonymous. The most obvious allusion to Johnson's grammar is when he criticizes the 'last *English* Grammar that hath been presented to the public, and by the Person best qualified to have given us a perfect one' for 'comprising the whole Syntax in ten lines' (1762: v). Two pages earlier he had questioned the assertion – again left anonymous – 'that our Language is in its nature irregular and capricious; not subject, or not easily reduceable, to a System of rules', calling it a 'charge [which] is wholly without foundation' (1762: iii). This is another reference to Johnson, who had written in his *Plan of a Dictionary of the English Language*, published in 1747 by Robert Dodsley among several others: 'The syntax of this language is too inconstant to be reduced to rules, and can be only learned by the distinct consideration of particular words as they are used by the best authors' (1747: 19). In the preface to the dictionary itself Johnson had written something of the same nature:

---

[1] One echo of Lily's grammar might be Lowth's decision to use the verb *to love* by which to illustrate various forms of the verb (e.g. 1762: 46, 47). Wallis used the verb *uro*, 'to burn'.

When I took the first survey of my undertaking, I found our speech copious without order, and energetick without rules: wherever I turned my view, there was perplexity to be disentangled, and confusion to be regulated; choice was to be made out of boundless variety, without any established principle of selection; adulterations were to be detected, without a settled test of purity; and modes of expression to be rejected or received, without the suffrages of any writers of classical reputation or acknowledged authority.

Having therefore no assistance but from general grammar, I applied myself to the perusal of our writers; and noting whatever might be of use to ascertain or illustrate any word of phrase, accumulated in time the materials of a dictionary (1755: sig. A2^r).

Lowth's 'little System' as he called it himself in his Preface (1762: xiii) should, I think, be considered as an answer to Johnson's 'charge' as Lowth put it, which in his view lacked any foundation. He clearly believed that he himself could do better than Johnson, certainly by providing a proper section on syntax.

But there was more that Lowth disagreed with. He also responded to Johnson's so-called 'charge' by criticizing his decision to collect dictionary material by 'the perusal of our writers', as Johnson had written in his preface. 'We have writers', Lowth countered in his own preface, 'who have enjoyed these advantages [i.e. "much practice in the polite world, and a general acquaintance with the best authors"] in their full extent, and yet cannot be recommended as models of an accurate style' (1762: vii), adding 'the greatest Critic and most able Grammarian of the last age, when he came to apply his Learning and his Criticism to an English Author, was frequently at a loss in matters of ordinary use and common construction in his own *Vernacular Idiom*' (1762: viii). Possibly the person referred to here was Dryden, who had died in 1700 and can thus be said to have belonged to 'the last age', and with whose work, including, as I will discuss below, his views of particular grammatical problems, Lowth was familiar. The 'English Author' in that case would have been Shakespeare, whose *Tempest* and *Troilus and Cressida* Dryden had revised (in 1667 and 1679, respectively); Dryden's usage was, moreover, frequently criticized by Lowth in his grammar. Lowth's response to Johnson was to adopt a different approach to grammar, and to syntax in particular, by basing himself not on the language of the best authors to illustrate correct usage – cf. Johnson's 'wells of English undefiled' (1755: C1^r) – but on their grammatical mistakes. By doing so he would be able to show not only that 'our best Authors for want of some rudiments of [grammar] have sometimes fallen into mistakes, and been guilty of palpable errors in point of Grammar' (1762: ix), but also to advertise his own grammar as a means to remedy this situation, 'to evince the necessity of the Study of Grammar in our own Language, and to admonish those, who set up for Authors among us, that they would do well to consider this part of Learning as an object not altogether beneath their regard' (1762: ix–x). By thus criticizing the very foundations of Johnson's authoritative dictionary, Lowth created a market for his grammar.

I have already argued that the addition of footnotes, in which Lowth illustrated grammatical errors by well-known writers, was an innovation within the English grammatical tradition, and that he appears to have picked up the idea for them from the *Monthly Review* and the *Critical Review*. I have also shown that this innovation was followed by many other grammarians after him. But the decision to adopt this approach to grammar, and particularly to syntax, had been inspired by Johnson's dictionary. Lowth, moreover, wrote in the preface to his grammar that the examples given in the notes 'are such as occurred in reading, without any very curious or methodical examination: and they might easily have been much increased in number by any one, who had leisure or phlegm enough to have gone through a regular course of reading with this particular view' (1762: ix). This interesting comment offers counter-evidence for the claim made by Biber, Conrad, and Reppen (1998: 55) when they state that 'unlike lexicography, grammar does not have a long tradition of empirical study'. In their book, the authors note that 'as early as 1755 ... Johnson used a corpus of texts to gather authentic uses of words, which he then included as examples in his dictionary of English' (1998: 21–2). Lowth had similarly 'gathered authentic uses of words', representing grammatical errors committed by authors already dead, but authentic all the same. As the above quotation suggests, Lowth collected his examples at random, believing that they could be considered representative of usage in general. This suggests that the grammar, unusually for its time, was based on a corpus that consisted of a collection of grammatical errors.

To view Lowth as a corpus linguist *avant-la-lettre* would go a little too far, but if, as Biber et al. (1998) do, Johnson's dictionary is taken as a starting point for the empirical study of language, Lowth's grammar demonstrates that such an approach to grammar is at least as old as that for lexicography. What is more, Lowth was not the only or even the first eighteenth-century grammarian who worked with a corpus: I know of at least three other grammarians published from the early 1760s onward who did so: White (1761), Ward (1765), and Fogg (1792–6), as well as Baker (1770). An empirical, corpus-based approach to language, if that is indeed what it was, appears to have been an eighteenth-century innovation which arose around the middle of the period, possibly originating with Johnson's dictionary and being almost immediately adopted by grammarians as well. That grammars thus have an equally long empirical tradition as dictionaries may have been obscured by the fact that eighteenth-century grammars are usually characterized as prescriptive, which presupposes the opposite. Like later writers on language, moreover, such as Otto Jespersen and F. Th. Visser, Lowth believed his corpus to be representative of actual usage. He clearly stood at the beginning of a tradition that had its culmination in the course of the twentieth century, but that came to an end with the advent of corpus linguistics, a discipline which placed new and more strict requirements on the nature of empirical linguistic research.

4.2 THE GRAMMAR'S SET-UP

Johnson's grammar is the only other grammar before Lowth's with the same system of parts of speech (Michael 1970: 225). James Douglas's 'Grammatical Manuscripts' (c.1720), also listed by Michael, should, I think be discarded as a possible source of influence, as the grammar was never published and probably wasn't available to either Johnson or Lowth. Johnson, however, Michael notes, 'does not enumerate the parts of speech, nor discuss them all', suggesting that he either 'took for granted the Latin classification of [Michael's] System 1', which comprises the noun (substantive, adjective, and article), pronoun, verb, participle, adverb, conjunction, preposition, and interjection, or 'adopted Wallis's indifference to the niceties of classification' (1970: 226). Wallis (1653) has been given a category of his own in Michael's classification, System 25, though this system is actually identical to the one adopted by Lowth. The question of whether or not there was any indebtedness from Lowth to Wallis here can, I think, be resolved as follows.

Wallis dealt with the parts of speech in the order noun substantive, article, preposition, adjective, pronoun, and verb, to each of which he devoted a chapter of their own, treating the remaining four parts of

Table 4.1 Systems of parts of speech used by Wallis, Johnson, and Lowth (and Lily)

Wallis (1653) System 25	Johnson (1755) System 10	Lowth (1762) System 10	Lily (1549)[2] (System 1)
Noun substantive	Article	Article	Noun (subst. + adj.)
Article	Noun substantive	Substantive	Pronoun
Preposition	Adjective	Pronoun	Verb
Adjective	Pronoun	Adjective	Participle
Pronoun	Verb	Verb	Adverb
Verb		Adverb	Conjunction
Adverb		Preposition	Preposition
Conjunction		Conjunction	Interjection
Preposition[3]		Interjection	
Interjection			

speech – adverb, conjunction, preposition and interjection – in a single chapter, Chapter XIII of the 1674 edition. (This is the most recent edition that would have been available to Johnson and Lowth.) This reflects a division into declinable and indeclinable parts of speech. See Table 4.1 for an overview.

Under the lemma *Accidence* in Johnson's dictionary (1755), there is a reference to 'the eight parts of speech'. This suggests Michael's System 1, which as a category includes Lily (see Table 4.1) and grammars of English from the earliest days onwards (Michael 1970: 214). It is therefore not surprising that this classification would have been foremost in Johnson's mind when searching for a definition of 'Accidence'. Much of Johnson's grammar, however, was a direct translation from Wallis, which may be attributed to lack of time on his part: writing the dictionary had taken much longer than expected and finishing the book had obviously taken priority over producing additional features to the book, such as a grammar (Tieken-Boon van Ostade 1988: 22–4). With the publishers putting pressure on him to conclude the overdue project, Johnson turned to Wallis's grammar, though he claims not to have done so uncritically (1755: sig. c1ʳ). In the opening lines to the section on syntax, however, he

---

[2] This same division into parts of speech is found in the 1702 edition of the grammar.

[3] It is odd that Wallis deals with the preposition twice. All he says about this category in Chapter XIII is that 'they are commoner in English than in Latin' and that he 'gave a full account of [them] earlier, when I was talking about the noun' (trans. Kemp 1972: 377).

referred to Wallis as an excuse for largely skipping the subject: 'The established practice of grammarians requires that I should here treat of the Syntax; but our Language has so little inflection, or variation of terminations, that its Construction neither requires nor admits many rules. **Wallis therefore has totally omitted it**' (1755: sig. c2^r). His section on etymology consequently deals with the same parts of speech as Wallis's grammar (though in a different order), i.e. articles, nouns substantive, adjectives, pronouns, and verbs, followed by a section called irregular verbs (also in Wallis), and derivation, syntax, and prosody. It is as if Johnson, rushed as he was and having copied Wallis's section on irregular verbs, stopped there and then, accidentally omitting the contents of Wallis's next chapter (Chapter XIII), which dealt with the indeclinable parts of speech.

Lowth's grammar follows Johnson, similarly including a section on irregular verbs, though the parts of speech are presented in a slightly different order, after which the indeclinable parts of speech – adverb, preposition, conjunction, and interjection – are treated separately (see Table 4.1). Lowth was thus inspired by Johnson's dictionary in the approach he took to his own grammar, but he treated his source critically. Finding that Johnson had presented an incomplete system of parts of speech would have confirmed to him the poor quality of the grammar. Lowth's inspiration from Johnson's grammar doesn't seem to have gone any further than his desire to improve upon it: he did not, for instance, adopt Johnson's definitions of the parts of speech, while Johnson, in his turn, claimed to have copied most of them from 'Clarke's Latin Grammar' (1733, or a later edition) (see the definitions of the different parts of speech in the dictionary). Priestley (1761), on the other hand, did adopt Johnson's definitions of the parts of speech.

Lowth did not adopt Johnson's division of the grammar into different sections either. Johnson, in the opening lines of his 'Grammar of the English Tongue', defined grammar as '*the art of using words properly,* [which] comprises four parts: Orthography, Etymology, Syntax, and Prosody' (1755: sig. a1^r). In smaller print, he added: 'In this division and order of the parts of grammar I follow common grammarians, without enquiring whether a fitter distribution might not be found.' Johnson was right in claiming that he had selected the most commonly used division into grammatical sections (Michael 1970: 36; Vorlat 2007: 504). We also find it, for instance, in Priestley's grammar (1761: 1), but it wasn't the only one in use, and Lowth was clearly aware of this. He similarly opened with a definition of grammar, which is not very different from Johnson's definition: 'GRAMMAR is the Art of rightly expressing our thoughts by Words' (1762: 1). He proceeded by distinguishing between Universal Grammar and 'the Grammar of any particular Language, as the English Grammar', and then concluded his opening section by stating:

Grammar treats of Sentences, and the several parts of which they are compounded.

Sentences consist of Words; Words, of one or more Syllables; Syllables, of one or more Letters.

So that Letters, Syllables, Words, and Sentences, make up the whole subject of Grammar (1762: 2).

This reflects the grammar's structure, which comprises the following sections: 'LETTERS' (1762: 2–6), 'SYLLABLES' (1762: 6–7), 'WORDS' (1762: 7–95), and 'SENTENCES' (1762: 95–153). Where exactly Lowth found this structure is unclear; it wasn't in Lily's grammar, which deals with 'Orthographia, Etymologia, Syntaxis, Prosodia' (Lily 1702: 1), but we find it in other eighteenth-century grammars, too. Perhaps he had encountered it in the *Bellum Grammaticale* (1712), a pamphlet which dealt critically with various recently published grammars. In particular, the *Bellum Grammaticale* criticized Greenwood (1711), according to Buschmann-Göbels (2008: 92), for being 'too complicated for young learners. He suggested,' she continues, 'the distribution into "*Letters, Syllables, Words,* and *Sentences*" instead, "which need no Manner of Explanation" (1712: 21)'. Originally writing for his son, Lowth may have taken this decision for similar reasons.

There is obviously considerable overlap between the traditional division into sections and the one adopted by Lowth: in the sections 'Letters' and 'Syllables' he in effect deals with orthography, in 'Words' with the parts of speech (etymology), and in 'Sentences' with syntax. The only section missing from Lowth's set-up is prosody. Instead, he included a section on punctuation (1762: 154–72) followed by what he called 'A PRAXIS, or Example of Grammatical Resolution' (1762: 173–86). This section presents six sentences of various lengths, taken from the Gospel of St Luke but slightly adapted in the process; the sentences are parsed as a means to illustrate how the rules presented in the grammar could be put into practice, as in:

IN the fifteenth year of the reign of Tiberius Cæsar... (1762: 173)

In is a Preposition; *the* the Definite Article; *fifteenth*, an Adjective; *year*, a Substantive, or Noun, in the Objective Case governed by the Preposition *in*; *of*,

a Preposition; *the reign*, a Substantive, Objective Case, governed by the Preposition *of*; *of Tiberius Cæsar*, both Substantives, Proper Names, Government and
Case as before ... (1762: 174–5).

Learning to parse a sentence was an important skill, and one that would
prepare the reader for similar work in Latin. Such practice sentences were
not unusual in grammars of English. Kemp (1972: 71) notes that Wallis
added a practice section to the fourth edition of his grammar (1674),
which comprised fifty-five pages of text from the Lord's Prayer, the
Apostles' Creed, and other texts. Though similar sections occur in other
grammars published before Lowth, such as Greenwood (1711), Jones
(1724), Barker (1733), Saxon (1737), Collyer (1735), and Newbery (1745), it
seems more likely that he got the idea for the 'Praxis' from Wallis, as there
are other correspondences between the two grammars as well. Lowth's
addition of the section agrees with the original aim of his grammar, to
prepare his son Thomas Henry for his Latin lessons once he would enter
school, something which, as Lowth said in his preface (762: xiii), he
expected would be of more general use as well. The addition of the section
on punctuation seems to have had a different reason.

  According to Michael (1970: 195), 'Punctuation is included in
about sixty per cent of the grammars, taken over the whole period', i.e.
1586–1800, and he adds that 'the proportion is a little higher during the
middle of the eighteenth century and rather lower during its last decade'.
Including a section on punctuation agrees well with the additional
purpose the *Short Introduction* acquired when it ceased to be merely a
grammar for young children like Lowth's own son or the son of his
patron Bilson Legge. In his preface, Lowth argued that his grammar
should be of particular use to 'those, who set up for Authors among us,
that they would do well to consider this part of Learning as an object not
altogether beneath their regard' (1762: x). This perspective fits in well
with that of his publisher, Dodsley, who was often held responsible for
the final version of texts he published. Tierney's edition of Dodsley's
correspondence contains several references to this, even in a letter from
Lowth himself:

But before you send the Book [*William of Wykeham*] to the press, I must beg the
favour of you to take the trouble of reading it over carefully yourself: & not only [to]
alter any mistakes in writing, spelling, &c. but to give me your observations,
& objections to any passages; & mark all improprieties of expression, obscurity,

&c. for all wch. I shall be much obliged to You (Lowth to Dodsley, September 1757; Tierney 1988: 290).

Another instance is from a letter to Dodsley from the clergyman George Tymms (1699–1781), which read:

N.B.: I give you an absolute power not only over the Title page, but every other page and Sentence of it; and beg of you at least to correct any blunder wch. you may observe, that your Friend may be as little exposed as possible (Tymms to Dodsley, 24 August–9 September 1758; Tierney 1988: 367).

I have, moreover, come across a passage in a letter from the novelist Sarah Fielding (1710–68), addressed to her friend the printer Samuel Richardson (bap.1689, d.1761), which suggests that correct punctuation, as well as the proper use of capitals, was the responsibility of the typesetter: 'I am very apt when I write to be too careless about great and small Letters and Stops, but I suppose that will naturally be set right in the printing' (14 December 1758; Battestin and Probyn 1993: 149). That this was the case is confirmed by the author of *The Printer's Grammar*, who writes that 'most Authors expect the Printer to spell, point, and digest their Copy, that it may be intelligible and significant to the Reader' (Smith 1755: 199). By providing clear rules for the use of punctuation, illustrated by examples from Addison, Milton, and Pope, Lowth intended to put an end to this – thereby undoubtedly accommodating to his publisher's needs – and make the correct use of punctuation the responsibility of the writers instead, in the same way as he said he hoped to do for the grammar of would-be authors.

  Lowth's division into different sections, though announced on page 2 of the grammar, may not have been as self-evidently clear to his readers as he appears to have thought. In July 1778, he received a letter from James Dodsley proposing the introduction of a table of contents (an 'index') to the grammar for the next reprint. As already discussed, Lowth believed the set-up of his grammar to be clear enough to be able to do without one: 'A Grammar always is, or ought to be, ranged so exactly under its proper heads in so clear a method, y^t. no one can be at a loss to find y^e. part on wch. it is to be consulted', he replied to Dodsley on 21 July. He had indeed provided the necessary headings – GRAMMAR, LETTERS, SYLLABLES, WORDS, ARTICLE, SUBSTANTIVE, PRONOUN, PRONOUNS (sic), PERSONS, CASES, ADJECTIVE, VERB, To HAVE, To BE, IRREGULAR VERBS, ADVERB, PREPOSITION, CONJUNCTION, INTERJECTION, SENTENCES,

(PHRASES, PRINCIPAL PARTS,) ADVERBS, PREPOSITIONS, (RELA-TIVES, CONJUNCTIONS, INTERJECTIONS,) PUNCTUATION, and PRAXIS – expecting that this would provide the reader with sufficient guidance (the headings in brackets occur as capitalized words within the text). When approaching the grammar as he seems to have intended it, with learners starting at the beginning and memorizing its contents (leaving the footnotes, I expect, aside), this set-up would indeed have been quite straight-forward, but for those who wished merely to consult the grammar on incidental features, or only to gain access to the usage problems discussed in the footnotes, one would have to be familiar with the way in which grammars were customarily arranged in order to be able 'to find y^e. part on wch. it is to be consulted'. It looks as if by this time the suggestion for an 'index' was made to accommodate readers interested in usage problems, as this had been the main reason for the grammar's immediate success. Though the reprint in question was published without an 'index', the suggestion to add one – and a table of contents had already been prepared to this end – would not, I think, have been a bad idea. In 1795, Murray's grammar was published with a table of contents, pointing the reader, for instance, to a separate section on double negation, which was regarded as a typical feature upon which the grammar might be consulted. A proper index was finally published about two hundred years later, by Reid (1977). Consisting of three pages of three columns each, it includes not only subjects treated in the 1762 edition of the grammar but also individual words, which greatly facilitates finding one's way in this edition of the grammar.

4.3 LOWTH'S PROSCRIPTIVE APPROACH TO GRAMMAR

Lowth's decision to base his *Short Introduction*, and particularly his section called 'Sentences', on the linguistic mistakes of the best authors suggests a proscriptive approach to grammar and usage. By showing what was wrong and correcting the mistakes made he provided, as it were, the rationale behind the stricture in the main text. A typical example is his discussion of the requirement that 'Every Verb, except in the Infinitive or the Participle, hath its Nominative Case, either expressed or implied: as, "Awake, arise, or be for ever fall'n: that is, 'Awake *ye*, &c.'". This grammatical rule is accompanied by the following footnote:

'Forasmuch as it hath pleased Almighty God of his goodness to give you safe deliverance, and *hath preserved* you in the great danger of Childbirth:' – Liturgy. The Verb *hath preserved* hath here no Nominative Case; for it cannot be properly supplied by the preceding word *God*, which is in the Objective Case. It ought to be, '*and He hath preserved* you;' or rather, '*and to preserve* you.' Some of our best Writers have frequently fallen into this, which I take to be no small inaccuracy: I shall therefore add some more examples of it, by way of admonition (1762: 122–3n).

Such an approach to grammar becomes quite typical of the second half of the eighteenth century, particularly after the 1760s. Sundby, Bjørge, and Haugland, in their *Dictionary of English Normative Grammar* (1991), made an inventory of the occurrence of proscriptive comments in 187 eighteenth-century grammars. Of all grammars which included a hundred or more such comments, 45 altogether, 11 were published in the 1760s, 6 in the 1770s, another 11 in the 1780s, and 15 in the 1790s. Only 2 of these, Greenwood (1711) and (1737), date from the first decades of the eighteenth century. The number of comments increases quite drastically, too, even in Priestley's grammar: while its first edition, according to Sundby et al., contains only 22 proscriptive comments, this number had gone up to 283 in the second edition of 1768. An increase in the number of proscriptive comments can also be found in Lowth's second edition, but this edition is not incorporated in Sundby et al. Compared to 243 proscriptive comments found in the first edition of Lowth's grammar, the higher figure for Priestley (1768) belies its widespread reputation as a descriptive grammar. Indeed, Jane Hodson has recently challenged this view, showing that Priestley's status in this respect is as iconic as that of Lowth as a prescriptivist. She traces the origin of the distinction to S. A. Leonard's influential *Doctrine of Correctness* (1929), which was published in the wake of de Saussure's *Cours de Linguistique Générale* (1916). De Saussure, according to Hodson (2006: 60), believed that 'the genesis of 20th-century linguistics lies in the rejection of 18th-century grammar'. Within what she calls 'the overarching narrative of 18th-century prescriptivism', Priestley was depicted by Leonard as 'a lone prophet of descriptivist linguistics in the wilderness of mid-18th-century prescriptivism' (2006: 63).

All of this is confirmed by Straaijer's (2009) analysis of the grammars by Priestley and Lowth. Analysing the use of deontic modals in the wording of the rules in these two grammars, Straaijer demonstrates that Lowth and Priestley, in spite of their different reputations, were both fairly equally prescriptive – as well as, significantly, descriptive – in their approach to grammar. Straaijer also found important differences between the language of the two grammars proper (in both the first and the second editions) and that of their footnotes, with the notes, not unexpectedly, being characterized by greater prescriptiveness than the main text of the grammars. Comparison by Straaijer of the first and second editions of Priestley's grammar showed that Priestley had become less descriptive and more prescriptive in the course of time, which agrees with the evidence presented by Sundby et al. (1991). In the light of these differences, it is unfortunate that Lowth's second edition was not included in their analysis as well. At the time when Sundby et al. did their research, the extent of the difference between Lowth's first edition and the later editions of his grammar had not yet been recognized. Whenever Lowth's grammar is identified as the cause of the disappearance of multiple negation from Standard English, for instance, this is generally – but mistakenly, as I have shown in Chapter 1 – assumed to be the first edition of 1762. Another example of this may be found in Molencki (2003), who claims that Priestley (1761) and Lowth (1762) were the first to criticize the so-called pleonastic perfect infinitive, as in the use of *I thought to have written last week* instead of *I thought to write last week* (2003: 188). The comments in question, however, only first occurred in the 1768 edition of Priestley's grammar and the 1769 edition of Lowth's. A notable exception to the practice of treating Lowth's grammar as a single entity over the years of its publication history is Percy (1997), who consulted various editions and reprints for her study of Lowth's use of the poetic register – 1762, 1763, 1764, 1771, 1781, and 1786 – noting many significant differences between them accordingly.

The example from Molencki (2003) suggests that it is not altogether certain that Lowth never read Priestley's grammar. It is perhaps more than a coincidence that a stricture against the pleonastic perfect infinitive appears in a reprint of Lowth's grammar the year after it first made its appearance in Priestley's grammar. It also confirms that Lowth's grammar became increasingly prescriptive in subsequent editions. For all that, the general picture of the eighteenth-century normative grammarians presented in Sundby et al. hardly warrant Lowth's exceptional status as an eighteenth-century icon of prescriptivism. In view of Murray's sixth place on the list in Sundby et al., with 363 proscriptive comments, Chapman

Table 4.2 **Error categories distinguished by Sundby et al. (1991), illustrated with examples**

Error category	Example
Ambiguity	Is it possible that I should not grieve for his loss? (the loss of him/what he has lost)
Collocation	Anger may be compared with fire (to fire)
Concord	I have not wept this forty years (these forty years)
Contraction	don't, sha'n't, in't, he's
Cooccurrence	He is thirty years old next Friday (will be)
Differentiation	His sermons are exceeding well written (exceedingly)
Ellipsis	Whitehall is opposite Ø the Horse Guards (opposite to)
Government	The horse carries both he and she (both him and her)
Inflection	citys, gooder, mought 'might', awaked
Phraseology	When the plague raged, we wanted it in Scotland (we had it not)
Redundancy	Thou art the most wisest boy I say (the wisest boy)
Sequence	The man that came here last week, and who was sick ... (who ... and who)
Tautology	We prefer the old original reading (i.e. the original)
Transposition	We always find them ready when we want them (we find them always ready)

(2008: 36) is right when he suggests that 'if we need an eighteenth-century icon for prescriptivism, a better choice than Lowth would be Murray', but the best candidate would have been Knowles (1796), who tops the list in Sundby et al. (722 comments). With only six editions down to 1801, four of which were published in Liverpool (Alston 1965: 78–9), he is, however, far less conspicuous than either Lowth or Murray.

The inventory compiled by Sundby et al. (1991) is based on so-called error categories, labelled 'Ambiguity, Collocation, Concord, Contraction, Cooccurrence, Differentiation, Ellipsis, Government, Inflection, Phraseology, Redundancy, Sequence, Tautology, and Transposition'. Examples of each category, taken from Sundby et al. (1991: 20–5), are provided in Table 4.2. Sundby et al. classified the instances of linguistic criticism encountered according to these fourteen categories. An example is when Lowth discussed a clash in grammatical concord between the relative pronoun *who* and the corresponding subject pronoun for which Shakespeare had used *it* instead of *he* when referring to a ghost in *2HenryVI* (III.ii.160). Lowth commented by saying:

If the Poet had said *he* instead of *it*, he would have avoided a confusion of Genders [i.e. masculine with neuter], and happily compleated the spirited and elegant Prosopopœia, begun by the Personal Relative *who*. The Neuter Relative *which* would have made the sentence more strictly grammatical, but at the same time more prosaic (1762: 35n).

This instance is classified as belonging to a subcategory of the main category Concord.

In view of Lowth's reputation as an icon of prescriptivism, it is interesting to see how often he is listed first in the different categories and subcategories in the *Dictionary of English Normative Grammar*. This will allow us to decide upon the innovative nature of his prescriptive comments. Lowth takes first position in 74 instances, divided over all categories except two (Contraction, Tautology). In view of the total number of excerpts on which Sundby et al. is based, some 18,000 altogether (1991: 453), and the large number of different categories and subcategories included in the book, this figure is not very high. Compared to the total number of instances in which Lowth occurs in the database, 234, Lowth's comments can be called innovative only in about one-third of his own total number of instances (31.6%). Strikingly, this figure is just as high as that for Priestley (1768), which is listed as coming first in 84 instances out of 283 altogether (29.7%). Again, the two grammars prove not to be very different in this respect.

Table 4.3. below shows that Lowth's 'first' comments mostly concern the categories Differentiation, Cooccurrence, Concord, Sequence, and Ellipsis. The apparent imbalance in the spread of the number of comments over the different error categories is due to the fact that most of the items under 'Differentiation' deal with irregular verbs, on which, from page 75 in the grammar onwards, Lowth cites many mistakes in usage. He notes, for instance, that 'Frequent mistakes are made in the formation of the Participle of this Verb [*sitten*] . . . But it is now almost wholly disused, the form of the Past Time *sat*, having taken its place' (1762: 75). Another example is when he discusses a group of verbs in which 'the Form of the Past Time is confounded with that of the Participle', a confusion, he writes, which 'prevails greatly in common discourse, and is too much authorised by the example of some of our best Writers' (1762: 85–6). The participles discussed in the accompanying footnote are *spoke*, (*inter*)*wove*, *bore*, *stole*, *rode*, *chose*, *began*, *sprang*, *spake*, *wrote*, *broke*, *arose*, *rose*, (*mis*)*took*, *shook*,

Table 4.3 Lowth (1762) first cited by Sundby et al. (1991) on particular usage problems

Category	Number of features	Page in the grammar (1762)	Label in Sundby et al.
Ambiguity	2	140–1, 138–9	harsh/inelegant (1), [none] (1)
Collocation	1	129	improper (1)
Concord	8	35, 104, 136, 120, 121, 120–1, 97 (2)	solecism (1), improper/ungrammatical (1), [none] (6)
Contraction	0		
Cooccurrence	12	151–2, 141, 152 (3), 151 (3), 150 (2), 153 (2)	improper/obsolete (2), inaccurate (1), improper (2), [none] (7)
Differentiation	23	126, 111, 151 (2), 94, 75, 87, 86 (2), 82, 89 (2), 90 (2), 86 (4), 88, 87 (4)	improper (2), obsolete (1), colloquial/ corrupt (15), barbarous (1), absurd/ offensive (1), [none] (3)
Ellipsis	7	137 (2), 149, 147, 123 (2), 17	colloquial/imprecise/inelegant (1), improper (1), inaccurate (2), [none] (3)
Government	4	143, 106, 97, 108	improper (1), [none] (3)
Inflection	4	91, 23, 39, 46	improper (1), obsolete (2), corrupt (1)
Phraseology	1	132	unidiomatic (1)
Redundancy	3	152–3, 124, 109	improper (3)
Sequence	8	35, 140, 136 (2), 117, 119–20, 118–19, 119	imprecise (1), harsh/inelegant (1), solecism (2), improper (1), [none] (3)
Tautology	0		
Transposition	1	127	colloquial (1)
	Total: 74		

and (be)fell, while the offending authors are Milton, Dryden, Atterbury, Clarendon, Addison, Pope, Prior, Swift, and Gay (1762: 86–8). With each of these criticisms counted separately in the total number of proscriptive comments, Lowth's position on the league list drawn up by Sundby et al. is perhaps unduly high.

The normative grammarians analysed by Sundby et al. (1991) used a wide variety of proscriptive labels. These were reduced for the purpose of classification (cf. Table 4.3.), though this does not always do justice to the grammarian in question. The labels in question range from relatively neutral, like 'not good English', 'not preferable', 'not grammatical', and 'not polite', to strong condemnations like 'most absurdly used', 'irreconcileable to sense', 'hardly to be approved of', 'to be most religiously avoided', 'we must not, with the vulgar say', and 'execrable vulgarism' (1991: 44–53). Many of the terms adopted imply social comment, such as 'mere shopkeepers cant', 'childish phrases', and 'shamefully adopted by the ignorant'. Lowth's labels are primarily of a linguistic nature, as when he notes that 'Some Writers have used *Ye* as the Objective Case Plural of the Pronoun of the Second Person; **very improperly** and **ungrammatically**' (1762: 33n), or that the 'Neuter Verb [*to lie*] is **frequently confounded** with the Verb Active *to lay*' (1762: 76n). Several times Lowth adopted the label 'mistake', as when observing that '**mistakes** in the use of [conjunctions] are very common; as it will appear by the following Examples' (1762: 149n). Occasionally, he expressed himself more forcefully, noting, for instance: 'This **abuse** has been long growing upon us, and is continually making further incroachments' (1762: 88–9); 'Here the sense is suspended, and **the sentence is unintelligible**, till you get to the end of it' (1762: 139n); and 'But the following Sentence **cannot possibly be understood** without a careful recollection of circumstances through some pages preceding' (1762: 140n). One particularly harsh comment is when he cites Richard Bentley on a particular usage problem in Milton's *Paradise Lost*: 'and this ***ugly and deformed* fault**, to use his own expression, Bentley has endeavoured to impose upon Milton in several places' (1762: 107n, Lowth's own italics). One interesting point is Lowth's discussion of the common but in his view mistaken notion that the genitival -*s* derives from the possessive form *his*, in the course of which he quotes Addison's contrary opinion on the matter:

'*Christ his* sake,' in our Liturgy, is a **mistake**, either of the Printers, or of the Compilers. – 'My paper is the *Ulysses his* bow, in which every man of wit or learning may try his strength.' Addison, Guardian N° 98. This is **no slip of Mr. Addison's pen**: he gives us his opinion upon this point very explicitly in another place. 'The same single letter [*s*] on many occasions does the office of a whole word, and represents the *his* and *her* of our forefathers.' Addison, Spect. N° 135. The latter instance might have shewn him how **groundless** this notion is: for it is not easy to conceive, how the letters *s* added to a Feminine Noun should represent the word *her*; any more than it should the word *their*, added to a Plural Noun (1762: 26–7n).

Here, however, and contrary to what is suggested in Sundby et al. (1991: 297), he is not discussing a usage problem but attacking a widespread opinion among fellow writers interested in English grammar. In the text of the grammar itself Lowth merely noted that '*Thomas's* book' should be pronounced as '"*Thomasis* book;" not "*Thomas his* book," as is commonly supposed' (1762: 26).

Other such instances, all listed by Sundby et al., are when he notes that 'anciently' plurals like *eyen, shoen, housen, hosen, sowen*, and *cowen* are found, with the last two being 'now always pronounced and written *swine, kine*' (1762: 23n), while elsewhere, in the main text of the grammar, he observes of the forms *himself* and *themselves* that they

seem to be used in the Nominative Case by **corruption** instead of *his self, their selves*: as, 'he came *himself*;' 'they did it *themselves*;' where *himself, themselves*, cannot be in the Objective Case. If this be so, *self* must be in these instances, not a Pronoun, but a Noun. Thus Dryden uses it:

> 'What I show,
> Thy *self may* freely on thy self bestow.'
> (Lowth 1762: 39).

Rather than providing illustrations of incorrect usage, Lowth is attempting to explain the origin of the forms by looking at their history. The word 'corruption' refers to the development of the forms rather than to mistakes in usage, and to classify this instance as an example of corrupt usage, as Sundby et al. do (1991: 302), is due to a misunderstanding of this, admittedly complicated, passage. Perhaps to clarify the text, Lowth added another example of the 'former' use of *his self* as he calls it in the second edition of the grammar, from Sidney (1763: 38n). A final example is Lowth's discussion of the verb forms *they loven* and *they weren* (Sundby et al. 1991: 313), of which he says that they were 'formerly in use' and that usage 'hath been long obsolete' (1762: 46n). Again, we have to do with a historical comment here and not with a usage problem. The classification made by Sundby et al. should therefore be interpreted with a certain degree of care, and in Lowth's case this applies to any instances found in sections other than the part in which he deals with syntax. Again, Lowth's prescriptivism is less evident from an analysis of the grammar than his treatment by Sundby et al. suggests.

Lowth can be outspoken in his condemnation of certain forms of construction, but also careful to avoid making outright statements. He is at his most critical when using the word 'solecism', of which I have found three examples in the first edition of the grammar, two of which are accompanied by a modifier: 'enormous' and 'manifest'. The third time he used the word is when he condemned the use of *never... so* for *ever... so*. Here, however, he is quoting Johnson: 'This Phrase, says Mr. Johnson, is justly accused of Solecism' (1762: 147n). The word *solecism* is defined by the *OED* as 'An impropriety or irregularity in speech or diction; a violation of the rules of grammar or syntax; properly, a faulty concord'. In its own right, the term does not imply particularly strong condemnation; it is due to the addition of the modifiers that it acquires strong disapproval. Lowth employed it in connection with the use of *you was*, which he called 'an enormous Solecism', adding 'and yet Authors of the first rank have inadvertently fallen into it' (1762: 48n). In a footnote on page 136 he criticized 'a confusion of Persons'. The confusion in question is due to the use of the relative *who*, as in '*Thou... Who* all my sense *confin'd*' instead of *confinedst*, branding it as 'a manifest Solecism'. The offender was Pope, who even failed to apply verbal concord twice in the same poem, 'The Universal Prayer' (1738): 'It ought to be *confinedst*, or *didst confine; gavest*, or *didst give*', Lowth commented (1762: 136n).

Johnson is mentioned a second time in the grammar, but indeed no more than that. It is also the only time when Lowth offers a sociolinguistic comment in his grammar. We find the comment in connection with the discussion of the use of the double comparative *lesser*: '*Lesser*, says Mr. Johnson,' Lowth writes, 'is a **barbarous** corruption of *Less*, formed **by the vulgar** from the habit of terminating comparisons in *er*' (1762: 43n). In this instance, too, Lowth paraphrased Johnson (see Johnson 1755, *never* and *lesser*). The word 'vulgar' in this quotation refers to the common people, which is indeed how Johnson defined it in his *Dictionary* (*vulgar*), and in thus referring to usage by others than the so-called polite section of society, it is a social comment. Elsewhere in the grammar the word 'vulgar' occurs in combination with 'use', as in 'They [Defective Verbs] are in general words of most frequent and vulgar use' (1762: 84). In this case the word has the sense of 'common, ordinary', which could similarly have a negative connotation. Here, however, the word does not have such a connotation, as the type of verbs in question, which include *be, can, go, may,* and the like, are simply very common indeed. A similar instance is found when Lowth comments on the phrase 'About *an* eight days' (Luke ix.28): 'But the expression is obsolete, or at least vulgar; and we may add likewise improper' (1762: 20n). The phrase may be in general use, he suggests, but that need not sanction it, even though it is found in the New Testament, otherwise a frequently cited model of linguistic correctness. On page 89 of the grammar he wrote, for instance, that the 'Vulgar Translation of the Bible...is the best standard of our language'. The label 'barbarous', defined in Johnson's dictionary as 'stranger to civility, savage, uncivilized', occurs two more times in the grammar, once on the same page as the comment on *lesser*, this time to condemn *worser* (1762: 43n). Lowth does not quote Johnson here, though Johnson used the same label; this use of 'barbarous' may therefore similarly have been inspired by Johnson's dictionary. The third instance of Lowth's use of 'barbarous' as a usage label can be found on page 90 of the grammar's first edition, where it is part of Lowth's strong condemnation of the use of what we now consider to be preterite forms as past participles:

We should be **immediately shocked** at *I have knew, I have saw, I have gave,* &c: but our ears are grown familiar with *I have wrote, I have drank, I have bore,* &c. which are altogether as **barbarous** (1762: 90).

I will return to this grammatical problem, as identified by Lowth, in Section 4.5. Checking Lowth's grammars in ECCO suggests that his use of the label 'barbarous' did not increase in later editions and reprints. A new term, 'vicious', made its appearance in the 1769 edition of the grammar in connection with Lowth's condemnation of the pleonastic perfect infinitive. This term is often interpreted today as a strongly proscriptive term, perhaps because of connotations with its present-day meaning. According to the *OED*, the word, when used in a linguistic sense, has the meaning 'Impaired or spoiled by some fault, flaw, blemish, or defect; faulty, defective, imperfect, bad; corrupt, impure, debased' (*vicious*). Johnson used it in his grammar to condemn the use of *do* in affirmative declarative sentences, which he called 'a vitious mode of speech' (see Tieken-Boon van Ostade 1987: 233n). To me, this seems a fairly general term of disapproval rather than a particularly strong condemnation, as indeed in the case of Lowth's criticism of the use of the perfect in *I thought to have written last week* (1769: 148). Johnson defined the word in his dictionary as 'corrupt; wicked', adding that 'it is rather applied to habitual faults, than criminal actions' (1755, *vitious*).

The majority of Lowth's critical comments are of a normative nature. There are as many as twenty-seven instances in the first edition of the grammar which in one way or another deal with the 'impropriety' of a particular usage. 'Propriety' is, indeed, a key notion in the grammar, for as Lowth had written in the preface, 'It is with reason expected of every person of a liberal education, and much more it is indispensably required of every one who undertakes to inform or entertain the public, that he should be able to express himself with propriety and accuracy' (1762: viii–ix). The first instance occurs as early as a footnote on pages 16–17, where he noted with reference to a quotation from the Bible (Acts xxii.4), 'And I persecuted this way unto *the* death', that 'the Apostle does not mean any particular sort of death, but death in general: the Definite Article therefore is **improperly** used'. Related terms of disapproval are 'a great **impropriety**', 'I doubt much of the **propriety** of...', 'the **impropriety** of the Phrase...is evident', and 'This manner of expression, however **improper**, is very common' (1762: 49n, 63n, 109n, 124n). In many instances he added 'it ought to be...', thus providing the correct alternative. I have noted this expression as often as twenty-two times in the grammar, along with a number of instances where the correct alternative is proposed rather more tentatively, as in 'and perhaps ought to be written as' (1762: 68n), 'Ought it not to be, by these means, by those means?' (1762: 120n; see also 1762: 19n), and 'perhaps ought to be written in this manner' (1762: 68n). In a normative text like Lowth's grammar, one would expect recommendations for correct usage to be phrased more strongly, and that he would have used the deontic modal 'should' instead; I have, however, come across this modal only once in the grammar, in the context of the criticism of *never so* where Lowth invoked the support of Johnson's dictionary: 'It **should** be, *ever* so wisely; that is, *how* wisely *soever*' (1762: 147n). The question is whether 'ought to' as used by Lowth in his grammar expresses weak obligation, as it does today. The examples given by Johnson in his dictionary to illustrate the different meanings of *ought* suggest that we have to do with epistemic rather than deontic modality (1755, *ought*):

(1) 'to be obliged by duty': Judges **ought** to remember, that their office is to interpret law, and not to make or give law. Bacon.

(2) 'to be fit; to be necessary': If grammar **ought** to be taught, it must be to one that can speak the language already. Locke.

Neither sense seems to fit Lowth's usage in the grammar. Myhill (1995) deals with the use of *ought* as a modal verb expressing weak obligation, just as Lowth used it in his grammar. This usage increased in American English only after the Civil War (1861–5), while *should* had occurred in this function previously, thus showing a decline in usage. Biber et al. (1998: 208) note that *ought* is rare before 1800 in the text types news, fiction, and drama, but my evidence from Lowth's grammar suggests that this is not the case for this particular text type (cf. Straaijer 2009). More research into the different uses of the two modals seems called for.

At times, Lowth appears to have lost his sense of objectiveness, allowing a value judgement to show through his condemnation of a particular item. Thus, on the use of *So* —, *as* instead of *So* —, *that*, as in 'This computation being *so* easy and trivial, *as* [that] it is a shame to mention it', he wrote that 'it seems improper, and is **deservedly** grown obsolete' (1762: 150n). He even seems cynical at times, as when he comments on what he identified as confusion between the subjunctive and the indicative in the use of *thou wert*:

Shall we in deference to these great authorities [i.e. Milton, Dryden, Addison, Prior, and Pope] allow *wert* to be the same with *wast*, and common to the Indicative and Subjunctive Mode? or rather abide by the practice of our best antient writers; the propriety of the language, which requires, as far as may be, distinct forms for different Modes; and the analogy of formation in each Mode; I *was*, Thou *wast*; I *were*, Thou *wert*? all which conspire to make *wert* peculiar to the Subjunctive Mode (1762: 52n).

In all the examples provided, *wert* was used in the indicative: wrongly, in Lowth's view. On mistakes in the use of the gerund, he wrote: 'I believe there are hardly any of our Writers, who have not fallen into this inaccuracy' (1762: 112n). As I will show in Chapter 7, even Lowth himself occasionally committed the error he complained of here.

Frequently, Lowth's critical comments are formulated carefully, sometimes even hesitantly, as in the case of his usage of 'ought' (in assertive sentences, but also in questions) rather than 'should'. There are other examples of this as well. On the lack of concord between subject and complement after a form of *be* ('*they are* an unanswerable argument'), for instance, Lowth commented: 'but as the Sentence stands at present **it is not easy to reconcile it** to any grammatical propriety' (1762: 121). When writing on the misuse of *because*, still a usage problem today (e.g. Burchfield 1996: 100), he noted: 'The Conjunction *because* used to express the motive or end, is **either** improper **or** obsolete.' Providing two examples, one from the New Testament and the other from Bacon, he added: '**We should now** make use of *that*' (1762: 93–4n). Similarly, in his discussion, already referred to, of Shakespeare's use of *who* and *it* for the ghost in *2HenryVI* ('Oft have I seen a timely-parted ghost... *Who*, in the conflict that *it* holds with death...'), he wrote that 'the Neuter Relative *which* **would have made** the sentence more strictly grammatical, but at the same time more prosaic' (1762: 35n). Often he noted that a particular usage '**seems** defective', that it '**seems** to be improperly accompanied with...', or '**seems** improper' (1762: 121n, 143n, 150n). All of these instances should in my view be interpreted as hedges rather than straightforward condemnations of a particular grammatical error. This tentativeness of expression is a far cry from the complacent self-assurance which Aitchison (1981) accuses him of in his approach to grammar.

Contrary to Aitchison's general qualification of Lowth as a mere prescriptive grammarian, there are many instances in which he makes a careful distinction between different levels of usage. I have already illustrated this in Chapter 1 with the way in which he approached the problem of preposition stranding, about which he had observed that it 'prevails in common conversation, and suits very well with the familiar style in writing', while its more acceptable counterpart, pied piping, in which the preposition preceded the noun phrase rather than following it, 'agrees much better with the solemn and elevated Style' (1762: 127–8). Well over two hundred years and much prescriptive comment later, this is indeed still Burchfield's 'final verdict' after a lengthy discussion of the phenomenon in his third edition of Fowler's *Modern English Usage* (1996: 619). What is also of interest is that Lowth wrote, after having illustrated preposition stranding with a few examples: 'This is an Idiom **which** our language is strongly inclined **to**'. We may readily, I think, identify this as a typical purist joke, similar to the – possibly apocryphal – statement attributed to Sir Winston Churchill, 'This is the sort of English up with which I will not put' (e.g. Crystal 1995: 194). (Priestley had made exactly the same joke a year earlier; see §3.6.) But it was not identified as such by Finegan (1992: 124), who wrote, with what looks like a sense of surprise: 'in the very sentence in which he says, "This is an idiom which our language is strongly inclined to," he uses the colloquial idiom himself, not the pied-piping he is recommending'. Lowth's immediate followers, such as Seally (1788), Story (1793), and Murray (1795), didn't recognize the proper intent of the sentence either, for they all corrected it into the stylistically more appropriate (for a grammar, that is) 'This is an idiom **to which** our language is strongly inclined' (Seally 1788: 44; Story 1793: 49; Murray 1795: 122).

Lowth's careful discussion of preposition stranding is not unique within the grammar: I have found a number of instances where he distinguished between the 'Polite' and the 'Familiar Style' (1762: 48n), 'common discourse' and the 'Solemn or Formulary Style' (1762: 131n), the 'familiar style' and the 'serious' (1762: 137n). This is a distinction he continued to make in subsequent editions of the grammar, for Percy (1997: 138) noticed an increasing number of references to different registers over time. He added, for instance, a footnote to his discussion of preposition stranding in the 1771 edition of the grammar in order to discuss another type of sentence in which preposition and noun are separated, as in 'To suppose the Zodiac and Planets to be efficient *of*, and antecedent *to*, themselves' (1771: 119–20n). This usage, he continued, 'should never be admitted, but in **Forms of Law** and the like; where fulness and exactness must take place of every other consideration'. Poetry, Percy argues, is particularly singled out in subsequent editions of the grammar as being characterized by different grammatical rules than prose. As an example, she discusses the use of *hath* and *doth* (1997: 140), on which Lowth, citing examples from poetry, commented: 'The nature of the style, as well as the harmony of the verse, seems to require in these places *hath* and *doth*' (1763: 53n). The comment does not occur in the first edition of the grammar, and is therefore another instance of how Lowth continued to update the work. Interestingly, as a search in ECCO demonstrated, he used *hath* himself in the grammar, though at a ratio of one to two in relation to *has* (23 vs. 47). *Doth* is much rarer, as I have found (using ECCO) only one instance of it as against fifteen of *does*. As in the case of his use of the subjunctive in the grammar, which occurs more frequently in this text than in his private usage (Auer and Tieken-Boon van Ostade 2007), he believed these forms to be appropriate to the formal style in which the grammar was written.

4.4 A CANON OF PRESCRIPTIVISM

Lowth's comments on grammatical mistakes made by 'our best Authors' predominantly occur in the footnotes to the grammar, and in particular in the section called 'Sentences'. As argued above, these comments formed the backbone of his treatment of syntax in the grammar. An inventory of them, published in Tieken-Boon van Ostade (2006a: 553–5), shows that they are all proscriptive comments, dealing primarily with grammatical features like problems of concord (or agreement) and government, for example that *let* should be followed by *me*, not *I* (1762: 117n), the proper case of pronouns following *than* (1762: 144–6n), the correct uses of *whom* and *who* (1762: 97n, 99n, 127n), the inconsistent use of moods and tenses (1762: 117–20n), the correct form of the gerund (1762: 107–8), adjectives mistakenly used as adverbs (1762: 124–5n), the distinction between preterite and past participle forms of irregular verbs (1762: 86–8n), and many other items, like the superfluous use of *to* as in *to see him to do it* (1762: 109n), double subjects in relative clauses (1762: 135n), *who* used for *as* as in *no man so sanguine, who...* (1762: 152), the 'improper' use of prepositions (1762: 129–31), and sentences 'abounding with Adverbs' (1762: 127n). There are occasional lexical features, though, as would be expected in a grammar, not many of them. Examples are the use of *lie* for *lay* (1762: 76n) and of *fly* for *flee* (1762: 77n). In addition, there are grammatical strictures that are only dealt with in the main text of the grammar, of which preposition stranding is a good example. As already discussed in Chapter 1, double negation only made its appearance in the second edition of the grammar, as did a more elaborate discussion of double comparison other than merely a reference to the 'barbarous' use of *lesser* and *worser*.

Many of these features became standard ingredients of later normative grammars. Yáñez-Bouza (2008) traced the history of preposition stranding in this respect, and González-Díaz (2008) that of double comparatives and superlatives; see also Molencki's (2003) work on the pleonastic perfect infinitive, and my own on double negation and the use of *shall/will* (Tieken-Boon van Ostade 1982, 1985). Vorlat (1996) analysed what she calls Lindley Murray's 'prescriptive canon'. Usage guides like Baker (1770), Burgess (1856), and Fowler (1926) include many of the same features that are discussed here – adjectives used as adverbs, *lie* for *lay*, preposition stranding, *lesser*, and many others that arose in the course of the nineteenth century and afterwards. Baker (1770) has been called the ancestor of the usage guide (Leonard 1929: 35); in anticipating the birth of this new text type, Lowth's grammar, and especially the footnotes in its syntax section, can be seen as a kind of usage guide *avant-la-lettre*. Often, as in the case of double negation and preposition stranding, Lowth's name is linked with the item in question, suggesting that the strictures originated with him. This is even the case with the split infinitive, though this grammatical shibboleth only arose in the course of the nineteenth century

(Beal 2004: 112; Tieken-Boon van Ostade 2010). Lowth neither used the construction himself nor expressed any interest in it: the time for objections against its use simply hadn't arrived yet.

In Section 4.3, I discussed the question of whether Lowth, with his reputation as the first to raise a particular linguistic problem, actually deserves the status of being an innovator in this respect. A closer analysis of the usage problems included in the inventory by Sundby et al. (1991) showed that this was only the case in a fairly small number of instances. Examples are the question of whether a 'Noun of Multitude' should show singular or plural concord with the finite, the confusion of *set* and *sit*, the use of the subjunctive after the conjunction *that*, the confusion of *whom* and *who*, and the long list of preterite forms used as past participles (e.g. *arose, began, bore, broke, drank, gave, held, mistook, spake,* and *sprang*), as well as the reverse (*begun, drunk, overrun,* and *run*). Many strictures did not originate with Lowth but with others. An interesting instance of this is preposition stranding, which Yáñez-Bouza (2008) discovered was first formulated more than a century earlier in a work – which was not a grammar but a treatise on poetry – by Joshua Poole (1657). Whether this is indeed where Lowth picked the issue up is unclear; it is more likely that he found it discussed in Dryden's *Defence of the Epilogue* (1672) (Bately 1964), which, as we know from his Will, he possessed. The stricture against participial *wrote*, as I've argued elsewhere (Tieken-Boon van Ostade 2002a), he similarly appears to have encountered in a source that was not an English grammar: Harris's *Hermes* (1751). Harris, as far as I know, discussed the issue for the first time, and Lowth likewise possessed his works. As discussed in Chapter 1, the same applies to his stricture against double negation, which he was not the first to include in his grammar and which was only brought to his attention after his grammar was first published. Only about 30 per cent of Lowth's strictures included in Sundby et al. (1991) were new in that they were evidently first formulated by him. This suggests that he must have found the remaining 160 or so features elsewhere. This does not imply that his grammar was derivative. There is, as far as I know, and as I will discuss in greater detail in Chapter 8, no direct link between Lowth, Baker, or even Fowler, and yet there is a substantial amount of agreement when it comes to the kind of usage problems they discuss. Lowth may have found many of the features he discussed in the *Monthly Review* where, according to Percy (2009), usage problems were regularly discussed. The *Monthly Review* was not included in the analysis of Sundby et al. (1991) or by Yáñez-Bouza (2008) and others, but it may prove to be an important source for this. Fowler likewise based his *Modern English Usage* upon his reading of the newspapers of his day (Burchfield 1996: vii–viii) rather than on a systematic analysis of similar works published previously.

Leonard (1929) marks Lowth in his Topical Glossary as having possibly brought about a change in usage with respect to four usage problems: the use of *broke* and *wrote* as past participles, of *you was*, and double negation. Changes in the use of *wrote* as past participle have been documented by Oldireva Gustafsson (2002*a*: 269) who, instead of the decrease she expected to find, identified an increase in the occurrence of this form. Lowth advocated *broken* and *written*, but the impact of his prescriptions in this respect was not found by Oldireva Gustafsson. My own analysis of *you was* in eighteenth-century English has shown that there was a sharp and considerable decrease of the construction in the decade 1761–70 (Tieken-Boon van Ostade 2002*b*), a development which may indeed be linked with the impact of Lowth's proscriptive comment: his condemnation of *you was* as 'an enormous Solecism' is one of the strongest in his grammar. Double negation, however, was already on the way out by the time the stricture started to appear in English grammars – first in that of Greenwood (1711), in other words, long before Lowth could have had anything to do with it – and the same is true of the double comparative (Tieken-Boon van Ostade 2008*b*). Sairio (2008) demonstrates that her informants, in particular Mrs Montagu, also started to avoid preposition stranding well before the normative grammarians could have been of influence.

There are other instances besides *you was* where the influence of normative grammarians, and perhaps that of Lowth, may have played a role after all. Use of the formally marked subjunctive, as in:

(3) If your ear **approve** of them, pray don't be afraid of using them freely (Lowth to Merrick, 27 March 1762).

showed a temporary peak around the 1760s, both in Lowth's own language and in that of his contemporaries. This may well have been due to the impact of his grammar and of others which dealt with the phenomenon (Auer 2006; Auer and Tieken-Boon van Ostade 2007). The increase, however, would only be a temporary one. Another instance is the development of the *be/have* periphrasis with mutative intransitive verbs, as in:

(4) Your Letter of the 26th **is** just **come** to my hands (Lowth to his wife, 31 October 1755).

(5) that **have** not **come** to my hands (Lowth to Robert Dodsley, 12 February 1758).

The phenomenon has been described in detail by Rydén and Brorström (1987). Taking up the subject twenty years later, McFadden (2007) discovered that usage, which had previously varied, as in (4) and (5), definitively 'tips' in favour of the *have* construction, the form the construction takes in Present-day English (PDE). In his paper, McFadden raised the question of what could have been 'the magic' that caused this tip, but he didn't consider the role that the normative grammarians might have played here. In my view, this is indeed what caused the tip. Lowth's contribution to the development was that he was the first who, still fairly tentatively, raised the problem in his grammar (1762: 62–3): while accepting the use of *be* with particular verbs in the main text of the grammar, he added in a footnote that he 'doubt[ed] much of the propriety' of the use of *be* with other verbs. Murray (1795) copied Lowth's discussion of the *be/have* periphrasis, adding a number of examples of which he wrote that they 'appear to be erroneous'. In the 1818 edition of the grammar, he offered a firm condemnation, writing 'It **should be**, "*have* swerved, *had* ceased," &c.' (Murray 1818: 177) (Tieken-Boon van Ostade 2002*c*: 168). In this case, the stricture did start with Lowth, but it was gradually turned into a proper prescriptive comment by Murray, who may thus have been the one who waved the magic wand here. There may well be many more such instances, and more research into the question of the relationship between normative grammar writing and actual usage should bear this out.

4.5 TREATMENT OF STRONG VERBS AND IRREGULAR VERBS

Oldireva Gustafsson (2002*b*) concludes her case study of the preterite and past participle forms of the verb *write* in the language of letters by saying that it is due to the codification of its forms in eighteenth-century grammars that the process of levelling (*write – wrote – wrote*, just as with weak verbs like *work – worked – worked*) came to an end. If it hadn't been for the normative grammarians, in other words, *wrote* might similarly have served both functions, and the same applies to other strong verbs as well. At the same time, Oldireva Gustafsson noticed a great deal of variation in the use of participle forms of this verb, with five different ones during the period 1680–1710 (*writ, writt, wrote, wrott, written*) and only three remaining during 1760–90 (*writ, wrote, written*). In her larger study of English strong verb forms, she wrote that 'the nature of this variation was incompatible with the aspirations of language codifiers' (2002*a*: 285), and the reduction of the number of forms for *written* in the course of the period analysed by Oldireva Gustafsson might be interpreted as a first result of the normative grammarians' influence.

'How many grades should a strong verb have?' 'Which should be kept, which scrapped?' 'Should the pret/pp contrast be maximized or minimized?' These are some of the questions Lass (1994: 88) addressed when analysing the strong verb system in the history of English grammar. In his study, he deals with a number of eighteenth-century grammars, i.e. Greenwood (1711), Kirkby (1746), and Lowth (1762), all of which show a certain amount of variation in preterite and past participle forms. For the verb *to write*, the forms identified were those shown in Table 4.4. Johnson had merely noted in his grammar: 'Many words have two or more participles, as not only *written, bitten, eaten, beaten, hidden, chidden, shotten, chosen, broken*; but likewise *writ, bit, eat, beat, hid, chid, shot, chose, broke*, are promiscuously used in the participle' (1755: sig. b2v), thus accepting the current status quo. Kirkby, some ten years earlier, had been of the same opinion, which neatly reflects the situation identified by Oldireva Gustafsson for the second half of the eighteenth century. In advocating only a single form for the participle, Greenwood anticipates Lowth by fifty years, while Lowth further reduced the amount of variation for the preterite. He is thus unusual among the grammarians studied by Lass in not allowing any variation but prescribing a separate form for each function of the verb. Lowth went even further than that, proscribing in his footnotes forms that had been considered acceptable in earlier grammars, i.e. preterite and participial *writ* (1762: 74n) and the

Table 4.4 **The different forms for *write* according to Greenwood, Kirkby, and Lowth**

	Infinitive	Preterite	Participle
Greenwood (1711)	write	writ, wrote	written
Kirkby (1746)	write	wrote, writ	wrote, writ, written
Lowth (1762)	write	wrote	written

participle *wrote* (1762: 87n). He denounced the general tendency to 'confound', as he phrased it, 'the Form of the Past Time... with that of the Participle' as 'a very great Corruption' (1762: 85). As his list of examples shows (1762: 86–8), he had had no difficulty finding illustrations of mistakes by different authors. He explained the problem as follows. Though English only has a fairly small set of verbs which distinguish between the preterite and past participle, the 'General bent and turn of the language is towards the other form, which makes the Past Time and Participle the same', a process we now call 'levelling'. 'This confusion', he continued, 'prevails greatly in common discourse, and is too much authorised by the example of some of our best Writers':

This abuse has been long growing upon us, and is continually making further incroachments.... in some [instances] Custom has established it beyond recovery. In the rest it seems wholly inexcusable. The absurdity of it will be plainly perceived in the example of some of these Verbs, which Custom has not yet so perverted. We should be immediately shocked at *I have knew, I have saw, I have gave*, &c: but our ears are grown familiar with *I have wrote, I have drank, I have bore*, &c. which are altogether as barbarous (1762: 88–90).

In his section 'Irregular verbs' (1762: 64–90), Lowth subdivided these verbs into three categories on the basis of their participle forms:

I.   Irregulars by Contraction (e.g. *beat, cast, cut, hurt, shut, wet*) (1762: 67–70).
II. Irregulars in *ght* (e.g. *bring, catch, teach, think, work*) (1762: 70–1).
III. Irregulars in *en* (e.g. *fall, shake, weave, hide, thrive, write, choose*) (1762: 71–81).

The third category is subdivided further into verbs that are 'Irregular only in the Participle' (e.g. *bake, load, saw, wax*) and verbs 'which change *i* short into *a* or *u*, and *i* long into *ou*' and that 'have dropt the termination *en* in the Participle' (e.g. *begin, fling, slink, swim; bind, find, wind; hang, come, win*). The so-called 'Defective Verbs' – *be, can, go, may, must, ought, quoth, shall, weet, will*, and *wist* – are treated separately (1762: 84–5). Each section is followed by a list of verbs, including the forms for the preterite and past participle, 165 of them altogether. Though he doesn't actually say so, these different lists should probably be memorized by readers of the grammar in order to rid the language of the undesirable forms, thus reducing the amount of variation in usage. Such practice is common in second language learning, and my copy of the *Longman Dictionary of Contemporary English* (1978) contains a list of about 230 verbs for this purpose.

Lowth's list is not, however, free from variation. Several verbs are marked with a cross, indicating that they 'have the Regular as well as the Irregular forms in use' (1762: 68n). Examples are *build*, *gird*, *heave*, *shine*,

Table 4.5 Comparison of Lowth's *cling – clang – clung* series with PDE (*Oxford Advanced Learner's Encyclopedic Dictionary*, 1992)

	Infinitive	Preterite	Participle
Lowth	begin	began/*begun	begun
PDE		began	begun
Lowth	cling	clang, clung	clung
PDE		clung	clung
Lowth	drink	drank/*drunk	drunk/drunken/*drank
PDE		drank	drunk
Lowth	fling	flung	flung
PDE		flung	flung
Lowth	ring	rang, rung	rung
PDE		rang	rung
Lowth	shrink	shrank/shrunk	shrunk
PDE		shrank/shrunk	shrunk
Lowth	sing	sang/sung	sung
PDE		sang	sung
Lowth	sink	sank/sunk	sunk
PDE		sank	sunk
Lowth	sling	slang/slung	slung
PDE		slung	slung
Lowth	slink	slunk	slunk
PDE		slunk	slunk
Lowth	spin	span/spun	spun
PDE		spun/span	spun
Lowth	spring	sprang/sprung	sprung
PDE		sprang	sprung
Lowth	sting	stung	stung
PDE		stung	stung
Lowth	stink	stank/stunk	stunk
PDE		stank/stunk	stunk
Lowth	string	strung	strung
PDE		strung	strung
Lowth	swim	swam/swum	swum
PDE		swam	swum
Lowth	swing	swung	swung
PDE		swung	swung
Lowth	wring	wrung	wrung
PDE		wrung	wrung

and *shave*. For others, he presents different forms of the participle in *-(e)n* (e.g. *hewen/hewn, lien/lain, stolen/stoln, stricken/strucken*). Variation is similarly found with some preterite forms (e.g. *clave/clove, tare/tore, sang/sung*). On the *cling – clang – clung* series, Lowth notes that 'the original and analogical form of the Past Time in *a* is almost grown obsolete; and the *u* prevailing instead of it, the Past time is now in most of them confounded with the Participle' (1762: 89). He lists the entries in Table 4.5 above by way of illustration (1762: 78–9, 86–90).

The forms with an asterisk were condemned by Lowth, and it is interesting to see that they have all disappeared. Comparison with PDE usage shows that the amount of variation still allowed by Lowth was reduced considerably, and that the preterite with *u* has become the standard form in eight out of the eighteen verbs. Lowth's comment on the prevalence of participial forms in *u* as a source of confusion for the forms in the preterite is confirmed by modern research. Hogg (1988), for instance, has shown that /ʌ/ developed into an iconic marker of pastness, while Cheshire (1994: 123) identified many such forms in non-standard English, which remained 'less affected by prescriptive ideas about usage'.

PDE, however, is still not completely free from variation. Examples are *mow – mowed – mowed/mown* and *saw – sawed – sawn/sawed*, in which strong and weak participial forms coexist, as, indeed, according to Lowth's grammar. A number of variant forms were explicitly banned by Lowth in his grammar, most of them, indeed, by means of examples from 'the best authors' in the footnotes (see Table 4.6). The second edition contains three additional instances, two from Shakespeare and one from Pope, while one of the examples from Clarendon was omitted. Table 4.6 suggests that more errors occurred, in Lowth's view, in the use of participles than in preterite forms, though Oldireva Gustafsson (2002a: 196), on the basis of her analysis of private

Table 4.6 **Verb forms (preterite and participle) proscribed by Lowth (1762)**

Preterite forms	Participle forms	Authors criticized
begun, drunk, o'er-run, run, writ	arose, bore, befell, begot, began, bid, broke, chose, drank, fell, got, hid, held, interwove, mistook, rode, rose, shook, spoke/spake, sprang, stole, took, wove, writ/ wrote	Addison (3), Atterbury (1), Authorized Version (3), Bolingbroke (2), Clarendon (4), Dryden (3), Gay (1), Milton (7), Pope (3), Prior (4), Swift (3)

writing during the period 1760–90, shows that they were equally frequent in both categories. I will show in Chapter 5 that Lowth himself used some of the proscribed forms in his letters, though only in his most informal ones. The errors dealt with by Lowth were illustrated from a variety of writers, as well as from the Authorized Version of the Bible; I will discuss the authors singled out for criticism in greater detail in Section 4.6.

One of the few books Lowth consulted for his grammar was Ward's *Four Essays upon the English Language* (1758), though he referred to it only once. The reference occurs in a footnote to his discussion of the problem of confusion between preterite and participle forms:

The whole number of Verbs in the English language, Regular and Irregular, Simple and Compounded, taken together, is about 4300. See Dr. Ward's Essays on the English Language; the Catalogue of English Verbs (1762: 83n).

Lowth's list of strong verbs contains items that are identical to those in PDE, as well as verbs that allow for more variation than today. It would be interesting to try and find out to what extent Lowth relied on Ward's catalogue of verbs, which would help us to decide whether or not Lowth was influenced by this work. To this end, I have compared Lowth's various lists of irregular verbs with the one compiled by Ward, which includes regular (i.e. weak) verbs as well and which has the advantage of being arranged alphabetically. In comparing Lowth's lists and PDE we should, however, reckon with the possibility that whenever there is agreement with PDE usage against the forms in Ward's catalogue, this was due to Lowth's prescriptions in the matter. I have, moreover, compared Lowth's list of strong verbs with those in the grammar by Lindley Murray (1795), who, as we know, largely relied upon Lowth for his grammar. For his list of irregular verbs, however, which is also presented in alphabetical order (1795: 68–73), Vorlat (1959: 119) claims that it was original, that is, not derived from any sources she was able to identify.

The results of my comparison are summarized in Table 4.7 below. My information on PDE usage derives from the *Oxford Advanced Learner's Encyclopedic Dictionary*. The data in Table 4.7. show that Lowth and Ward agreed in only about half the number of verbs listed (18 + 3 + 66 + 5 = 92). If Lowth used Ward's catalogue, he did not copy the list uncritically. At the same time, he decided to deal with the different categories systematically, rather than merely present them in alphabetical order like Ward's list (and as Murray would do after him). When the *Four Essays upon the English Language* (1758)

Table 4.7 Comparison between the strong/irregular verbs in Lowth (1762), Ward (1758), Murray (1795), and PDE

Agreement/ differences	Verbs	Total
Lowth = Ward	bake, bear, beat, bend, burst, clothe, heave, geld, knit, ought, quoth, rent, ring, sing, sink, steal, swear, swim	18
Lowth = Ward = Murray	shred, sling, tear	3
Lowth = Ward = Murray = PDE	be, begin, bleed, breed, bring, buy, can, cast, come, cost, cut, do, fall, feed, feel, fight, find, flee, fly, forsake, gird, give, go, grind, grow, have, hit, hurt, know, lead, leave, lend, let, make, may, meet, must, put, read, rend, rise, run, see, seek, sell, send, set, shall, shed, shoot, shrink, shut, sleep, speed, spend, spread, spring, stand, stick, stink, take, teach, tell, think, throw, will	66
Lowth = Ward = PDE	hang,[4] mean, shew [= show], slit, sow	5
Lowth = Murray	awake, bereave, break, crow, deal, dwell, lade, lie, rive, shear, slide, speak, spin, spit, sweat [Lowth: swet], thrive	16
Lowth = Murray = PDE	blow, catch, choose, draw, drive, eat, fling, freeze, rid, shake, slay [slayn = slain], smite, sting, string, thrust, win, wind, write	18
Lowth = PDE	bid, bite, guild [= gild], hide, mow, ride, saw, slink, stride, swell, swing, wet, wring	13
Ward = Murray	bite, grave, hold, swing	4
Ward = Murray = PDE	bind, drink, shine	3
Ward = PDE	crow, hew, lift, load, melt, shave, sit	7
Murray = PDE	build, chide, cling, creep, dig, get, strive, wear	8
Lowth ≠ Ward ≠ Murray ≠ PDE	abide, cleave, dare, dream, seethe, shrive, straw/strew/ strow, strike, tread, wax, weave, weet, wist, work	14
	Total	175

was published, Ward was already in his late seventies – indeed, he died that same year (Michael 1970: 584) – so the list may contain forms that were by that time already old-fashioned. An interesting example of this is the fact that he lists *shog* as an alternative form of *shake*, which the *OED* labels as 'Now chiefly *dial.*'. One of the eighteenth-century illustrations provided in the *OED*,

---

[4] In the second edition of his grammar, Lowth added a footnote explaining the differences in meaning between the strong and the weak forms of this verb (1763: 85).

1787 <u>W. H. MARSHALL</u> *Norfolk* (1795) II. 388 To *Shug*, to shake; as hay, &c.,

suggests that this may already have been the case in the eighteenth century. That Ward's list includes outdated forms seems confirmed by the fact that there is more agreement between Lowth and PDE than between Ward and PDE ($66 + 5 + 18 + 13 = 102$ for Lowth vs. $66 + 5 + 3 + 7 = 81$ for Ward). There are also fourteen verbs in which neither agrees with the other, nor with PDE or Murray.

The same conclusion may be drawn for the question of whether Murray made use of Lowth's lists of strong verbs for his own: just over a hundred verbs are the same in both lists ($3+ 66 + 16 + 18 = 103$). Lowth provides verbs that do not occur in Murray's grammar and vice versa: Murray's *beseech, climb, hear, keep, lay, light, lose, pay, say, show, spill, split*, and *weep* were not listed by Lowth, while Lowth's *bake, dream, geld, heave, help, lift, mean, melt, ought, rent, shrive, weet, wet*, and *wist* are not in Murray's grammar. Most verbs in the latter list (except for *ought*) either disappeared or became regular and weak in the thirty years intervening between the two grammars. If, again, Murray did draw on Lowth here, he did not do so uncritically. Like Lowth, he seems to have been aware of changes in usage. For all that, his list is not closer to PDE usage than Lowth's. In fact, Lowth has more verbs that are the same today than Murray ($66 + 5 + 18 + 13 = 102$ for Lowth vs. $66 + 18 + 3 + 8 = 95$ for Murray), while they overlap only in 103 verbs (59%). Ward, too, shows considerable similarity with PDE (81 verbs), overlapping with Lowth in 92 verbs (53%) and with Murray in 76 verbs (43%). An interesting difference between the three works is the verb *climb*, for which Ward offered what developed into the established preterite *climbed*. The verb *climb*, however, is only first included in the second edition of Lowth's grammar (1763: 78), with the preterite *clomb* and the participle *climbed*; the form also occurs in Murray's list, alongside the regular form. A full-text search in ECCO shows that *clomb* was indeed still in use at the time, though much less frequently than the weak preterite *climbed*; but a large number of hits for *clomb* occur in eighteenth-century editions of the work of Milton, which thus confirms the obsolescence of the form. If Lowth had been persuaded to include the form on the basis of attestation in Milton's language, this was not the right decision; what is more, despite Vorlat's claim as to the originality of Murray's list of irregular verbs, the presence of the form *clomb* in his list does seem to point to Lowth's grammar after all.

Lowth may well have made use of Ward – and Murray, in his turn, of Lowth – when drawing up their lists of irregular verbs. There is, in any case, a considerable amount of overlap between the three works. There is even some independent agreement between Murray and Ward, though the seven verbs in question (4% only) may be the result of mere chance. There is, moreover, evidence that suggests fairly conclusively that Murray did not use Ward as a source for his grammar. Upon being accused of plagiarism in the *Critical Review* in October 1797 (Jones 1996: 66), Murray immediately supplied his sources in the next edition of the grammar, published in 1798: Harris, Johnson, Lowth, Priestley, Beattie, Sheridan, and Walker (1798: 7). If Ward (1758) had been one of them, Murray would certainly have acknowledged the book. Table 4.7 shows that the PDE list of strong and irregular verbs does not have its ancestry in either Murray or Lowth, or indeed Ward, alone. Oldireva Gustafsson (2002*a*: 274) concludes her analysis of strong verb forms in eighteenth-century private documents by saying that 'the standardisation of each irregular verb had its own story', and this is confirmed by the analysis presented here.

4.6 'OUR BEST AUTHORS' CRITICIZED

Lowth's practice of condemning grammatical mistakes committed by what were considered to be established and authoritative writers formed the basis of the section on syntax in his grammar. The practice was innovative, and he had adopted it as a means of demonstrating Johnson's premise – mistaken, in his view – that usage 'can be only learned by the distinct consideration of particular words as they are used by the best authors' (Johnson 1747: 19). Altogether, the first edition of the grammar contains 260 acknowledged quotations, only 27 of which occur in the main text. The vast majority are found in the section called 'Sentences'. An overview of the authors quoted in the first edition of the grammar is presented in Table 4.8.

In view of Lowth's policy only to include examples of grammatical errors from authors already dead, it is interesting to realize that Thomas Sherlock (1677–1761), who is cited three times, had died just before the grammar was published, and could thus be safely included. In addition to the names in Table 4.8, Lowth referred to Bentley, Harris, Hickes, Johnson,

Table 4.8 Authors (and the Authorized Version) in Lowth (1762), (1763), and (1764) (Tieken-Boon van Ostade 1997; Navest 2006)

First edition (1762)	Total	Main text	Footnotes	Criticized	Older use	Second edition (1763)	1764 edition
Bible	48	10	38	23	4	25	2
Old Testament	19	6	13	6	1	9	
New Testament	25	4	21	15	3	14	2
Apocrypha	4		4	2		2	
Swift	39		39	39		4	6
Addison	22	4	18	16		11	5
Dryden	20	4	16	16		7	2
Milton	20	1	19	16		14	
Pope	18	2	16	14		8	1
Clarendon	17		17	17			
Prior	14		14	14		1	
Tillotson	12		12	12		1	
Bacon	11	1	10	6	6	1	1
Atterbury	6		6	6		6	1
Bolingbroke	6		6	6			
Shakespeare	6	2	4	1		38	
other religious texts	5		5	3		1	
Chaucer	3	2	1		3	1	
Middleton	3		3	1			
Sherlock	3		3	1			
Hobbes	2		2	1	1	6	
Locke	2		2	2	3		
Raleigh	2		2	1	1	1	
Shaftesbury	2		2	1	1	2	
Congreve	1		1	1		1	1
Gay	1		1	1			
Hooker	1		1			4	
Sidney	1		1			3	
Spectator 32 [Steele]	1		1	1			
Spenser	1	1					
Temple	1		1	1			
Total 28 authors/ texts	268	27	241	200	19	135	19

Ward, and Wilkins, though strictly for the purpose of providing a scholarly reference in his text.

Not all authors in Table 4.8 were criticized for their bad language. Those
that occur in the main text of the grammar are always cited to illustrate
good usage, such as Addison, Dryden, Pope, Shakespeare, Milton, and
Spenser, but as the above figures show, they did not constitute an un-
equivocal model of grammatical correctness to Lowth: quite the opposite
in fact, for they were all criticized as well, and some of them very
frequently indeed. The case of Swift is particularly interesting in view of
the fact that his language was criticized most in the grammar. This is
striking, for in his preface Lowth had remarked that he was 'one of our
most correct, and perhaps our very best prose writer' (1762: ii). In a
footnote on page 150, Lowth sounds more doubtful: 'Swift, **I believe**, is
the last of our good Writers, who has frequently used this manner of
expression [*so . . . as*]: it **seems** improper and is deservedly grown obsolete'
(1762: 150n). Lowth's critical treatment of Swift in the grammar had also
provoked a comment by Melmoth when he returned the manuscript of the
grammar which he had been asked to read to Robert Dodsley on 20
November 1759:

I was pleased to find several instances of gross inaccuracies produced from Swift:
a writer w^m. I have always looked upon as enjoying a reputation much higher
than he deserves, in many respects. I am persuaded, if he had flourished in these
times . . . that he w^d. not have been held in much esteem as a prose writer. In
poetry I acknowledge his excellence (Tierney 1988: 429).

Milton presents another interesting case, for six of the ungrammatical
instances which Lowth identified in *Paradise Lost* he attributed to Bentley's editorial intervention (1762: 107n). Other writers who came in for
substantial criticism were Addison, Dryden, Pope, Clarendon, Prior, and
Tillotson (all, like Milton, with more than ten citations). Lowth's equivocal attitude to the status of Addison, Milton, and Pope as models of
correctness is also evident from the fact that in his section on 'Punctuation', he provides example sentences from these authors' writings (1762:
154–72).

Table 4.8 also presents additions made to the second and 1764 editions
of the grammar. A collation between these three editions performed by
Navest (2006) demonstrates that the number of quotations in the second
edition was increased by more than 50 per cent, and the 1764 edition by a
further 5 per cent. The new quotations in the second edition added nine

new authors to the above list (Thomas Burnet, John Donne, Simeon Dunelm, Sir John Mandeville, John Philips, Wentworth Dillon, Earl of Roscommon, Thomas Sprat, Edmund Waller, and an anonymous author), but also many quotations from Shakespeare and the Bible, as well as from Addison, Dryden, Milton, Pope, and Swift. The increase of grammatical errors from these writers, presumably the result of suggestions made by his readers, suggests that Lowth's critical attitude to these authors' language was widely shared. Wright (1994) shows that Addison, during much of the eighteenth century, was a model of linguistic correctness, but the evidence from Lowth's grammar suggests that by the early 1760s his role in this respect had changed, as had Swift's. Even the language of the Authorized Version of the Bible, which Lowth considered 'the best standard of our language' (1762: 89), came in for criticism. The large number of additional examples from Shakespeare suggests that his language similarly came in for attack at this time. Though not yet in the first edition of the grammar, which contains only one critical quotation from Shakespeare, this had already been observed as early as the late seventeenth century, when Dryden, revising Shakespeare's *The Tempest* and *Troilus and Cressida*, had corrected his language in the process (Tieken-Boon van Ostade 1990). In many ways, Dryden anticipates the normative grammars that were produced in such numbers in the course of the eighteenth century. Swift heads the list of the authors most criticized in the eighteenth-century normative grammarians analysed by Sundby et al. (1991: 35–7), followed by the Bible. Addison, with 177 instances, Pope (155), Shakespeare (118), Dryden (97), and Milton (90) also occur in the top ten. The high league positions of these authors may to some extent be due to Lowth's influence on later grammarians, who in adopting his strictures, adopted his critical examples as well. The list in Sundby et al. also includes Johnson (26 instances), Melmoth (23), and Harris (21), all of whom were still alive when Lowth's grammar was in its early years and thus simply couldn't come in for overt criticism. Melmoth's large number of critical comments is due to Baker (1770), who commented on his linguistic errors twelve times in the first edition of the *Reflections* alone. Dodsley is included in the list as well, though with only five references. Even Lowth himself occurs on the list, with six instances; no doubt it would have pleased him, in view of their vicious dispute, if he had been in a position to know that Warburton, with eleven instances, occupied a higher position on the list.

Six of Lowth's most criticized authors, including the Bible, are among the authors most frequently invoked by Johnson to illustrate *good* usage.

Lowth's canon of bad writers thus curiously – though no doubt deliber-
ately – coincides with Johnson's canon of good writers. According to
Brewer (2007: 107), there are only seven sources in Johnson's *Dictionary*
which between them make up almost half his total number of quotations:
Shakespeare (15.5%), Dryden (10%), Milton (5.7%), and Bacon, the Bible,
Addison, and Pope (< 4.5% each). She observed the same phenomenon
for the *OED*, where the most frequently cited sources for quotations are
Shakespeare, the Bible, Sir Walter Scott, Milton, *Cursor Mundi*, Chaucer,
Dryden, Dickens, and Tennyson (2007: 125), a peculiar list to say the least.
Due to extensive research carried out on the *OED*, we now know that the
nature of this list may be explained by the personal preference of, primarily, the volunteer readers for the *OED*. This, according to the *OED* website,
accounts for the large number of quotations from Shakespeare, and
particularly from *Hamlet*, which is the most cited play in the dictionary.
In Johnson's case, the criteria by which illustrations were selected were
highly personal: he claims only to have included quotations from 'the
wells of English undefiled', dating from before the Restoration, noting that
the reason he decided to 'admit no testimony of living authours' was
that he did not want to be accused of partiality by including some writers
but not others. 'Nor', he continued, 'have I departed from this resolution,
but when some performance of uncommon excellence excited my venera-
tion, when my memory supplied me, from late books, with an example
that was wanting, or when my heart, in the tenderness of friendship,
solicited admission for a favourite name' (1755: B2^v). Such favourites can
indeed be identified, for Keast (1957) noted a sizeable number of contemporary quotations, from Richardson as well as, significantly, Johnson
himself.

Lowth's selection of examples served a different purpose, that is, to
illustrate not good but bad usage, so in his case different selection criteria
obtained. The most important of these was that his authors were no longer
alive; in addition, he appears to have believed that his selection of instances was fairly representative of usage generally. Baker's focus on
Melmoth as a source of bad English, which I believe is due to the fact
that he happened to be reading Melmoth's work while gathering material
for his *Reflections*, thus stands in sharp contrast to Lowth's rather more
unbiased approach. Lowth appears to have had no inclination to focus on
any particular individual, not even, it would seem, Swift. And since it was
especially the grammar's critical footnotes that appealed to readers,
Lowth's call for comments at the end of the preface to the grammar

produced many additional examples of grammatical errors. Lowth arrived at his list of grammatical errors as a result of his own very wide reading. The inventory of the books in his Will shows that he had a very well-stocked private library. He possessed not only a copy of Johnson's *Dictionary*, but also James Harris's works, as well as the works of Swift, Addison, Dryden, Pope, Milton, and Shakespeare, and Clarendon's *Life* and *History*, Sherlock's *Sermons*, and an eight-volume edition of the *Spectator*. Cash (2002) published an analysis of the readership of the British Library during the period 1753 to 1836. In 1759, 135 people visited the library, and one of them was Robert Lowth. This was the time when Lowth was engaged on his grammar, and we can just visualize him poring over books of which he did not possess a copy himself, collecting additional examples for his critical footnotes. Another important source must have been the *Monthly Review* and *Critical Review*: this, as has recently been shown by Percy (2008: 137–9; 2009), is where many authors were publicly criticized for linguistic errors they had committed. In contrast to the authors in Lowth's grammar, however, these were still very much alive, and thus had to live through the unpleasant experience of having their language savagely butchered.

4.7 CRITICAL, TRADITIONAL, INNOVATIVE

Though a product of its age, Lowth's grammar presented a significant innovation in the English grammatical tradition due to his use of a corpus of linguistic mistakes as a basis for his grammar. Lowth adopted this approach in reaction to Johnson's notion that the usage of the best authors could be used as a basis for describing the language in his *Dictionary*. Not thinking very highly of Johnson's grammar to begin with, Lowth noted that the same authors – Swift, Addison, Pope, and Milton as well as, later, Shakespeare – were capable of committing gross linguistic errors, which he attributed to the fact that 'a Grammatical Study of our Language makes no part of the ordinary method of instruction which we pass thro' our childhood' (1762: vii). His grammar, he believed, could remedy this situation. Due to the invitation in his preface for readers to submit additions to his grammar, the *Short Introduction* not only grew, and continued to grow, in subsequent editions, it also turned into what we might now term an interactive grammar. It was precisely the inventory of linguistic errors that caused the immediately favourable reception of the grammar: a few years previously, in 1758, the *Monthly Review* had called attention to the fact that there was at the time no good grammar available. In view of the detailed linguistic criticism that regularly appeared in the public press at the time, this may be interpreted as a call for what we nowadays call a reference grammar, such as Quirk et al. (1985) or Huddleston and Pullum (2002), or indeed the type of usage guide that would not have its origin until Baker published his *Reflections on the English Language* in 1770. As a reader of the *Monthly Review*, Lowth may well have seen this article, and his decision to write a grammar himself may have been taken accordingly. It might therefore be argued that the public press created a market for a grammar like Lowth's. In an important sense, therefore, offering linguistic advice to those in need of it or, indeed, people who were interested in the approach offered, the grammar was a product of its time. Through its critical footnotes, Lowth's grammar filled a clear gap in the market, and this to some extent determined its popularity at the time, though it would also lead to Lowth's present-day status as an icon of prescriptivism. Usage guides proper, however, were not to appear until about a decade after Lowth's grammar appeared; as a text type they effactually belong to a different stage in the standardization process, the prescription stage rather than that in which the English language was codified.

The grammar as such was written within the Latin grammatical tradition. Though Lowth didn't slavishly follow any predecessors – I have not detected any instances of unacknowledged copying, for instance – the grammar's set-up is traditional, with its system of parts of speech not differing radically from what Michael (1970) classifies as the 'Latin systems'. After Johnson (1755), Lowth's was the first grammar to adopt what Michael would come to classify as 'System 10', and it may have been through discontent with Johnson's approach that, either directly or indirectly, he drew upon the latter's major grammatical source, Wallis (1653). In this light, it is odd that Lowth doesn't mention Wallis in his grammar. He does refer to other grammatical sources, in particular Ward (1758), which he nevertheless did not use uncritically. One of the interesting aspects of Lowth's treatment of strong and irregular verbs is his attempt to provide a systematic classification of these verbs. This, too, disproved Johnson's observation that 'our speech [is] copious without order, and energetick without rules' (1755: sig. A2^r). Despite its origin and its popular reception, Lowth's grammar was thus primarily a grammar for scholars, and this is how it was received, being turned by reviewers of later grammars into a kind of benchmark of what a good grammar should be.

Lowth's *Short Introduction* is not the stable, monolithic normative grammar that modern scholars take it for. There are many important differences between the first edition and the second, where we find additions such as the strictures against double negation and double comparison, along with many other changes. Additions, moreover, continued to appear, in agreement with Lowth's own claim in his Memoirs that he continued to correct his grammar in subsequent editions. Examples are the discussion of the pleonastic perfect infinitive and the increasing awareness of the different grammatical characteristics of the registers of prose and verse, as well as the addition of more instances of grammatical errors by the 'best' authors. The second edition may in some respects be regarded as Lowth's definitive edition, though it is important to be aware of the fact that changes continued to be made. Lowth's status today as a prescriptivist needs to be reinterpreted: proscriptive pronouncements primarily occur in his footnotes, which are not part of the grammar as such. Closer inspection of the rules in the grammar proper demonstrates unequivocally a descriptive approach to language. Such rules are often presented very carefully, allowing for different usage depending on medium (speech or writing) or the formality of the utterance. There are many instances, moreover, which lack the forcefulness of expression that is usually attributed to Lowth, and that would be expected of the staunch prescriptivist that he is customarily taken for. In his comments he rarely, if ever, offers any socio-economic judgements, in contrast to later normative grammarians. This is a very different picture of Lowth as a grammarian than that which is usually presented of him. The normative approach he took to language was the result of deliberate choice, as he explained in a letter to his friend and fellow scholar James Merrick, with whom he argued strongly over the grammatical acceptability of particular linguistic features. As a grammarian, Lowth felt called upon to let grammatical propriety prevail over custom. My analysis of his treatment of the strong verb and of irregular verbs has shown that he allowed for a certain amount of variation in usage, which indeed we still encounter in English today, despite some 250 years of prescriptivism.

Leonard (1929: 169) claims that 'the language described by the grammarians and rhetoricians of the eighteenth century was **of course** that of gentlemen'. This, however, turns out to be the kind of language that is most criticized in Lowth's grammar. Contrary to Johnson's opinion on the matter, Lowth did not think very highly of writers that were believed to make up what Brewer (2007: 107) refers to as the 'pantheon of literary giants', as these were, in fact, guilty of many linguistic errors. Socially ambitious as he was, Lowth was strongly aware of the existence of different linguistic norms of correctness, and we will see in Chapter 6 that even in his own language he carefully distinguished between different degrees of formality, not only in matters of grammar but also in spelling. Thus, his most formal language shows a minimal amount of variation, and is free from features that we nowadays characterize as non-standard language. In this, we can see him accommodating to the linguistic norm in use among the highest social classes – the aristocracy, in other words. The norm he advocated in his grammar appears to have been that of the aristocracy, not that of the class of gentlemen, as Leonard claims. Evidence of this may be found in pronouncements made by Sir Horace Walpole (1717–97), for instance, who had strong opinions on the ungrammaticality of *between you and I* (Tieken-Boon van Ostade 1994), while he also upbraided Robert Dodsley, whom he branded as a 'decent, humble, inoffensive creature' who was 'little apt to forget or disguise his having been a footman' (*ODNB*, 'Sir Horace Walpole'), for his use of preposition stranding: 'Line 449, and line 452 [of a poem by Dodsley], should I think be corrected, as ending with prepositions, disjoined from the cases they govern' (Tierney 1988: 161). Dating from November 1753, this quotation also shows that criticism of preposition stranding had been in the air well before Lowth dealt with it, though it was through Lowth's grammar that the stricture became part of the canon of prescriptivism. Walpole occupies the very lowest position on the list of authors in Sundby et al. (1991) who were criticized in the grammars of the period, and Oldireva (1999: 280) notes that his language in so far as she analysed it 'stands out... as an example of the minimum variability associated today with a cultivated command of grammar'. Whether Lowth and Walpole were personally acquainted is something which I will go into in Chapter 5, but I believe that it is Walpole's language as well as that of his peers that formed a model for Lowth and which he therefore laid down as a norm of correctness in his grammar.

RECONSTRUCTING LOWTH'S SOCIAL NETWORK

5.1 GAINING ACCESS TO A SOCIAL NETWORK

On 11 April 1772, James Boswell made the following entry in his journal:

Sir Alexander Dick had given me a letter of recommendation to Dr. Lowth, the Bishop of Oxford. I had called for him and left it, and he had called for me when I was abroad. I called again this morning and found him at home in his house in Duke Street, Westminster. He seemed to be a neat, judicious little man in his conversation with me. His abilities as a writer are well known (Wimsatt and Pottle 1960: 112).

Lowth evidently had a house 'in Town', something which he was expected to have as a bishop alongside his episcopal residence, Cuddesdon (near Oxford), at this time in his career. This is clear from his correspondence with Edward Pearson, his secretary during the few months that he was Bishop of St Davids in 1766, who informed him that 'the officers at y^e. Post office will charge all Your Letters directed to my House', adding '(as you have no House in Town as yet)' (Pearson to Lowth, 15 August 1766). The quotation from Boswell's journal is important for several reasons. To begin with, it illustrates one of the means by which people in those days sought to establish acquaintance with others, by calling upon a friend of a friend, Sir Alexander Dick in this case. This is an important means, even today, of gaining access to a social network to which one doesn't belong oneself (Milroy 1987: 57). Dick is described by Wimsatt and Pottle (1960: 112n) as 'One of Boswell's closest

friends of the older generation', and we have already come across a reference
to the fact that he was acquainted with Lowth as well. Boswell had attempted
the same strategy when seeking an introduction to his much admired Dr
Johnson, approaching Thomas Sheridan (1719?–88) with whom he had got
acquainted in Edinburgh. However, this plan fell through as, according to the
entry on Boswell in the ODNB, 'Johnson and Sheridan had become es-
tranged, and the eventual famous first meeting came unexpectedly, when
Johnson suddenly entered as Boswell was drinking tea in [the bookseller
Thomas] Davies's back parlour (16 May 1763)'. In the case of Lowth, the
attempt was more successful, and a meeting eventually came about. It
appears from another note in Boswell's journal from 14 June 1785, when
he recorded 'Visited Bishop of London' (Lustig and Pottle 1982: 309), that the
acquaintanceship even lasted for some time, but the two men never became
really intimate.

The above quotation also illustrates a particular problem in reconstructing
a social network from the more or less distant past: Boswell became part of
Lowth's social network, but as far as I know they never exchanged any letters.
Though a highly valuable source of information in this respect, a correspondence, when analysed to this end, can never be expected to provide the
complete picture, for people usually only corresponded with each other
when they were apart and unable to communicate in person. The only letters
from Lowth to his wife, for instance, date from when he was away from home
in 1755; that no other letters to her have come down to us suggests that they
were never afterwards separated from each other for any lengthy stretches of
time. At the same time, it is only through the letters that we can reconstruct
visiting patterns between Lowth and the people he was acquainted with,
which is an important means of establishing the strength of tie between two
people (cf. Milroy 1987: 141–2; Vickery 1998). Boswell's journal provides useful
additional information here, though on Lowth it is very limited indeed.

It is peculiar at first sight that Boswell did not seek acquaintance with
Lowth through Dr Johnson, whom by then he had known a considerable
number of years. Lowth and Johnson were both friends with the same
publisher, Robert Dodsley, who published books by both, and the men
shared an interest in the same subject, the codification of the English
language. But though both regularly visited Dodsley's bookshop, and
referred to each other's work (Nagashima 1968), they never seem to have
been acquainted personally, or not to the extent that a meeting between
them was ever recorded – in Boswell's Life of Johnson (1791), for instance.
They did exchange letters, though I have located no more than one from

each, with Johnson trying to secure preferment with Lowth as Bishop of London for 'a Friend in distress' (Johnson to Lowth, 13 July 1780). Johnson's attempt was unsuccessful: 'I am sorry,' Lowth replied,

that Mr. Stockdale has given you this trouble in his affair: he might have told you the reasons for my not accepting him as a Candidate for Priests Orders, which I believe would have satisfied you. He knew I had no personal exception to him, as I told him a year or two ago, that I would readily accept him as such, whenever he would bring me a proper Title. What he brings now is no Title at all (Lowth to Johnson, 15 July 1780).

There is no indication in the two letters to suggest that the men had ever met in person. Unlike in the case of Boswell, to whom he returned a call, Lowth apparently felt no personal interest in meeting the man with whose approach to grammar he fundamentally disagreed. At the same time, it is interesting that Boswell approached Sir Alexander Dick with his request for an introduction. I have come across only a single letter from Dick to Lowth, which is a reply to an earlier, unattested, letter from Lowth in which he consulted Dick in his capacity as a physician on 'the Painful and wasting complaint of the Stone' which had been afflicting him (Dick to Lowth, 9 April 1783). The letter suggests familiarity with Lowth and his family, so the two men were on fairly intimate terms:

My Lord, as I see your Lordship does not make use of an Amanuensis as I do – I entreat you not to venture to write me any Letter with your own hand, but if your Son [Robert], or any of the young Ladies [Frances or Martha] will do me that honour, to enform me now & then how you are, it will be great consolation to me and all this Family; and if I am alive when my Son (who is recreating here) goes to London to the Guards, he will come to receive your Lordship's Blissing, and bring with him his Cousin the Earl of Balcarras's Brother, M[r]. Lindsay from Oxford, or perhaps M[r]. Gregory, both bred to the Church, and who are both extreamly well disposed to do credit to the Cloth (Dick to Lowth, 9 April 1783).

The note in Boswell's journal, however, suggests that Lowth and Dick had been close enough for at least a decade longer for Boswell to draw upon the relationship as an introduction to Lowth's social network. If it hadn't been for Boswell and his journal, I would have been unable to assess the nature and longevity of the relationship between Lowth and Dick.

In this chapter I will attempt to reconstruct Lowth's social network – or networks, as, particularly with people of Lowth's social standing and ambitions, a network is never a stable entity. I will do so first and foremost on the basis of an analysis of his correspondence, but I will draw on data from other sources as well, such as the two lists of presentation copies for *Isaiah* (1778), for the first as well as for the second edition (1779). The main aim of this is to try and provide a basis for an analysis of his communicative competence as it can be reconstructed from the language of his letters; this will be the subject of Chapter 6. At the same time, my reconstruction of Lowth's social network will help identify his views on language, particularly from the perspective of the linguistic norm he aspired to in his own writing and which is presented in his grammar. This topic will be dealt with in Chapter 7. As I argued in Chapter 4, I believe that it is people from the class of Sir Horace Walpole whom Lowth aspired to associate with, something in which he eventually succeeded when he obtained his desired bishopric. As far as I can tell, however, an actual acquaintance with Walpole never seems to have come about: there are no letters between the two men which have come to light, and Lowth refers to Walpole only once in his entire correspondence, in a letter to Robert Dodsley:

However, in the mean time I should be obliged to You, if you could get, or borrow for me, S^r. Thomas Smith, Of the correct writing of English: printed in 1568; of what size, I know not; but suppose 'tis a small Treatise. **Your Friend M^r. Walpole** may perhaps be able to give You some information about it (Lowth to Robert Dodsley, 9 January 1761).

Despite Walpole's somewhat condescending attitude to Dodsley, commented on in Chapter 4, Lowth's qualification of Walpole as 'Your Friend' here is not cynical: Lowth needed to consult a particular book, and he drew upon Dodsley's very extensive social network to get hold of it. Like Boswell, he employed what in terms of the model of social network analysis is called a second-order contact, a friend of a friend, in order to bring about what is usually referred to as a transaction (Milroy 1987: 47–8): receiving a book in his case and acquiring a contact in that of Boswell. Having a man like Walpole as a first-order contact would have been highly desirable to him at this time of his life, when he still hadn't secured a bishopric. At the same time, Lowth may have had reservations about the usefulness of Walpole as a network contact in view of the latter's reputation as a gossip (cf. Christie 1954). Being acquainted with someone like Walpole might in the end have done more harm than good. That such considerations played an important role in his social ambitions will be discussed further in Section 5.4. In the same section I will argue that Lowth engaged in what Fitzmaurice (2000b) calls coalition formation, precisely in order to acquire contacts like Walpole (though not Walpole himself). His efforts to this end were very direct: at the time when he had just been nominated Bishop of London, he needed to secure the support of men in strategic positions in society, and having just published *Isaiah, A New Translation*, he took the opportunity of doing so by distributing presentation copies of the book – a costly affair, but to Lowth no doubt well worth the expense. Whether or not his efforts served to consolidate his new status as Bishop of London is something which I will discuss below.

5.2 LOWTH'S CORRESPONDENCE

Living in an age which has been called 'the great age of the personal letter' (Anderson and Ehrenpreis 1966: 269), and having many private and ecclesiastical responsibilities, Lowth must have written and received an enormous number of letters in the course of his lifetime. Given the unlikelihood that any correspondence from whatever period in the past would be preserved intact – there are many reasons why letters did not survive, such as that people were not in a position to preserve the letters they received or that they did not care to do so (Tieken-Boon van Ostade 2005: 114–16) – my expectations of discovering a very large number of letters written either by Lowth himself, called 'out-letters' by Baker (1980: 123), or addressed to him, 'in-letters', were relatively modest. Lowth was very different from Horace Walpole, who must have spent much of his time writing letters, often merely for the sake of maintaining a particular relationship or to be able to discuss a particular topic (Henstra in preparation). Walpole's correspondence comprises 'over four thousand letters to about two hundred correspondents' (Baker 1980: 13), and it was published in a 48-volume edition by Lewis et al. (1937–83). Another prolific letter writer from the period was Elizabeth Montagu, who worked hard according to Sairio (2009) at building and maintaining social relationships, and of whose letters some 3,500 have come down to us (2009: 52).

As said, I did not expect to be able to unearth what might be considered Lowth's 'complete correspondence'. This is something Tierney (1988) did aim for in his edition of Dodsley's correspondence; having calculated that he might expect to locate at least about a thousand letters, he managed to retrieve no more than 393 (1988: 51). For all that, since the publication of *The Correspondence of Robert Dodsley* twenty years ago, no new letters have come to light (Tierney, personal communication). In Lowth's case, due to the purpose for which the letters will be analysed here, it was not strictly speaking necessary to have his complete correspondence at my disposal – even if this had been a realistic aim to begin with. What I need for my linguistic analysis of Lowth's correspondence in Chapters 6 and 7 are letters written in different styles, formal and informal, intimate as well as written with greater or lesser distance. In this, I believe I have succeeded well enough for the purpose of the present study: on the basis of internal evidence, by searching the collected letters for keywords like *Letter, Favour* (= 'letter'), *yours* (= 'your letter'), *sent*, and *wrote* and by proceeding upon the assumption that every letter written produced an answer if only to acknowledge its receipt, I calculated that I located over 50 per cent of what at best I might have hoped for. Letters that were referred to in the correspondence as having been written, sent, and received were not always located for reasons already mentioned, but also because they might have miscarried due to the in-securities of the postal system (Tanskanen 2004). Though individual letters may continue to surface, all major collections of Lowth's letters that are currently available through the National Register of Archives as well as many minor sources have been transcribed for the purpose of my analysis.

Altogether, I have collected 330 letters: 250 out-letters and 80 in-letters. The out-letters range from 1748 to 1785, and the in-letters from 1754 to 1785. (Lowth died two years later.) According to Bailey (1996: 17), during the early nineteenth century, the average person in England and Wales received about four letters a year. Baker (1980: 36) provides a similar figure for John Wesley, though for his correspondence with a single person only, a Mrs Eliza Bennis from Limerick, during the period 1763–76. Both must have received many more letters than that, and this is true for Lowth, too. Lowth corresponded with almost fifty people, for some of whom I found fewer than Baker's figure of four or five, while for others, such as his wife, considerably more than that. We can only speculate about the number of letters that were written but that have not come down to us.

The majority of the letters found are autograph letters, in that they are in Lowth's own hand: for only ten out-letters and three in-letters have I been unable to locate the original documents. Having recourse to auto-graph letters rather than edited ones for the analysis of a person's language is essential (Lass 2004; Dury 2006): editors usually have different objec-tives in reproducing letters than linguists. Whether intentionally or not, they may have normalized or corrected a particular linguistic feature, despite changes in the process of the correspondence in the feature in question, which might have formed an important object of analysis for linguists. An example of this is the spelling of *'d* in weak verb forms, preterites and participles, in the letters of Hester Lynch Thrale (1741–1821), which the editors of the correspondence, Edward and Lillian Bloom, normalized because she only used it 'intermittently': according to Bloom and Bloom (1989–2002: 41), 'it was a usage that she came to see as outmoded'. Another instance, commented on by Smend (2004: 59n), is that in one transcription of Lowth's letters to Johann David Michaelis, past tense *begun* had silently been corrected into *began*, thus obscuring the fact that even Lowth used a form that he proscribed in his own grammar (see Table 4.5). Editors may, moreover, have made mistakes in the transcription of letters. An example of this is the word *Grammer* in one of Lowth's letters to Dodsley (Tierney 1988: 461), which would suggest a writing slip on Lowth's part. Checking the autograph letter, however, showed that Lowth spelled the word correctly; his <e>s may at times be hard to read, but in this case there is no doubt about the word's spelling.

Of the letters I have located, only those to Robert and James Dodsley were published previously (Tierney 1988; Tieken-Boon van Ostade 2001: 90–2), as well as Dr Johnson's single letter to Lowth (Anon. 1941), a letter to John Brown (1715–66) published by Lowth himself (1766: 137–41), the letters by Sir Joshua Reynolds (1723–92) (Ingamells and Edgcumbe 2000), and eight of the letters to the Wartons, two to Joseph and six to Thomas (Wooll 1806); Wesley's letter to Lowth is from Telford (1931). For all remaining letters, including those to and from Robert Dodsley, I have used the original, in the majority of cases, autograph documents. In addition to Lowth's English correspondence, I have identified a number of letters in Latin – according to Smend (2004: 58–9) Lowth used to correspond with Johann David Michaelis in Latin between 1762 and 1770, after which he switched to English 'nachdem Michaelis erklärt hat, daß er damit keine Probleme habe' – and even some in French. These have been excluded here for reasons that are self-evident.

The letters I retrieved are rather unevenly spread over Lowth's lifetime (see Figure 5.1 below). This must be taken into account when analysing his language as it may well have changed during the thirty to forty years of his correspondence. The graphs in Figure 5.1 contain a number of peaks: the one for the out-letters produced during the year 1755 – between 1 March and 15 November – is with sixty-four out of sixty-five letters almost solely due to the preservation of Lowth's letters by his wife. Molly wrote about equally many letters to her husband, but Lowth did not keep them. For someone who travelled as much as he did during this time, and who may consequently have lived out of a trunk for many months, it may have been impossible to preserve this enormous collection of letters, even for sentimental reasons. For Molly, at home, things were of course very different. The smaller peak in the graph in Figure 5.1. for the year 1762 is with one exception due to the letters Lowth wrote to his friend and fellow scholar James Merrick. The letters, which today are part of a single manuscript (Bodleian Library MS Eng. Lett. C. 573), contained important information which Merrick needed for the revision of his translation of the Psalms, and this must have been why he kept them. All the letters written during the years 1768 and 1769 were addressed to Glocester Ridley, who together with Lowth and Edward Rolle was co-executor of Joseph Spence's Will (Spence had died in 1768) (Wright 1950: 174). The peak for the year 1781 is largely due to Lowth's correspondence with the Scottish historian Sir David Dalrymple (1726–92), which ensued after Lowth sent him a presentation copy of his *Isaiah* in 1778.

The highest peak for the in-letters in Figure 5.1 represents the letters Lowth received from his secretary Edward Pearson during the brief period when he was Bishop of St Davids. With fifteen letters written in two months (early July to 1 September 1766, averaging over seven letters a month), the intensity of the contact between Pearson and Lowth was almost as strong as that between Lowth and his wife in 1755. With an almost equal number of letters written by his wife, the strength of contact

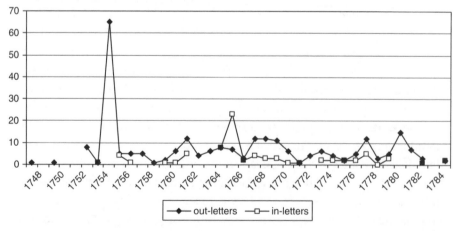

FIG. 5.1. The number of out-letters and in-letters compared (English letters only)

during this period was reciprocal; in the case of Pearson and Lowth this is less certain, as I have found references to only two letters – untraced – that Lowth wrote to him; but there may well have been more. The letters Molly wrote to her husband were not the only ones Lowth received during his absence from home in 1755 but which he failed to keep: I have calculated that he must have received at least nearly a hundred letters altogether, none of which have come down to us: in addition to the letters from his wife there are references to letters sent by Thomas Cheyney, Dean of Winchester, who was his wife's father's cousin and her guardian (10), Lowth's sisters (6), his brother-in-law Dr Eden (3), Dr Leslie, later Bishop of Limerick (4), Richard Trevor, Bishop of Durham (2), Benjamin Hoadly, Bishop of Winchester, Joseph Spence, a Mr Bailey, and an apothecary in Sedgefield (1 each).

There are thus clusters of letters, whether they actually came down to us or not, which were written or received by Lowth during a particular year, but there are also sets of letters addressed to or received from a single correspondent. In addition to Lowth's wife (64 out/65 in) there are Glocester Ridley (30 out/2 in), James Merrick (15 out/8 in), Sir David Dalrymple (14 out/9 in), Edward Pearson (2 out/15 in), and Thomas Cheyney (2 out/10 in). Furthermore, there are the letters to and from James Dodsley (16 out/4 in) and Robert Dodsley (18 out/1 in), William Warburton (9 out/7 in), and John Brown (1 out/1 in). As the Dodsleys were Lowth's publishers, their correspondence mostly deals with his books, though letters exchanged with Robert Dodsley also deal with other matters. Lowth's relationship with Robert was of a very different nature than the one with James; in the course of the years it developed from a business contact to a friend to whom he would pass on his wife's greetings. The correspondence with Warburton and Brown took place during the years 1756 and 1765 (until the end of January 1766), and it deals with the controversy between them which I have described in Chapter 2. Though I have been able to locate the autograph manuscripts of the letters to and from Warburton, the correspondence also exists in printed form, the anonymously published *Letter to the Right Reverend Author of The Divine Legation of Moses Demonstrated* (1765). The author is referred to on the title page as 'A Late Professor in THE UNIVERSITY of OXFORD', so Lowth's identity is all too apparent. The publication of the letters renewed the hostilities between the two men. 'My Lord,' Lowth wrote to Warburton on 1 December 1765 from Bath:

I have just now received Your Letter dated Novr. 21, wch. has been transmitted to me hither from Durham.

As to my publishing Your Letters, I hold myself fully justified by the Injury You had done me, in abusing me infamously & atrociously in Your Appendix: an Injury of that kind, which, tho' less in degree, would, by those very Laws of Society wch. You say I have violated, have cancelled y^e. obligation to Secrecy, wch. You absurdly pretend I lay under in the present case: a case, wch. arose from a haughty demand of Satisfaction ab^t. a matter antecedently before the Public, & of which it became in the event proper that the Public sh^d. be informed of the whole circumstances.

A series of eight letters were exchanged between the two men between 21 November 1765 and 31 January 1766, and they were likewise published, this time by Warburton in 1766. The earlier letters to the author of *The Divine Legation of Moses* were reissued by Lowth as a fourth edition in 1766, with an additional letter to John Brown. Brown belonged to Warburton's circle of friends, and according to Samuel Hallifax (1733–90) in a letter to Lowth dated 17 December 1765, 'it seems, [he] has taken upon him to fight the Bp's battles'. Brown's role in the affair is also referred to in a letter to Lowth from his close friend Benjamin Kennicott from around the same time: 'I cannot write a word farther without expressing my Joy at having <u>stole</u> Yesterday's News Paper, & inclosd it here for <u>your own proper possession</u>, & <u>speedy</u> as well as <u>certain</u> Sight of it – words are not at hand . . . whereby to express ye admiration of 45 Men of Oxfd, at the Letter here printed from <u>the Bp of G's Admirer</u>. Read, & be happy' (Kennicott to Lowth, December 1765). As discussed in Chapter 2, Lowth was even reprimanded for his part in the affair by the Archbishop of Canterbury, Thomas Secker, a letter to which Lowth replied in turn. The dispute between Lowth and Warburton produced more letters than those between the men involved alone.

Apart from the controversy with Warburton, distinct topics of Lowth's correspondence are therefore the publication of his books (in addition to Robert and James Dodsley, he also corresponded with printers), the inheritance of Joseph Spence as well of that of Thomas Cheyney (mostly exchanging letters with Samuel Speed, but also with Philip Barton and John Eames), the editing of Merrick's translation of the Psalms, his career in the Church (mostly the letters to his wife, but also those in which he acknowledged his promotion, on two occasions, to Thomas Pelham-Holles, the Duke of Newcastle), news of family and friends (the letters to his wife, but also to his relatives and his friends) the publication of *Isaiah* (letters exchanged with Sir Joshua Reynolds and John Thomas Troy, the Bishop of Ossory), the exchange of presentation copies, his own and those written by others (letters with e.g. Sir George Baker, Shute Barrington, the Bishop of Landaff, Sir David Dalrymple, William Duncombe), handling Church affairs in his capacity of a bishop (with a variety of people with whom he barely had a personal relationship other than in his official capacity, including Samuel Johnson and James Beattie), and a variety of other topics. Contrary to what I had hoped to find, the grammar is not dealt with in his correspondence very often, apart from his letters to and from the Dodsleys and those to his friends James Merrick and Joseph Spence, whom he invited personally to send suggestions for an improved second edition. The grammar brought him the reputation of a language expert in general, as appears from a request he received towards the end of the year 1780 from Thomas Brudenell-Bruce (1729–1814), Earl of Ailesbury, to check the language on a column Ailesbury had erected in commemoration of his elevation to the earldom.

Two other interesting letters are the very first items of the correspondence I have identified. The letters are addressed to Sir Francis Dashwood (1708–81), and they report on Lowth's two European tours in the late 1740s, early 1750s. In the second letter, Lowth describes his visit to Herculaneum, where he apparently was among the earliest visitors from England, and where Dashwood had been himself as well (ODNB, 'Dashwood'). According to Kemp (1967: 95), Charles Lyttelton (1714–68), dean of Exeter and Fellow of the Society of Antiquaries,

may well have received a copy of Lowth's letter, and may have handed it round privately, and Dashwood must surely have shown it to members of the Dilettanti Society. But Lyttelton did not communicate it to the Society of Antiquaries, which was not yet interested in Herculaneum, nor to the Royal Society, which was.

Though the letter in question was part of the private correspondence between Lowth and Dashwood, what happened to it subsequently illustrates the way in which letters tended be treated at the time: they often contained news that was of interest to other parties than the immediate addressee, and would be passed round to others who might be interested in the topics discussed as well. Another example of this can be found in a note by Lowth to Lord Ailesbury, returning to him 'with many Thanks the Letter from India' (Lowth to Brudenell-Bruce, 4 May 1781). If the author was aware of this possibility – in this case, Lowth even suggested in his letter to Dashwood that Lyttelton would be interested in what he wrote – this has important consequences for identifying the relatively private nature of the language used.

5.3 TYPES OF LETTERS

Most of the time, Lowth's handwriting is clear and legible. Apart from the draft letters, Lowth's out-letters have a meticulous appearance: they are, for instance, always dated, which is not always the case with eighteenth-century letters. This fits in well with Boswell's qualification of him as 'neat' and 'judicious'. The letters can be classified into formal notes and letters proper. Formal notes can be distinguished from letters by a number of features, such as the size of the sheet on which they are written, their corresponding shortness and terse style, the absence of the opening and closing formulas that are typical of letters and of a signature, and the lack of features expressing personal involvement, like the use of first and second person pronouns singular, of intensifiers such as *very*, and of so-called private verbs like those in *I think* and *I hope* (see Nurmi and Palander-Collin, 2008, for a discussion of letters as a text type). A typical example is the following note addressed to Thomas Cadell:

The B^p. of Oxford's Comp^{ts}. t[o] M^r. Cadell; & acquaints ^{him} that a [?] Card to M^r. Le Grand was to desire him to present both to y^e. D. of Gloucester & y^e. D. of Cumberland; & Two Sermons sh^d. have been sent with it. That he knows nothing himself concerning the publication, or the advertising; but has written to M^r. Prince, desiring him to satisfy M^r. Cadell, as to the particulars mentioned in his Letter.

Cuddesdon,
Octr. 31. 1771.

Formal notes also differ from proper letters in having more short forms such as *Comp^{ts}.*, *y^e.*, and *sh^d.* than was considered acceptable in formal letters (Tieken-Boon van Ostade 2006*b*). I have come across eight such notes altogether among Lowth's out-letters, all in his own hand, and only two among the in-letters. People possibly didn't think them worth preserving, due to their impersonal and merely functional nature. Those that have come down to us deal with an acknowledgement of receipt of *Isaiah* by Reynolds and with ecclesiastical business, and may therefore have been considered important enough by Lowth to preserve. Lowth himself must have written many more notes than I have located; one such note might have read something like 'The B^p. of Oxford presents his Comp^{ts}. to M^r. Boswell; & requests the pleasure of his company whenever convenient to him. Duke Street, Apr. 7. 1772'. Having found Lowth out on his initial visit, Boswell, as his journal entry quoted in Section 5.1 indicates, felt encouraged by this note to try and visit Lowth again at a later time.

So far, these formal notes have not received much scholarly attention as a text type: having encountered one in Robert Dodsley's correspondence, Tierney (1988: 474n) comments on its 'unusually impersonal air'. The author, Richard Graves, and Dodsley were after all on friendly terms. Lowth's notes, insofar as I have found any, were addressed only to Thomas Cadell, James Dodsley (2), Richard Burn, a certain 'M^r. De Precetes', Charles Woide (1725–90), Thomas Brudenell-Bruce, and John Nichols (1745–1826). They mostly concern affairs of business, relating to printing and Church matters. The note to de Precetes is a request to 'send herewith a Packet of Books wch. he [Lowth] begs y^e. [favour?] of M^r. de P. to order to be conveyed to Madrid by way of Paris under his protection. The Packet is addressed to M^r. Wadilove Chaplain to L^d. Grantham' (Lowth to de Precetes, late 1778); it seems unlikely that the two men were personally acquainted. That Lowth sent a formal note to the Earl of Ailesbury even after they had exchanged ordinary letters suggests, I think, that their acquaintance never developed into a closer relationship:

> The Bp. of London presents
> his Comp^{ts}. Ld. Ailesbury; & returns
> with many Thanks the Letter from
> India; & adds what occurs to him on
> the Orthography of the Inscription.
> Fulham, Friday Night.
> (Lowth to Brudenell-Bruce, 4 May 1781)

With James Dodsley, for one reason or another, Lowth never developed as close a relationship as with his brother Robert. The superscriptions to the letters, for instance, as well as the formal notes he sent to him suggest that their relationship remained strictly business.

All formal notes found date from after Lowth's appointment as Bishop of Oxford: possibly, he felt that this form of communication befitted his new social status. He even sent such notes to James Dodsley, though they had previously communicated by ordinary letter. We don't know if he ever made use of such tools, but Lowth would have been able to acquire the appropriate style of such notes, 'cards' or 'billets' as they were called, from popular manuals like *The Compleat Letter Writer* (Anon. 1756). The third edition of this particular manual, for instance, contains an Appendix with about twenty examples of different types of formal notes. At the same time, Lowth would have become acquainted with their style in his daily circumstances: it is very likely that he received many such notes in the course of his lifetime, particularly as he rose along the social ladder. That the medium did not always suit him is evident from the fact that a proper letter follows a note addressed to James Dodsley, reading:

Dear S^r.
On second thoughts I do not much like y^e. correction wch. I sent you last: be pleased to strike it out & let Stanza IX. line 4 stand as it did. I am much obliged to You for your good wishes: I am now, I thank God, pretty well recovered.

    Dear S^r.
        Your most faithful humble
            Servt.
                R. Oxford.
Cuddesdon,
Augt. 11. 1774.

The note, which had been sent less than a week previously, had read:

The B^p. of Oxford presents his Comp^{ts}. to M^r. Dodsley: he sent him some time ago his Corrections of y^e. Choice of Hercules, wch. he hopes came in time. He was forced to give y^m. by memory; not being able to find his corrected Copy of at least 30 years standing, wch. he has just ^{now} light upon. He finds, he has sent all y^e. material emendations, except the following, wch. he desires him to insert.
Stanza IX. line 4. read,
      Unbath'd with tears thy cheek, with sweat/ thy brow.
He desires a Line to know, if the Corrections came in time.

Cuddesdon
Augt. 5. 1774.

Compared to the other notes he sent, this one is of a less formulaic nature and deals with too much actual content for the medium adopted.

In his introduction to Wesley's letters, Baker (1980: 38) notes that 'like most careful writers, Wesley usually prepared drafts for his more important letters, and also kept fair copies for reference'. Lowth similarly drafted his more important letters, for I have found several of them, twenty-five altogether, that can be identified as such. There are a number of indications for this, the most obvious one being lengthy sections of text that were struck out, as in the case of a letter to William Duncombe, of which about half the amount of text was erased; we can only speculate about Lowth's reasons for doing so. Other indications are the occasional omission of an opening formula. Such draft letters make it hard to identify the addressee, but also those in which the formula used merely reads 'My L^d.' or 'D^r. S^r.' from which the endorsement, which would have contained the name and address of the correspondent in question, is lacking. Examples are:

My L^d.

Y. L^P. must certainly wonder at my negligence, in suffering Your last obliging Letter to ~~xxx~~ ^continue so long with^t. my Acknowledgem^ts. & Thanks (Lowth to ?, 30 November 1773).

and:

S^r.

I have taken the liberty to send by [no name filled in] a Box directed to You. It contains Basket's Great <u>Bible</u> in 2 Vols. As I am informed, that you have nothing of y^t. kind upon y^e. Communion Table in N.C. Chapel, I thought it might be no improper ornament for y^t. place. If you sh^d. think it ~~such~~ so, I sh^d. be ~~happy~~ glad if y^e. Coll. w^d. do me y^e. favor to accept ~~it I ...~~ it as a small Memorial of my late dear Son: ~~& with that ...~~ to explain wch. design have ~~xxx~~ written his Name in it. I desire to refer this matter intirely to Your judgem^t. (Lowth to ?, after 7 June 1778).

On the basis of internal evidence the former letter can be dated at around 1773, as there is a reference to Lowth's *Sermon Preached before the Society Corresponding with the Incorporated Society in Dublin* which was published in that year, while the latter refers to the recent death of his son Thomas Henry in 1778. The first addressee was either a fellow bishop of Lowth's or one of his aristocratic acquaintances, as 'My L^d.' was the proper title by which to address such men (Anon., *The Compleat Letter Writer*, 1756: 55–7). The addressee of the second letter was possibly a master at Winchester College where Thomas Henry had been a student, though not John Burton (fl.1759–71), with whom Lowth was on considerably more friendly terms than to address him with a plain 'S^r.'. Draft letters usually also lack a subscription, such as 'I have y^e. honour to be –' (Lowth to ?, after December 1778), or they contain only his initials by way of a signature, as in a draft letter to Warburton dated 14 October 1756: 'the sincerity wth. wch. I am, Dear S^r. Your most faithful & Affectionate humble Servt. R.L.'.

As the two examples above show, draft letters can be identified by the presence of large numbers of self-corrections – obliterations and rephrasings in the form of superscriptions – but also by a much higher than usual number of short forms and abbreviations, particularly of names. Occasionally, moreover, draft letters were written on paper scraps, which were usually of a smaller size than that of the paper used for fair copies of letters. In some cases, both the draft version and the letter's fair copy have come down to us, which allows us to study the differences between them. This will help us identify letter-writing practice that is peculiar to draft letters for which no fair copy exists. The opening sentence of a letter to Warburton, dated 9 September 1756, reads: 'Our good Friends D^r. C. & M^r. S. have agreably to your desire communicated to me some particulars of y^e. conversation wch. you have lately had with them relating to me', while we similarly find abbreviations in Lowth's reply to Archbishop Thomas Secker's reproof of Lowth's behaviour in the affair: 'I beg Y. G. to accept of my sincerest thanks for your most obliging Letter. Y. G. expectations f^m. me do me great honour, but xxx discourage me' (Lowth to Secker, 9 December 1765). These letters can therefore be identified as drafts. Apart from Warburton and Secker, my corpus contains draft letters written to a Mr Day and a certain Richard Eastman, both of them Lowth's parishioners, Robert Darley Waddilove (1736–1828), chaplain to the British ambassador in Madrid, a certain John Roberts, a Mr Walter, de Precetes, Michaelis, Troy, and Shute Barrington. In some cases, such as his correspondence to Warburton and Secker, which dealt with rather precarious affairs, we can thus see that Lowth carefully drafted his letters beforehand. Such drafts show him formulating his thoughts as he went along, phrasing and rephrasing his sentences to the best possible effect, but they also provide evidence on his different attitudes towards informal (draft letters) and formal (fair copies) usage. Along with the letters received from Warburton, Lowth later used his own draft letters for the publication of their correspondence in 1765, and Warburton did similarly with the second part of their correspondence a year later.

Draft letters occasionally show linguistic corrections made by Lowth, some of which are of particular interest. In one instance, Lowth changed the spelling of the participle *rejoiced* into *rejoic'd* (Lowth to his wife, 6 July 1755). He was thus aware of the stylistic differences between the two spellings which were then still current. Osselton (1984) found evidence for the existence of two spelling systems at the time, the one characterizing printed texts and the other private documents like letters. Forms like *rejoic'd* are typical of what he terms 'epistolary spelling'. A different type of spelling change is when Lowth corrects *you* into *You* (Lowth to Day, 6 April 1770). Capitals are sometimes hard to distinguish in the letters, but this instance suggests that Lowth was in the habit of capitalizing *You* for reasons of politeness. All instances of *you* in his letters to Johann David Michaelis, with whom he conducted a friendly but polite exchange of letters, are indeed capitalized. Capitalizing the second person pronoun singular for this purpose was quite common in my own language, Dutch, down to approximately forty years or so ago; for English, however, the practice has never been described. In a letter to Spence of 29 September 1761, on a poem on which Lowth was engaged at that time, he likewise insisted upon 'You, with a Cap[l].'. In a letter to Merrick, I found a correction of *lays* into *lies*. The question whether it should be *lie* or *lay* was, and still is, a linguistic shibboleth, and the fact that the letter in which the correction occurs is dated 30 December 1761, only about one month before his grammar was due to appear, indicates that Lowth's linguistic awareness was particularly acute at this time. In the final correspondence with Warburton, five years later, his mind was clearly occupied by more important things than linguistic correctness, for the letter which he clearly laboured over extensively eventually included an instance of the gerund in a form disapproved of by Lowth in his own grammar.

5.4 EPISTOLARY FORMULAS AS AN INDEX OF SOCIAL RELATIONSHIPS

5.4.1 *Opening formulas*

For the large variety of opening formulas attested in Wesley's letters, Baker (1980: 48) describes what he calls 'a hierarchy of terms', ranging from salutations expressing least to greatest intimacy:

> Sir/Madam
> Dear sir/Dear madam
> My dear Mr.–/Mrs.–/Miss X
> My dear brother/sister
> Dear James/Jane, etc.
> Dear Jemmy/Jenny, etc.

Lowth was equally meticulous in his use of address forms, and we find a similar though a both somewhat more elaborate and more restricted system in his letters (see Table 5.1). For an overview of Lowth's correspondents, see Appendix 2. In terms of intimacy, Lowth's address forms can be divided into three categories, the two main categories being those used to family members and those to non-family members. The latter category can be subdivided into forms expressing a distant and forms expressing a close, or at any rate closer, relationship. While the forms 'My Lord', 'Sir', 'Gentlemen', and 'Rev.ᵈ Sir' express greatest distance, or, in terms of the politeness theory developed by Brown and Levinson (1987), negative politeness, those which have an additional modifier, 'good' in 'My good Lord' and 'dear' in 'Dear Sir', indicate greater closeness, thus expressing positive politeness. 'Dear Brother Spence' is the most intimate address form I have found in Lowth's letters to non-family members; it correlates with terms of affection in the letter itself, such as 'Mʳ. Professor' as Lowth teasingly calls him in a letter from 29 September 1761. The address forms used to his wife, his son Tom, and his brother are as one would expect them to be in view of their relationship. As in the case of Wesley's letters, Lowth usually repeated the salutation of the address form in the closing formula, except for his letters to his wife, which he invariable ended with 'My Dearest Molly', irrespective of

Table 5.1 **Lowth's use of address forms**

My Lord	Hartington, Pelham-Holles, Osborne, Secker, **Warburton**, Wentworth, Yorke, two unidentified addressees
Sir	**Burn**, Eames, Dalrymple, Day, **Robert Dodsley**, Duncombe, Jenkinson, Johnson, Michaelis, Nourse, Roberts, Reynolds, **Speed**, two unidentified addressees
Gentlemen	unidentified addressees
Rev.ᵈ Sir	Eastman, Morant, **Percy**, Walter, one unidentified addressee
My good Lord	Barrington, Brudenell-Bruce
My dear Lord	Troy
Dear Sir	Barton, **Burn**, Cadell, Chapman, Dashwood, James Dodsley, **Robert Dodsley**, Merrick, **Percy**, Rotheram, Ridley, **Speed**, Sturges, Waddilove, **Warburton**, Joseph Warton, Thomas Warton, Woide, three unidentified addressees
Dear Brother [surname]	Spence
Dear Brother	brother
My dear Molly/Tom	wife, son
My dearest Molly	wife
My dearest (Love)	wife

the opening formula used. This reflects both the extent to which he missed his wife and his worries for the well-being of his family.

Some people occur twice in Table 5.1, Warburton, Burn, Robert Dodsley, Speed, and Percy. In the case of Warburton, the relationship worsened over the years, which is indeed expressed in the epistolary formulas used. At the same time, Lowth adopted the appropriate 'My Lord' as soon as Warburton acceded to the bishopric of Gloucester. His relationship with Burn, his secretary when he was Bishop of London, Robert Dodsley, and Percy clearly became more intimate over the years, while in the case of Speed we see the opposite, presumably due to some tension that arose over the administration of Thomas Cheyney's Will. Another form worth commenting on is 'Dear Sir', with which Lowth addressed Sturges despite the fact that he was Sturges' uncle. Possibly, Lowth considered the fact that they were fellow clergy members to be of greater significance than their blood relationship. The contents of the letter do show greater intimacy than that usually found between Lowth and the other members in this category:

We begin printing a New Edition of Isaiah next week: the three parts separately, to go on together, for dispatch. If You have noted any mistakes of any kind, **communicate**. If at the beginning of either of the parts, immediately: for I have already given the first sheets of each to the Printer, who begins on Monday.

All our **Love** to You and Yours; & $^{\&\ our\ Bob.}$; Fanny thanks Isabella for her Letter. I suppose You have paid M^{rs}. Eyre.

Yours most Aff^{ly}.

R. London (Lowth to Sturges, 5 December 1778).

In a letter to a more distant addressee Lowth would more likely have used a polite form like 'be pleased to communicate ...' than the short 'communicate', and this is confirmed by the lack of a verb form in the sentence following. Nor would he have used such an intimate form to express his greetings: apart from the letters to his wife, 'Love' in this context is found only in letters to Dashwood, Spence, his son Tom, and his brother William.

To try and find out whether Lowth's relationship with his addressees was conceived as being reciprocal, I have listed the address forms used by his correspondents in Table 5.2 below. Again, see Appendix 2 for an overview of the correspondents. In contrast to Table 5.1, the correspondents are all non-family members. As above, a division can be made into forms expressing greater and lesser politeness, but a complicating factor in this is that from 1766 onwards Lowth had to be addressed with a form that reflected his new status. This was true even for old friends like Benjamin

Table 5.2 **The address forms used by Lowth's correspondents**

My Lord	Baker, Beattie, Cooke, **Hallifax**, Jenkinson, Johnson, Kennan, **Kennicott**, **Morant**, Nicolls, Pearson, Pitt, Prince, Reynolds, Roberts, **Secker**, Speed, Tookie, Trew, Woide, one unidentified correspondent
Sir	Gilpin, Michaelis, **Warburton**
Revd Sir	**Morant, Warburton**
My good Lord	Lincoln
My dear Lord	Barrington, Pelham-Holles
Good Dr. Lowth	**Secker**
My most respected Lord Bishop	Dick
Dear Sir	Burton, Robert Dodsley, **Hallifax**, **Kennicott**, Merrick, **Warburton**, Joseph Warton, Thomas Warton
My dear Brother	Spence

Kennicott, who, upon Lowth's appointment as Bishop of Oxford, became one of his chaplains (see *ODNB*, 'Benjamin Kennicott'). Indeed, all letters in which Lowth was addressed as 'My Lord' date from after he had become a bishop. This explains the different forms used previously by Morant, Hallifax, and Kennicott. An interesting illustration of what Lowth's new station in life entailed in the eyes of his friends is a teasing letter he received from an unidentified but evidently very close friend, which presumably dates from soon after his accession to the see of London:

To The Lord Bishop of London,
            D^r. Lowth
Can your Lordship take in good humour a piece of pleasantry the only thing I ever was conscious of producing extempore. I am sure that it is not a symptom of any diminution of my respect for your Lordship.

> Lowth's Learning! what is it to me,
> Who never yet his soup could see.
> Of Sacred Poesy he writes;
> But me to dinner ne'er invites
> To Christian Bishop sure belongs
> More – Hospitality than Songs.
> So, till his Lordship takes my cue
> I'll hold him as an Hebrew – Jew (? to Lowth, after 1777).

Secker's use of 'Good Dr. Lowth' may be taken as an act of positive politeness, the function of which was to soften the tone of his letter of reproof in relation to the Warburton affair. The formula used by Sir Alexander Dick similarly expresses positive politeness. Warburton is least constant in his use of address forms, which may be linked to their changing, though in the end definitively deteriorating, relationship.

Comparing the forms in Table 5.2 with those in 5.1, it may be concluded that the relationship between Lowth and Spence, Robert Dodsley, the Wartons, and even Secker can be called reciprocal (though not always equal), whereas it is also noticeable that Lowth made fewer attempts at showing positive politeness than his correspondents, particularly Barrington and Pelham-Holles ('My **dear** Lord'), and even Spence ('**My** dear Brother'). This confirms my suggestion as to Lowth's extreme social sensitiveness: he considered it safer to stick to the prescribed formulas, even in his problematical relationship with Warburton, than to risk varying on the expected forms.

5.4.2 Closing formulas

The closing formulas of letters, according to Baker (1980: 59), were expected to contain three elements, 'the address (usually repeated from the opening salutation), the "compliments" or "services" (normally introduced by the phrase "I am" or "I remain"), and the signature'. This is true for Lowth's letters, too, though the signature is usually lacking from the letters which have only come down to us in draft form. Lowth's signature varies from 'Robt. Lowth', 'R. Lowth', or 'R.L.' to 'R. S^t. Davids', 'R. Oxford', and 'R. London'; adopting the name of a bishop's episcopal diocese as part of his signature was common practice at the time (cf. Smend 2004: 58). The fullest form of Lowth's signature mostly occurs in the initial stages of a correspondence, and as he never used his first name even when writing to his wife, this suggests that the use of his full name indicates distance rather than closeness. Two other frequently occurring elements in the closing formulas are the invocation of God's blessing and words of prayer, particularly in the letters to his wife (e.g. 'God bless & preserve thee, My Dearest Love, & grant us soon a happy meeting', Lowth to his wife, 27 May 1755), as well as the passing on of greetings, either from his wife to the addressee or from himself to a common acquaintance. The presence of greetings in a letter's conclusion signifies considerable closeness with the addressee, and helps establish the nature of Lowth's relationship with the addressee in question when other means are lacking.

The variation in Lowth's closing formulas is much greater than that in the opening formulas to his letters. They are therefore not only more

interesting to analyse, but are also of great use in determining his relationship with the addressee, serving as a signal for any change in relative
closeness. This is important for the classification of his writing styles
which I will present in Chapter 6. The most frequent conclusion found
is the one containing the phrase 'Dear S^r. Your most Affectionate humble
Servt. R. Lowth'. It occurs with slight variations ('Believe me, Dear S^r.',
'I am, Dear S^r.', 'I am ever, Dear S^r.') in letters addressed to Robert Dodsley,
Merrick, Ridley, Speed, and the Wartons. Another frequent formula is
'I have the honour to be with great ['the greatest'] Respect, S^r. Your most
Obedient humble Servt. R. London', in which, depending on the status of
the addressee, the words 'My Lord' and 'Your Lordship's' are substituted
for 'S^r.' and 'Your'. We find this formula in letters addressed to Dalrymple,
Jenkinson, Johnson, Yorke, and Osborne. In general, it can be said that the
longer the closing formula is, the more polite the tone of the letter in
question and the more distant Lowth's relationship with the addressee.
I have observed the same phenomenon in the correspondence of John Gay
(1685–1732) (Tieken-Boon van Ostade 1999), so this seems to have been
common practice at the time. Examples of lengthy closing formulas are
'I have the honour to be with the highest Gratitude, My Lord, Your Grace's
Most obliged & most Obedient humble Servt. Robt. Lowth' in Lowth's first
letter in my collection to Thomas Pelham-Holles, Duke of Newcastle
(2 December 1765), and 'I am, My Lord, with all possible Respect &
Gratitude, Your Excellency^s Most Obliged & most Obedient humble
Servt. R. Lowth', addressed to Lord Hartington (15 November 1755). Both
men were his patrons, and Lowth was expected to express himself to them
in terms of the utmost politeness.

We find the opposite, too. While we do indeed find Lowth's shortest
conclusions in the letters to the people he was closest to, such as his wife
(e.g. 'Ever Your's R. Lowth') and his friends Merrick and Ridley (e.g. 'I am,
Dear S^r. Your's most Aff.^{ly} R. Oxford'), very short formulas also occur in
the last letters to Warburton ('My Lord, Your humble Servant'). There is
also an uncharacteristically short concluding formula in Lowth's last letter
to Samuel Speed in my collection (14 July 1764):

S^r.

Be pleas'd to deliver to M^{rs}. John Dison any Title deeds or Writings belonging
to me, & his receit shall be Your discharge from
>Your humble Servt.
>Robt. Lowth.

While all other letters to Speed end with a formula containing the word *affectionately* and greetings were even exchanged from home to home, as in 'We & our little folks are, I thank God, all well; & join in our best respects to M^{rs}. Speed & Yourself' (Lowth to Speed, 14 December 1760), the change in formula suggests that relations between the two men had soured in the process of the concluding stages of the administration of Thomas Cheyney's Will, in which both were involved. Other changes in Lowth's relationship with the addressee are evident when he switches to a formula containing the word *affectionate*, as in the case of Robert Dodsley, Percy, and, temporarily, Warburton. Lowth's letters to Robert's brother James, however, continue to show greater distance, usually concluding with 'I am, (Dear) S^r. Your most Obedient humble Servt. R. Lowth'. Lowth's use of *esteem* in closing formulas, as in 'I am with the greatest Respect & Esteem, Dear Sr. Your most Obedient humble Servt. R. London' (Lowth to Rotheram, 9 February 1781), similarly signals positive politeness. Apart from Rotheram, it is also found in his letters to Woide. In his letters to Merrick *esteem* is even combined with *affectionate*. Usage of the latter word is a sign of extreme closeness: apart from the letters to his nearest and dearest, we find it in the closing formulas of letters addressed to Spence and Chapman (along with the use of *Brother*, a term expressing particular intimacy), Dashwood, Robert Dodsley, Merrick, Ridley, Speed, Percy, and the Wartons, as well as Warburton, though only once.

The use of the word *Servant* in closing formulas was quite common, even in letters to friends, but Lowth never used it in letters to his wife, his son, his nephew John Sturges, or his close friend Spence. In letters to Ridley and Merrick, likewise friends of his, he varied between the formula 'Your's most Affectionately' and variants upon 'your most Affectionate humble Servant'. In the correspondence, *Servant* always collocates with *humble*, while *humble Servant* is variously modified by the addition of *obedient, affectionate, faithful, obliged*, nothing (in letters to Warburton and Speed), or, indeed, *most*. Several of these adjectives could even be combined in the same formula, as in the most polite formulas quoted above. In such formulas the intensifier *most* might occur twice. Compared to Lowth's complete corpus of correspondence, *most* typically occurs as an intensifier of concluding formulas: a concordance search of the letters, performed with the help of WordSmith Tools, produced 320 instances, as many as two-thirds of which were found in the formulas. Though *sincerely* today indicates distance when used in closing formulas, this was not the case in Lowth's time (Tieken-Boon van Ostade 1999; Bijkerk 2004): in seven letters the word collocates with *affectionately*, once with *ardently* (Lowth to Pelham-Holles, one of his patrons), and once with *very* (Lowth to Speed).

While variation in the closing formulas offers important clues to changes in his relationships, Lowth's use of these formulas is at times invariable: his letters to Dalrymple always end with the formula 'I have the honour to be with great Respect, S^r. Your most Obedient humble Servt. R. London'. Presumably their relationship did not change sufficiently in the course of their correspondence (1779–82) to call for a change in formula. In his letters to Michaelis, Lowth similarly sticks to the concluding formula 'Your most obedient and most obliged humble servant' (with some slight variations) throughout the English part of their correspondence (1770–82). Though Smend (2004: 58) believes that the two men were friends until the moment of Lowth's death, Lowth's use of this fairly formal formula suggests that their relationship never became truly close. His letters to his wife, however, do show a variety of different formulas, but in all cases they express his love for her and the extent to which he missed her. Striking examples are 'Believe me, My Dearest Love, Most impatiently Your's R. L.' – the word *impatiently* occurs only once more in the letters, when he enquires about the well-being of his family ('I long most impatiently to hear how the dear little Tom does; & the little wench & her little Mama', 24 October 1755) – and 'My dearest Molly, Your's intirely R.L.' (10 May 1755). The word *adieu*, which Gay used only in letters to his closest friends (Tieken-Boon van Ostade 1999), is likewise exclusively found, with seven instances, in Lowth's letters to his wife, always collocating with 'My dearest (Love)'. It therefore similarly reflects extreme closeness.

As for the closing formulas used by Lowth's correspondents, there are on the whole too few letters by individual correspondents to allow for an analysis as detailed as that for the letters by Lowth himself. For all that, a few interesting comments can be made. The one person who never varied in his use of closing formulas is Pearson, Lowth's secretary during the summer of 1766. All his letters end with 'I am My Lord Your Lordship's Most Obedient & very much Obliged Humble Servant Edwd Pearson', which confirms the purely functional as well as essentially unequal nature of their relationship. A second point that may be made is that most of the in-letters conclude with a formula containing the word *Servant*, which, as in the case of Lowth's own letters, most frequently collocates with *humble* and less frequently with *affectionately, obliged, dutiful, faithful,* or *obedient*. Only Burton (in one of the two letters located), Kennicott, Secker, Spence, and Thomas Warton do not use the 'Servant' formula. One letter, clearly expressing the desperation of the writer, ends with 'Your Lordship's most humble and distress'd Servant' (Kennan to Lowth, 14 October 1766). Secker, Spence, and a certain John Lincoln, one of Lowth's parishioners, use 'Brother' in their closing formulas, but in Spence's case alone is the use of the term reciprocated by Lowth, thus confirming their intimacy.

A combination of the above-mentioned premodifiers signals greater negative politeness, as in the case of Johnson's 'I am, My Lord Your Lordship's most obedient and most humble Servant Sam: Johnson' (13 July 1780) – note the repetition of the intensifier *most* here, which, as in the case of Lowth's own letters, occurs predominantly in the letters' concluding formulas – and in that of Pearson already referred to. Negative politeness can also be expressed by the addition of phrases indicating respect ('with most profound respect', 'with the most sincere Respect', 'with the highest Respect and Esteem', 'with the greatest respect'). Such forms we find with Beattie, Hallifax, Reynolds, Trew, and Woide. Others, such as Barrington, Pelham-Holles, and Pitt add the words *esteem* or *affectionate* in their superscriptions (Pitt even used both), presumably to mitigate the possible effect of extreme negative politeness. Pelham-Holles was one of Lowth's patrons, and his other letter seems to end slightly more positively polite than the first: 'assuring you of The Regard, and Affection, with which I am, My Dear Lord, Your Lordship's most Obed^t. Humble Servant Holles Newcastle' (19 May 1767). Sir Alexander Dick used the word *Friend* in his closing formula: 'Your Lordship's most devoted Friend & Servant Alex^r Dick' (9 April 1783), which confirms their intimacy, already commented on. As in the case of the out-letters, positive politeness is expressed by shorter conclusions than usual. An extreme case, with as many as three words suggesting closeness between the two men, is the only letter from Spence I have found: '**A Dieu.** Your most **affectionate Bro^r**: Jo: Spence' (31 August 1756). Other short formulas worth mentioning here are Thomas Warton's '& believe me to be, Dear Sir, You<rs> truly' (18 April 1770) and Kennicott's 'I am, . . . Yours most affectionately' (30 December 1760), 'Ever Yours most affectly' (c.1766), and 'ever Y^r Lp's gratefully' (23 February 1772). All these anticipate the development of the formula *yours sincerely*, thus indicating that this formula originated as a positive politeness device, subsequently developing into a negative one. The variation in the formulas used by Kennicott confirm his closeness with Lowth, despite their difference in Church ranks. From the year 1766 onwards, when Lowth had become a bishop, their newly arisen social inequality called for greater negative politeness, despite their personal relationship. The epistolary formulas adopted by Alexander Dick further illustrate this point: the letter dates from 1783, when Lowth was Bishop of London. I will discuss in Chapter 6 whether this also had an effect on the language used in the letters proper. Similarly, writing top-down, as in the case of Secker and Pelham-Holles when addressing Lowth, could produce seemingly more intimate formulas – and, presumably, language – than when Lowth addressed these men in turn. Neither Secker's use of 'Loving Brother' in his closing formulas nor Pelham-Holles's use of *affection* should therefore be taken to indicate a reciprocally close relationship with Lowth. Warburton's closing formulas are as similarly and equally rudely short during the final phase of their relationship as Lowth's. In the earlier stage of their correspondence he concluded a letter with 'I am Dear Sir your very faithfull **affectionate** Humble Servant W. Warburton'. This letter is dated 12 October 1756, and it induced Lowth to reciprocate by likewise using the 'affectionate Humble Servant' formula in his reply written two days later. But Lowth would never do so again.

5.4.3 *More epistolary evidence*

Both the opening and the closing formulas used by Lowth and his correspondents could be adapted to express greater or less negative or positive politeness. As already said, the longer the formula, the greater the social distance between writer and addressee, or, in the case of Lowth's in-letters dating from after he was appointed bishop, the more the writers observed the accepted rules of politeness in this respect. Conversely, very short formulas usually express closeness, particularly if they included words expressing affection as such. Lowth's meticulous use of epistolary formulas facilitates the isolation of his different styles of writing which I will analyse in Chapter 6. An additional way of determining closeness between Lowth and his addressees is the presence of greetings in the closing formula, which suggests that the relationship in question was not confined to Lowth and the addressee, but that it included, for instance, Lowth's wife as well. We find such greetings in letters addressed to Chapman, Robert Dodsley, Speed, Barton, Joseph Warton, Spence, Ridley, and even Secker, as well as, obviously, in his letters to his son Tom, his brother, and his nephew John Sturges. Occasionally, greetings also concern the wife of the addressee, as in the case of Speed, Barton, Eames, Joseph Warton, and Ridley, thus suggesting even greater closeness. Lowth's relationship with Ridley encompassed their entire families, who eventually came to be on visiting terms, as is evident from the following letter:

Dear S^r.

If You can let me know, that You are not engaged on Saturday next, I will do myself the pleasure of waiting on You at Poplar [nowadays in Greater London]. If I find, y^t. I can get at You by the back road, M^{rs}. Lowth, who is advised to make use of every opportunity of taking the air, may perhaps accompany me, & wait of M^{rs}. Ridley. We shall set out as soon as we have breakfasted, & come home to a late Dinner.

    I am, Dear S^r.
              Your most Affectionate
                  humble Servt.
                      R. Oxford.
Argyle Street,
Jan. 31. 1769.

Even their respective daughters became friends: one letter, dated nearly eight months later, includes the line 'M^{rs}. Lowth & my Girls desire to join in Comp^{ts}. to M^{rs}. Ridley & the Young Ladies' (Lowth to Ridley, 15 August 1769). By 'my Girls' Lowth must have referred to Frances (aged eleven) and Martha (aged eight); Mary and Charlotte were both dead by this time, while Margaret had died only five months previously. Another indication of the closeness between two families may be found in Lowth's letter to his nephew John Sturges in Winchester: 'All our Love to You and Yours; & our Bob. Fanny thanks Isabella for her Letter' (5 December 1778). At sixteen, and with his father being situated in London, 'Bob', or Robert Junior, had stayed behind in Winchester to live with his relatives there. Though not of the same generation, Isabella (aged sixteen) and Fanny (aged twenty-one) corresponded together as if they were cousins.

5.5 LETTERS AS EVIDENCE OF LOWTH'S SOCIAL NETWORK

On the basis of my analysis of the epistolary formulas (opening and closing formulas) used by Lowth and his correspondents I have classified the addressees of his out-letters into the following categories, which reflect a decreasing amount of closeness: Relatives, Close friends, Friends, Fellow

Table 5.3 **A classification of Lowth's correspondents (fifty altogether) according to their relationship (based on the out-letters)**

Relationship	Addressee
Relatives	Mary Jackson (wife), Thomas Henry Lowth (son), William Lowth (brother), John Sturges (nephew)
Close friends	Chapman, Dashwood, **Spence**, **Joseph Warton**, **Thomas Warton**, unidentified correspondent
Friends	**Robert Dodsley**, **Hallifax**, **Merrick**, Percy, Ridley, **Speed**, Troy
Fellow scholars	Dalrymple, Michaelis, **Woide**, Woog
Work-related contacts (publishing)	Cadell, James Dodsley, Robert Dodsley, Nichols, Nourse
Work-related contacts (church)	Burn, Day, **Eastman**, **Jenkinson**, **Johnson**, **Roberts**, Rotheram, Walter, Yorke
Patrons	Hartington, **Pelham-Holles**, Secker
Acquaintances	Barton, Duncombe, Eames, **Morant**, Percy, **Reynolds**, Waddilove, Wentworth
Bare acquaintances	**Barrington**, Brudenell-Bruce, Osborne, de Precetes
Enemies	Brown, **Warburton**

scholars, Work-related contacts (publishing and the church), Patrons, Acquaintances, Bare acquaintances, and Enemies. The most difficult category is that of patrons, as any relationship with such men would involve both a certain amount of closeness and social distance at the same time. This ambivalence is reflected in Lowth's language use, as I will demonstrate in the following chapter. Table 5.3 presents the names of the various correspondents ranked according to these relationships.

In some cases, the relationship between Lowth and his correspondents changed over the years, mostly from less close to closer, in which case I have included the names twice (Robert Dodsley, Thomas Percy). Lowth's relationship with Warburton, though temporarily fairly amicable, was mostly hostile, and it has been classified accordingly. Though not exactly a patron, Thomas Secker's relationship with Lowth was probably similar to that with his actual patrons, Lord Hartington and Thomas Pelham-Holles. In the category 'Close friends' I have placed an unidentified correspondent alongside Chapman, Dashwood, Spence, and the Wartons, as Lowth closes the letter in question with the formula 'Rev^d. S^r. Your & Their very **Affectionate Brother**, & most faithful humble Servt. R. S^t. Davids' (Lowth to ?, 4 August 1766). Particularly his use of 'Brother', as also in his letters to Spence and Chapman, signals an intimate relationship. Another difficult person to classify was John Thomas Troy. Only a draft letter to him has come down to us, and it lacks a closing formula. I have categorized him as a 'Friend' because of the opening formula 'My D^r. L^d.' and because of a little joke Lowth makes ('My Is. [*Isaiah*] is very much obliged to you for your kind & favourable reception', Lowth to Troy, 15 May 1779), which is a play on a common politeness formula. Jokes are not always easy to identify as such in a letter, as there is always the risk that they are misunderstood. To be able to make one thus presupposes a considerable amount of shared intimacy between writer and addressee (see Brown and Levinson 1987: 124).

I have similarly tried to classify Lowth's correspondents on the basis of the in-letters (Table 5.4). Several names occur in both lists; these have been highlighted in bold in the tables. Lowth's relationship with Thomas Warton is characterized by a double bond and can thus be considered to have been particularly strong: they were old friends, and had collaborated on the publication of a book. As Warton puts it himself: 'I esteem it an honour of my Life to have my labour joined with your's in this Edition; & I hope we shall always *act together*, as becomes Friends joined by such a bond of union' (Thomas Warton to Lowth, 18 April 1770). In Chapter 6 I will discuss the question of whether Lowth's different relationships with his addressees correlates with his language use in the letters, and as such can be taken to reflect his communicative competence.

Many of Lowth's correspondents were members of the clergy (see Appendix 2 for an overview of their professions): his male relatives (Thomas Lowth, William Lowth, and John Sturges) were all clergymen,

Table 5.4 A classification of Lowth's correspondents (thirty–eight altogether) according to their relationship (based on the in–letters)

Relationship	Addressee
Close friends	Kennicott, **Spence, Joseph Warton, Thomas Warton**
Friends	Dick, **Robert Dodsley, Hallifax, Merrick, Speed**
Fellow scholars	Gilpin, **Woide**
Work-related contacts (publishing)	Prince
Work-related contacts (church)	Pearson, Beattie, Cooke, **Eastman**, Gore, Hodgson, **Jenkinson, Johnson**, Kennan, Lincoln, Neve, Nicolls, Pitt, **Roberts**, Tookie, Trew, Walsh, Wesley
Patrons	**Pelham–Holles, Secker**
Acquaintances	Baker, Burton, **Morant, Reynolds, Barrington**
Enemies	**Warburton**

and so were Barrington, Barton, Chapman, Gilpin, Hallifax, Kennan, Kennicott, Morant, Percy, Ridley, Rotheram, Secker, Speed, Trew, Troy, Waddilove, Walter, Warburton, Wesley, and Woog. The list includes bishops and future bishops (Barrington, Hallifax, Percy, Troy, and Warburton) as well as the Archbishop of Canterbury, Thomas Secker. With many others Lowth corresponded on diocesan affairs: Burn (his secretary as Bishop of London), Cooke, Day, Eastman, Gore, Hodgson, Lincoln, Neve, Nicolls, Pearson (his secretary as Bishop of St Davids), Tookie, and Walsh. Samuel Kennan wrote to Lowth on the matter of his own ordination. Many of Lowth's correspondents belonged to the class of the nobility: Sir George Baker; Brudenell-Bruce, the first Earl of Ailesbury; Lord Hartington, the Duke of Devonshire; Sir David Dalrymple; Sir Alexander Dick; Francis Osborne (Duke of Leeds, Marquess of Carmarthen); Thomas Pelham-Holles, Duke of Newcastle; and Philip Yorke, the second Earl of Hardwicke. With some of these, Lord Hartington and Pelham-Holles, Lowth was in closer contact than with others: these men were his patrons, and his relationship with them was thus never one of equality; by the time Lowth had become Lord Bishop of London and greater equality would have been possible, the two men were dead. Lowth's relationship with Pearson, on the other hand, though also unequal due to their different positions in the Church hierarchy, nevertheless appears to have been relatively close: this is evident from the tone of their correspondence – in so far as we can deduce this on the basis of Pearson's share in it – as well as from the topics discussed and the language used. Pearson's letters, for instance, contain more abbreviations than was considered acceptable in letters to people higher up on the social scale. His relationship with Lowth seems very typical of that between modern executives and their secretaries: relatively informal without becoming as intimate as between actual friends.

Other groups of correspondents are the people involved with the publication of Lowth's books and those he corresponded with on scholarly matters. The latter I have classified as 'Fellow scholars'. The former group consists of Robert and James Dodsley and Thomas Cadell, whose names appear on the title pages of his books; no letters appear to have come down to us to or from Andrew Millar, co-publisher with the Dodsleys of *The Life of William of Wykeham*, the grammar, and a sermon published in 1779. John Nichols, also in this group, had printed one of Lowth's sermons, published in 1779, and also *Isaiah*. According to the *ODNB*, John Nourse (bap.1705, d.1780) was a London bookseller, and he occasionally supplied

Lowth with books; he also sold Lowth's *De Sacra Poesie*, which, contrary to his other books, had been published in Oxford. The following letter from Lowth to Nourse highlights this particular group of members of his social network:

Winchester May 15. 1753.

S^r.

   My Brother [William Lowth] informs me that you
desire to have a few Copys of my
Book to send abroad. Please to
write to M^r. **Daniel Prince** at M^r.
Clements's Bookseller in Oxford, who
will send you whatever number you
shall want for exportation; as for y^e.
home-sale, you know I am engaged to
M^r. **Dodsley** & M^r. **Millar**. You will
account to me for them at the same
price that they do: that is, 10.^{s} p Book,
or 12.$^£$ for 25.

I am,

S^r. Your most humble Servt.

Robt. Lowth.

Cover: To M^r. **Nourse**
      Bookseller in the
            Strand
                  London.

The letters from Daniel Prince to Lowth all concern the publication of the third edition of *William of Wykeham*, which was published in Oxford at the Clarendon Press in 1777. The group comprising Lowth's fellow scholars consisted of Sir David Dalrymple, James Merrick, Charles Geoffrey Woide, but also Johann David Michaelis, the editor of the Leipzig edition of Lowth's *De Sacra Poesie*.

With an overlap of eighteen names, the lists in Tables 5.3 and 5.4 comprise sixty-nine different correspondents (and an unidentified one); see Appendix 2 for an overview of them. Lowth's social network – or networks at different points during his lifetime – must have been considerably larger than that. This is, for instance, evident from the fact that he occasionally sent his greetings to friends or acquaintances shared with the addressee of a particular letter. In his two earlier letters to Dashwood, for instance, he presents his compliments 'to L. & Lady Sandys & y^e. Young

Ladys' (11 May 1748, 25 April 1750), and in other letters he sends his greetings to a Mr Wheeler, John Loveday, and Lord Lincoln (1720–94). Henry Fiennes Pelham-Clinton was the ninth Earl of Lincoln and nephew of the Duke of Newcastle, one of Lowth's patrons (*ODNB*, 'Henry Fiennes Pelham-Clinton'). Loveday was a close friend of both Merrick and Lowth, as is confirmed by Lowth's particular request to 'present my best Respects to M^r. Loveday, when You have opportunity'. He is frequently referred to in the correspondence with Merrick, and though, as far as I know, no letters between Lowth and Loveday have come down to us, Loveday's interest in Lowth is evident from the fact that he kept track of the different editions of the grammar that were published (see Chapter 3). A document in the Hampshire Archives reads that Lowth was appointed domestic chaplain to the politician Samuel Sandys in 1743 (11M70/B4/131), and Dashwood is described in the *ODNB* as one of Sandys's followers.

The question presents itself whether Lowth's correspondence in so far as I have collected it can be considered representative of Lowth's network contacts over the years. Baker (1980: 28), for instance, raises the same question in relation to his collection of Wesley's correspondence, which was ten times as big. The lists of names in Tables 5.3 and 5.4 clearly suggest that it is not, for apart from Lowth's wife they include not a single woman. Lowth did, however, correspond with women, as I have found references to letters he received from both his sisters, Mrs Coltman, and a Mrs Hercules, while he himself corresponded with his wife's father's cousin Anne Covey, the main beneficiary of Thomas Cheyney's Will. There is also evidence that Lowth corresponded with Hannah More, one of the members of the Bluestocking Circle (Staves 2003: 82), and their friendly relationship is also referred to in the *ODNB*, but no letters have come down to us. Women obviously did make up part of his social network, for apart from the women already referred to, there are several references in the letters to Molly to their 'friends in the Close' in Winchester, such as a Miss Stevens, possibly one of Molly's cousins as her mother's maiden name was Stevens; to the nurse helping Molly with the children ('you believe you & Nurse caught your Coughs of Tom', Lowth to his wife, 13 May 1755), Mrs Legge, his patron's wife ('M^{rs}. Legge is in Town, but not at home', Lowth to his wife, 1 March 1755), the Duchess of Devon ('Their <u>Graces of Devon</u> are well: the Dean sent word he would dine there tomorrow; I may possibly do the same unless I stay at home in respect of the Lady of the House', Lowth to his wife, 1 March 1755), his friends the Wartons' mother Elizabeth, and many others. Again, however, I have been unable to trace any letters to or from any of these women. As the letters to his wife represent his most informal style of writing, it will, moreover, be impossible to take the factor gender into consideration in any systematic way when analysing Lowth's language.

The 'Young Ladies' Lowth presented his compliments to in his letters to Dashwood from 1748 and 1750, along with their very wealthy mother, Lady Sandys, may well have been of marriageable age (their parents had married in 1725), and there is furthermore the mysterious 'M^{rs}.' or Miss Molyneux, whom Lowth knew well enough to present with a copy of *Isaiah* in 1778. There is a draft letter addressed to William Duncombe dated 18 May 1758, which contains the following passage, struck out, it appears, on second thoughts:

I am much obliged to You for the honour You ᶜhave done **my little Latin Ode** by your very elegant Translation, & for the pleasure You have given me in communicating it to me. I think it is the same that I remember to have seen some years ago in a Magazine,. I then shew'd it to **the Lady to whom it was originally address'd**, as much the best Translation of several that I had met with. She, who was an excellent Judge, approv'd it much on the whole; but complain'd that the Translator had wrong'd her, by suppressing & even reversing the greatest Compliment that was made to her in it: namely, in ᵞᵉ· last Stanza, [. . .] matter to right. This led me on to offer [?] a few other alterations, wᶜʰ. I submitt intirely to your Judgement. You will be so good, as to excuse the liberty I have taken, & impute it to the foolish fondness of a parent towards his Favourite Child; for such I must own it to be: not fᵐ. any conceit of its superior merit, but fᵐ. the great regard wᶜʰ. I have for the [+] Person abovemention'd, to whom it more properly belongs.
I beg You to present my Compliments to Your Son, & believe me,

      S^r. Your most Obedient
        humble Servant
          Robt. Lowth.

+ **Miss Moli-
-neux of Win-
-chester**.

Could it be that this 'Miss Molineux of Winchester' was a young woman Lowth had had his eyes on as a possible bride, well before he became acquainted with Molly? Two Misses Molyneux, one called Diana, as well as their mother Mary, a widow, were mentioned in Thomas Cheyney's Will, so they belonged to Cheyney's social network. What exactly happened will probably remain a mystery forever.

5.6 OTHER EVIDENCE FOR RECONSTRUCTING THE NETWORK

5.6.1 *Wills*

Letters are not the only source by which a social network can be reconstructed. Another important source are wills, which present the testator's closest network members at the time of death. In Lowth's case, however, only his wife, his daughter Martha, and his son Robert are mentioned as private beneficiaries of the Will. Witnesses to the Will were his brother William, his secretary Richard Burn, and a certain 'St. Eaton' (Stephen?), possibly the 'M^r. Eaton' who is mentioned as the bearer of a message from Charles Woide in a letter of 4 November 1777. The codicil to the Will was signed by Burn and two other men, Thomas Foster and John Warne, whom I have been unable to identify. Thomas Cheyney's Will was much more informative in this respect. Of only Richard Burn does Lowth's correspondence contain any letters.

5.6.2 *Subscription lists*

A third source for reconstructing social networks are subscription lists. Publication by subscription was common in the eighteenth century. Gaskell (1972: 181) describes it as 'essentially a method of persuading customers to help with the cost of producing a book by offering them a substantial discount if they would agree to pay all or (more usually) part of the price in advance'. Subscription lists were, according to Speck (1982: 47), published in the books themselves, and they enable us 'to find out something about the readership for a certain type of book in the eighteenth century'(1982: 51). Hannah Glasse's *The Art of Cookery, Made Plain and Easy* (1747), for instance, contains a five-page list of subscribers, mostly middle-class women, the typical audience for this kind of book. But the lists also throw important light on the social network of the author in question, for writers would usually canvas among their own friends and acquaintances for potential buyers of the book. Thus, Wright (1950), when discussing the publication by subscription of Joseph Spence's *Polymetis* in 1745, notes that 'the length of the list [717 names for 816 copies] and the dignity and importance of many of the names therein testify to the extent of Spence's acquaintance among literary and aristocratic circles'

(1950: 87–8). Lowth drew upon his network contacts in order to supply James Merrick, who was an invalid, with subscribers for his translation of the Psalms. In a letter dated 25 October 1764, Lowth sent Merrick a list with the following names: 'the (late) Duke of Devonshire, Lord John Cavendish, Lady Eden, of Durham, Rev^d. D^r. Dickens, Rev^d. M^r. Spence, Rev^d. D^r. Burton, Rev^d. D^r. Vane, Rev^d. D^r. Douglas, 2 Copies, Church Library of Durham, Francis Page Esqr. of Middle-Aston Oxfordshire, George Garnier Esqr. of Wickham Hants'. Most of these names were indeed friends or acquaintances of Lowth. From Merrick's perspective, and in terms of the model of social network analysis, the people on Lowth's list might be referred to contacts belonging to a 'second-order zone' (Milroy 1987: 48), but from that of Lowth it shows the extent to which he felt he could draw upon them. None of Lowth's books, however, were published by subscription as none of them include subscription lists, but he did publish one of his sermons by subscription, as appears from the following quotation from a letter to the bookseller Thomas Cadell, written on 14 September 1771:

A Sermon, wch. I lately preached before the Governors of the Radcliffe Infirmary, being the first on the occasion, is to be printed. There will be added a Short acc^t. of the Establishment, **List of Subscribers**, & the Acc^ts. of the ^1st. year ending at Mickss. The Demand for Presents is usually large on these occasions; as to the Sale, You ^are the best Judge: & ^I beg Your Opinion, with regard to the Number of Copies, wch. it w^d. be proper to print.

Lowth himself also subscribed to books, as the following quotation from a letter to Robert Dodsley bears out: 'I must [beg] of You to send... The first Volume of Duncombe's Horace, wch. M^r. Duncombe says he order'd for me, as a Present; & pra[y] enter my name as a Subscriber for [the] same' (9 June 1758). A search in ECCO for Lowth's name on subscription lists produced some twenty-five more works, which testify to his interest in particular books as well as to the extent of his acquaintance, as various titles suggest that he had been encouraged to enter his name on a certain subscription list by one of his acquaintances. An example of this is Ann Yearsley's book of poetry, published in 1785. This 'milkwoman poet', as Clarke (2000: 172) calls her, had been Hannah More's 'discovery' and protégée, and More had tried to gain Yearsley some money by publishing her poetry through subscription. Over a thousand people subscribed to the book (2000: 177), including Lowth and, separately, his wife.

5.6.3 *Presentation copies*

The above quotation also refers to 'Presents', or presentation copies, a specialized sense of the word not mentioned by the *OED*. Exchanging such 'Presents' is yet another promising source for the reconstruction of social networks, particularly of published authors. As is still the case today, handing out presentation copies was an important means by which authors consolidated or initiated relationships with fellow scholars and other people. On 9 August 1757, Lowth wrote to Robert Dodsley as follows:

Dear S^r.

I have been obliged to **publish a Serm[on]** preach'd at y^e. meeting on occasion of the Pub[lic] Infirmary at Newcastle. It is printed the[re] & I have taken the liberty of putting You[rs] & Mr. Millar's name in the Title-page. I have order'd 150 to be sent to You, of wch. be so good as to send a part to M^r. Millar with my humble Service & request that he would be so kind as to assist in y^e. sale. 'Tis publish'd for the Benefit of the Infirmary, & if it produces any gain, it will so far do some good.

I must further beg the favour of you [to] send a few **Presents** of them for me, [?] wch. I will give you a List inclos'd (Tierney 1988: 287).

Dodsley was yet to become Lowth's publisher, of his *Life of William of Wykeham* a year later and of his grammar in 1762, while *Isaiah, A New Translation* was to be published well after Robert's death by his brother James and Thomas Cadell in 1778. Lowth had published this sermon privately, and with the letter he employed Dodsley and Millar in their capacity as booksellers. Any money Lowth would gain by the sale of the sermon was to benefit the Newcastle hospital. What is of further interest here is that Lowth wished to give away presentation copies of the sermon, to which end he had drawn up a list of names. The list, however, is missing, 'probably torn off for R[obert] D[odsley]'s convenience', as Tierney (1988: 288) suggests, and so is the 'List [of Per]sons to be Presented [with a copy of his *De Sacra Poesi Hebraeorum Praelectiones*], with all necessary [directi]ons about it' (1988: 150). In the spring of 1762 Lowth wrote to his friend James Merrick that he would ask 'M^r. Dodsley to send to You A Short Introduction to English Grammar, wch. I suppose may by this time be ready for publication', and Loveday's copy of the first edition of the grammar, in which he recorded changes made in subsequent editions (see Chapter 3), may similarly have been a presentation copy. It seems likely that Spence had received a copy of the grammar, too: 'I am very glad You approve of Tom's Grammar, on its appearance in y^e. world', Lowth replied on 2 March 1762 to what must been Spence's acknowledgement of his presentation copy. Lowth himself also received presentation copies, as the following acknowledgement in a letter to Sir David Dalrymple illustrates: 'I beg Your acceptance of my best Thanks likewise for the honour of Your Presents of Lactantius De Iustitia; & of Christian Antiquities, which latter I presume comes from the same hand' (7 June 1779). Another recipient of a 'Present' of the grammar must have been Henry Bilson Legge, whose request for a copy was the reason why the grammar got published in the first place.

The actual presentation list of the grammar – if such a list ever existed – has not come down to us, nor has that of *William of Wykeham*. There is, however, an indication of the size of the list for the latter book, for in September 1757 Lowth wrote to Dodsley: 'This has put me in mind to look over my form[er] List of Presents; & I find I cannot reduce it [to] under Fourscore for Wykeham' (Tierney 1988: 290). Lowth thus counted some eighty people as part of his circle of acquaintances around the year 1757 when the book was published. This does not seem inconsiderable, but who these people were we can only speculate about. We are more fortunate with respect to the publication of *Isaiah* some twenty years later, for in my search for Lowth's letters I came across a document in the Bodleian Library (MS Eng. Lett. C. 574, ff. 1–139), which contains two long lists of names, at ff. 113–14 and 114–15, both composed in Lowth's own hand. (The lists are provided in Appendix 3.) On the first list, which is somewhat shorter than the second one, a note has been added in a different hand, which reads 'List of Names/ app for "Isaiah." copies'. *Isaiah* came out in October 1778, as appears from the following quotation from a letter to Lowth from an unidentified correspondent who informed Lowth that he looked 'forward to October with impatience, on account of <u>Isaiah</u>' (17 August 1778). The book was immediately popular, for only about two months later, on 5 December of that year, Lowth wrote to his nephew John Sturges:

We begin printing a New Edition of Isaiah next week...If You have noted any mistakes of any kind, communicate. If at the beginning of either of the parts, immediately: for I have already given the first sheets of each to the Printer, who begins on Monday.

This confirms that *Isaiah* was not published on the basis of subscription, as it would have taken too long to collect a substantial list of names in such a short space of time. That the lists of names are presentation lists rather than subscription lists is also evident from the order of the names. Both lists are headed by the Royal Family, and are almost immediately followed by the Cavendish family: the members of this family continued to play an important part in Lowth's life, even long after the death of his former patron in 1764. The people on the list are primarily listed by their function, e.g. 'Bp. of Durham', 'Dean of Bristol', rather than their personal relationship with Lowth.

As there are two lists, it seems reasonable to assume that one would have been intended for the first edition and the other for the second. Though there is considerable overlap between them, the lists are not identical. In view of the request to his nephew John Sturges quoted above, it may be concluded that the list which carries Sturges's name, the longer one, would have been intended for the first edition of *Isaiah*: Sturges must have possessed a copy of the first edition of the book if he was to pass on any corrections of mistakes. The relative shortness of the other list – merely referring to 'Arch B^{ps}. & B^{ps}. in Town' rather than individual bishops as on the other list – suggests that Lowth felt that not every acquaintance of his needed to receive a new copy of his book. That he did send a number of them a copy of the second edition after all shows his pride at the immediate popularity of his book.

The first list contains ninety-three names, as well the Royal Family and several libraries, with 136 copies altogether: to the Royal Family, for instance, he sent five copies and to the Cavendish family seven. The second list contains eighty names for about a hundred copies. The exact number on this list is hard to assess as Lowth merely mentions the 'Arch Bps. & Bps. in Town' without specifying the number of copies required. In the list for the first edition of *Isaiah*, he had been more specific, mentioning the Bishops of Winchester, Durham, Chichester, Bristol, Llandaff, Bangor, Chester, Ossory, and Oxford; the name of the Bishop of Gloucester, William Warburton, is conspicuously absent: more than a decade after their big clash, their relationship hadn't been patched up. Some of the names on the second list have been provided with addresses, such as 'D^r. Owen, S^t. Olave Hart Street'. The libraries to which Lowth sent presentation copies are New College Library and the Bodleian Library in Oxford, the libraries of the Royal Society and of Sion College (now incorporated into Lambeth Palace Library), and the British Museum. Taking the overlap between the two lists into account, they contain 146 names of individuals. If Lowth had adopted the same principle in drawing up his list of presentation copies for *William of Wykeham*, the number of his social contacts would have grown considerably in the intervening years. However, the question arises to what extent Lowth knew all the people on the lists personally, and if so, how well he knew them. The second list, for instance, contains a note against the names of the Duke of Montagu, the Marquess of Carmarthen, and Dr Bell saying that their copies are 'to be sent to me wth. those for y^e. R. Fam'. This suggests at first sight that Lowth was in close contact with members of the Royal Family. As long-standing Chaplain to the King, he might have known the King and the members of the royal household personally, meeting them on a fairly regular basis. He had, moreover, dedicated *Isaiah* to King George III, so it would have been fitting to present the King with a copy of the book. However, the above note contains the clue as to how this was actually done: George Brudenell Montagu (1712–90) was one of the King's courtiers, who had been made a member of the Privy Council in 1776 (*ODNB*, 'George Brudenell Montagu'). Lowth thus handed his presentation copies not to the King himself but to one of the members of the Privy Council. This is why the Duke of Montagu appears on both lists: Lowth may have learnt about the proper way to present his book to the King from the first time presentation copies of *Isaiah* were distributed. As Lowth never mentioned a meeting with a member of the Royal Family in his correspondence, his contacts with the Royal Family thus have to be relegated to a second-order zone, in spite of his dedication of *Isaiah* to the King.

Many of the names on the lists suggest that Lowth distributed his 'Presents' for strategic or political reasons. Both lists contain the names of Lord North, Prime Minister at the time and a Tory, and Charles Wentworth, Marquess of Rockingham, who had been Prime Minister from July 1765 to July the following year. Like Wentworth, with whom he had corresponded in 1761 on the subject of the latter's coin collection, Lowth was a Whig, though as I've argued in Chapter 2 his interests were less with matters of politics than with scholarship. For similar reasons he included the Lord Chancellor, the Lord Mayor, and the Speaker of the House of Commons in the second list of presentation copies. None of these men, Edward Thurlow (1731–1806), Samuel Plumbe (fl.1778), and Sir Fletcher Norton (1716–89), are referred to in his correspondence, nor is the 'Ld. Primate of Ireland' (both lists), James Hewitt, first Viscount Lifford (1709/16–89), who occurs on both lists as well. Sir Joshua Reynolds is included (first list) because he was president of the Royal Academy, and this resulted in a brief correspondence between the two men, unlike in the case of the majority of the other beneficiaries of *Isaiah* copies. The lists furthermore include many ecclesiastical functionaries, in particular bishops and deans. Most of the deans on the list, of Bristol, Exeter, Windsor, Peterborough, Rochester, Salisbury, and Winchester, only received a copy of the second edition of *Isaiah*. An exception is the Dean of Carlisle, who received copies of both. The newly appointed Dean of Carlisle was Thomas Percy (1729–1811), who had become a friend of Lowth's, and was thus apparently felt to merit a copy of the second edition as well. As for the bishops and archbishops on the shorter list, copies of the second edition of the book apparently only went to those who happened to be around at the time of publication.

One interesting name in the first list of presentation copies is that of 'M^r. Jones, Temple'. The same name occurs on the second list as 'W^m. Jones Esqr., Temple'. Both names refer to the 'orientalist and judge' Sir William Jones (1746–94), who, as a scholar, is familiar to historical linguists in relation to what is often referred to as the 'discovery' of Sanskrit (see, e.g., Baugh and Cable 2002: 20). Jones, however, did not receive his knighthood until a few years after the publication of *Isaiah*, in 1783 (see *ODNB*). Further research into the relationship between Lowth and Jones demonstrates that Jones regarded Lowth as his 'very good friend' (Cannon 1970: 407), and that one of his major works, *The Moallakát, or, Seven Arabian Poems* (1782), was partly modelled on Lowth's *Isaiah*. Their closeness is confirmed by the insertion of Jones's name in both presentation lists: as in the case of Thomas Percy discussed above and others, Lowth only appears to have done so in special circumstances. Unfortunately, however, I have not come across any letters between the two men that would be able to confirm the nature of their relationship. Thus, even the evidence from a valuable source like the presentation lists for the reconstruction of Lowth's social network doesn't tell the complete story. For all that, it is of considerable interest to realise that these two important eighteenth-century scholars were acquainted with each other and that they seem to have got on well together.

Garside (2003) argues it is not always easy to 'ascertain social groups' on subscription lists:

Aristocratic subscribers are generally obtrusive: sometimes found in separate clusters at the head of lists... In a few cases a whole list appears to consist of an aristocratic group followed by dependents and hangers-on. Members of the gentry are also fairly perceptible, through titles (Sir, 'Bart', etc.), territorial designations, and the appendage of 'Esq.' (though the latter appears to have been a somewhat fluid term). A large professional component is inferable through the presence of titles such as Dr, and related factors such as a high proportion of clergymen, administrative post-holders, and serving officers.

To some extent, this is also true for Lowth's presentation lists: I have already commented on the clustering of royalty, Lowth's patrons, and the bishops at the top of both lists. In addition, a fair number of aristocrats are included, such as the Duke of Marlborough, Lord Dartmouth, Lord Suffolk, Lord Ailesbury, Lord Dacre, and Lord Sandys. They are listed consecutively, and they all received copies of both editions of the book. Edwin, Lord Sandys was the eldest son of the Lord Sandys to whom Lowth had passed on greetings in his letters to Dashwood. The 'hangers-on' that Garside refers to are lacking, which seems due to the different nature of the two lists: they were entered on Lowth's personal initiative, not as the result of any canvassing activities as in the case of subscription lists. There is indeed a large professional component in both lists as well, though it is larger than the group designated by the title 'Dr.': both lists comprise well over twenty such titles, though not always followed by the same names. They do not always refer to clergymen: Sir George Baker (bap.1723, d.1809), who occurred on the first list as Dr Baker, was physician to George III, and so was Anthony Addington (1713–90). We have come across Addington before, when Lowth reported in a letter to his son, dating from about a year earlier, about having consulted him on the nature of his complaints. Tom died less than six months afterwards, before the publication of *Isaiah*.

Garside (2003) also mentions that it is difficult to decide about the status of the women on subscription lists. In the case of Lowth's list, this is much easier, for the same reason given above: apart from any possible members of the Royal Family, who are, however, left unspecified, we find the name of only one member of the aristocracy, the Countess of Hillsborough (both lists). This was Henry Bilson Legge's widow, who had remarried four years after her husband's death in 1768. In addition, we find the names of Mrs Covey, Mrs Smythe, Mrs Molyneux, Mrs Cooper, Mrs Lucas, and Mrs Kennicott, all on the first list. The number of women is thus – disappointingly – low. Of these women, I have only been able to identify as members of Lowth's social network Anne Covey, his wife's father's cousin and godmother to their daughter Margaret, and Mrs Molyneux, who had also been mentioned in Thomas Cheyney's Will, though it is unclear whether the reference is to Mary, the widow, or to either of her daughters: until the late eighteenth century, according to the *OED*, 'Mrs' could be used 'as a title of courtesy applied, with or without inclusion of the first name, to elderly unmarried ladies' (*OED Online*, Mrs 1.b). Mrs Kennicott may have been Ann Chamberlayne (d.1831), the wife of Lowth's friend and fellow scholar Benjamin Kennicott: they were married seven years previously (*ODNB*, 'Benjamin Kennicott'). Kennicott himself appears on both lists. It is striking, however, that neither Lowth's sisters, nor his wife, his daughter Martha, or his son Robert occur on either of the lists. Perhaps it was considered enough to have one copy of the book, Lowth's own copy, in the family. The only members of his family who did receive a copy were his nephew John Sturges (first list) and his brother William (second list). Two names, moreover, that are of interest here are those of 'D^r. Michaelis', who as the editor of the German edition of Lowth's *De Sacra Poesi Hebræorum Prælectiones* deserved a copy of *Isaiah*, too, and 'M^r. Koppe', who was to publish a translation of *Isaiah* into German a few years later. The 'M^r. Michaelis' on the first list refers to Michaelis's son, who had visited England in the late 1770s.

It would have been polite to acknowledge the receipt of a presentation copy. Lowth usually did so himself: my collection of his letters contains some ten references to this effect (e.g. to Thomas Warton: 'Accept of my best thanks for your kind present of your Life of Bathurst'; 28 June 1761). But the collected correspondence contains no more than four such letters: from Sir Joshua Reynolds, Samuel Hallifax, George Baker, and Shute Barrington. There must, however, have been other such letters as well, like the letter from John Thomas Troy, the Bishop of Ossory, referred to in Section 5.5. And in his first letter to Sir David Dalrymple, Lowth replies to an acknowledgement of Dalrymple's receipt of *Isaiah*:

I have the honour of Your Letter; & am much obliged to You for the kind & candid reception, wch. You have been pleased to give to my Isaiah. The approbation of such Readers cannot but give me particular pleasure (Lowth to Dalrymple, 7 June 1779).

As far as I have been able to discover, Sir David Dalrymple is the only case in which Lowth's distribution of presentation copies led to any tangible results. For one thing, Dalrymple sent Lowth Volume 2 of his *Annals of Scotland* (1779), for which Lowth thanked him in the same letter:

I have the honour of Your Present of the Second Volume of the Annals of Scotland. In the multiplicity of my business & various avocations here, I have been obliged to defer the pleasure of reading it till I get into the Country, where I intend to take the first opportunity of perusing the whole Work. I beg Your acceptance of my best Thanks likewise for the honour of Your Presents of Lactantius De Iustitia; & of Christian Antiquities, which latter I presume comes from the same hand (Lowth to Dalrymple, 7 June 1779).

For another, the result was a prolonged correspondence between the two men, with fifteen letters from Lowth written between June 1779 and November 1782, and at least nine from Dalrymple, though they are left untraced.

As said, several names, like Warburton's, are lacking from the lists. Three others are worth mentioning: Sir Francis Dashwood, Samuel Johnson, and James Boswell. Lowth and Dashwood had been close friends, at least down to the early 1760s, and according to Kemp (1967), both men had belonged to a close group of friends with Merrick and John Loveday. Merrick had died nearly ten years previously, and Loveday did receive a copy of the book. The reason why Dashwood didn't seems due to the fact that since the early 1760s he had become interested 'in black magic, outlandish orgies, and obscene parodies of the rites of Rome' (*ODNB*, 'Sir Francis Dashwood'). Such activities turned him into a dangerous person to be associated with for someone in Lowth's position. As for Dr Johnson, it is interesting to see that Lowth felt he had no reason for sending him a copy of *Isaiah*. Johnson did not belong to Lowth's circle of professional contacts, the clergy, and I have argued in Chapter 4 that Lowth didn't particularly agree with Johnson's approach to grammar in his *Dictionary*. Lowth's Will shows that he possessed a copy of Johnson's *Dictionary*, but Johnson appears to have been merely the author of a standard work of reference: Lowth had nothing to gain by trying to win Johnson's personal acquaintance as he had with most of the other people on the presentation lists. Johnson perhaps felt differently about this: approaching Lowth as Bishop of London in an attempt to intercede in an ecclesiastical appointment for a friend of his, Johnson possibly believed that they shared a certain amount of common ground that would justify this attempt. That Boswell wasn't presented with a copy of *Isaiah* either suggests that his attempt at gaining access to Lowth's social network had not been successful after all. We can only speculate as to the reasons for this; possibly, Lowth associated him too much with Johnson, though, again, Lowth may have felt there was nothing to gain from the acquaintance.

Lowth had been appointed Bishop of London just one year before *Isaiah* came out. This explains why he decided to dedicate the book to the King. It also, I think, explains both the length of the presentation lists and kind of names that occur on them. Lowth's prime purpose in deciding what names were to be included on the lists appears to have been the wish to establish and strengthen political and professional alliances. In other words, he appears to have been engaged in so-called coalition building. Coalitions can be defined as 'strategic, planned alliances', which are formed with specific people 'for particular purposes, for a particular period of time' (Fitzmaurice 2000*b*: 273). No longer in need of actual patronage himself, Lowth clearly felt that his appointment as Bishop of London called for alliance making, which explains the presence on his list of many key players on the political scene at the time: the current (Tory) and a previous (Whig) Prime Ministers, the Lord Chancellor, the Lord Mayor, the Speaker of the House of Commons, the Lord Chancellor of Ireland, and the President of the Royal Academy. The publication of *Isaiah* came at an appropriate time in his career, and Lowth clearly saw the distribution of presentation copies of the book well worth the enormous expense involved.

5.7 COALITIONS, SOCIAL NETWORKS, AND THE CHURCH

A coalition is a specific type of social network, formed not spontaneously but for a particular purpose. It consequently differs significantly from social networks comprising family members or friends. At the same time, the presentation lists of *Isaiah* do not include merely the names of people Lowth sought to form a coalition with, they also include people from his wider social network who were his friends, and whom he wished to present with a copy of his book as a token of the friendship he felt for them. Social networks, according to Milroy (1987), are unbounded, and this must have been the case for Lowth as well. The two presentation lists combined contain the names of around 160 people from different social backgrounds, men and women, but he must have been acquainted, in one form or another, with many more people. A full-text search of the *ODNB* produced the names of a number of people who are described by the authors of the entries as 'friends' of Lowth: the physician Nathan Alcock, the religious writer William Bromley Cadogan, the lawyer Samuel Rose, and the writer Thomas Tyers. The author and literary hostess Elizabeth Montagu is likewise referred to as a friend or an acquaintance, though not in her own entry but in that of Archibald Alison, while the singer and organist Joseph Corfe is mentioned as a friend of a friend (James Harris), another second-order contact in terms of social network analysis. Other interesting references in the *ODNB* include the following: Lowth appears to have 'encouraged and materially supported' the biblical scholar Alexander Geddes in his work, and counted the classicist Jonathan Toup among his scholarly acquaintances. I have not, however, found any confirmation of the existence of links between Lowth and these people or any of those that are linked to him in the *ODNB* (see §2.3) in the sources that have been available to me. Lowth's name is also mentioned in the *ODNB* in relation to the marriage of his niece Mary Eden to the banker Ebenezer Blackwell; this, however, seems to be no more than an example of namedropping, as there seems to have been no reason for the reference to Lowth as such. The same applies in the case of the political writer John Lind (1737–81), whose 'style of writing', the *ODNB* entry reads, 'was much praised by Lord Grenville, Bishop Lowth, and Samuel Parr'. One interesting piece of information in the *ODNB* entry for Ebenezer Blackwell, however, is that 'it was at the Blackwells' home that Lowth and Wesley met and exchanged courtesies on 24 November 1777, the day after Wesley preached a sermon for the Humane Society in Lewisham church'. This interesting piece of information suggests that Wesley and Lowth had already been acquainted before the date of the only letter by Wesley to Lowth that has come down to us (1780). As in the case of Boswell's attempts to seek an introduction to Lowth, this confirms that letters alone never tell the complete story.

Appendix 2 lists Lowth's correspondents, but as he wrote to many more people, this list can hardly be taken to be representative of his social network. My analysis of the other sources that were available to me has already shown that he knew many more people. Baker (1980: 29) calculated that Wesley's known correspondents probably numbered around sixteen hundred. His *Works of John Wesley* was intended to contain 3,500 letters, though he believes that this was 'still only a fraction of [Wesley's] actual output' (1980: 28). According to Baker, so many letters have come down to us because Wesley's many 'eager devotees' cherished his letters and kept them accordingly, but also 'because improved postal services had led to a general increase in letter-writing' during Wesley's lifetime (1980: 29). Even Wesley and Lowth exchanged letters, though perhaps never more than a few of them. A correspondence like Wesley's would thus offer far greater opportunities for reconstructing a person's social network. The number of Lowth's actual correspondents I have been able to identify is not much smaller than that of Robert Dodsley, who, according to Tierney (1988: xxxvi–xxxvii) corresponded with eighty-nine people. But in view of the different types of correspondents I have been able to isolate, ranging from people he was highly intimate with to formal acquaintances only, Lowth's letters are nevertheless representative of a number of different styles of writing. As such they form a more than adequate basis for my analysis of his communicative competence, and I will show in Chapters 6 and 7 that they will allow us to gain valuable insight into Lowth's abilities at stylistic variation and linguistic accommodation depending on the nature of his relationship with the addressee in question.

COMMUNICATIVE COMPETENCE AND THE LANGUAGE OF THE LETTERS

6.1 DIFFERENT STYLES OF WRITING

WHEN Lowth wrote in his grammar that preposition stranding 'prevails in common conversation, and suits very well with the familiar style in writing', adding that what we now call pied piping 'agrees much better with the solemn and elevated Style' (1762: 127–8), he shows an awareness of the fact that different styles of speech and writing have different linguistic requirements. What Lowth conceived to be 'the solemn and elevated Style' may be illustrated by the opening sentence of the preface to his grammar:

(1) The English Language **hath** been much cultivated during the last two hundred years (1762: i).

Hath, though still part of the verbal paradigm for *have* in his own grammar (1762: 48) as well as that of Murray's grammar more than thirty years later (1795: 45), never occurs in his letters, not even in his most formal ones. The same applies to *doth*, and a full-text search of the grammar in ECCO – which never, unfortunately, produces wholly reliable results – yielded only a single instance. The language of the grammar is similarly characterized by a more frequent use of the subjunctive than his private letters: there are as many as eight instances of the inflectional subjunctive in the grammar, in the third person present tense, as in (2), where the subjunctive form is triggered by *unless*:

(2) In Spelling, a syllable in the beginning or middle of a word ends in a vowel, unless the consonant *x* **follow** it (1762: 7).

Two more instances were found after *unless*, four after *if*, and one after *whatever*. In the letters, the inflectional subjunctive is far less frequent: it was found in only about 10 per cent of the instances in which it might have occurred, as against over 60 per cent in the grammar (Auer and Tieken-Boon van Ostade 2007). In the letters, *unless* likewise triggered the subjunctive, as in:

(3) **unless** the aggressor **were** by one resolute & decisive stroke absolutely disabled f^{m}. repeating his attack (Lowth to Secker, 9 December 1765).

(4) **unless** it **be** for giving them an easy & elegant Translation (Lowth to Dalrymple, 15 August 1781).

but it occurs with the indicative as well:

(5) **unless** he **wants** the Chancellorship for some Layman (Lowth to his wife, 26 September 1755).

Example (5) was taken from a letter by Lowth to his wife, whereas his addressees of the letters in (3) and (4) were men with whom, as I argued in Chapter 5, he had a formal relationship: as the Archbishop of Canterbury, Secker was far superior to Lowth in terms of Church hierarchy, and Dalrymple, who was a fellow scholar, never became more than that. The use of the subjunctive in the letters thus correlates with formality of style, as it does in the case of the grammar.

Lowth was therefore not only aware of the existence of different styles, he also knew how to differentiate between formal and informal styles of writing or the 'solemn and elevated' vs. the 'familiar' styles as he called them himself – even in his letters. This phenomenon is known as communicative competence, which is defined by Milroy and Milroy (1991: 119) as 'the capacity of persons to select and recognise the language variety appropriate to the occasion'. The study of communicative competence is typically the domain of sociolinguistics, which aims to identify and analyse different speech styles, ranging from least to most formal. In practice, however, it is virtually impossible to gain access to a speaker's most informal, vernacular style, as this can as a rule only be found in situations that cannot by definition be captured during an interview – a phenomenon known as the Observer's Paradox. To solve the problem, sociolinguists attempt to monitor the linguistic output of their informants by focusing on linguistic differences between speech styles that reflect greater or lesser formality rather than on absolute distinctions in formality. It is sometimes claimed that the Observer's Paradox as such does not need to be reckoned with in the field of historical sociolinguistics (see, for instance, Nevalainen and Raumolin-Brunberg 2003: 50), as, after all, data have come down to us as they happened to be recorded rather than as having been elicited in more or less artificial interview situations. It is nevertheless a concept that must be taken into account when analysing linguistic data from the past, though in a different form than that which has been described in modern sociolinguistic research.

Historical sociolinguists are as interested as modern scholars in this field in identifying and studying the least formal styles of language, but for obvious reasons they have access only to the written medium. Though spontaneous speech did not become available for analysis until after it was possible to record the spoken language, this is not to say that no speech has ever been recorded. In presenting a variety of text types from the Early Modern English period, Cusack (1998) argues that speech can be identified in, for instance, court depositions and presentments, even with a view to gaining insight into local pronunciation. For the Late Modern English period, a particularly promising resource is the Old Bailey Online, which makes available the records of '197,745 criminal trials held at London's central criminal court', dating from between 1674 and 1913 (Old Bailey Online website). Careful analysis of these records is currently still in its infancy, but there are many instances of recorded dialogue that have more than just a realistic ring to them, as examples (6) and (7) illustrate:

(6) I don't know, I did not see it that night, **nor** the ring **neither** (Catherine King, Mary Collings, Theft > pocketpicking, 15 September 1756).

(7) She was going to set stamps with **them two six-pences**, and to leave off making shillings (Ann Whitmore, Royal Offences > coining offences, 19 February 1752).

Data like this, however, only lend themselves for grammatical or lexical analysis, and their significance for the study of the history of English is yet to be explored in detail.

The language of letters is currently considered by historical sociolin-guists as the best possible material for accessing natural language, language that, in contrast with published texts, was not in principle intended for a wider reading public than that of the immediate addressee. Often, letters are studied as a useful substitute for the analysis of speech, which is otherwise hard to gain access to. Though this is indeed how many letter writers considered the opportunity of corresponding with one another, as in the case of Betsy Sheridan (1758–1837), who told her sister: 'to you my dear Love I write as I talk in all modes and tempers' (1788; Lefanu 1960: 123), letters are not speech. This is primarily due to the fact that they represent communication that is written down, with all its concomitant restraints on the spontaneous nature of such utterances. What is more, during the eighteenth century, letter writing was considered an art, which meant that the best letters were those that were produced according to a set of rules that, paradoxically, were to give the impression that they had been written spontaneously (Anderson and Ehrenpreis 1966). This is, in my view, one of the forms the Observer's Paradox takes when the language of documents like eighteenth-century letters is studied (Tieken-Boon van Ostade 2000b). This is not to say that the language of such letters cannot be analysed, rather that it should be approached with a fair amount of caution, as seemingly spontaneous letters might prove to contain highly polished language.

In all this it needs to be taken into account that eighteenth-century letters had an important function of exchanging information that was of more general interest than to the addressee alone. At the time, letters often served as carriers of news, and they were thus frequently handed round among friends and relatives of the recipient. An example from Lowth's correspondence is his second letter to Sir Francis Dashwood, dated 25 April 1750, which relates his visit to the excavations at Herculaneum. As discussed in Section 5.2, the letter was passed on to readers with similar antiquarian interests, but whether Lowth was aware of this possibility when he composed the letter is unclear.

For all this, it is still possible to identify relatively spontaneous letters that are worth analysing linguistically as evidence of a writer's most vernacular language (see Tieken-Boon van Ostade 2005). In the case of Lowth's correspondence, the letters to his wife may be identified as such. They represent his most informal written style, and their language proba-bly closely reflected the way they normally spoke. There are various indications of this in the letters themselves, such as when he wrote 'If I say much more I shall be too late for the Post' (Lowth to his wife, 3 June 1755). This suggests that he did not as a rule look over his letters to his wife carefully and correct them before sending them off. Other letters, particularly those of which the draft versions have come down to us, illustrate the care with which he formulated his sentences, which was particularly important when addressing a superior or a person with whom he was negotiating an affair that required a certain amount of tact. The correspondence with Warburton is a good illustration of this. Such letters represent a very different style of writing.

Letters may be analysed as evidence of the interaction between speaker and writer, both from a pragmatic perspective, as explored by, for instance, Fitzmaurice (2002), and from a linguistic one. A pragmatic study of letters allows, for example, for the study of a correspondence along the lines of modern conversation analysis, though taking place across greater distance and, significantly, time. An example from Lowth's correspondence would, again, be the exchange of letters between Warburton and himself, which in its first stage dealt with an argument between the two men which was temporarily patched up only to revive again nearly ten years later, with consequences that were fatal to their relationship. The second phase of the correspondence took place between 21 November 1765 and 31 January 1766, with letters being exchanged daily between 1 and 5 December. This reflects the vehemence of the conflict, and reading the letters in their context produces a considerable sense of immediacy to the modern reader.

To enable the study of linguistic aspects of letters, a large-scale corpus was set up by the Helsinki Research Unit for Variation and Change led by Terttu Nevalainen. While the original Corpus of Early English Correspondence covered the period 1410 to 1681, an extension is being compiled in order to span the eighteenth century as well. At this point, the Corpus of Early English Correspondence Extension (CEECE) includes nearly 5,000 letters written by well over 300 correspondents, comprising 2.2 million words (Nurmi and Palander-Collin 2008: 30). The corpus allows for socially stratified searches, as it can be subdivided for non-linguistic variables like gender, profession, social rank (e.g. gentry vs. non-gentry), and family membership compared to letters written by others. The ultimate aim of CEECE is to provide a source for carrying out research that is intended to be representative of the language of eighteenth-century letter writers.

Representativeness is the aim of most large-scale text corpora. AR-CHER, which is a joint project in which various universities collaborate, is a case in point, as indeed its full name, 'A *Representative* Corpus of Historical English Registers', indicates. Striving to compile representative corpora, however, calls for a selection process, which, no matter how carefully conducted, inevitably omits material of which the validity can rarely be assessed beforehand. For instance, until Lowth's letters to Sir Francis Dashwood came to light, which happened at a fairly late stage in my research, I was under the impression that Lowth never used double negation. The second letter to Dashwood, however, proved to contain the following sentence:

(8) it is about the size of a common two penny brown Loaf, has the same form & appearance, & does **not** look so very stale **neither** (Lowth to Dashwood, 25 April 1750).

If, for the purpose of compiling a large-scale letter corpus, I would have had to make a representative selection from Lowth's out-letters, the chances that this very letter would have been excluded would have been quite high. After all, the correspondence contains letters to other close friends, like Joseph Spence or the Wartons. An analysis of such a corpus would have suggested that Lowth never used double negation – not very surprising in the light of the fact that his name is often linked with the disappearance of the construction from Standard English. The letter in question, however, not only shows that Lowth did use double negation, an interesting fact in its own right, but also that he ceased to do so at a certain point in his lifetime, even in the letters to his wife, which represent his most informal usage.

My aim in the present chapter and in Chapter 7 is not to analyse a representative corpus of letters, but to study the language of the letters of a single man in all its available forms. Studies of linguistic idiolects of eighteenth-century writers are fairly rare: in addition to my own work on the language of James Boswell, Lady Mary Wortley Montagu (bap.1689, d.1762), Betsy Sheridan, and Sarah Fielding, I know of relatively few other such studies. Some examples are Wright (1994) on Joseph Addison (1672–1719), Mizono (1991) on James Boswell, Percy (1996) and other publications on Captain James Cook (1728–79), Urhström (1907) on Samuel Richardson, and Sairio (2008, 2009) on Elizabeth Montagu. Studying my collection of Lowth's letters allows me to analyse his communicative competence, an approach to the language of writers of the past that is not usually taken, and which has, to my knowledge, never before been studied as systematically as I propose to do here. The main reason for taking this approach is to investigate to what extent his language agrees with the norm he presented in the grammar, something which has been greatly speculated about but never studied.

6.2 LOWTH'S LINGUISTIC REPERTOIRE

All speakers, according to Milroy and Milroy (1991: 120), have access to what is known as a 'linguistic repertoire', which they define as 'the totality of styles (both spoken and written) available to a community', and speakers draw upon this repertoire 'in order to fill various communicative needs'. To be able to do so, Milroy and Milroy argue, 'is likely to be crucial in [some-one's] general career and social advancement'. There is no need to assume that Lowth's case would have been different from that described in modern sociolinguistic studies. After all, he was a speaker and writer – though highly educated, as it happens – like any other person, then as now, and he was, moreover, a particularly ambitious one. In the light of his attempts to rise in the Church, which, as I have argued several times above, moti-vated many of his actions throughout his lifetime, it would be particularly relevant for him to be aware of the existence of different styles of writing – as well as, of course, speech – and to deploy them carefully. The letters that have come down to us in draft form illustrate how he carefully attempted to negotiate between the different linguistic choices available to him. I have also argued above that his grammar came to have the function of providing access to the norm of language in use among members of the highest social classes.

Lowth's language, variable as it is, correlates with formality of style: his most informal letters, particularly those addressed to his wife but also those to his closest friends, are characterized by a large amount of linguis-tic variation compared to the developing standard language. This is true for his spelling and morphosyntax, but even in his use of vocabulary it is evident that usage varies according to the nature of his relationship with the addressee and the topic discussed. An obvious example is that with one exception the word *dearest* only occurs in the letters to his wife. (The exception is found in the conclusion to the single letter to his son in the corpus.) A less obvious example is his use of the contraction *'tother* ('the other'), as in:

(9) I was talking with our good friend the B^p. of Chester **'tother** day of the present state of Ecclesiastical affairs (Lowth to John Sturges, 5 December 1778),

which similarly correlates with informality of style or intimacy of relationship: in nine of the ten instances recorded, the word was found in letters to his wife (6), to his nephew John Sturges (1), his friend James Merrick (1), and the second letter to Thomas Percy (1) dating from the time when they had drawn closer to each other. The only exception is from an early letter to Robert Dodsley (1753), which concludes with the conventional formula 'Your most faithfull Humble Servt.'. There are, however, many other indications in the language of these early letters to Dodsley that suggest that despite the fairly formal conclusion, their relationship had already developed into a relatively intimate one.

The language of Lowth's letters not only reflects a patterned variability, it also changed over the years: his out-letters span a period of nearly forty years, and even though the earliest letters date from the time when he was approaching his fortieth birthday, it is unrealistic to expect that his language would remain unchanged, the more so since at this period in his life he was fully engaged on his upwardly mobile career in the Church. I have already mentioned the loss of the double negative from his language, which may well be a linguistic consequence of his social advancement. That his language was not stable over the years is also evident from the fact that his use of the subjunctive shows a peak during a short period after the publication of his grammar in 1762. This was apparently a time in his life when he was most focused on producing grammatically correct language in his letters (Auer and Tieken-Boon van Ostade 2007).

In Chapter 5, I classified Lowth's correspondents according to their relationship with him, as a basis for studying his communicative competence. I thus distinguished eight categories of letters, i.e. in decreasing order of formality: letters addressed to his wife (64 letters, 24,138 words), to Close friends such as Dashwood and Spence (19 letters, 10,900 words), to Friends (53 letters, 19,825 words), Fellow scholars (40 letters, 12,125 words), Work-related contacts, both in the Church and in publishing (33 letters, 7,035 words), his Patrons (6 letters, 1,650 words), Acquaintances (9 letters, 2,661 words), Bare acquaintances (3 letters, 687 words), and Enemies (8 letters, 7,650 words). Unfortunately, these subsets of letters are of varied length, which means that the problem should be reckoned with that the results obtained for the smaller sections, particularly the letters to the bare acquaintances, are possibly skewed and must be interpreted with great care. For the analysis, I included the draft letters in the collection but not those for which fair copies have come down to us as well. Whenever a relationship changed in the course of time, as with Robert Dodsley and Thomas Percy, I have placed the letters in question in the relevant category, with the exception of Lowth's letters to Warburton. I included all these in the category Enemies because, in spite of Lowth's conclusion of one of the letters as 'Your most faithful & **Affectionate** humble Servt.' (Lowth to Warburton, 14 October 1756), the relationship continued to be strained. The formal notes (8 items, 760 words) I have placed into a separate category, as their language is so different from ordinary letters that they should be considered as a text type of their own.

In order to analyse the letters I have made use of WordSmith Tools, which is a commercially available concordancing program developed by Michael Scott from the University of Liverpool. The software allows for the study of frequency of usage, collocation patterns between words, and the analysis of the salience of particular words in their context (keyness). In making use of this program, as in the case of the application of any such software, the results of data searches should be treated with the care they deserve. Thus, in looking at the frequency of a word like *set*, the context should be taken into account to determine whether the form in question is a noun or a verb, and even, in the latter case, whether it might be an instance of the past tense of *to sit*, as in:

(10) It has a long time **sett** heavy on my conscience that I have not wrote to You (Lowth to Dashwood, 25 April 1750).

Another example is the occurrence of *I think*, which might be interpreted as an instance of an evidential verb functioning as a hedge, or as a verb indicating a thought process. The two usages are not always easy to distinguish, as example (11) demonstrates:

(11) much older than I imagined, by what, **I think** I had heard from You (Lowth to Ridley, 29 November 1768).

A considerable amount of manual analysis was therefore required for the interpretation of the results.

In what follows, I will focus on Lowth's spelling and his use of vocabulary. His variation in usage with respect to morphosyntax will be dealt with in Chapter 7, where I will relate his own usage to the rules in his grammar. First, however, I will test to what extent my subdivision of the letters on the basis of Lowth's relationship with his addressees agrees with the amount of involvement demonstrated vis-à-vis the recipient of his letters. According to Sairio (2005: 24), in her analysis of the correspondence of Dr Johnson, 'the more involved the letters are, the stronger the writer's attachment to the recipient is'. Though she found this to be the case for Dr Johnson's letters, the situation for Lowth is more complicated, due to the fact that my analysis comprises categories of letters not included in Sairio's study.

6.3 LINGUISTIC INVOLVEMENT IN THE LETTERS

Chafe (1985), in his study of the linguistic differences between speech and writing, argues that there are different degrees of involvement between writer and addressee in speech compared to writing. He distinguishes between three different types of involvement:

- involvement of the speaker with himself, that is, ego involvement;
- involvement of the speaker with the hearer, that is, concern for the dynamics of interaction with another person;
- and involvement of the speaker with the subject matter, that is, an ongoing personal commitment to what is being talked about (Chafe 1985: 116).

These different types of involvement take linguistic shape in a variety of ways, but to facilitate comparison I will adopt the same categories as those employed by Sairio (2005): the occurrence of first person pronouns (*I, me, my, mine, myself*) to study the first type of involvement, that of second person pronouns for the second type (*you, your, y'., yourself*), and of evidential verbs and degree adverbs for the third type. It is unclear from Sairio (2005) whether she included the oblique forms of the pronouns as well. For my own analysis I have decided to exclude all instances of *your's/ yours* that are part of the closing epistolary formulas as they occur so often that the results would be skewed if they had been included. Evidential verbs include verbs that 'mark knowledge as having been arrived at through some kind of reasoning' (Chafe 1985: 119), and Sairio analysed the occurrence of *think, know, believe, suppose, find, (be) sure,* and *doubt.* They therefore include hedges such as *you know, I suppose,* and *I think.* As for degree adverbs, Sairio's analysis included *very, so, quite, pretty,* and *really,* to which I have added *such.* Examples of each of these categories are the following:

(12) 'Twas **my** intention to write to **You** as soon as **I** had taken such a general survey of this place as might enable **me** to say something more to **you** than just that **I** was arriv'd here (Lowth to Dashwood, 11 May 1748).

(13) Pray **my** Dear keep up **your** spirits, & don't frighten **yourself** with every thing **you** hear (Lowth to his wife, 11 March 1755).

(14) **You** may **be sure** that **I** have taken much consideration upon this occasion (Lowth to his wife, 18 March 1755).

(15) & that the dear Tom is **so** well & **such** good company to **you** (Lowth to his wife, 12 June 1755).

The results of my analysis of Lowth's involvement in the different categories of letters are presented in Figures 6.1 (ego and interpersonal involvement) and 6.2 (degree adverbs and evidential verbs). In order to be

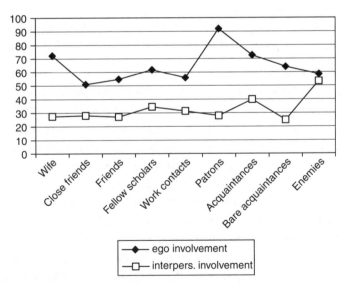

FIG. 6.1. Ego and interpersonal involvement in Lowth's letters according to relationship with the addressee

able to compare the different categories of letters, I normalized the raw data to occurrence per 1,000 words. The results, however, become less reliable the smaller the size of the individual subcorpora.

The graphs in Figure 6.1 show that first person pronouns in Lowth's letters are always much more frequent than second person pronouns. This was also the case in Sairio's analysis. Only for the subcategory of Enemies are the two figures remarkably similar. This is confirmed by a keyword analysis of this category of letters in the light of the complete correspondence. Keyness is a function of WordSmith Tools that allows for the identification of 'salient language differences in texts' (Baker 2006). To carry out a keyword analysis for a particular corpus one needs a substantially larger reference corpus. For the present purpose, when analysing subsets of letters I used the collection of out-letters as a whole as my reference corpus. Accordingly, the second highest keyword in Lowth's letters to Warburton is *Job*, which is, after all, the object of their controversy. But the list is headed by the pronoun *you*, which highlights the accusatory tone of most of the letters, as may be illustrated by the following passage:

(16) **You** seem to think I ought to have quoted **you**, or refer'd to **your** Book: & a Friend of **yours** charges me with writing against **you** & being afraid of **you**. **Your** Friend is mistaken in both these particulars, & the ground of **your** complaint I cannot possibly comprehend. Why should I single out **you**, & attack **you** for opinions wch. were common to **you** with twenty other Authors of note? w^{d}. this have been a mark of respect to **you**? (Lowth to Warburton, 9 September 1756).

Keywords in Warburton's letters (5,310 words), compared to the in-letters as a reference corpus (32,330 words), similarly include *you*, but also *me*. When the out-letters are used as a reference corpus, the keywords include *religion, your* (*your letter*), and *say*. This last verb collocates with *you* (*you say, say you*) ten times. All this confirms the reciprocal nature of the quarrel. *You* is similarly the third most frequent word in Lowth's published letter to Brown, one of Warburton's supporters.

There are many other striking differences between the two graphs in Figure 6.1. To begin with, Lowth's personal (ego) involvement with his wife is higher than that with his Close friends, Friends, Fellow scholars, and Work-related contacts, as would be expected given the intimacy of their relationship, but not as high as that with his Patrons. Perhaps this is not surprising after all, as in these letters he was concerned with himself in relation to the ways in which Lord Hartington, Archbishop Thomas Secker, or the Duke of Newcastle might be able to assist him or had already assisted him in the advancement of his career. Lowth's letters to his Acquaintances are characterized by both a high personal and a higher than usual interpersonal involvement. The category of Acquaintances comprises Barton, Duncombe, Eames, Morant, Percy, Reynolds, Waddilove, and Wentworth. Possibly, the data found are evidence of a higher amount of effort than usual on Lowth's part to express involvement with the addressees in question.

Lowth's relatively low amount of interpersonal involvement with his wife seems odd: the contents of the letters suggest otherwis, as he is greatly concerned for his family's well-being and always eager for news from home. Keywords are, indeed, *love, Tom, Dean* (Thomas Cheyney), and *friends* ('My Love to Tom, & all Friends', 1 March 1755). Possibly, the establishment of personal involvement by focusing on the use of second person pronouns alone is insufficient. An additional way of doing so is by looking at expressions of affection to those concerned, though not only his wife and children but also those in their immediate surroundings, such as close friends. In Chapter 5, I argued that passing on greetings from home to home is a way of expressing closeness between writer and addressee. To this end, I looked at the words expressing affection for the addressees themselves and those who were close to them, in particular the use of words like *love, respects,* and *compliments* (including its abbreviated form). Examples are the following:

(17) **Love** to Friends in the Close, Miss Stevens, & Tom (Lowth to his wife, 17 May 1755).

(18) I beg my best **Respects** to all of your Family, in which my Wife joins with me (Lowth to Chapman, 11 September 1756).

(19) & to have desired You to present my **Comp^{ts}**. & Thanks to him (Lowth to Robert Dodsley, 19 June 1760).

I next compared Lowth's letters to his wife to those to his close friends and his friends. The results, which are presented in Table 6.1, confirm the relevance of taking this feature into account: particularly the high frequency of the word *love* in Lowth's letters to his wife, similar in meaning to the more formal use of *respects* or *compliments*, illustrates this. The only other three instances of *love* were found in Lowth's letters to his son Tom, his brother William, and his nephew John Sturges.

The formal notes contain no instances of first or second person pronoun usage: for both, third person NPs are used. See, for instance, example (20):

Table 6.1 Lowth's use of words for passing on greetings correlated with addressee

Addressee	*love*	*respects*	*compliments/ comp*^{ts}*.*	Total (normalized/1,000 words)
Wife	74	2	1 + 4	81 (3.6)
Close friends	4	4	5	13 (1.2)
Friends	0	11	0 + 11	22 (1.1)
All letters	*81*	*24*	*8 + 26*	*139 (1.5)*

(20) **The Bp. of London** [first person] presents **his** [first person] Comp^{ts}.
Ld. Ailesbury [third person]; & returns with many Thanks the Letter from India; & adds what occurs to **him** [first person] on the Orthography of the Inscription (Lowth to Brudenell-Bruce, 4 May 1781).

Calculation of Lowth's involvement through his use of third person NPs showed an interpersonal involvement of 39.5 per 1,000 words and a personal involvement of 65.8; the notes, however, comprise not even 1,000 words altogether, so these figures are probably not very reliable. They contain no instances of degree adverbs or evidential verbs either, in contrast with the letters proper (see Tables 6.2 and 6.3 below). This confirms that they are altogether a different text type from letters.

In Figure 6.2 I have presented the data for my analysis of degree adverbs and evidential verbs that Lowth used in the different categories of letters.

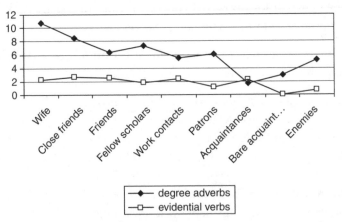

Fig. 6.2. Degree adverbs and evidential verbs in Lowth's letters according to his relationship with the addressee

Table 6.2 **Lowth's use of degree adverbs in the different letter categories (normalized to 1,000 words)**

Addressee	very	so	such	quite	pretty	really	Total
Wife (64) 24,138	149	75	4	14	15	2	259 (10.7)
Close friends (19) 10,900	57	19	2	8	6	1	93 (8.5)
Friends (53) 19,825	70	47	6	2	1	0	126 (6.4)
Fellow scholars (40) 12,125	42	34	1	2	1	0	80 (6.6)
Work-related contacts (33) 7,035	21	13	0	0	0	0	34 (4.8)
Patrons (6) 1,650	6	4	0	0	0	0	10 (6.1)
Acquaintances (9) 2,661	2	0	0	0	0	0	2 (0.8)
Bare acquaintances (3) 687	2	0	0	0	0	0	2 (2.9)
Enemies (8) 7,650	18	20	1	0	0	1	40 (5.2)
Formal notes (8) 760	0	0	0	0	0	0	0
Out-letters (250) 90,725	377	241	25	64	29	5	741 (8.2)

The graphs in Figure 6.2 are based on the distribution of the various adverbs and verbs as presented in Tables 6.2 and 6.3.

Figure 6.2 shows that the use of evidential verbs is most homogeneous and remarkably similar for all categories of letters with the exception of Bare acquaintances and Enemies. As the amount of text available for the letters to the Bare acquaintances is very small indeed, the lack of data for this category is probably not very significant. As for the letters to the Enemies, it would

Table 6.3 **Lowth's use of evidential verbs in the different letter categories (normalized to 1,000 words)**

Addressee	think	know	believe	suppose	find	am sure	doubt	Total
Wife (64) 24,138	18	0	14	20	3	1	0	56 (2.3)
Close friends (19) 10,900	13	1	10	4	1	0	0	29 (2.7)
Friends (53) 19,825	20	0	9	21	0	1	0	51 (2.6)
Fellow scholars (40) 12,125	5	0	6	10	2	0	0	23 (1.9)
Work-related contacts (33) 7,035	3	0	5	9	0	0	0	17 (2.4)
Patrons (6) 1,650	1	0	1	0	0	0	0	2 (1.2)
Acquaintances (9) 2,661	3	0	1	2	0	0	0	6 (2.3)
Bare acquaintances (3) 687	0	0	0	0	0	0	0	0
Enemies (8) 7,650	2	0	1	2	0	0	0	5 (0.7)
Formal notes (8) 760	0	0	0	0	0	0	0	0
Out-letters (250) 90,725	66	1	47	69	6	2	0	191 (2.1)

seem that Lowth used fewer hedges – *I think, I believe, I suppose* – in these letters, presumably in an attempt to come across assertively. Sairio (2005: 26) found that Dr Johnson's use of evidential verbs correlated with the age of the addressee: Johnson used significantly fewer instances of such verbs in his letters to the much younger Queeney Thrale (1764–1857), who is character-ized in the *ODNB* as the 'protégée of Samuel Johnson' (*ODNB*, 'Hester Maria Elphinstone'), than to his other addressees. As in the case of Lowth, this seems due to a desire, unconscious or otherwise, to express authority. As for Lowth's use of degree adverbs as evidence of involvement, the data indicate strongest involvement in the letters to his wife. His usage in the other categories is fairly similar, with the exception of the categories Acquaintances and Bare acquaintances; again, this is not unexpected, for one would expect a lower degree of involvement with people Lowth was barely intimate with than with others, but it is striking that this is more evident from the distribution of degree adverbs than for any of the other features I have analysed here.

6.4 SPELLING IN THE LETTERS

Of the features that were studied by Sairio (2005) as a measure of linguistic involvement in eighteenth-century letters, only the occurrence of first person pronouns and of degree adverbs appeared to correlate in Lowth's case with the nature of his relationship with the addressee. The single exception to this, Lowth's use of *you* in the letters to Enemies, was confirmed by a keyword analysis of the letters. Another way of analysing involvement, or in any case of a lack of formality in a writer's approach to the addressee, is by studying the use of contracted forms and abbreviations in a letter, as in example (21):

(21) I **can't** conclude without informing you, **y^t**. Mr. Legge was 4 days last week at Potsdam, **w^{ch}**. itself is a mark of great favour; he constantly din'd & supp'd with **y^e**. King, & had frequent & long private conferences with him (Lowth to Dashwood, 11 May 1748).

The use of short forms like *can't*, *w^{ch}*. 'which', *y^t*. 'that', *y^e*. 'the', and many others besides was not considered acceptable at the time, or, at any rate, not in the case of a formal correspondence. John Carter, for instance, in his *Practical English Grammar* (1773), wrote that '*Contractions*, except for private Use, should be as much as possible avoided. They argue Disrespect to Superiors, and are puzzling to others' (1773: 137). In a later work, *The Scholar's Spelling Assistant* (1796), Thomas Carpenter wrote about 'Contractions used in Writing and Print' that 'it is to be remembered, except in Addresses and Accompts, such Contractions in the Body of a Letter, are improper' (1796: 110).

Two kinds of contractions can be distinguished, those that reflect pronunciation such as *can't* in (21) but also *don't, I'll, there's*, and *won't* (all of which were used by Lowth), and those that serve as convenient abbreviations in the letter writing process. Of the former, Carter noted that they 'appear disrespectful and too familiar' (1773: 140). As the advice concerned someone 'writing to [their] Superior', this suggests that they might not be out of place in informal letters. This, as I will show below, is indeed the case with Lowth's letters. Examples of the latter type of forms are w^{ch}., y^t., and y^e. from (21), but there are many others. In Lowth's letters I have come across a large variety of such forms, which I have subdivided into the following categories:

- names of the months: *Feb., Mar., Apr., Aug^t/Aug., Sep^r./ Sept., Oct^r., Nov^r., Dec^r.*
- titles and forms of address: *Ab^p./ArchB^p./Arch-B^p./Archb^p, B^p./Bp.*,[1] *Capt., Col., D.* 'Duke', *D^{ss}.* 'Duchess', *D^r., Lieut./Lieut^t./Lieut^{nt}., L^d., Lordsh^p./L^p., M^r., M^{rs}., Prof^r., R^t. H^{ble}.* 'Right Honourable', *R^t. R^d.* 'Right Reverend', *S^t.*
- forms that are part of epistolary formulas: *Affect./Affect^{ly}./Aff^{ly}., Broth^r./B^r., humb., P.S., Servt.*
- verb forms: *c^d.* 'could', *rec'd/rec^d.* 'received', *s^d.* 'said', *s^d./sh^d.* 'should', *w^d.* 'would'
- pronouns: *w^{ch}.* 'which', *w^m.* 'whom', *y^r.* 'your'
- prepositions: *ab^t., ag^t., f^m., wth., with^t.*
- personal names and placenames: *Fred^c* 'Frederick', *H.* 'Hartington', *L.* 'Lowth', *N.* 'Newcastle', *Robt./R.* 'Robert', *Thos., W^m.* 'William' and 'Wykeham', *B.* 'Brunswick', *D./D^m.* 'Durham', *Hants., Wint.* 'Winchester'
- words typical of letters: *acc^t.* 'account', *Comp^{ts}.* 'compliments'

---

[1] Whether or not <p> is superscript in these forms in Lowth's letters is not always easy to see.

- words characteristic of the written medium: *B.* 'book', *ibid*, *i.e.*, *N.B.*, *viz.*
- books of the Bible (only in Lowth's letters to Merrick): *Deut.*, *Ezek.*, *Gen.*, *Heb.*, *Jud.*, *Num.*
- general nouns: *A-Deaconry*, *Bprick/B^p.rick*, *Coll.* 'College', *Comp.* 'Company', *D.* 'Deacon', *H.* 'House' as in 'H. of Commons/Lords', *N.T.* 'New Testament', *Parl^t.*, *Preferm^t.*, *Univ^{ty}.*, *y^{rs}.* 'years'
- words relating to scholarly matters: *ant.* 'anterior', *Cap^l.* 'Capital', *col.* 'column', *Heb.* 'Hebrew', MS and MSS, *p.* 'page', *Ps.* 'Psalm', *v.* 'verse'
- titles of books: *D.L.* 'Divine Legation', *Hom. Edit. Rom.*, *Antiq. Sacr.*
- *pounds*, *shillings* and *pence*: *ll.*, *s.* and *p.*
- *&* and *&c.*
- 'y' words, with the letter <y> being a relic of mediaeval practice: *y^e.* 'the', *y^m.* 'them', *y^n.* 'than', *y^s.* 'this', *y^t.* 'that' (conjunction, demonstrative, and relative).

Some forms are indeed puzzling, as Carter writes, such as those for the titles of books; these could only be freely used in letters to addressees able to identify them easily, fellow scholars, for instance. The reason it was considered unacceptable to use abbreviations like the ones listed here was their very function, the means to speed up the writing process. To betray one's haste in writing was, for obvious reasons, considered impolite: it reduced the serious purpose of the job in hand. Not surprisingly, abbreviations occur in great numbers in draft letters – Carter indeed made an exception 'for private Use'. As the above list shows, Lowth used various abbreviations for single words, while different forms were used by his correspondents, such as *Febry,* and *Sat.* for *Saturday* (which Lowth always used in its full form). Letter writers either sought no guidance in the matter, or the use of abbreviations depended on their individual inclinations.

When abbreviations do occur in Lowth's letters, or indeed in those he received, their number can be shown to correlate with formality of style. Elsewhere (Tieken-Boon van Ostade 2006b), I have already demonstrated this on the basis of an analysis of Lowth's usage to representatives of the different categories of correspondents, his wife, Spence (Close friend), Merrick (Friend), Dalrymple (Fellow scholar), Jenkinson (Work-related contact), Pelham-Holles (Patron), Morant (Acquaintance), and Warburton (Enemy). For Warburton I also analysed Lowth's draft letters to him, as well as the formal notes. The results are shown in Table 6.4.

Table 6.4 Contractions and abbreviations in Lowth's out-letters (Tieken-Boon van Ostade 2006*b*: 240)

Addressee	Amount of text	All abbrev.			Gram. words			Excluding &		
		N	N/1,000	Rank	N	N/1,000	Rank	N	N/1,000	Rank
Lowth's wife	24,138	1,295	53.7	8	1,139	47.2	5	604	25	5
Spence	3,228	231	71.6	3	216	66.9	3	127	39.3	3
Merrick	5,333	324	60.8	5	291	54.6	4	147	27.6	4
Dalrymple	1,943	92	47.4	9	77	39.6	8	23	11.8	8
Jenkinson	351	13	37	10	8	22.8	10	3	8.6	9
Morant	297	16	53.9	7	9	30.3	9	5	16.8	7
Pelham-Holles	477	26	54.5	6	22	46.1	6	3	6.3	10
Warburton (fair copies)	2,480	168	67.7	4	109	44	7	47	19	6
Warburton (draft)	3,129	238	76.1	2	223	71.3	2	133	42.5	2
Formal notes	409	46	112.5	1	33	80.7	1	23	56.2	1

The figures in Table 6.4 show that it is important to exclude *&* and *&c* from the data: *&* occurs with overwhelming frequency in all letters, irrespective of their formality. I have found 2,023 instances of *&* as against only 208 of the full form *and*, and 68 instances of *&c, etc.* or *etcetera* never occur. The ampersand thus constitutes a normal writing habit to Lowth and did not have the same function as his other short forms. The table also shows that there are no great differences whether grammatical words (e.g. *can't, don't, w^{ch}*.) are included or not, except for Morant and Pelham-Holles; here, however, the amount of text analysed is very small. The figures also show that abbreviations in formal notes do not correlate with formality: their frequency can only be accounted for by the limitations of space of the message. This, again, confirms their status as an independent text type.

If short forms correlate with formality of style and hence with politeness, it is clear that Lowth was most polite in his letters to Jenkinson (Work-related contact), Pelham-Holles (Patron), Dalrymple (Fellow scholar), and Morant (Acquaintance), and less so to Merrick (Friend) and Spence (Close friend). That he should use fewer short forms in the letters to his wife (rank: 5) suggests, perhaps, that he thought that their use served to indicate familiarity between men, with whom he was after all more used to correspond by letter, than in letters to her. Perhaps he also thought that they might indeed be 'puzzling' to her. The 'private' function of the use of abbreviations and contractions is evident from a comparison between the draft letters to Warburton and the fair copies (Table 6.4). Another illustration may be found in the letters to Michaelis, where usage between draft letters and fair copies is completely reversed. With short forms making up 72 per cent of the total number of instances in the draft letters, full forms included, they only represent 27 per cent of the instances encountered in the fair copies:

- Lowth–Michaelis drafts (943 words): y^e. (26) / *the* (8), y^t. (6) / *that* (6) (both functions), y^n. (2) / *than* (1), w^{ch}. (9) / *which* (–), f^m. (5) / *from* (2), *with*^{t}. (1) / *without* (–), w^{th}. (1) / *with* (4), sh^d. (2) / *should* (–), w^d. (1) / *would* (–), *abt.* (1) / *about* (–). Index: 54/21 (72%);

- Lowth–Michaelis fair copies (1,008 words): y^e. (7) / *the* (4), y^t. (1) / *that* (11), y^n. (–) / *than* (3), w^{ch}. (5) / *which* (5), f^m. (–) / *from* (9), sh^d. (–) / *should* (2), *abt.* (–) / *about* (1). Index: 13/35 (27%).

If we look at Lowth's in-letters, the same conclusion can be drawn as for the out-letters, with one important difference. The writers selected for analysis were a Close friend (Spence), a Friend (Merrick), a Fellow scholar (Woide), Work-related contacts (Beattie, Pearson, and Prince), and Patrons (Pelham-Holles and Secker) (Table 6.5). With the exception of Pearson, Lowth's correspondents used far fewer short forms than Lowth. Beattie, Prince, Secker, and Woide even have none at all in the third column. Woide's practice may perhaps be disregarded: as a foreigner he was probably unfamiliar with current practice in this respect. Example (22) shows that he was not aware of the practice of capitalizing the first pronoun *I* either:

Table 6.5 Contractions and abbreviations in Lowth's in-letters (Tieken-Boon van Ostade 2006*b*: 242)

Addressee	Amount of text	All abbrev. N	N/1,000	Rank	Gram. words N	N/1,000	Rank	Excluding & N	N/1,000	Rank
Spence	538	21	39	3	15	27.9	3	4	7.4	2
Merrick	2,487	71	28.6	6	39	15.7	5	8	3.21	4
Beattie	429	0	0	8	0	0	7	0	0	5
Pearson	4,588	380	82.8	1	343	74.8	1	247	53.8	1
Prince	699	23	32.9	5	12	17.2	4	0	0	5
Pelham-Holles	437	19	43.5	2	14	32	2	3	6.9	3
Secker	480	16	33.3	4	7	14.6	6	0	0	5
Woide	564	3	5.3	7	0	0	7	0	0	5

(22) May j lay it before Your Lordship, with the preface j intend to prefix
to the Egyptian Grammar, now finished (Woide to Lowth, 29 July
1777).

If the use of abbreviations and contractions serves as an index of politeness, Lowth's correspondents were more polite to him than the other way
around, which is something I have already observed in relation to their use
of address forms. That Lowth's usage in the third column is similar to that
of Pelham-Holles, even though the absolute figures are small, suggests that
he took his cue as to what was socially acceptable usage from the language
of his patrons. Secker even used none at all (third column). Pearson's
usage is truly exceptional. As Lowth's secretary, letter writing to him had a
different function than for Lowth's other correspondents. Writing on such
a regular basis – fifteen letters in two months – as well as in a capacity in
which social distance played a less important role than in the case of the
other correspondents, using a great deal of short forms served a purely
functional purpose. For someone in Pearson's position, writing letters
probably made up a large portion of his daily activities.

If we look at Lowth's use of short forms in more detail, there is more to his
usage than merely demonstrating greater or lesser politeness, for it also
changed over the years. This development only affected forms reflecting
pronunciation, i.e. *can't, don't, I'll, here's, there's, she's, 'tis, 'twas,* and *'twould,*
none of which occur after the 1760s:

- *can't* (8) / *cannot* (87): *can't* is found only in letters to Dashwood
  (1748), Robert Dodsley (1753), his wife (5, 1755), and Merrick (1762),
  and never again after that;
- *don't* (39) / *do not* (65): *don't* only occurs in letters to Robert Dodsley
  (2, 1753; 2, 1757), his wife (23), Spence (5, 1761; 2, 1765), Merrick (3,
  1762; 1, 1763), and Ridley (1768); it no longer occurs after 1768;
- *'ll* (21) / *will* (191), *shall* (229):
  o *I'll* (13): his wife (12, 1755) and Merrick (1, 1763); it is never found
    after 1763. The full form *I will* occurs 96 times, and *I shall* 211 times;
  o *you'll* (8): Dashwood (1, 1748), his wife (2, 1755), Robert Dodsley (4,
    1757 and 1758), and Spence (1, 1761); it is never found after 1761; *you
    will* occurs 94 times, *you shall* 18 times;
  o the forms in *'ll* disappear completely after 1763;
- *won't* (3) / *will not* (51): his wife (2, 755) and Robert Dodsley (1, 1757);
  it never again occurs after 1757;

- *here's* (1), *there's* (1): both to his wife (1755); *here is* was attested twice throughout the letters, and *there is* 39 times;
- *she's* (1) / *she is* (12): his wife (1, 1755); *he's* does not occur, but the full form occurs in large numbers throughout the letters (52);
- *'tis* and *'twas*:
  - *'tis*: 47 instances: Robert Dodsley (5, 1753; 1, 1757; 3, 1758; 1, 1761), Woog (1753), his wife (27, 1755), Warburton (1756), Duncombe (3, 1758), Spence (2, 1761), Merrick (2, 1762), and Ridley (1769); this form disappears after 1769; 95 instances were found of *it is* in all types of letters, throughout the correspondence;
  - *'twas* (6): Dashwood (1748), his wife (3, 1755), Speed (1761), and Spence (1761); the form no longer occurs after 1761; *it was* was found 54 times in all types of letters;
- *'twould* (3): only to his wife (1755); *it would* was found 10 times, also in the letters to his wife.

The forms *I'm, you're, he's, we're, they're, shan't, couldn't, shouldn't, wouldn't, haven't, hasn't, hadn't, didn't, isn't, wasn't,* or those with *'d* 'would', were not found in the letters. With the exception of *'tis,* which occurs in formal and informal letters alike, and several instances in the early letters to Robert Dodsley, all the above forms exclusively occur in Lowth's letters to his wife and to people I have classified as his Close friends or Friends. They can therefore be called informal spellings. (I have already commented in Chapter 5 on the fact that Lowth's early letters to Robert Dodsley display an informal type of language that is not as yet matched by his use of epistolary formulas at that time.) My collection contains informal letters dating even from after the 1760s, addressed to Percy, Troy (draft), and Thomas Warton (manuscript letter), and to Lowth's son Thomas, his nephew John Sturges, and his brother William, but none of them contains any instances of the forms discussed. The short forms no longer occur in the draft letters from after this period either. The case of Michaelis confirms all this, for, as already illustrated, the draft letters contain many more short forms and abbreviations than the letters that were actually sent. I have, moreover, come across one instance of the spelling *farther* in a draft letter to Michaelis which was changed to *further* in the fair copy:

(23)   a P.S. I have no **farther** intelligence yet of the Edition of y^e. 70
          Version of Daniel of Rome (draft letter to Michaelis, 12 July 1771)

    b P.S. I have no **further** intelligence of the Edition of **the** 70 Version
       of Daniel from Rome (fair copy).

Note also that, along with the omission of *yet* in (23a), *y^e^.* was changed
into *the*. I have come across a similar example of such a change in a letter
addressed to Dalrymple in which Lowth caught himself at having inadvertently written the same words twice over:

(24) I believe You will get no satisfaction from Nourry, as to the point, ~~as
      to y^e^. point~~ wch. You want to examine (Lowth to Dalrymple, 21
      January 1782).

This instance suggests that Lowth regularly varied between the two forms,
but also, since he crossed out the phrase containing *y^e^.*, that he considered the
full form more appropriate to the style of this particular letter. As for the
spelling *further*, this is by far the more frequent form in Lowth's letters: I have
come across 47 instances of it, compared to 6 instances of *farther*, all in
informal letters, addressed to Dashwood (1748), his wife (3, 1755), Chapman
(1756), and Speed (1760). The form *farthest* was found only once, again in a
letter to his wife; *furthest* did not occur. The change as illustrated by example
(23) suggests that Lowth was aware of the informal status of the spelling of
words, including that of *y^e^*.

    The short forms discussed here are not the only spelling forms that
correlate with formality of style in Lowth's letters: I have found many
spelling variants, none of which are still acceptable today, that are primarily and at times even exclusively found in his informal letters. A good
example is the use of <tt> in, primarily, monosyllabic verbs or nouns,
of which I have identified 94 tokens altogether: *admitt, committ, cutt,
(for)gett/(for)gott, hitt, lett, mett, omitt, sett,* and *submitt.* The forms with
single consonant, 267 items, far exceed this number. Osselton (1984: 132)
considers these forms to be instances of older spelling, surviving as part of
private spelling that was distinct from the system found in printed texts.
This is indeed what we find in Lowth's letters, too: with only four exceptions,
three early ones, *committ* and *sett* in a letter to Robert Dodsley (1753) and
sett to Hartington (1755), and one later instance of *gott* to Michaelis (1775),
all instances are found in his informal letters. *Gott,* for instance, occurs 25
times in the letters to his wife as against only four instances of the form
with single <t>. The latest instance found, *submitt,* occurs in a draft letter
to Shute Barrington (1778): though the corpus doesn't include a fair copy
of this letter, it is more than likely that this form would have been copied

as *submit*. Another old-fashioned spelling which only occurs in the informal letters is the word *pacquet*, both in the sense of 'packet boat' and 'parcel': the only two instances are found in a letter to his wife (1755) and in one to Robert Dodsley (1762). With 52 instances, *packet* is Lowth's normal spelling of the word.

There are other interesting spelling variants in the letters, particularly those used for the past tense and past participle suffix *-ed* and for the third person singular present tense of verbs in *-y*, and those for the plural in nouns ending in the same vowel. To start with the first, Osselton (1984: 133) identified the following different spelling forms for *-ed* in printed texts from around 1600: *saved, sav'd, sav d, lackd, lackt*, and *lack't*. The forms with the apostrophe reached about 50 per cent by the middle of the eighteenth century, after which their usage sharply declined. As for practice in letter writing, he noticed a more conservative tendency compared to that of the printers of the time. In Lowth's letters, the form in *'d* is by far the most common, but I have also found forms like *clapt* and *fixt*, forms that were sanctioned by his own grammar (1762: 66, *snatcht, checkt, snapt, mixt*), and *wheeld* – again only in the letters to his wife (1755), and to Dashwood (1748) and Spence (1761). Lowth's practice was therefore no exception to what Osselton found: he is similarly more conservative in his usage than the printers of his age, but that is not all. In the letters I have identified 567 verb forms in *'d* as against 877 in *-ed* (from these data I excluded forms in *-ted, -ded*, as well as words like *learned* and *supplied* which do not as a rule end in *'d*). If the general picture is that Lowth used *'d* in slightly more than 1 in every 3 instances of the forms concerned, usage in the letters to his wife is much higher: I found 250 instances of *'d* as against only 51 of *-ed* (83.1%), which is about twice as frequent as Osselton's figure of some 40 per cent in letters from the 1750s. Apart from the letters to Lowth's wife, *'d* is found primarily in draft letters: 94 to Warburton (1756), 14 to Duncombe (1758), 2 to Secker (1766), and 1 each to Michaelis (1771), Barrington (1778), and Troy (1779). Lowth also used *'d* in letters to Close friends and Friends (Chapman, Robert Dodsley, Merrick, Ridley, Speed, and Spence[2]), and to his brother William. There are a few exceptions, 4 instances in a letter to Hartington (1755), 1 in a

---

[2] I have found only a few instances in Lowth's letters to the Wartons. Most of these, however, are from Wooll (1806), and the possibility must be reckoned with that Wooll, like Bloom and Bloom (1989–2002) in their edition of the Piozzi letters, expanded the use of *'d*.

letter to two unidentified gentlemen (1771), and 4 instances in letters to James Dodsley (1763, 1764). After 1755, with the last letter containing '*d* being addressed to his patron Lord Hartington, no more instances are found in any of his formal letters. His letters to Michaelis, written between 1770 and 1782 (fair copies only), do not contain a single instance of '*d*. Lowth's change in this respect mirrors that which affected printed texts of the time and may have been brought about as a result of his reading, which would explain why it lags behind printers' practice; but his usage also varies according to his relationship with his addressee and thus with formality of style. Lowth wasn't alone in showing a changing preference for -*ed* compared to '*d*: I have found the same for Lady Mary Wortley Montagu, Samuel Richardson, and Dr Johnson. Another letter writer whose language was similarly influenced in the course of his lifetime by the spelling of printed books was James Boswell (Tieken-Boon van Ostade 1996*c*).

Lowth's use of -*ys* for -*ies*, both in plural nouns and present tense verb forms, similarly correlates with relative formality of style. I have come across 88 instances of what are now regular plurals in -*ies* in a variety of nouns, and 57 in -*ys*. The latter category comprises *Babys* (23) (only in letters to his wife, 1755); *civilitys* (2) (draft letter to Woog, 1753; his wife 1755); *cntrys* 'countries' (1) (draft letter to Waddilove, 1774); *countrys* (Spence, 1775); *copys* (7) (5 in a letter to Robert Dodsley 1753; 2 in a draft letter to Woog, 1753); *difficultys* (3) (his wife 1755); *en/inquirys* (6) (2 to Dashwood, 1748; 1 to Robert Dodsley, 1753; 3 to his wife 1755); *inaccuracys* (1 to Robert Dodsley, 1753); *Ladys* (4) (2 to Dashwood 1748, 1750; 2 to his wife 1755); *Mollys* (1, his wife 1755); *opportunitys* (3) (1 each to Robert Dodsley, 1753; his wife, 1755; and a draft letter to Warburton, 1756); *partys* (2) (to his wife, 1755); *perplexitys* (1) (to his wife 1755); *Preliminarys* (1) (to Dashwood 1748); and *uncertaintys* (1) (to his wife 1755). With the exception of 8 instances in the early letters to Robert Dodsley, plurals in -*ys* only occur in draft letters (5), letters to his wife (38) or to close friends (6). In addition to *Babys*, I have also found two instances of *baby's* in the letters to his wife (*babies* does not occur). As for the spelling of present tense forms, I have come across 3 instances in -*ys* (*complys*, *signifys*, *implys*), again all in letters to his wife. With 9 instances, *lies* (7), *specifies*, and *carries*, the forms in -*ies* are more common.

Related to the features discussed here is the occurrence of forms in -*yd* rather than -*ied*, i.e. *carry'd, envy'd, lay'd, marry'd, pay'd, satisfy'd, suppy'd, stay'd*, and *vary'd* (13 altogether), solely in the letters to Dashwood and

Lowth's wife. Here, Lowth doesn't apply the spelling rule, which is now obligatory, according to which final -*y* in past tense forms and participles of weak verbs changes into -*ie*-, similar to that of the formation of the plural of nouns ending in the same vowel, or into -*i*- as with *pay*. Failure to do this typically occurs in Lowth's informal letters, and we similarly find *carry'd*, *deny'd*, *signify'd*, and *(un)satsfy'd* in the draft letters to Warburton. The regular modern forms in -*ied* or -*aid* are found in fairly large numbers throughout the correspondence: there are 35 instances of them altogether, both in his formal and his informal letters. This suggests that variation in this spelling feature does not characterize his formal letters but only his informal ones. The word *said*, with 64 instances, never occurs in a different spelling. The form *staid*, found only once and in a letter to Dashwood, is now no longer used, but it occurred in an example sentence in Lowth's grammar: 'You *and* I rode to London, *but* Peter staid at home' (1762: 93).

Other interesting patterns of variation are the following. There are 10 instances of *compleat(ed)*, 6 of which occur in informal letters, while of the 3 instances of the present-day spelling (*complete/completed/completely*) 1 occurs in a draft letter and 2 in formal letters. Of the adjectives ending in -*full* in what would nowadays be -*ful* (*beautifull, carefull, doubtfull, dreadfull, distressfull, faithfull, joyfull, successfull*), 6 are found in letters to his wife, 1 in a letter to Chapman, and 1 in a draft letter to Warburton; the remaining 3 occur in formal letters. Forms in -*ful* are more frequent: I found 41 instances, most of which are *faithful* (20), which occurs as part of epistolary formulas. Lowth's variation in the use of -*ick/ic* spellings is of interest as the -*ick* spelling was becoming old-fashioned during the period of Lowth's correspondence, despite the fact that Dr Johnson prescribed it in his *Dictionary* (and preferred it in his private letters) (Osselton 1963; Tieken-Boon van Ostade and Bax 2002). There are 14 instances of this spelling in the letters: *Bishoprick(s)/B^p.rick* (7), *italicks* (2), *lyrick, Musick, politicks* (2), and *relick*. Nine were found in the letters to his wife (mostly *Bishoprick(s)/B^p.rick*, as acquiring a bishopric was a major topic in their correspondence), 2 in letters to close friends, 1 in a letter to a friend, and 2, both instances of *italicks*, in the early letters to Robert Dodsley. This makes the -*ick* spelling, old-fashioned though it was, an informal spelling. The spelling no longer occurs after 1768, when only the -*ic* spelling is found, of which the out-letters contain 87 instances. This suggests, as in the case of *farther* and other spellings such as monosyllables ending in double *t*, that the process of obsolescence progressed from a form's general acceptability to usage in informal contexts (including private usage in draft letters) and its eventual disappearance.

A few remaining spelling variants are worth mentioning here. The modern form *show* makes its single appearance in 1778 in a – formal – letter to Sir Joshua Reynolds: Lowth's regular spelling is *shew* (also *shewed/shewing/shewn*), of which I found 24 instances altogether. The *OED* marks *shew* as 'also dial.', but Lowth's letters suggest that the spelling was still quite common despite the fact that Johnson in his *Dictionary* prescribed *show*. The in-letters confirm this: the instances with *shew* outdo the modern form by two to one. It is striking that Reynolds used *show* in his letter to Lowth from 7 November 1778. Lowth's only instance of this form occurs in a reply to this letter of two days later. This confirms Lowth's sensitivity to what would appear to him to be prestigious patterns of usage, that of members of the aristocracy. Lowth, moreover, varies between *(dis)agreable* (26 instances) and *(dis)agreeable* (9 instances). Though the spelling with double <ee> is the one preferred in PDE, and was indeed prescribed by Johnson, Lowth clearly preferred the old-fashioned form (the *OED* unfortunately does not offer a spelling history of the word). Though the modern form also occurs in his informal letters, it is striking that Lowth consistently wrote *(dis)agreeable* in his fairly formal correspondence with Michaelis.

As a final instance of variation: we now associate spelling variants in *-ise/ize* or *-our/or* with the different spelling systems operating in British and American English. Lowth varies in his letters between both forms, and if we focus on two verbs, *authorise* and *surprise*, we can see that though he prefers forms in *-ise* (9) to those in *-ize* (4), the preference does not correlate with relative formality of style: both *authorized* and *authorised* occur in formal letters, while *surprize* is found in formal and informal letters alike. As for the *-our/or* spellings, the forms in *-our* far outnumber those in *-or*. I came across only two words showing variation: *candor/candour* and *honor/honour*. With a distribution of 7 to 2, Lowth clearly preferred the form *candor*, in formal and informal letters alike, while the only instance of *honor* (as against 11 with *-our*) occurred in a draft letter. Johnson's dictionary prescribed *candour* as well as *honour*, and this is how the words are spelled in British English today. In the light of Lowth's other spelling habits, *honor* can be called an informal spelling which was clearly no longer current, while his preference for *candor* was perhaps an idiosyncratic one. A similar case, from a present-day perspective, is the word *center*, which occurs twice in what would now be considered the American spelling of the word (*centre* was not found). Johnson's dictionary prescribed *centre*. It is clear that it never occurred to Lowth to consult Johnson's dictionary for these instances, despite the fact that he owned a copy of the work.

Lowth's single instance of *show* suggests conscious influence from a member of his social network, and from one he considered by that time, as Bishop of London, to be of similar social status. Such an instance of conscious change is known as 'change from above' (Labov 1994: 78). Another case of influence from the language of members of his social network is the following. In Lowth's correspondence, the modern standard spelling of the word *immediately* is first found from 1768 onwards in his letters to Ridley, someone who has been categorized as a friend. Altogether, I found 40 instances of the word, 28 spelled without the intermediate <e> (*immediatly*) and 12 with. Unfortunately, no spelling variation for this word has been recorded in the *OED*, but the spelling was also common with, for instance, James Boswell (Tieken-Boon van Ostade 1996c). In the in-letters, only the spelling *immediately* occurs. Lowth first started to vary between the two forms in his letters to Ridley (2 without <e> in 1768 and 5 with). He would have encountered the modern spelling in letters dating from around this time written by the Archbishop of Canterbury (1765, 1766), Samuel Hallifax (1765), and Pelham-Holles (1766). As the language of the Archbishop of Canterbury and the Duke of Newcastle represented that of the social class to which Lowth aspired in those days, he would likewise have considered their usage prestigious enough to adopt it. This is therefore another instance of change from above affecting his usage.

6.5 SPECIAL LEXIS

In Section 5.2, I noted that different topics were discussed by Lowth in letters to different correspondents. To begin with, there is the advancement of his career in the Church and the well-being of his family in the letters to his wife, while other topics are his controversy with Warburton in the letters to Warburton himself, to some of his own friends, and to the Archbishop of Canterbury, the publication of his books in letters to the Dodsleys and one or two printers, the administration of the inheritance of Joseph Spence and of his wife's guardian Thomas Cheyney in letters to

Glocester Ridley and Samuel Speed respectively, the exchange of presentation copies with several of his acquaintances, old and new ones, scholarly matters, such as the editing of Merrick's translation of the Psalms and the publication of Michaelis's translation, in instalments, of the Bible, Church affairs, such as suggestions for preferment, to which he replied, in letters on the subject by Samuel Johnson and James Beattie, and his efforts at learning German, which he reported on in his correspondence with Johann David Michaelis.

Special topics require specialized lexis, and in some cases even what Görlach (2001: 153) calls 'occupational jargon'. Particularly his more scholarly letters are full of such lexis, and some examples are: *Deuteronomy, Genesis, Pentateuch,* and *Septuagint; Alexandrium, Anthiochene, Aramæan, Egyptian, Heliopolitan,* and *Syriac; apostrophe* and *preposition; collate/ collating/collation(s); dialect(s)* and *language(s); orient(al);* and various words for library, *bibliotheca, bibliothek(e), Bibliotheque.* Primarily, such words express his concerns as a biblical scholar and philologist. The word *grammar* occurs seventeen times in his correspondence altogether, though in fifteen cases it refers to his own grammar, in which case the word is part of his correspondence with the Dodsleys. The word *lexicon* occurs twice, once in a letter to Michaelis and once to Merrick, who, though I have classified him as a friend, was also a fellow scholar. Where lexis is concerned, it is hard to work with discrete categories in this respect. The word *dictionary* similarly occurs in more categories than in that of the letters to fellow scholars alone: on one occasion, in a letter to Robert Dodsley, Lowth refers to Johnson's *Dictionary* on a spelling issue, and twice he informs Michaelis of the use he has been making of his German dictionary, which is not exactly a scholarly reference in the sense of the words listed earlier. Thirteen of the fourteen instances of the word *German* in the correspondence were found in the letters to Michaelis: this clearly reflects a significant topic in the exchange of letters between the two men; WordSmith consequently designates it as a keyword. Lowth's correspondence contains a single instance of the word *Spanish*: in a letter addressed to Robert Darley Waddilove, chaplain to the British ambassador in Madrid, he wrote: 'I am become a dabbler in Spanish' (Lowth to Waddilove, 16 September 1774). All this confirms his interest in languages, an interest that is typical of Lowth the philologist.

Professional jargon is also found in Lowth's letters to his publishers and printers. I have already referred to the frequency of his use of *grammar* in these letters. Words exclusively found in these letters are *copper plate, corrector, fables* (Robert Dodsley published a collection of them, to which Lowth contributed as well), *frontispiece, imagery, italicks* (the one instance of *italics* occurs in the printed letter to Brown), *outworks*, and *proof sheets*. A good example illustrating this type of professional lexis comes from the following letter:

(25) Last Month my Affairs were entirely at a stand for three weeks: my **Composer** was crippled with the Rhumatism, my **Corrector** taken ill of the Smallpox, & my principal agent forced to fly from it. They are hard at work now, & promise me to finish with all possible expedition: every thing is **printed off**, but the **Outworks, Contents, Index** &c.; & I believe I may depend upon being ready to **publish** early next Month. I find my Expenses will rise higher than I imagined; & they tell me at Oxford that I cannot afford to sell under 12^s. unbound: I suppose You will allow me 10^s. I will order them to be sent according to your directions (Lowth to Robert Dodsley, 16 January 1753).

The word *Outworks* has no entry in the *OED*. Other words regularly, though not exclusively, found in this selection of letters are *advertise/advertisement/ advertising, appendix(es), book(s), bookseller, copy/copies/copys, dedication, preface, drawing(s), edition(s), engrave/engraver/engraving, errata, bound* (collocating particularly with *handsomely* and *neatly* but also occurring in the phrases *bound & letter'd* and *bound together*), *plate(s), print, spell/ spelling,* and *subscribed/subscriber(s)*. A particularly interesting word is *presents*, as in:

(26) Pray send by the first opportunity one of my Books (sow'd) to the Revd. Mr. Ridley at Rumford Essex: I forgot him in my List. Are all y^e. **Presents** deliver'd? (Lowth to Robert Dodsley, 7 March 1753).

In Chapter 5, I discussed the importance of presentation copies in Lowth's attempts at coalition building; in turn, he received many such 'presents' himself. The word occurs nineteen times in this particular selection of letters; in the larger correspondence, the word collocates ten times in the singular with *kind* and twenty times with *of*, as in:

(27) Accept of my best thanks for your **kind present** of your Life of Bathurst, and the pleasure it has given me in the perusal (Lowth to Thomas Warton, 28 June 1761).

(28) And it is above a year ago, that I was honoured with a **Present of** Your very elegant & ingenious Work on the Song of Solomon.

I received it from Dodsley according to your orders soon after it was published, & should then have returned You my best thanks for it, had I known Your direction (Lowth to Percy, 3 July 1765).

Lowth is not alone in using the word: a note has come down to us from Sir Joshua Reynolds acknowledging the receipt of a presentation copy of Lowth's *Isaiah*:

(29) Sir Joshua Reynolds presents his most respectfull Compliments to the Bishop of London, and begs leave to return his thanks for the very flattering **present** which he has had the honour of receiving from His Lordship.

        Leicesterfields   Nov 4th 1778.

It thus warrants an entry in the *OED* in this specialized sense.

Apart from occupational jargon, Görlach (2001: 150–2) also distinguishes 'upper-class jargon and "low" words'. As 'low' words Görlach, quoting McKnight and Emsley (1928: 412), lists *banter, cocksure, dumbfound, doodle, enthusiasm, extra, flimsy, flippant, flirtation, fun, gambling, hanker, helter-skelter, humbug, jilt, kidney, mob, nervous, noodle, palming, pell-mell, prig, quandary, shabby, sham, shuffle, topsy-turvy, touchy, turtle,* and *twang.* Tucker (1967), in her study of eighteenth-century vocabulary, lists several more, including intensifiers like *confoundedly, cursedly,* and *damnable.* From Görlach's selection, Lowth's entire correspondence included no more than two, *fun* and *kidney.* The latter word, however, only occurs in Lowth's letters to his wife with reference to the bodily organ, in which case it is unlikely to be a 'low' word. McKnight presumably referred to the use of *kidney* as in *a man of my kidney,* i.e. 'type', though Johnson doesn't mark the word as low. Johnson does, however, label *fun* as 'a low cant word'. It need therefore come as no surprise that the only instance of the word occurs in a letter to Spence, who, apart from Dashwood, appears to have been his closest friend. The context in which the word occurs illustrates this:

(30) To compleat all & to put him effectually to shame, I w^{d}. refer to your <u>Book & your Name: but in this I will be directed by you</u>. I shall not spare him & depend upon it, I w[ill] give him two or three **jerks** extraordinary for your sake. <u>I have some **Fun** wth. him; but I don't enjoy half</u> of it for want of a Friend to laugh with over it. **I wish You were here.** Let me hear from You soon (Lowth to Joseph Spence, 10 June 1765).

Spence was clearly a friend Lowth could have a laugh with, and he missed his presence at this time. The only other person to whom he expressed similar feelings of longing was his wife. The above quotation also highlights the word *jerks*, which has a particular colloquial ring to it. If the word means 'lash of sarcasm, cutting jibe', Lowth's use here represents a post-dating to the history of the word provided by the *OED*.

In his letters, Lowth didn't use intensifiers of the kind mentioned by Tucker (1967); presumably, words like *cursedly* and *damnable* would be out of the question for a devoutly religious and socially ambitious man like him. This is not to say that he didn't use strong language: in his letters to Spence I encountered *brutal, scurrilous, shocked*, and *vile*, as the only such instances in the entire correspondence. No strong words occur in the letters to Dashwood, in which the strongest word I have encountered was *abhorrence*. The earliest letters, dating from 1748 and 1750, report on Lowth's travels on the Continent, and the topics Lowth dealt with relate to accounts of people he met or heard about and on whom he reproduced local gossip, operas he attended, and the excavations at Herculaneum. The letters to Dashwood are the only ones to contain lexis pertaining to music, such as *fidler*, the word *music(k)* itself, *Handel*, and *opera*. Even the word *bellows* is used in a musical context:

(31) there is no nobody that is eminent, nobody that has any name at all, nobody that is worthy to **blow the bellows to** M^r. Handel (Lowth to Dashwood, 25 April 1750).

The expression *blow the bellows to*, the meaning of which seems to be something like 'comes close in reputation to', has a particularly colloquial ring. The *OED* does not provide the expression, saying only that the compound *bellows-blower* may refer to 'an unskilled assistant whose part is merely mechanical like that of the blower of an organ' (*OED, bellows*). There are not many words that similarly suggest colloquial usage in the letters to Dashwood, apart perhaps from the verbs *reckon* and *vex*, the use of *charms*, and that of *unawares*, the only instance of which in the correspondence occurs in (32), which also illustrates the gossipy contents of the letters to Dashwood, as is confirmed by the change in tense from past to present:

(32) Before y^e. conclusion of the affair Barbarini repented of her bargain; she goes to y^e. King, throws herself at his feet, & begs his protection; in short, y^t. his Majesty would by his Authority release her from an

~~Obligation~~ Engagement & Bond, wch. Mr. Algaroti had drawn her into **unawares** (Lowth to Dashwood, 11 May 1748).

Strong language does occur in the letters to Warburton, and the following passage illustrates this. The underlining, doubled at times, is Lowth's own:

(33) You say, I had <u>grossly insulted</u> You in a Latin Note to the New Edition of my Lectures. The charge is absolutely False: unless <u>You</u> are y^e^. Author of a Book intitled, <u>A Free & Candid Examination of the B^p^. of London's Sermons</u>. But had <u>You</u> been y^e^. Author, where is the **gross insult**? As You declare, that You have not yet, & believe You never shall, read the Letter to <u>You</u>, wch. has lately been published by <u>Me</u>, (of wch. Concession You may make whatever use You please) I will ask You here, How come <u>Your</u> Opinions, even when vented by other persons as their own, to be **uncontrovertible, inviolable**, & sacred? And had such an Act of self-defence, as my Note here referred to was, really been an <u>insult</u>, had it been even a **gross** ^insult^ on an <u>inoffensive</u> person; how c^d^. it justly be esteemed such an One, who has in a manner so notorious, so **licentious**, & singularly **scandalous**, especially in one of his profession & order, abused Writers of all ranks & characters, civil & ecclesiastical, living & dead, as <u>You</u> have done? (Lowth to Warburton, 1 December 1765).

The words highlighted in (33), *gross* (inspired by the letter from Warburton to which Lowth replies), *inviolable, licentious, uncontrovertible,* and *scandalous,* occur only in this part of Lowth's correspondence. Other strong words only found there are *aggravate, atrociously, despise, detest, immoderate, indiscretion, infamously, inviolable, menaces, nonsense, overhauled, perverse(ness), presumptive, uncharitable, unsatisfactory, unworthy, violated,* and the like. In the light of the correspondence as a whole, Lowth's use of strong language to Warburton is truly exceptional. I will show below that Lowth also had other means of expressing his displeasure with his rival.

Cant and slang, two other lexical categories distinguished by Görlach (2001), I did not encounter in Lowth's letters, not surprisingly in view of his character, nor did I find any instances of malapropism: Lowth was too highly educated to be prone to such usage. Regional lexis, highly marked at the time according to Görlach (2001: 157), is hard to identify, and perhaps unexpected in the correspondence of a man like Lowth. I have, however, encountered many instances of words that are typical of Lowth's informal letters only, with a specific group of expressions that might be characterized as private language, as they are only found in the letters addressed to his wife or to his closest friends. I have, for instance, come across ten instances of (')*tother* in Lowth's letters, nine of which occur in an informal context (6 to his wife, and 1 each to Merrick, Percy, and Sturges). The remaining instance occurs in one of the early letters to Robert Dodsley. The word collocates with *day, night, time*, or *side*, as in:

(34) My Lord told me '**tother day**, that he had mention'd the Worcester Scheme to the Duke of Newcastle, who approves of it (Lowth to his wife, 6 May 1755).

The word was marked as a vulgarism in 1797 by Jonathan Burr in his *Compendium of English Grammar* (1797: 60), and the *OED* labels it as 'Now dial.'. The restricted use of this form by Lowth in his letters suggests that the development by which *tother* eventually became obsolete in Standard English may already have been in evidence in his time.

A rarer instance is what looks like a colloquial use of the verb *skip* in a letter to Dashwood:

(35) Lombardy has lost much of it glory in **being skip'd of** the two great Collections of Pictures, y^t. of Parma & Modena (Lowth to Dashwood, 25 April 1750).

The expression *being skipped of* refers to the fact that the collections used to be there, but had, regrettably, been moved. Possibly, this sense comes closest to that in *OED* for *to skip* 2b, 'to hasten, hurry, move lightly and rapidly; to make off, abscond', but for which no eighteenth-century examples are given. The *OED* labels this sense as 'Now *colloq.*', but to me it seems that it was already so in Lowth's time. The same letter contains the following instance of what similarly looks like a colloquial use of the phrasal verb *hit off*:

(36) a Gentleman that saw it since observ'd some Letters upon it, wch. he was told no body could make out; he viewd it very narrowly, and with supplying a few Letters at the beginning, wch. I shall mark, is confident that he has **hitt it off** completely & truly as follows: SILIGO C RANII E CICERE.

Though the *OED* lists the meaning 'to describe, represent, or reproduce successfully or to a nicety' for *hit off* (*hit* v. 25c), which fits the context of

(36) very well, it doesn't mark its use as informal, which it clearly was here. The verb *hit(t)* does not occur elsewhere in Lowth's letters (nor in the in-letters). A similar case is Lowth's use of the idiomatic expression *put to the blush*, as in:

(37) If he writes to the Bp. in the same style, I think he will **put** his Lordsh^P. a little **to the blush** (Lowth to his wife, 16 August 1755).

The *OED* does list it, with the sense 'put to shame' (*blush* n. 4.b), but its use by Lowth in a letter to his wife suggests colloquial usage at the time. A final example of a colloquialism in Lowth's correspondence is his use of the idiom *be upon the tramp*, as in (38):

(38) All this Morning I have^{been} **upon the tramp** (Lowth to his wife, 24 April 1755).

This usage antedates the first quotation in the *OED* (sense 3b, 'on one's way from place to place on foot, esp. in search of employment, or wandering as a vagrant') by five years. All this shows that informal correspondence, like Lowth's letters to his closest friends or his wife, are a useful source of additional information for the *OED*.

Example (39), also from a letter to his wife, is similarly of interest, though it provides a post-dating to the information in the *OED*, rather than an antedating, as in the case of (38):

(39) my affairs seem to be at a dead stand, **without** we can turn this offer to some advantage (Lowth to his wife, 15 March 1755).

There are no such instances in Lowth's other letters, nor, indeed, in the in-letters. The *OED* writes about the use of *without* as a conjunction ('unless') that it was 'Formerly common in literary use, most frequently with verb in subjunctive; later *colloq.* ("not in use, **except in conversation**" J[ohnson] 1755) or *arch.*, and now chiefly *illiterate* [sic]' (*without* C2). The reference to Johnson's label of the word confirms the approximation of Lowth's letters to his wife to actual conversation. The letters contain many instances that one would not come across outside the intimacy of such a private exchange of letters. Striking examples are *in your tomorrow's letter* (Lowth to his wife, 8 March 1755) and *the well-days* (Lowth to his wife, 27 May 1755), which refers to the fact that his wife was greatly advanced in her pregnancy. His use of the word *jant* seems to be a similar case:

(40) I have been a little sort of a **jant** these three days (Lowth to his wife, 7 August 1755).

The form only occurs in the *OED* as an obsolete variant of the adjective *gent*, and Finegan (1998: 573) cites evidence to show that *gents* was considered a 'vulgarism' around the late nineteenth century, but the instance in (40) indicates that usage was already restricted in Lowth's time. All this suggests that this *OED* entry could be fruitfully revised, too. Lowth's use of *agreables*, in the sense of 'agreeable things', as in:

(41) I long to be with you, & can hardly persuade myself to sit to write **agreables** to tell you (Lowth to his wife, 16 July 1755),

provides an antedating to the *OED* by nearly sixty years.

Words that occur only in the letters to his wife are *wench* (9), which refers to the newborn baby and always collocates with *little*, *thrive* (4), *mama* (13), *papa* (2), and *biggin* (1), a type of children's cap. Such words would hardly have a function outside a family correspondence. The word *love* (81) likewise mostly occurs in the letters to his wife (75), as in *Dearest Love* and *Love to all*. Not surprisingly, the word *dearest* (130) is found only there, too, usually collocating with *my* and *Molly* (92). The closing formula *adieu* (7) is similarly restricted as an address form to his wife: this agrees with usage in the correspondence of John Gay, who only used it once to address a very close friend, while Wesley did similarly (Tieken-Boon van Ostade 1999: 104). I think, therefore, that usage of *adieu* around this time reflects particular closeness, more so than is suggested by the *OED* (which, however, lacks an eighteenth-century example). Another usage that is typical of Lowth's most informal language is the word *folks*, as in:

(42) I left the Lewisham **folks** very well yesterday (Lowth to his wife, 22 March 1755).

Four of the five instances encountered occurred in the letters to his wife, and the fifth in one of the more intimate letters to Samuel Speed. The *OED* notes that the word denotes 'the people of one's family, parents, children, relatives' and 'friends, intimates' (*folk* 4a and b), but the instance in (43) suggests that Lowth's private usage was wider than that:

(43) he has enquir'd here of Leslie's Character, and consulted some Principal **folks** (My L^d. Chancellor, &c) upon the propriety of his Promotion to a B.^{P}rick (Lowth to his wife, 10 May 1755).

There is very little truly intimate language in the letters between Lowth and his wife, except for the references to the breastfeeding of baby Molly:

(44) I am sure she is a good Girl by her taking to **sucking** so well (Lowth to his wife, 19 June 1755).

(45) How I shall long to hear that y^e. dear Tom is got quite well, & y^e. little Girl & her Mama after **weaning** (Lowth to his wife, 17 October 1755).

One striking feature, as an expression of affection, is Lowth's use of the diminutive *-kin* and the plural suffix combined with the definite article, as in:

(46) My Love to all in the Close & at home to y^e. little **Mollykin**, & y^e. Dear Boy Tom (Lowth to his wife, 13 August 1755).

(47) to leave **the Toms** behind for 2 months (Lowth to his wife, 19 October 1755).

Another feature of interest is his occasional use of the pronoun *thee*, which I found three times, but only in the letters to his wife:

(48) God bless & preserve **thee**, My Dearest Love, & grant us soon a happy meeting (Lowth to his wife, 27 May 1755).

The pronoun *thou/thee* was no longer in general use, except as in Richardson's novel *Clarissa*, where it is used to signal a male camaraderie between Lovelace and Belford (Stevick 1971: 61). Lowth, though, observed in his own grammar that it was no longer used 'in the Polite, and even in the Familiar Style' (1762: 48n). It is therefore striking that the pronoun could still be used to express extreme closeness between a husband and his wife.

As a final expression of affection I'd like to mention the occurrence of jokes, which we find in the letters to his wife, as in (49) and (50), but also in letters to friends, as in (51)–(53):

(49) I congratulate you on Tom's new Tooth: I suppose you expect I should insert so joyfull an event in the Gazette (Lowth to his wife, 8 March 1755).

(50) I suppose you have put her into the same quart pot that you stood in upright with the lid shut down. If she will but make as proper & as good a little woman I shall be quite satisfy'd (Lowth to his wife, 13 August 1755).

(51) The D. of Modena has not one piece of painting left; except his own Face (Lowth to Dashwood, 25 April 1750).

(52) At y^e. same time, I don't expect, that Authors of any kind, & especially You Poets, will once in twenty times regard what I say. But seriously, I am in my conscience persuaded ... that <u>Thou wert</u> in the Indicative is an Absolute Solecism (Lowth to Merrick, 4 May 1762).

(53) & if you will but allow me to be taller than you, your right [to the cane formerly owned by Spence] will be indisputable (Lowth to Ridley, 1 October 1768).

If making jokes may be interpreted as an expression of positive politeness, which thus characterizes the tone of Lowth's most intimate letters, the opposite of positive politeness, negative politeness, also features in the letters. In Section 5.4 I have already discussed the way in which the use of different types of epistolary formulas can function as such. But negative politeness is also evident in the use of particular words which are part of what McIntosh (1986) calls 'courtly-genteel prose'. Typical words that belong to this category are *deserve, duty, favour, goodness, honour, interest, merit, obligation, obliged, pleasure,* and *serve,* which according to McIntosh express a relationship between people that is reminiscent of the feudal age. The standard epistolary formula 'your most obedient humble Servant' (37 instances) that Lowth used in his less intimate letters is a good illustration of this type of language, and his variation upon this formula by adopting the word *affectionate* in order to signal greater intimacy shows deliberate attempts at expressing positive politeness. As shown, the opposite effect was produced by adopting extreme curtness, and writing 'your humble Servant' only.

But Lowth also exploited the effect which the greater or lesser use of courtly-genteel language could have in his letters. This may be illustrated by a comparison between letters of different degrees of intimacy, those to his close friend Dashwood (2,660 words), Michaelis, whom I have classified as a fellow scholar (8,100 words), and his enemy Warburton (6,500 words). While the letters to Michaelis contain 81 instances of courtly-genteel usage, *favour* (6), *honour* (41), *interest* (1), *obligation* (2), *obliged* (15), *pleasure* (15), *serve* (1), there are only 7 in the letters to Dashwood (2,660): *favour* (3), *goodness* (1), *obligation* (2), *pleasure* (1). When normalized to 1,000 words, this shows that Lowth's language is indeed characterized by greater politeness in the letters to Michaelis (10/1,000 words) than in those to Dashwood (2.6/1,000 words). In the letters to Warburton, however, he used not more but fewer courtly-genteel words: with a normalized frequency of only 2.5 items per 1,000 words – *favour* (5), *deserve* (2), *honour* (3), *merit* (1), *obligation* (1), *obliged* (2), and *pleasure* (2) – Lowth's language can be classified as downright rude, a rare attitude for a man who, as I have already pointed out several times, was extremely status conscious and constantly strove not to step on anyone's toes.

6.6 SPELLING AS AN INDEX OF INTIMACY

Lowth's use of vocabulary in his letters confirms what we have learnt about him so far: in his contacts with fellow scholars he comes across as a philologist, while we also see him as a loving husband and as a man careful to avoid offence. Like the language of any speaker and writer, then as much as now, his choice of words reflects the topic of the letters he wrote as well as the person he addressed, and he knew how to exploit ways to express positive and negative politeness effectively, even showing the effect of refusal to observe the common rules of politeness. Warburton cannot have failed to notice Lowth's anger in the letters he received. If letters were to serve as a means of conversation between writer and addressee, as indeed the letter writing manuals of the time prescribed, according to Fens-de Zeeuw (2008), the varied use of lexis as it appears from my analysis of Lowth's correspondence suggests that this is how he conversed with the people that he was in touch with. His letters to his wife – along with those to his dearest friends such as Dashwood and Spence – illustrate this most closely, as appears from the fact that he once used the weak pronoun form *'m* in a letter addressed to her:

(54) let *'m* do what they please with me (Lowth to his wife, 7 August 1755).

Apart from its extreme rarity, the form is similar to the other short forms reflecting pronunciation discussed in Section 6.4. Normally, Lowth used either *them* (184 instances) or y^m. (47), the latter form only occurring, as usual, in his informal or draft letters (1 instance was found in a formal note as well). Today, *'m* is typical of spoken usage, and the instance in (54) suggests that this was true for the eighteenth century, too. Fitzmaurice's transcription of a letter by Charles Sackville, Earl of Dorset, addressed to his intimate friend Charles Montagu, similarly includes an instance of *'em* (Fitzmaurice 2008: 101, l.13), and the *OED* provides another example from an eighteenth-century letter.

There is nothing unusual in all this: the ability to use different vocabulary depending on topic or the nature of one's relationship with the addressee is merely characteristic of someone's fairly regular linguistic repertoire, even if it shows that Lowth was never very outspoken even in his most intimate letters. What is more striking is his spelling, which correlates to an important extent with the style of his letters such as I have defined it. His most formal letters are characterized by a spelling that lacks variation and that is virtually identical to that which we are used to finding in PDE. Osselton (1984) distinguishes two spelling systems for eighteenth-century English, an epistolary spelling and one found in printed texts. My analysis of Lowth's spelling suggests that the situation must have been more complicated than that, as Lowth's most private spelling habits, as attested in the letters to his wife, his closest friends, and his friends, as well as in his draft letters, show a degree of variation that is comparable to what modern sociolinguists usually identify for different speech styles, with the amount of variation from Standard English correlating with formality of style. This has come to light by my analysis of the letters as evidence of Lowth's communicative competence, which showed that they represent a full array of styles which he was able to deploy to the best possible effect.

My analysis has also brought to light that Lowth's spelling habits were not stable, but that they changed over the years, presumably as a result of his exposure to the different spelling habits of those he exchanged letters with. In this he was particularly sensitive to the language of those who were highly placed in society, and the developments in his spelling thus to a certain extent reflect change from above. One thing that struck me is that his spelling in the early letters to Robert Dodsley, whom I originally classified as a work-related contact on the basis of the letters' closing formulas, is identical to that of the later letters to him which date from the time when their relationship had developed into a distinctly closer one. Possibly, Lowth's spelling already anticipated the developing relationship, while his more positively polite closings of the later letters was still to follow as a means by which he could formally signify their increased closeness. Spelling variation in eighteenth-century letters by educated writers such as Lowth, sociolinguistically salient as I have shown it to be, can thus serve as an important means of gaining insight into the nature of the relationship between different correspondents. But Lowth's variation in different aspects of his letter writing was not limited to lexis and spelling: I will show in Chapter 7 that we will find the same phenomenon in his use of morphosyntax, my analysis of which will demonstrate that he deviated most from his own prescribed norms of grammatical correctness in his most informal letters.

LOWTH'S OWN USAGE AND THE GRAMMAR'S NORM OF CORRECTNESS

7.1 EIGHTEENTH-CENTURY USAGE PROBLEMS

S. A. Leonard's *Doctrine of Correctness in English Usage 1700–1800* (1929) contains an appendix in which he provides a list of topics which were the subject of debate among eighteenth-century grammarians and other writers on usage. The topics range from whether an expression like *cut a joke* was considered acceptable – it wasn't – to an inventory of writers in favour of or against the preverbal placement of *only* when it did not function as a clause modifier, as in:

(1) I **only** saw her yesterday.

This is a topic which still incites many speakers today (cf. Crystal's 'Grammatical Top Ten', 1995: 194), who argue that the correct version of the sentence in (1) is that in (2) because it is felt that as an adverb, *only* 'should be placed immediately next to the word it modifies' (Mittins et al. 1970: 58):

(2) I saw her **only** yesterday.

The items in Leonard's 'Topical Glossary', some 540 altogether, are classified into 20 major categories comprising usage problems with respect to agreement, redundancy, tense sequence, purism, national usage, and many other types. Of these items, Lowth is listed in 71 instances as the first grammarian to express his opinion on their acceptability, in 46 of which he heads the list of opponents and in 25 that of the advocates of a particular usage. In 4 instances – the use of *broke* and *wrote* as past participles, *you was*, and double negation – Lowth was not only the first to deal with the item in question, but he is also labelled as having 'possibly influenced a change in usage' (1929: 251). As already discussed, Leonard was wrong in attributing the disappearance of double negation to Lowth, and also in giving him credit for being the first to discuss it as a usage problem.

A more modern overview of usage problems discussed in eighteenth-century books on grammar is Sundby, Bjørge, and Haugland's *Dictionary of English Normative Grammar* (1991), already dealt with in detail in Chapter 4. According to this inventory, Lowth was not the first to condemn the use of *wrote* as a past participle either. As a usage problem it had previously been treated by James Harris in *Hermes* (1751), who wrote:

It would be well therefore, if all Writers, who endeavour to be accurate, would be careful to avoid a **Corruption**, at present so prevalent, of saying, *it was wrote*, for, *it was written*; *he was drove*, for, *he was driven*; *I have went*, for, *I have gone*, &c. in all which instances a Verb is **absurdly** used to supply the proper Participle, without any necessity from the want of such Word (1751: 186n).

Lowth was familiar with Harris's work, and he presumably found this stricture in *Hermes*. Though he doesn't actually quote Harris in his section on problems relating to the forms of irregular verbs, he similarly used fairly strong words of condemnation, including the words *corruption* and *absurdity* highlighted in the above quotation from Harris (Lowth 1762: 89–90), so the link between the two is fairly clear. Problems with the use of *broke* – and other verbs – as a past participle were discussed in the same section in Lowth's grammar, and here Lowth is indeed credited by Sundby et al. as the first to condemn the form. But whether he actually influenced a change in usage is hard to say. Other grammarians adopted his strictures in this respect, such as Coote (1788: 123), who frequently referred to Lowth in his grammar and provided the same examples from Milton and Addison, though with many others besides. Murray (1795: 68–73) similarly prescribed *written* and *broken*, and current usage in Standard English may be the result of the combined influence of the grammarians from the 1760s onwards.

A different case is the change in usage with respect to *you was*, apparently proscribed by Lowth for the first time and in no uncertain terms ('an enormous Solecism', 1762: 147n). An earlier grammar cited by Sundby et al. (1991) is Fisher (second edition 1750), which includes *you is* among the examples of bad English provided in the grammar. It is, however, unlikely that Lowth picked up this stricture from Fisher's grammar, as I doubt if he was familiar with the work. As for the possible influence of Lowth's strong condemnation of *you was*, I have identified a sharp decrease in usage immediately after the publication of the grammar. This decrease is all the more striking because it follows a steep rise in frequency of the construction during the 1750s. All this is shown in Figure 7.1, which presents data I collected from forty-four eighteenth-century novels by sixteen different writers, male as well as female, included in the Chadwyck-Healey Eighteenth-Century Fiction Full-Text Database (1996); for details, see Tieken-Boon van Ostade (2002*b*). The decrease is so striking that Lowth's grammar as a source of influence seems very likely, given its enormous popularity at the time. This is not to say that *you was* disappeared altogether, but its relegation to non-standard registers seems the direct result of its stigmatization by Lowth in his grammar. The evidence from the language of William Clift (1775–1849), a surgeon's apprentice originating from Cornwall, during the early years of his stay in London confirms this (Austin 1994: 290–2).

Sundby et al. (1991) do not mention Lowth as the first to condemn the misplacement of *only*, unlike Burchfield in his third edition of Fowler's *Modern English Usage* (1996: 551), who does. But though Burchfield refers to the first edition of Lowth's grammar, the stricture only first occurred in the second, like those on the use of double negation and double comparatives. Sundby et al. did not include the 1763 edition in their survey, having failed to notice its significant extension since the first edition had been published. The added stricture reads: 'The Adverb, as its name imports, is generally placed close or near to the word, which it modifies or affects; and its propriety and force depend on its position' (1763: 138–9). It is accompanied by a footnote in which examples of mistakes in the placement of the

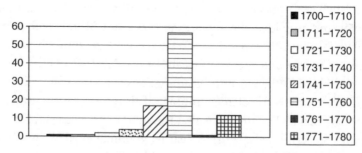

FIG. 7.1. *You was* in eighteenth-century novels (Tieken-Boon van Ostade 2002*b*: 95)

adverb are corrected. The example from Dryden that Lowth provides there is, according to Sundby et al., found in two later grammars, Bell (1769: 309) and Murray (1787: 138), and in one other work called *English Grammatical Exercises* (Alderson 1795: 142). The addition to Lowth's second edition is part of the elaboration of the passage on adverbs in the syntax section of the grammar, about which he had merely written in the first edition that 'ADVERBS have no Government' (1762: 126). The fuller section also came to comprise the passage on double negation.

The case of *only* may serve as an example of the main question addressed in this chapter as to the relationship between the norm of correctness which Lowth presented in his grammar and his own usage. Aitchison (1981: 23–4) suggests that Lowth's rules were based on his 'personal stylistic preferences', which I interpreted as a mere assumption made due to Lowth's iconic status as a prescriptivist. If we look at the use of *only* in his letters, we see that he showed only a slight preference for the 'proper' placement of *only*, 'close or near to the word, which it modifies or affects', and that Aitchison's statement thus barely holds water.

I have come across twenty-seven instances of the type of construction illustrated by (3), as against twenty, or 43 per cent, of the other variant, as in (4):

(3) they publish **only** Daniel, as an Anecdote (Lowth to Michaelis, 22 October 1770).

(4) I **only** note the most obvious & y^e. most necessary (Lowth to James Dodsley, 9 December 1767).

Nor is the less acceptable of the two constructions, the one in (4), which should have read 'I note **only** the most obvious…', more common in his most intimate letters, as we might expect on the basis of the findings presented in Chapter 6: there, the distribution is virtually identical to the pattern of usage in the letters generally, with 42 per cent of instances that are not considered acceptable by the prescriptive grammarians. The stricture as such thus neither correlates with his own usage, nor is Lowth's deviance of his own rule of correctness in this respect only attested in his informal usage. In this chapter I will demonstrate that the case of *only* is no exception. By analysing a variety of grammatical constructions that came to be formulated as linguistic strictures, both in his own grammar and in the course of the developing canon of prescriptivism, I will argue that Lowth's norm of correctness was not so much based on his own usage but that he must have found it elsewhere. My analysis of Lowth's use of grammar in his informal letters will show that, as in the case of his spelling, his private usage is characterized by features that would be proscribed in the centuries to come, largely as a result of the strictures in his own grammar that were formulated in increasingly prescriptive terms by his followers.

7.2 LOWTH'S LINGUISTIC AWARENESS

Lowth's letters contain a number of self-corrections. These are of particular interest in that they can be used as an index to his awareness with respect to certain usages at the time. I have already discussed several of them, a change of -*ed* into '*d* as the latter seemed more appropriate to the style of an informal letter he was writing, and of *you* into *You* in order to express greater politeness. One that is grammatically relevant is the following:

(5) I should be very glad to contribute any assistance, that ~~lays~~ **lies** in my power (Lowth to Merrick, 30 December 1761).

Lowth nowhere else in his letters confuses the two verbs, but it is interesting all the same to see that he nearly did so here, and also that the slip occurred in a letter to a friend. He did not bother to make a copy of the letter so that he could have refrained from incriminating himself linguistically in the eyes of Merrick. Perhaps this shows that confusion of *lie* and *lay* wasn't considered a shibboleth yet, but merely a grammatical mistake, the result of a 'frequent confounding', as he wrote in the grammar (1762: 76n), of two closely related verbs. A similar case is the confusion between the verbs *to fly* and *to flee*, on the differences between which he had expounded in a letter to the would-be publisher of the grammar, Robert Dodsley (see §3.1). Yet he would mix up the two verbs himself as well, as is clear from the following quotation:

(6) my Composer was crippled with the Rhumatism, my Corrector taken ill of the Smallpox, & my principal agent forced to **fly** from it (Lowth to Robert Dodsley, 16 January 1753).

This grammatical mistake, as he was to see it later, dates from before he had started on the grammar. Two other interesting self-corrections are the following:

(7) wch. I have not had time of late to consider. ~~them~~ (Lowth to Merrick, May 1762).

(8) And this is a grievous Consequence of such a ~~xxx~~ marriage, $^{\text{wch. you have}}$ $^{\text{not mentioned}}$ y^{t}. y^{e}. Issue ~~are~~ is liable to be declared Illegitimate (Lowth to Roberts, 20 November 1775).

In (7), Lowth corrected what would have been a double object construction, not untypical of spoken usage, and in (8) he was clearly confused as to the grammatical status of the word *issue*, which might refer to more than one child born of the marriage discussed. 'A Noun of Multitude, or signifying many', he had written in his grammar, requires a plural verb (1762: 104–5). In the event, Lowth appears to have decided that *issue* was different from a word like *mob*, for which he did recommend a verb in the plural.

In contrast to the *lie/lay* confusion, double negation was a linguistic shibboleth at the time, as this is the only explanation I could find for the fact that the eighteenth-century normative grammarians include a stricture against its use in their grammars despite the fact that it was no longer characteristic of relatively educated usage (Tieken-Boon van Ostade 2008*b*). It is, again, no coincidence that the only instance of double negation in Lowth's letters occurred in a letter to one of his closest friends, and that it never made its appearance again. Usage of double negation would have been inappropriate for someone with Lowth's social aspirations. He did not use any double comparatives either, but there is one case which suggests that he was trying to avoid the stigmatized *lesser*:

(9) The Appendix I suppose you will print on a **less** Letter (Lowth to Robert Dodsley, 24 February 1758).

Less is used here in the sense of 'smaller', and *lesser* would have been more appropriate, but in view of Johnson's condemnation of the word, which, as discussed in Section 4.3, Lowth himself fully endorsed in his grammar, he presumably thought it prudent to avoid the form altogether. In effect, he thus produced an instance of hypercorrection as a result.

The following instance similarly smacks of hypercorrection, though it isn't:

(10) We have lost our good Friend D^{r}. Chapman, **than whom** no man had better pretensions to long life (Lowth to Robert Dodsley, 19 June 1760).

The problem with the use of *than whom* here is the question of whether *than* functions as a conjunction or as a preposition. In the latter case, the pronoun following should have the oblique form, as in (10), and in the former the nominative form. In his grammar, though only in its second edition, Lowth argued in favour of *than* being a preposition: 'the Relative *who*,...when it follows *than*, is always in the objective Case' (1763: 159–60). In this light, stilted though it seems today, the form in (10) is entirely correct, and it is interesting to see that it occurs in a letter to Robert Dodsley dating from the time when Lowth was engaged on his grammar. As in the case of his discussion of the *fly/flee* problem in an earlier letter to Dodsley, Lowth seemed anxious at this time to present himself to his publisher as an expert on grammar. The construction occurs nowhere else in his letters, neither with *whom* nor with *who*, nor did any of his correspondents use it. His other pronouns always occur in their correct case form in the letters as well, as one might expect from someone raised as a classical scholar. The general rareness of the *than whom* construction is commented on by Görlach (1997: 283), who also notes that Lowth was the first to include the stricture in his grammar. The stricture is similarly found in Murray's grammar, based, as usual, on Lowth. It is, however, striking that the stricture doesn't occur until the fourth edition of Murray's grammar, published in 1798, which shows that, like Lowth, Murray continued to revise his grammar. It is also striking that in the sixth edition consulted by Görlach, Murray had added: 'The phrase *than whom* is, however, avoided by the best modern writers' (1800: 75, as quoted by Görlach 1997: 284). Comments on the construction, according to Görlach, became rare after 1860; for all that, it did not cease to be part of the prescriptive canon, for it is still included in Partridge's *Usage and Abusage* (1965: 339).

Lowth's linguistic awareness, as I argued in Section 6.1, is also evident from his increased use of the subjunctive, though this waned when the immediate effect created by the grammar and its popularity was less acutely felt. But Lowth could also produce grammatical mistakes, that is, in the light of his own prescriptions. One such error was produced in the heat of the moment, when he was engaged in his vehement argument with Warburton. In the final letter between the two men, dated 24 January 1766, Lowth had written:

(11) I now in My turn desire, that You would consent **to my publishing Your part of the said Correspondence** together with my own.

This is how the sentence appeared in the printed version of the letter, as published by Warburton in *The Second Part of a Literary Correspondence, between the Bishop of Gloucester and a Late Professor of Oxford* (Warburton 1766?: 15). The draft version of the letter suggests that Lowth originally intended to write '... give me leave to publish Your part of it' but that he changed the sentence into one containing a gerund:

(12) I now ^{in} My turn desire, that You would ^{consent} ~~give me leave~~ to ^{my} publish^{ing} Your part of ^{the} ~~it~~ $^{said\ Correspondence}$ together with my own.

However, by his own account of the gerund in the grammar, the resulting sentence is an example of the kind of construction he would normally have aimed to eradicate:

The Participle, with an Article before it, and the Preposition *of* after it, becomes a Substantive, expressing the action itself which the Verb signifies: as, 'These are the Rules of Grammar, by *the observing of* which you may avoid mistakes.' Or it may be expressed by the Participle, or Gerund; 'by *observing* which:' not, 'by *observing of* which;' nor, 'by *the observing* which:' for either of these two Phrases would be a confounding of two distinct forms (1762: 111–14).

He illustrated the rule with an example from Addison, 'the best authority', he wrote, but his own error shows the difficulty of putting the rule, simple though it might have appeared to Lowth as a grammarian, into actual practice. The problem with the gerund as Lowth described it is that the present participle has both nominal and verbal characteristics depending on the grammatical context in which it occurs. Confusion, therefore, is only to be expected, and Görlach (2001: 115) in his introduction to eighteenth-century English confirms that this was indeed common practice, even in the next century. But it is interesting to notice such confusion also in the language of a grammarian like Lowth, who tried to formulate clear rules for the correct use of the construction and who commented that 'there are hardly any of our Writers, who have not fallen into this inaccuracy' (1762: 112n).

The instance in (12) is not exceptional: upon searching Lowth's letters for the occurrence of the gerund after the definite article as well as after possessive pronouns, I found that what Lowth referred to as 'a confounding of two distinct forms' was fairly common practice in his own language: out of 37 instances, only 8 took the required form, as illustrated by (13) and (14):

(13) But is not **the taking of** Harmon in a Metaphorical, & Zion in a proper sense...a greater inconvenience than that wch. it designs to remove (Lowth to Merrick, 30 December 1761).

(14) particularly with a view to **the reconciling** ^of the Dissenters to the Church of England (Lowth to Michaelis, 12 April 1773).

We find the correct form in his formal letters but also in those to his wife and his closest friends, and, conversely, the form which he criticized in the grammar in his informal and formal letters alike, as illustrated by (15) and (16).

(15) He told me he had heard from the Dean, & just mention'd **his preferring** the Worcester Scheme to the other (Lowth to his wife, 8 June 1755).

(16) & see if I am chargeable with the absurd reasoning, **the mistaking** y^e. question, y^e. misrepresentations...wch. you impute to me (Lowth to Warburton, 6 October 1756).

But example (14) is of particular interest in that the construction in its final form is the result of a self-correction, the insertion of *of* upon rereading the sentence. This confirms Lowth's linguistic awareness already commented on. Görlach (2001: 115) notes that Lowth's 'guidance does not appear to have had much influence', and in PDE (13) would simply read *taking Harmon in a metaphorical sense*, while in (14) the noun *reconciliation* would probably be used rather than the gerund.

7.3 GRAMMAR AND EPISTOLARY STYLE

If Lowth has gone on record – at least according to Leonard (1929) – as the first to condemn the use of *broke* and *wrote* as participles, the following examples from his letters may seem surprising, as they illustrate that he used these forms himself:

(17) It [a statue] was found at the Theatre, where there was the Fellow to it, wch. was **broke** all to pieces (Lowth to Dashwood, 25 April 1750).

(18) I have accordingly **wrote** to Leasinby (Lowth to Ridley, 2 January 1769).

Both Dashwood and Ridley belong to the categories of addressees to whom Lowth wrote informal letters (Close friends, Friends), so the question arises as to whether the proscribed forms *broke* and *wrote*, and perhaps others as well, similarly correlate with formality of style as his use of informal spelling discussed in Chapter 6. To investigate this, I collected all non-standard participial forms listed by Oldireva Gustafsson (2002*a*: 304), combined with the list of forms condemned by Lowth in the footnotes on pages 86–8 of the first edition of his grammar. The results show that he regularly used non-standard forms, and also that they all occurred in his informal letters only. I found as many as 13 instances of participial *wrote* (10 instances to his wife, and 1 each to Chapman, Dashwood, and Ridley), compared to 27 instances of *written*. In addition to participial *broke* (1 instance to Dashwood), the letters produced *drove* (1 instance to his wife), *spoke* (1 instance to his wife), and even *went* (1 instance to his wife):

(19)   The ship wch. I was to have **went** in today did not sail for want of a
       fair wind (Lowth to his wife, 14 October 1755).

Example (19) is the only such instance I have come across in the letters, which otherwise produced *gone* (27) or *come* (34), which he might have used instead. Participial *went* must have been a common form, for it was condemned by Harris, as is shown by the quotation from *Hermes* in Section 7.1. To find it in Lowth's letters to his wife is therefore not surprising, as the letters contain other instances of the forms condemned by Harris, such as participial *drove* and *wrote*. A form similar in its frequency to *wrote* is *forgot*, as in:

(20)   as I had *forgot* to do it before I sent it to you (Lowth to Robert
       Dodsley, 17 October 1757).

The letters, formal and informal ones alike, produced 14 instances. The form *forgotten* was attested only once, in a formal letter from 1781, so *forgot* seems to be his preferred form irrespective of style of writing. In his grammar, Lowth doesn't discuss this verb (nor did Murray thirty years later), but as for the simplex verb *get* he does provide *gotten*, he may also, by analogy, have considered *forgotten* to be the correct participle to use. This suggests a mismatch between precept and practice in his own language. Oldireva Gustafsson (2002*a*: 304) found 3 instances of *forgott* down to 1710 and none after that, so Lowth's preference for the short form appears to have been quite idiosyncratic.

Apart from the use of *broke* as a past participle, example (17) also illustrates a different distribution in Lowth's letters of the auxiliaries *be* and *have* with mutative intransitive verbs. Rydén and Brorström (1987) show that this was the case for eighteenth-century English in general, for which, on the basis of their analysis of letters and plays, they report a frequency of *have* with the verbs *alter, (a)rise, arrive, become, change, come, elapse, enter, escape, fall, flee/fly, get* (in different senses), *go, grow, improve, pass, recover, return, run,* and *turn* that amounts to only 25.7 per cent in relation to that of *be* with the same verbs. For the nineteenth century, they report the opposite, 72.1 per cent of *have*. (The figures for letters only are fairly similar.) Not all these verbs occur in Lowth's letters, but an analysis of those that do shows an even lower relative frequency of *have*: only 15 per cent was found to occur with *have* (17 instances), the overwhelming majority having a form of *be* (97 instances), as, indeed, in example (17) above. The most frequently attested mutative intransitive verbs in the letters are *arrive* (4 with *have*, 8 with *be*), *come* (3 with *have*, 30 with *be*), *get* (1 with *have*, 10 with *be*), and *go* (3 with *have*, 10 with *be*). Examples are the following sentences:

(21) to say something more to you than just that I **was arriv'd** here (Lowth to Dashwood, 11 May 1748).

(22) Your Papers **are** now **come** safe (Lowth to Speed, 10 November 1766).

(23) I din'd with them, & **am** now **gott** to mine Host's (Lowth to his wife, 1 March 1755).

(24) he I believe **is** now **gone** to Bath (Lowth to James Dodsley, 8 November 1763).

All this at first sight suggests that Lowth's usage was conservative in relation to the development described by Rydén and Brorström, but when correlated with the style of the letters, the situation proves to be quite different. With 2.42 and 1.1 instances per 1,000 words respectively, mutative intransitive verbs are most frequently construed with *be* as the auxiliary of the perfect in Lowth's letters to his wife and to his close friends, the remaining categories of letters varying between 0.39 and 0.75 instances per 1,000 words, as Figure 7.2 below illustrates. The raw figures for the occurrence of *have* in Lowth's letters are very low: only the letters to his friends have over 5 instances. (The peak for the bare acquaintances is deceptive: it reflects only one instance in 687 words.) If we separate the informal letters, those to his wife and his Close friends, from the rest, it appears that Lowth's usage generally was not conservative at all: with 12 instances of *have* against 39 altogether (*be* and *have* included), this comes down to a relative frequency of 31 per cent, which is not very different from that for the second half of the eighteenth century (33.2%), according to the figures in Rydén and Brorström (1987: 232). The data supplied by Rydén and Brorström are, however, of a rather diverse nature, comprising individual writers as well as collections of letters, with the letters of individual writers stretching well into the nineteenth century. All this makes their results hard to compare with my own data. Lowth's informal letters, and particularly those to his wife, do show a conservative usage with 6.6 per cent *have* (5 vs. 70 instances of *be*), which fits in well with the situation already described several times, both in relation to Lowth's spelling and to his usage of grammar in these letters: the informal letters are characterized by a very different usage from that discussed in the grammar or, in the case of spelling, from that of contemporary printed texts. Thus, even if his usage in these letters is conservative, the discrepancy with the rules in the grammar suggests little correspondence with his most informal private usage.

Rydén and Brorström (1987: 209) suggest that normative criticism against the usage of *be* with mutative intransitive verbs started, once again, with Lowth. The verbs in question are called 'Neuter' verbs, which Lowth defined in his grammar as verbs that 'signify some sort of motion, or

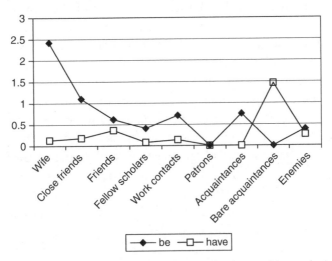

FIG. 7.2. Distribution of *be* and *have* with mutative intransitive verbs in Lowth's out-letters

change of place or condition', and as examples he gives *I am come, I was gone, I am grown,* and *I was fallen* (1762: 63), all of which are mutative intransitive verbs. From his discussion in the main text of the grammar, it appears that he accepted the use of *be* with these verbs, but in the footnote to the passage he expressed his doubt as to 'the propriety of the following examples', taken from Tillotson, Swift, and Atterbury, which contain the verbs *swerve, cease,* and *amount* along with a form of *be.* The third edition of the grammar, published in 1764, contains an additional example from Addison, with the verb *enter.* Lowth's disapproval of *be* with 'Neuter' verbs is thus not categorical, applying to a limited set of verbs only. Murray (1795) copied parts of Lowth's stricture, as found in the 1764 edition (or later), in different places of his grammar, on pages 67 and 113. In the latter instance an additional example occurs, with the verb *desert,* but Murray's formulation of the stricture has become more strictly prescriptive. While Lowth had merely written that he 'doubted much of the propriety' of the examples given, Murray wrote that they 'appear to be erroneous' (1795: 113). In a later edition of the grammar, published in 1818, Murray even added: '**It should be,** "have swerved, had ceased," &c.'. Lowth, who customarily corrected ungrammatical sentences in this way in his grammar, had refrained from doing so here, and this confirms his uncertainty with respect to the categorical unacceptability of *be* with mutative intransitive verbs, and this is mirrored by his own usage.

On the use of preposition stranding, Lowth was quite tolerant: as discussed in Chapter 4, he allowed for the use of the construction in more informal styles, spoken and written, noting that pied piping 'agrees much better with the solemn and elevated Style' (1762: 127–8). His own usage conforms to this, as I found by analysing his letters as to the occurrence of what Sairio (2008) calls 'high-frequency prepositions': *for, to, of, in, into, at, upon, from, by,* and *with.* To Sairio's list I added the prepositions *about, after, under,* and *without* as they are fairly frequent in the letters, too. For PDE, Huddleston and Pullum (2002: 627) distinguish a variety of constructions with preposition stranding and pied piping, showing that some of them favour while others disfavour preposition stranding. In the eighteenth-century this may have been the case, too. Lowth illustrated his discussion of preposition stranding with examples of relative clauses, adding: 'This is an Idiom which our language is strongly inclined to', a sentence which might occur with a zero relative, too. The present analysis focuses on sentences with *wh-* and zero relatives as well as *that,* sentences with embedded interrogatory *what,* and main clauses with prepositional complements. For the analysis, the formal notes have been left out of consideration as their language was shown to be very different from that of letters proper (see Chapter 5). Examples are the following:

(25) the Dear little Tom, **whom** I look **upon** . . . as quite restor'd to us from y^e. Dead (Lowth to his wife, 6 November 1755).

(26) one **for whom** I am much more concern'd (Lowth to Warburton, 6 October 1756).

(27) & Visitations of ye. Sick, **wch.** You ought to provide **for** by ye. Assistance of some Neighbouring Ministers (Lowth to Eastman, 24 March 1774).

(28) as I see by a Note to his French Translation, **for w^{ch}.** he quotes Synops, (Lowth to Dalrymple, 5 November 1782).

(29) such [a] one you hint **at** (Lowth to Roberts, 20 November 1775).

(30) I shall otherwise have no Copy to correct **by** (Lowth to Robert Dodsley, 24 February 1758).

(31) **by what** person in London his Correspondence with Hercules was carried on (Lowth to Ridley, 1 October 1768).

(32) **what** his Gold Watch is valued **at** (Lowth to Ridley, 31 August 1768).

(33) Christian Virtues sh^d. rather be enlarged **upon** (Lowth to Ridley, 2 August 1769).

(34) One or two of them I have still some little doubt **about** (Lowth to Merrick, 30 December 1761).

(35) hardly any **that** she w^d. look **upon** as desireable Furniture (Lowth to Ridley, 17 September 1778).

Only for *that* relative clauses did the corpus not yield any examples with pied piping, which suggests that preposition stranding, as in (35), was obligatory in such sentences then as much as now.

The results of my analysis are presented in Table 7.1. The raw data in the table show first of all that some propositions – *in, of, to, for,* and *with* – more readily occur in the kind of construction discussed here, while others were attested only fairly rarely (*from, under, about, at, after, into*) or not at all (*without*). They also show that preposition stranding is much less frequent than pied piping in the letters. Except for *into, under,* and

Table 7.1 Instances of preposition stranding and pied piping in Lowth's letters

Prepositions	Stranded	Pied piping	Total
*about/ab*ᵗ.	1	3	4
after	1	2	3
at	2	2	4
by	2	13	15
for	7	22	29
from	1	4	5
in	2	47	49
into	3	0	3
of	19	24	43
on	2	7	9
to	11	31	42
under	4	1	5
upon	13	5	18
with	13	14	27
*without/with*ᵗ.	0	0	0
Total	81 (32%)	175 (68%)	256

upon, moreover, pied piping is always preferred in the letters, while there is a fairly equal distribution between the two constructions only with the prepositions *at* and *with*.

If the occurrence of either construction is studied in the light of the addressee type, and hence in the different epistolary styles employed by Lowth, the picture shown in Table 7.2 emerges. (As Lowth's language to

Table 7.2 Instances of preposition stranding and pied piping according to addressee type (with $p < 0.025$, these differences are statistically significant)

Addressee	Preposition stranding		Pied piping		Total
Wife + son	25	53%	22	47%	47
Close friends	13	35%	24	65%	37
Friends	22	33%	44	67%	66
Fellow scholars	12	27%	32	73%	44
Work-related contacts	4	24%	13	76%	17
Patrons	2	17%	10	83%	12
Acquaintances	0	—	9	100%	9
Bare acquaintances	0	—	6	100%	6
Enemies	4	22%	14	78%	18
Total	82	32%	174	68%	256

Dodsley reflects relative closeness throughout their correspondence, despite changes in epistolary formula, I have classified him as a Friend here.) The figures in the table show that Lowth varied considerably in his use of the two constructions. Variation is even found within a single letter, as example (36) shows.

(36) You may possibly meet with some things wch. you cannot honestly approve **of**... with regard to the State & Variations of the H. MSS. **of w^{ch}**. the Learned are not well aware (Lowth to Woog, c.1753).

For all that, he always preferred the pied piping construction in his letters, irrespective of the addressee, except when he wrote to his wife, where we find a higher proportion of preposition stranding. In view of Lowth's comment in the grammar that preposition stranding 'prevails in common conversation, and suits very well with the familiar style in writing', this suggests that the letters to his wife more closely resemble conversation than those to his other correspondents, which agrees with my analysis of Lowth's use of lexis in these letters (§6.4). Usage of preposition stranding in the letters to his Close friends and Friends is similarly higher than average, as expected; that in the letters to his Enemies is almost identical to the figures for the letters to his Fellow scholars and Work-related contacts. Preposition stranding is rarest in the letters to his Patrons: these men represented the linguistic norm he strove after, and it is clear that his usage of this construction reflects this.

Sairio (2008) noticed on the basis of her analysis of the language of Elizabeth Montagu and her circle a decrease in preposition stranding across time, the variant of the construction that became stigmatized in the grammars of the period. Pied piping, on the other hand, increased considerably, even prior to the appearance of normative strictures in grammars like Lowth's. The question therefore presents itself as to whether such changing patterns of usage are also evident in Lowth's language. To this end, I subdivided his letters into five-year periods and classified the instances accordingly. The results are presented in Table 7.3.

The results are presented as absolute figures (N), normalized figures per one thousand words, and percentages indicating the relative occurrence of the one type of construction compared to the other. The smaller the size of the subcorpus in question, the less reliable the interpretation of the data is in view of the results as a whole; this is particularly true for the final time period, shortly before Lowth's death in 1787, when he wrote very few letters. No instances of either construction were recorded for this period.

Table 7.3 Distribution of preposition stranding and pied piping over five-year time periods of the letter corpus (with *p* < 0.03, these differences are statistically significant)

Period	Size	Preposition stranding			Pied piping			Total
		N	/1,000	%	N	/1,000	%	N
1748–52	2,500	2	0.8	40%	3	1.2	60%	5
1753–57	36,500	35	1	41%	51	1.4	59%	86
1758–62	12,800	11	0.9	32%	23	1.8	68%	34
1763–67	8,900	7	0.8	18%	33	3.7	82%	40
1768–72	11,700	15	1.3	36%	27	2.3	64%	42
1773–77	7,600	8	1.1	40%	12	1.6	60%	20
1778–82	9,425	3	0.3	10%	26	2.8	90%	29
1783–87	525	0	–	–	0	–	–	0
Total (c.90,000 words)		*81*	*0.9*	*32%*	*175*	*1.9*	*68%*	*256*

In Table 7.3, I have highlighted the figures that stand out in relation to the average figures for the letter corpus as a whole. This allows us to see that the use of preposition stranding indeed decreased over time, though this is only clear at the very end of the period, when also the instances with pied piping have gone up. There is, however, earlier evidence of this change, during the period 1763–7. This is especially clear from Figure 7.3 below, which presents only the normalized frequencies. There is a slight dip in the occurrence of preposition stranding for this period, accompanied by a strong, and at first sight rather unexpected increase in pied piping. The years 1763–7 coincide with the publication and immediate popularity of Lowth's grammar. Though Lowth didn't proscribe preposition stranding in his grammar, his qualification of pied piping as 'more graceful, as well as more perspicuous; and agree[ing] much better with the solemn and elevated Style' may have made him more stylistically conscious when using the construction himself at that time. The majority of the letters during this period were relatively formal, addressed to James Dodsley (Work-related contact) and, significantly, to Warburton and Brown (Enemies), and Secker and Pelham-Holles (Patrons). This linguistic sensitivity was brought about by his newly acquired status as a grammar expert, and the same effect was found with respect to the temporary increase in his use of the subjunctive during the 1760s (§4.4). Eventually, the effect wore off, which accounts for the decrease of pied piping in the period 1773–7, after which usage picked up again. All along, preposition stranding continued to decrease. The figures also show that the development of the two

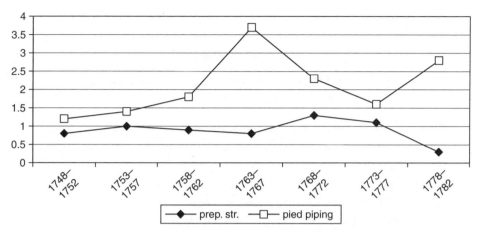

FIG. 7.3. Normalized frequencies of preposition stranding and pied piping over five-year time periods of the letter corpus

constructions took place independently of each other, which was also evident from the data presented by Sairio (2008). Sairio showed a similar overall development of usage across time in the language of Elizabeth Montagu, which suggests that Lowth's usage was not after all unusual at the time.

In contrast to preposition stranding and pied piping, double negation was never very frequent in the letters: with one instance in a letter to Dashwood from 1750, it is no longer found after that date, nor do we find any double comparatives in the letters. Lowth perhaps avoided them consciously, even hypercorrecting to produce *less* when he should have used *lesser* instead. For the comparison of adjectives as such he provided a simple rule in his grammar, which includes a number of well-defined exceptions:

> Monosyllables, for the most part, are compared by *er* and *est*; and Dissyllables by *more* and *most*: as, *mild, milder, mildest*; *frugal, more frugal, most frugal*. Dissyllables ending in *y* easily admit of *er* and *est*; as *happy, lovely*. Words of more than two syllables hardly ever admit of *er* and *est* (1762: 42).

In the second edition he added that disyllables in 'in *le* after a mute, as *able, ample*; or accented on the last syllable, as *discreet, polite*; easily admit of *er* and *est*' (1763: 42). The rule is in effect not very different from that found today (cf. Huddleston and Pullum 2002: 1582–5). Lowth's own usage largely coincides with the rules of his grammar, to the extent that – alongside *big, long, old, small, wise,* and *young* – even *righter* occurs, a form which nowadays, according to Huddleston and Pullum, 'does not inflect' and is even specifically listed as such.

(37) Or if you should think it **righter** to stay at home with the Toms...
      (Lowth to his wife, 15 March 1755).

More in Lowth's letters, indeed, collocates with adjectives like *agreable, probable, satisfactory,* and *suitable,* and *most* is similarly used with polysyllabic adjectives (*affectionate, faithful, humble, obedient,* and *obliged*), though it is striking that the latter forms only occur as part of the closing formulas of the letters. Lowth's letters also contain the forms *busier, easier, happier,* and *prettier,* forms that are covered by Lowth's own rule and that are still considered acceptable today. The letters to his wife also produced *handsomer* and *narrower,* which today vary with their periphrastic counterparts, though not in equal proportions: a search of the BNC produced 7 instances of *handsomer* as against 22 of *more handsome* and 50 instances of *narrower* compared to 13 of *more narrow.* In a letter to Dalrymple, Lowth used *properer,* which nowadays requires periphrasis. Huddleston and Pullum (2002: 1584n) write that such forms were still occasionally found in the nineteenth century. As for superlatives in *-est,* Lowth's letters produced a variety of monosyllables – like *grandest, oldest, poorest, slightest,* and *truest* – but also *earliest, prettyest, properest, readiest, severest,* and *sincerest.* Except for *prettiest,* all these forms, as a BNC search demonstrated, nowadays also occur with their periphrastic counterparts, though *earliest* and *readiest* are more frequent, while the corresponding forms with *most* today outdo *properest* and *severest; sincerest* (11) and *most sincere* (12) occur with equal frequency. In Lowth's letters, all 6 instances of *sincerest* collocate with *thanks,* which suggests that the word was part of a politeness formula at the time. In the BNC this is only the case for two of the instances attested.

In his section on adverbs, Lowth wrote that 'they admit of no Variation; except some few of them, which have the degrees of Comparison [of adjectives]: as, "often, oftener, oftenest;" "soon, sooner, soonest"' (1762: 90–1). *Sooner* is indeed fairly common in the letters (14 instances), but the other forms do not occur. In a footnote to the passage on adverbial comparison, Lowth proscribed sentences with the forms *easilier* and *highliest* as being used 'Improperly, for *more easily, most highly'.* Neither form is attested in his own letters. In his syntax section, Lowth also dealt with the proper use of adjectives and adverbs: 'Adjectives are sometimes employed as Adverbs,' he wrote, adding, 'improperly, and not agreeably to the Genius of the English Language' (1762: 125n). He provided examples from Dryden ('*extreme* elaborate'), Clarendon ('*marvellous* graceful'), Swift ('*extreme* unwilling', '*extreme* subject'), Addison ('live... *suitable* to'), and Pope ('Homer describes this river *agreeble* to'). In all these instances, the adverb should have ended in -*ly*. Lowth's own usage agrees with this, with only two exceptions. One is an instance of *new* used for *newly*:

(38) so that 'twould be better to have [the Ring] **new** sett (Lowth to his wife, 8 March 1755).

The other exception is Lowth's use of the phrase *is like to*, as in (39), which is found sixteen times in the letters, fourteen of which were addressed to his wife and one to his close friend Thomas Chapman:

(39) I don't know that any body **is like to** trouble them from abroad (Lowth to his wife, 22 May 1755).

The remaining one occurs in an early letter to Robert Dodsley, the language of which already anticipates their developing closeness despite the greater distance expressed by the epistolary formulas. The form with *likely* is also found, though only twice, in a letter to Thomas Warton and in one to Michaelis, both of them from 1770. There is yet another interesting instance with *like to*, though of a somewhat different nature:

(40) I have seen D[r]. Hallifax: he says [Mrs.] Lawman has lately had a bad fit, & **had like to have** fallen into the fire, & been burnt (Lowth to Ridley, 23 April 1769).

The construction is a subtype of the counterfactual perfect analysed by Kytö and Romaine (2005), which was rare in the history of English and which disappeared in the course of the nineteenth century. The instance in (40) seems part of a quotation from Samual Hallifax ('he says ...'), who was at that time a Fellow at Trinity Hall, and who had been consulted on an aspect relating to Joseph Spence's inheritance. This confirms Kytö and Romaine's findings, who believe that the construction was more typical of speech than of writing. Personal letters like this one – Ridley has been classified as a 'Friend' – may thus contain valuable information even on the spoken language of the period.

7.4 GRAMMAR RULES IN THE MAKING

In his discussion of mistakes in the use of adverbs, Lowth also condemned the use of the words *godly* and *heavenly* as adverbs, as in 'We should live soberly, righteously, and **godly** in this present world' (Tillotson) and 'O Liberty, Thou Goddess **heavenly** bright' (Addison). Leonard (1929: 253) observes that Lowth was the first to criticize the use of *exceeding* as an adverb, noting that George Campbell, in his *Philosophy of Rhetoric* (1776), had been the first to 'face' the problem of the adverbial use of adjectives like *heavenly, godly*, and others (1929: 71). Strictly speaking, it was believed, it would be more grammatically correct to write *heavenlily* and *godlily*, and Leonard refers to Dr Johnson's similar preference for *lowlily*. Lowth, however, had dealt with the problem elsewhere before, including an elaborate account of it in the second edition of his grammar, still well before Campbell took it up. Lowth's problems with the adverbial use of adjectives in -*ly* comes up in his correspondence with James Merrick, whose draft translation of the Psalms he was reading critically. Merrick raised the problem in connection with his own use of *heav'nly fair*, for which he had clearly consulted Lowth's grammar:

Psalm 85, l. 35. I have here used the expression heav'nly fair, corresponding with Mʳ Addison's heav'nly bright. You seem. Sir, not satisfied with this expression **in Your late Work**: But as heav'nlily has not so good a sound, and I seem to remember an instance or two in Greek of a syllable omitted in the same manner, observed either by Priscian or some other antient Grammarian, I am inclined to retain this form in one or two words of Our language. The word early You would not perhaps Yourself except to, when thus applied: as e.g.

 O early wise —

I think also, that I find somewhat of the same kind in a couplet which You must give me leave to be much pleased with:

 Truths more sublime, yet easier understood

 Confucius taught; He made his hearers Good.

Easilier, it is evident, could not be used. The words hourly, daily, yearly, are all both Adjectives and Adverbs, which together with heav'nly... early, may possibly be the **more easily** tolerated, as our Language, in a word not ending in ly, comprehends both the adverb and the adjective, the word Late being used in both senses. As the double use of the above-mentioned words ending in ly seems analogous to that of late, and may sometimes be very convenient, I should hope it may be allowed a place in Our language (Merrick to Lowth, early May 1762).

Merrick did not agree with Lowth's treatment of adverbs in the grammar, arguing that there are other words, such as *late*, which can similarly function both as adjectives and as adverbs. There is consequently no reason why *heavenly* should not be used as an adverb either. Merrick even argues in favour of the use of *easier* as an adverb in his own translation, which he preferred to *more easily* – used by himself in the above letter – for metrical reasons. *Easilier*, he knew, would not meet with Lowth's consent, as Sir Walter Raleigh had been criticized for this word in 'Was the *easilier* persuaded' as 'Improperly, for *more easily* ...' (1762: 90–1).

Lowth was not convinced by Merrick's arguments, for he replied three days later:

As to the word <u>heavenly</u> used as an Adverb, I am still perswaded that it is wrong; tho' [to] consider it thoroughly, & to set it [...]ll light, may require more time [&] examination that I can allow it a[t present.] However, be pleased to consider whether the Adverbial termination <u>ly</u>, when added to a Substantive, does not carry a different idea, from what it does, when added to an Adjective. <u>Hourly</u>, <u>daily</u>, <u>yearly</u>, (& I believe <u>early</u> will appear to be of the same sort, if we can come at the true Etymology of it) that is, <u>by</u> the hour, day, year; it here carries no idea of <u>manner</u> or <u>likeness</u>; as in <u>wantonly</u>, <u>piously</u>, &c in a wanton <u>manner</u>, <u>as</u>, or <u>like</u>, a pious person, &c. Adverbs in <u>ly</u> are naturally formed from Adjectives: I believe it will be found that very few Substantives admit of being converted into Adverbs by such addition. I think, <u>Heaven</u>, & <u>God</u>, do not. The Phrase to live <u>godly</u> in this world, has all the advantages on its side, that it is possible for any Phrase to have: it comes recommended on the best authority, & we have been familiariz'd to it by daily use from our infancy: & yet I [...] any English ear with reflection [...] of it or even to endure it (Lowth to Merrick, 4 May 1762).

Heavenly, Lowth argued, cannot function as an adverb because, like *godly*, it derives from a noun, and in his opinion 'very few Substantives admit of being converted into Adverbs' by the addition of the suffix -*ly*. For all that, he was willing to accept *godly* in the phrase 'to live <u>godly</u> in this world', his reason being that its source is the New Testament (Titus ii. 12), which he considered his 'best authority'. Lowth does concede that the topic 'requires more time [&] examination that I can allow it at present', something which he was to do in the preparation of the second edition of the grammar, for there we find an elaborate discussion of the issue at hand:

The Termination *ly*, being a contraction of *like*, expresses *similitude*, or *manner*; and being added to Nouns forms Adjectives; and added to Adjectives forms

Adverbs. But Adverbs expressing *similitude*, or *manner*, cannot be so formed from Nouns: the few Adverbs that are so formed have a very different import; as, *daily*, *yearly*; that is, day by day, year by year. *Early*, both Adjective and Adverb, is formed from the Saxon Preposition *ær*, *before*. The Adverbs therefore above noted are not agreeable to the Analogy of formation established in our language, which requires *godlily*, *ungodlily*, *heavenlily*: these are disagreeable to the ear, and therefore could never gain admittance into common use.

The word *lively* used as an Adverb, instead of *livelily*, is liable to the same objection; and not being so familiar to the ear, immediately offends it. 'That part of poetry must need be best, which describes most *lively* our actions and passions, our virtues and our vices.' Dryden, Pref. to State of Innocence. 'The whole design must refer to the Golden Age, which it *lively* represents.' Addison, on Medals (Lowth 1763: 137–8n).

Even if Lowth was not convinced by Merrick's arguments, for reasons explained here, the added passage shows the extent to which he had profited from the discussion with his friend and fellow scholar.

Another linguistic feature that led to a lot of discussion among eighteenth-century grammarians was the use of the auxiliaries *shall* and *will*. I have analysed the discussion of the problem by eighteenth-century grammarians in detail elsewhere (Tieken-Boon van Ostade 1985). Many grammarians simply copied what they had found in Wallis (1653), and this, with only a minor change, is indeed what we find in Lowth's grammar, too:

WALLIS:

In primis personis *shall* simpliciter praedicentis est; *will*, quasi promittentis aut minantis.
In secundis et tertiis personis, *shall* promittentis est aut minantis; *will* simpliciter praedicentis (1653 [1765]: 106).

LOWTH:

Will in the first Person singular and plural promises or threatens; in the second and third Persons only foretells: *shall* on the contrary, in the first Person simply foretells; in the second and third Persons commands or threatens (1762: 58–9).

In the second edition, Lowth, possibly in response to suggestions made to him for improvement of the grammar, added:

But this must be understood of Explicative Sentences; for when the Sentence is Interrogative, just the reverse for the most part takes place: Thus, 'I *shall* go; you *will* go;' express event only: but, '*will* you go?' imports intention; and '*shall* I go?' refers to the will of another. But again, 'he *shall* go,' and, '*shall* he go? both imply will, expressing or referring to a command (1763: 62–3).

Lowth was criticized for this by Fogg (1792–6: 129), who commented that 'The reversing of interrogations in the future, added by the latter grammarian [Lowth], seems to me to have little foundation. *Will I do a thing?* is nonsense – also *shalt thou?*'. Fogg, however, seems to have misinterpreted what Lowth meant by the 'the reverse': instead of simply reversing *shall* and *will* in questions, which would indeed convert *I shall do a thing* into the nonsensical *Will I do a thing*, Lowth referred to the fact that the meaning of *shall* in the first person in a question changed from expressing the future, as it did in 'Explicative Sentences', to asking permission. The rule as phrased by Lowth and many others coming both before and after him led to the famous dictum, first expressed by Mackintosh in his grammar of 1797 and later immortalized by Mencken, 'I shall drown: nobody will save me; I will drown: nobody shall save me' (1919: 537), in which the first part expresses futurity for the speaker (Lowth: it foretells) and the second volition or intention (Lowth: it promises/commands or threatens).

'But,' Mencken continues, 'the simplicity of this is deceptive, for like most of the other rules of grammar, those governing *will* and *shall* are subject to many exceptions.' And this is true of Lowth's own usage, too. *Shall*, indeed, occurs in the majority of the cases with the first person singular (242 instances) and plural (9 instances), but *will* is also found in a sizeable number of instances, 102 altogether (101 first person singular, 1 first person plural). In example (41), for instance, both *shall* and *will* refer to the future, though *will* may additionally express intention.

(41) I think **I shall** be in Town on Thursday: for **I will** sett out early Monday Morning (Lowth to his wife, 31 October 1755).

The shortened form, *'ll*, is also attested, and predominantly in Lowth's letters to his wife (§6.4); whether it stands for *shall* or *will* is of course impossible to determine. As for the second and third persons, *will* is far more common in Lowth's letters in the first person than *shall*: there are only 36 instances of second and third person *shall* as against as many as 446 of *will*. In (42), third person *shall* refers to a future state of events, and so does (43), which illustrates *shall* used with a second person singular pronoun:

(42) I have the honour of Your Letter, recommending M^r. Knyvett for the place of Gentleman of the Chapel Royal, when there **shall** be a Vacancy (Lowth to Jenkinson, 11 December 1781).

(43) [The Pre]face is done; & you **shall** have it...(Lowth to Robert
    Dodsley, September 1757).

But in (43), *shall* also implies a promise, so that here we have to do with
the same kind of 'inversion' of senses that Lowth described for interrogative sentences: *shall/will/will* applies with reference to the future, and *will/
shall/shall* to modal uses other than or, as in (41) and (43), in addition to,
the future.

Things are therefore not as straightforward as the grammatical dictum
emerging from the eighteenth-century normative grammars suggests. For
all that, the grammars appear to have had a considerable impact on usage.
Around 1680, according to Schlauch (1959: 143), there had been a 90 per
cent preference for first person *will* and 10 per cent for *shall*, but my
analysis of Lowth's letters suggests that by his time usage had changed,
with a preference of about 70 per cent for first person *shall* and of even 93
per cent *will* for the second and third persons. Phillipps (1970: 125) likewise
claims that the grammarians' rule is 'generally applicable to Jane Austen's
usage', while Facchinetti (2000: 128) discovered that first person *shall* for
the future predominates in nineteenth-century English as well, even with
Irish writers. The latter group used to be among those targeted by the
normative grammarians for failing to apply the rules correctly, and Fries
(1925) attributes the change in usage to these grammarians' influence. For
all that, the old rule is no longer adhered to as stringently today as during
the nineteenth and much of the twentieth centuries: Mittins et al. (1970),
basing themselves on a survey of usage carried out in the late 1960s, note a
general acceptance rate of 56 per cent for sentences like *I will be twenty-one
tomorrow*, which I expect will have increased considerably since then. Even
for this particular issue, Lowth can thus no longer be made to bear any
blame, whatever his role in the rise of the stricture may have been.

A grammatical rule that was similarly first formulated in the course of
the eighteenth century is that for the use of periphrastic *do*. The process by
which this came about I have described in detail in Chapter 9 of my study
of periphrastic *do* in eighteenth-century English (Tieken-Boon van Ostade
1987). By the end of that century, we find the rule such as we still know it
today and which is described by the acronym NICE to indicate in what
type of constructions the use of *do* is obligatory today: Negation, Inversion
(including questions), Code, and Emphasis. Though providing the NICE-
properties in a different order, Murray's grammar may serve as a suitable
illustration here:

Do and *did* **mark the action itself, or the time of it, with greater** energy and positiveness [Emphasis]; as, 'I do speak truth;' 'I did respect him;' 'Here am I, for thou didst call me.' **They are of** great **use in negative sentences** [Negation]; as, 'I do not fear;' 'I did not write.' They are **almost** universally employed in asking questions [Inversion]; as, 'Does he learn?' 'Did he not write?' **They sometimes also supply the place of another verb, and make the repetition of it, in the same or a subsequent sentence, unnecessary** [Code]; as, 'You attend not to your studies as he does;' (i.e. as he attends, &c.) – 'I shall come if I can; but if I do not, please to excuse me;' (i.e. if I come not.) (Murray 1795: 55).

But here, too, Murray was indebted to Lowth's grammar, and in the above quotation I have highlighted which parts of the rule derive from his source. Murray's source for this had not been the first edition of the grammar, which lacks the specification that *do* can be used to 'supply the place of another verb, and make the repetition of it, in the same or a subsequent sentence, unnecessary', but the second edition, where Code is dealt with for the first time (1763: 61–2), or indeed a later one. Again, this addition was part of the major revision that the grammar underwent after it was first published. In the process of adopting the rule from Lowth's grammar, Murray edited it slightly and supplied it with examples, as he did throughout his grammar, not only with Lowth's material but also with that of others (see, for instance, Navest in preparation).

My analysis of eighteenth-century usage of periphrastic *do* (Tieken-Boon van Ostade 1987) shows interesting stylistic differences in the occurrence of sentences with *do* (the modern pattern) and those without, a pattern of usage that was receding. In Figure 7.4 I have rearranged the data from my analysis of the construction with the largest number of instances, *do*-less negative sentences, according to the authors' date of birth (cf. Osselton 1984: 134). For an illustration, see (44):

(44)   whom you mean, **I know not** (Lowth to Roberts, 20 November 1775).

Figure 7.4 also includes data from Henry Fielding's letters, which were not previously available to me (Battestin and Probyn 1993). The data were obtained from his most intimate letters along with the principles set out in Tieken-Boon van Ostade (1987: 23–4). The resulting graph demonstrates that the data are not easy to interpret as evidence of a single, straightforward disappearing process. The data do show that the majority of authors distinguish in their usage between different styles of writing, though not uniformly so. In the case of some authors (Addison and Gibbon) the stylistic differences are not very large, whereas with others (Swift and

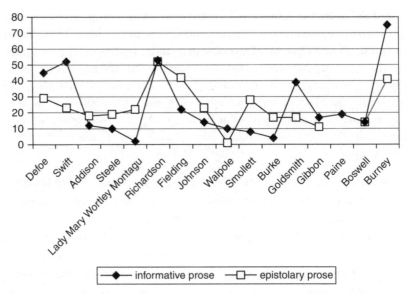

FIG. 7.4. Percentages of *do*-less negative sentences in the writings of eighteenth-century authors (arranged by date of birth) (Tieken-Boon van Ostade 1987: 187).

Burney) they are considerable. Two authors, Richardson and Boswell, make no distinction at all. The case of Burney is especially striking since she is the youngest of the authors studied, while her usage in informative prose is by far the highest of all. Her usage, however, was influenced to an important extent by that of Dr Johnson, particularly that found in his periodical *The Rambler*, which we know she read (but which was not part of the above study). In view of the ongoing development at the time, her usage should therefore possibly be interpreted as evidence of hypercorrection, which is also the case for the unusually high figures in both styles of writing for Richardson (see Tieken-Boon van Ostade 1991).

Lowth's usage of *do*-less negative sentences is not very high: in his letters, I found 12 instances as against 135 sentences with periphrastic *do*. At only 8 per cent, his epistolary usage is thus much lower than that of his contemporaries (from Fielding onwards, who was born in 1707), except for Walpole (1%). As in the case of eighteenth-century usage generally, the majority of the *do*-less negative sentences contain the verb *know*: along with *doubt*, found only once in Lowth's letters, this verb showed greatest resistance to the new pattern of usage. Other verbs found were *ask*, *become*, and *think*. The main verb *have*, moreover, was still commonly constructed without *do* at the time, and Lowth's usage was no exception. Seven of the

12 *do*-less negative sentences occur in Lowth's more formal letters, addressed to Dalrymple (1), Johnson (1), Michaelis (2), Roberts (1), Walter (1), and Warburton (1). His informal usage of *do*-less negative sentences is, at 11 per cent, slightly higher (letters to his wife, his Close friends, and his Friends). Lowth's own usage of *do*-less negative sentences is considerably lower than that found generally: 19 per cent for the second half of the eighteenth century as a whole (Tieken-Boon van Ostade 1987: 165). This is confirmed by the in-letters, which produced 8 *do*-less negative sentences, 6 of which with *know* and one with *doubt*, as against 38 sentences with periphrastic *do* (17%). Lowth's usage was thus advanced in relation to that of his contemporaries, and this is reflected by his own grammar rule.

7.5 'WHAT IS CUSTOMARY AMONG OUR SUPERIOURS'

On the use of periphrastic *do*, Lowth wrote in his grammar that *do* and *did* 'are also of **frequent** and **almost necessary use** in Interrogative and Negative Sentences' (1762: 58). This statement is so general that it covers the usage of negative *do* for the majority of the authors presented in Figure 7.4, including his own and that of his correspondents. Only in the case of Lady Mary Wortley Montagu's informative prose and Walpole's letters is usage of *do* well-nigh categorical in negative sentences. Lowth's informal usage is virtually identical to that of Gibbon, who was, however, younger than him by a generation, but also to that for Walpole's informative prose. Henstra (2009), moreover, having analysed the use of *be/have* with mutative intransitive verbs in Walpole's circle of close friends, shows that from the period 1739–41 to 1741–71 usage of *have* increased from 21 to 44 per cent. Lowth's letters, those to his wife and his Close friends excluded, show a usage of *have* of 31 per cent (the figure is much lower for his informal letters). Lowth's usage, reflecting his more formal language between the early 1750s and his death in 1787, thus does not seem far removed from the development Walpole's language was undergoing around the same time. Another instance where Walpole comes in here is his correction of a case of preposition stranding in Robert Dodsley's poetry (§4.7), thus demonstrating a preference for pied piping as being more appropriate in such a linguistic context. This view agrees both with that which Lowth presented in his grammar and with his own usage: particularly his letters to his wife represent usage – and not only that of preposition stranding – that comes close to 'common conversation', while usage in poetry and the language of his more formal letters can be considered more representative of 'the solemn and elevated Style', the two levels of usage he distinguished with respect to the question of the acceptability of preposition stranding.

Walpole is only a single representative of the aristocracy, but I believe that usage of the social class to which he belonged represented a clear linguistic model to Lowth, both in his own writing and in the rules that he presented in his grammar. Sairio (2009: 316), too, found a correlation between the language of members of the upper classes and the norm presented in the normative grammars of the period. Actual influence from Lowth's more highly placed correspondents on his own language has proved impossible to detect due to the limited amount of material I have at my disposal from the in-letters. Perhaps such influence is hard to identify through systematic analysis in any case. I have, however, found two instances which confirm that he was influenced by people he considered to be his 'superiors', whether socially or within the Church: he once, unusually, given his general practice, employed the word *affectionately* in a closing formula to a letter to Warburton. He seems to have done so in response to a similar use by Warburton, thus demonstrating his anxiousness to establish better terms with his opponent. The second instance is the single instance of what is now the standard form *show* in a fairly formal letter to Reynolds. As this is the form commonly employed by Reynolds himself – Lowth always used *shew* instead – he seems to have accommodated in his language use to that of a man whose acquaintance he valued so much as to present him with a copy of the newly published *Isaiah*. Such instances of linguistic accommodation may have occurred unconsciously, but the self-corrections in Lowth's letters show that changes were made consciously, too. Some of these even reflect grammatical issues that were then currently criticized, and they therefore occupy a rightful place in the grammar.

According to James Beattie, in his *Theory of Language*, 'we naturally approve as elegant what is customary among our superiours' (1783: 298). Beattie refers to Lowth's *Isaiah* in this work, as well as to the grammar, which inspired him to a discussion of several pages on a problem in the translation of the New Testament that he blamed on a mistranslation of the original Greek. As for using 'what is customary among our superiours' as a model of correctness, this is indeed what Lowth appears to have done in his letters as well as in his grammar. Beattie thought highly of Lowth's grammar, describing its author as a 'learned Bishop' and calling the grammar 'excellent' (1783: 490), but in referring to 'the example of approved authors' as representing a standard of linguistic correctness, he followed Johnson rather than Lowth, whose purpose with the grammar had been to show that these 'approved authors' were prone to grammatical error, and that they would do well to take the study of English grammar seriously. Lowth himself, however, did use the language of his 'superiours' as a linguistic model, but to him this class of people represented not literary or other writers but his *social* superiors and those who occupied a higher position in the Church than he did. In this, he shows himself a true social climber, and this view made his grammar more than a scholarly document that would benefit men like Beattie and many others: it served as an instrument that would be of use to those with similar social ambitions as his own.

THE GRAMMAR
AND THE RISE OF
PRESCRIPTIVISM

8.1 LOWTH AMONG THE
PRESCRIPTIVE GRAMMARIANS

I N Chapter 7, I discussed fifteen grammatical problems each of which, in one way or another, Lowth dealt with in his grammar: the placement of *only*, *you was*, preterite and participial forms of strong verbs, *fly/flee*, *lie/ lay*, *less/lesser*, double negation, the double comparative (including the formation of comparatives and superlatives generally), the *than whom* construction, the gerund, the *be/have* periphrasis, preposition stranding, adjectives used as adverbs and vice versa, the use of *shall/will*, and periphrastic *do*. Many more such items are dealt with in the grammar (for a list based on the first edition, see Tieken-Boon van Ostade 2006a: 553–5), but apart from allowing me to demonstrate that Lowth's pronouncements frequently did not match his own usage in his letters in a straightforward way, they illustrate the striking phenomenon that eleven of them, that is, all items except *you was*, preterite/participle forms of strong verbs, *fly/flee*, and the *be/have* periphrasis, still occur in the third edition of Fowler's *Modern English Usage* (Burchfield 1996). Four of them, moreover, are part of Crystal's 'Grammatical Top Ten' (Crystal 1995: 194), which is a list of usage problems that are typical of the kind of grammatical errors people encounter in speech or writing and complain about in the media: the placement of *only*, double negation, preposition stranding, and the use of *shall/will*. Lowth is often claimed to have been the first to deal with a particular issue, and while I have shown that this is indeed the case with some grammatical strictures, it is by no means true for all those that carry his name, nor were they usually formulated as proscriptive strictures, contrary to widespread belief.

To test to what extent Lowth was indeed the prescriptive grammarian that he is generally taken for, I looked at the number of proscriptive comments in his grammar in relation to those found in the other eighteenth-century grammars analysed by Sundby, Bjørge, and Haugland (1991). This produced the league table presented in Figure 8.1, the most striking conclusion from which is that Lowth does not even belong to the ten most proscriptive grammarians of the period. The list is headed by Knowles (1796), with 722 comments. This is about three times as many as the number of comments in Lowth's grammar (243) at the other end of the scale (the list is obviously much longer, but I stopped at Lowth for the sake of the argument). Even Priestley's grammar, with 283 comments in the second edition, a considerable increase compared to the first, takes up a higher position in the table than Lowth. This remarkable phenomenon confirms the need to review the iconic status of both grammarians and their work. With the number of proscriptive comments gradually increasing down to the publication of Angus (1800) with 422 comments until they take a big leap with Brittain's (1788) 531 comments and finally Knowles (1796), another striking phenomenon in the list in Figure 8.1 is

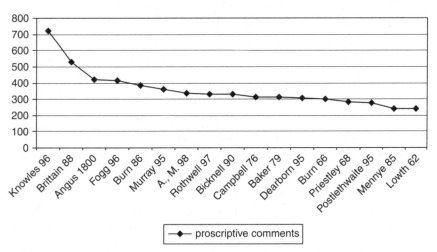

FIG. 8.1. Numbers of proscriptive comments in the grammars analysed by Sundby et al. (1991)

that ten of the seventeen grammars included there date from the final decade of the eighteenth century (Campbell 1776, however, is not a grammar but a philosophical treatise on language). Despite Lowth's early prescriptive approach to grammar, prescriptivism is thus clearly a feature of the very end of the eighteenth century, and, due to what Michael (1997) called the 'hyperactive production of English grammars' in the century following, this became a typical phenomenon of the nineteenth century. Fowler's *Modern English Usage* of 1926, with 742 pages of pre-scriptive comment (864 pages in the third edition revised by Burchfield), of both a lexical and a grammatical nature, can be considered a culmina-tion of the development, of which the early stages are represented by Figure 8.1. The popularity of usage guides like Fowler's continued throughout the twentieth century and into the twenty-first, with the reissue of the first edition – even twice – in 2003 and 2009 by Oxford University Press, with an introduction by Simon Winchester and David Crystal, respectively.

In this chapter I will place the development illustrated by Figure 8.1 into the wider context of the standardization process which the English language was undergoing at the time. Grammar writing in the history of English represents one of the final stages in this process, though it would still be followed by the stage that gave us usage guides like Fowler's and, on punctu-ation, Lynne Truss's *Eats, Shoots and Leaves* (2003). I will show that Lowth's grammar, though not a usage guide as such, can be considered a usage guide *avant-la-lettre* due to the innovative step of including a wealth of proscriptive comments in its footnotes. While I have repeatedly shown here that the grammar itself is not straightforwardly prescriptive, the way in which its rules were adopted and adapted by later grammarians turned Lowth's strictures into more outspokenly pre- and proscriptive comments. As the century wore on, grammars became increasingly prescriptive, as is illustrated by Priestley's revision of his grammar, of which Straaijer (2009) demonstrates that it was more prescriptive than the first edition, as well as by the fact that the grammar by Burn occurs twice in the league table in Figure 8.1, with the first edition of 1766 and the fourth of 1786 (see Alston 1965: 52–3). Lowth's second edition should have been included as well, for, as I have discussed above, there are several strictures that first made their appearance only in the second edition of the grammar (double negation, double comparison, the *than whom* construction, adjectives used as adverbs, and the rules for the use of *shall/will* and of periphrastic *do*). Sundby et al. were obviously not aware of the extent to which the two editions of the grammar differed.

The league table in Figure 8.1 also includes Baker (1779), the second edition of Robert Baker's *Reflections on the English Language, In the Nature of Vaugelas's Reflections on the French*, first published in 1770. This book has been called 'the ancestor of those handbooks of abuses and corrections which were so freely produced in the nineteenth century' (Leonard 1929: 35), and it can be considered the first usage guide proper. Baker's book is unusual and idiosyncratic, but it shows links with Lowth's grammar as well as with the many usage guides published after him that are too important to ignore. There is, I think, a good explanation for this, which will similarly help explain the great divide between modern linguistics and normative linguistics, the branch of linguistics that deals with phenomena like the topic of the present book. Usage guides are a new but important type of text that is a typical product of the prescription stage, the stage in the standardization process which, as I will argue more fully in Section 8.2, started in the 1770s and which continues to the present day.

Lowth's grammar is a normative grammar: it takes as its starting point a norm of correct usage for which grammatical strictures are formulated in such a way that they are often interpreted as prescriptive statements. In Chapter 7, I have argued that Lowth's norm of correctness was that of the aristocracy – or such as he perceived it to be – not that of his middle-class peers, as Leonard (1929: 169) claims. Characteristically, but against Aitchison's (1981) belief, this is an external rather than a private norm, one to which he, and the users of his grammar, aspired, and which often went against his own practice. Normative grammars carry the stigma of being prescriptive, yet according to Azad (1989: 3) 'to prescribe correctness was to describe usage'. It is increasingly recognized that many eighteenth-century normative grammarians are far from being single-mindedly prescriptive, but that they have a basis in usage, too: this has been demonstrated by Vorlat (1979), Tieken-Boon van Ostade (1987, 2000a; 2006b), Azad (1989), Rodríguez-Gil (2003), and Hodson (2006, 2008). In formulating this norm, Lowth rejected the then current practice of accepting the usage of 'our best Authors' as a standard model of linguistic correctness. We see the same phenomenon in Baker's *Reflections on the English Language*, where, like Lowth but quite independently of him, Baker described what he considered to be grammatically correct on the basis of errors from well-known literary authors. Fowler, too, based himself on popular writing, particularly that of newspapers. In doing so, these men all share an approach that is characteristic of the type of writing they engaged in and by which they aimed at offering their readers guidelines for grammatical correctness. In order to understand why their approach was so similar, we should begin by looking at the final stages of the standardization process, codification and prescription.

8.2 EIGHTEENTH-CENTURY GRAMMARS AND THE STANDARDIZATION PROCESS

It has frequently been commented upon, for instance by Sundby et al. (1991: 14), Fitzmaurice (1998: 326), and Beal (2004: 90), that there was a phenomenal increase in grammar writing in the course of the eighteenth century. I have calculated elsewhere that the second half of the century saw the publication of nearly four times as many grammars as during the entire period preceding it (Tieken-Boon van Ostade 2000*a*: 877). Figure 8.2 illustrates this development.

The data presented in Figure 8.2 include not only new titles but also reprints, thus confirming the growing interest in grammar writing. The most striking increase occurred during the 1760s, and especially during the early years of that decade, when many new grammars were launched onto the market. Alston (1965) lists six new titles for the years 1760–2 alone: Ash (1760), Wells (1760), Henson (1760?), Priestley (1761), Buchanan (1762), and Lowth (1762). Of these, Ash and Lowth would become the most popular, the former to a certain extent due to the fact that it was republished as an introduction to Lowth's grammar. With its

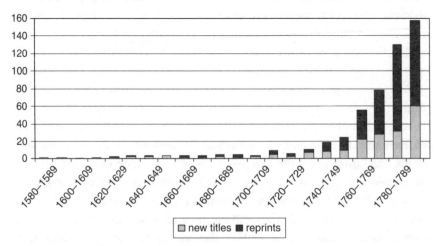

FIG. 8.2.   English grammars published by decade (reprints and new titles) (based on Alston 1965; Tieken-Boon van Ostade 2008*a*: 106; 2008*c*: 2)

new subtitle, *The Easiest Introduction to Dr. Lowth's English Grammar*, the work is advertised in, for instance, the *St. James's Chronicle* of 8 November 1766 and in the *Public Advertiser* of 15 December that same year ('17th–18th Century Burney Collection Newspapers'). A detailed analysis of the publication history of Ash's grammar will be found in Navest (in preparation). Percy (2008: 128) notes that the increase in grammar production even drew the attention of the *Critical Review*, where writers expressed their concern at the fact that grammar books seemed to 'multiply *every month*' (1765), commenting on the '*infinite number* of English grammars' (1771) that were making their appearance. Auer (2006: 45) notes a slight increase in the occurrence of the inflectional subjunctive during the second half of the eighteenth century, and Sairio (2008: 151) similarly identified an increase in the occurrence of pied piping coupled with a decrease of preposition stranding in the letters of Elizabeth Montagu during this period. This may well correlate directly with the enormous output of grammars at the time, though I will argue below that there may have been other factors at play as well.

At this point in the history of English, the language was being codified, with its rules of usage being laid down not only in grammars but also in dictionaries like the one by Dr Johnson (1755). Codification is generally recognized as a stage in the standardization process that languages undergo, though different models to describe this process have been in existence. The one most widely used was that developed by Haugen in the 1960s, and in his view it comprises 'four aspects of language development ... isolated as crucial features in taking the step from "dialect" to "language", from vernacular to standard', i.e.

a. selection of norm
b. codification of form
c. elaboration of function, and
d. acceptance by the community (Haugen (1966 [1972]: 110).

Twenty years later, a different model was presented by Milroy and Milroy (1991; first edition 1985), who adopted a stricter interpretation of the term 'standardisation', one of which the 'chief characteristic ... is intolerance of optional variability in language' (1991: 26). Their model consequently distinguishes seven stages of what they consider to be 'the implementation of the standard' (1991: 29): selection, acceptance, diffusion, maintenance, elaboration of function, codification, and prescription. Though Milroy and Milroy point out that 'these hypothetical stages do not necessarily follow one another in temporal succession', while they may at the same overlap with each other (1991: 27), I have shown elsewhere that in the history of the English language these seven stages closely reflect the linguistic developments from the beginning of the fifteenth century onwards, when a relatively focused formal written variety of English came into being, down to the eighteenth century when the language was codified (Nevalainen and Tieken-Boon van Ostade 2006).

The Milroy model has the additional advantage of including a stage following that of the codification of the language, the prescription stage. During this stage, according to the Milroys, 'speakers have access to grammars and dictionaries, which they regard as authorities', even to the extent that in the popular mind 'the "language" is enshrined in these books . . . rather than in the linguistic and communicative competence of the millions who use the language every day' (1991: 27). Beal (2008, 2009) notes a revival of prescriptivism during the late twentieth, early twenty-first centuries, which she attributes to the fact that the codifiers 'have left us with a legacy of "linguistic insecurity"' (Beal 2004: 123). While she focuses on the current revival of interest in elocution and 'good' pronunciation, Lowth's grammar demonstrates that the question of using correct language in point of grammar has remained an issue of unremitting interest since normative grammars first began to be written, and particularly so since the early eighteenth century. This is in line with the perspective taken by Milroy and Milroy (1991) that the standardization process when applied to language by definition remains unfinished: as they put it, 'the only fully standardised language is a dead language' (1991: 22). While suppression of variability will never be achieved, attitudes to particular usage problems, as Mittins at al. (1970) have demonstrated, have grown increasingly milder with the passage of time. But with the current culture of 'self-improvement', one of the factors mentioned by Beal (2008: 35–8) when trying to account for the upsurge of prescriptivism during the past few decades, it seems unlikely that linguistic intolerance will ever disappear.

8.3 THE BIRTH OF THE USAGE GUIDE

Figure 8.3 below, based on a combination of Michael's (1991) inventory of nineteenth-century grammars and Alston's (1965) data for the eighteenth

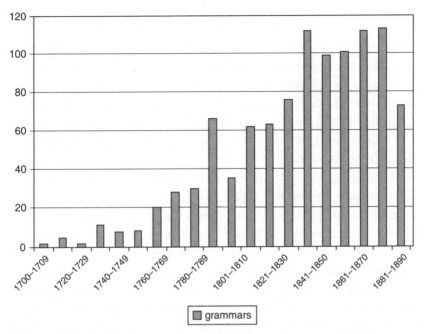

FIG. 8.3. English grammars published between 1700 and 1900 (cf. Tieken-Boon van Ostade 2008*c*: 4, based on Alston 1965 and Michael 1991)

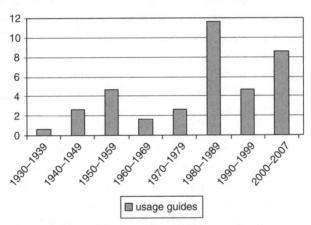

FIG. 8.4. The publication of usage guides since Fowler, based on Busse and Schröder (2008, Appendix 1)

century, shows that grammars continued to appear after the turn of the century, and in ever-increasing numbers.

Detailed overviews of these nineteenth-century grammars are provided by Michael (1997) and Görlach (1998). Meanwhile, usage guides started to appear as well: for example, Baker (1770), *Five Hundred Mistakes of Daily*

Occurrence in Speaking, Pronouncing, and Writing (1856), *The Queen's English* (1864) by Dean Alford, the Fowler brothers' *The King's English* (1907), Henry Fowler's *Modern English Usage* (1926), and many others. Busse and Schröder (2008, Appendix 1) identified over forty such works following Alford (1864) down to 2007, and not including subsequent editions such as those of Fowler. The increase of titles over the years, as presented in Figure 8.4, shows a dip in the 1960s and 1970s followed by a peak in the 1980s, which confirms the growing climate of linguistic anxiety identified by Beal (2004, 2008).

Grammars and usage guides should be kept strictly apart, because they are essentially different text types: they are different in form, their meta-language differs, and they have a different function. *Modern English Usage*, and many other works like it, takes the form of a dictionary in which the various items have been arranged alphabetically. Though an alphabetical ordering can hardly be called a systematic approach to the subject, given the wide scope of features dealt with in the book this is an easier format for anyone wishing to consult it on a usage problem. By contrast, Walton Burgess, the presumed author of *Five Hundred Mistakes*, notes that the items in the book are 'grouped miscellaneously, *without classification*' (Burgess 1856: iv), the alleged reason being that 'a division of subjects would render no assistance to those for whom the book is specially designed'. His readership comprises 'persons...who from deficiency of education, or from carelessness of manner, are in the habit of misusing many of the most common words of the English language, distorting its grammatical forms, destroying its beauty, and corrupting its purity' (1856: iii). Yet how such persons would benefit from the advice offered in the book other than by reading it from cover to cover is hard to imagine. Burgess distinguished different categories of usage problems in his book: 'abuses of grammar, misapplications of words and phrases, improprieties of metaphor and comparison, misstatements of meaning, and faults of pronunciation' (1856: iv), and the first page typically lists the following items: that it is impossible to say that one would be *enjoying* bad health, that it is *corporal* not *corporeal punishment*, that *notable* for *careful* in *She is a notable woman* is obsolete, that *advertisement* is to be pronounced with the stress on *vert*, not *ise*, that *up* in *rose up* is superfluous, and that *set* ('sit') in *set down* is wrong as '*setting* is said of the sun in the west, but cannot be properly applied to a person taking a seat' (1856: 19). The latter item suggests the tongue-in-cheek approach that typically characterizes usage guides: as Henry and Frank Fowler put it in their preface to *The*

King's English: 'We try to throw in a little elegant flippancy here & there, but grammar is a very solemn theme' (cited by McMorris 2001: 59). 'Elegant flippancy' is likewise evident throughout *Modern English Usage*, as may be illustrated by Fowler's classification of English speakers into five categories depending on the attitude they take to the split infinitive: '(1) those who neither know nor care what a split infinitive is; (2) those who do not know, but care very much; (3) those who know & condemn; (4) those who know & approve; & (5) those who know & distinguish' (1926: 558). 'Elegant flippancy' would also aptly describe the tone adopted by Truss in *Eats, Shoots and Leaves. Five Hundred Mistakes* was published in New York, which shows that usage guides were also popular in America. But as many of the items included are the same as in its overseas counterparts, the book clearly springs from the same tradition. A more modern version of an American usage guide, enjoying a phenomenal popularity even today according to Pullum (2008) is *The Elements of Style* (1918/1959), widely referred to as 'Strunk and White'.

Knowles's *Principles of English Grammar* (1796) is the fourth, considerably enlarged, edition of a grammar that was originally published in 1785 (Alston 1965: 78–9). The majority of the proscriptive comments which gave it its high position in Figure 8.1 appear to have been taken from a section called 'Of verbal criticism', which according to Sundby et al. (1991: 8) includes 'some 460 "improper" sentences... presented in alphabetical order, the "proper" form of... each sentence being given on the right'. Here, at least, the usage problems are presented in a way that would appear to be of use to the inquisitive reader. As the number of proscriptive comments in Figure 8.1. is considerably higher, additional instances were presumably taken by Sundby et al. from the book's appendix with 'Exercises of False Construction', which, according to Sundby et al., served to 'afford the schoolboys and teachers for whom the grammar was intended ample opportunity for testing their linguistic ability, improved (it may be supposed) by diligent study of the first two lists'. Some examples of Knowles's 'Improper expressions', followed by corrections labelled 'Proper', are the following:

(1) The Articles were as *follow*.   *follows*
    It is no more *but* was expected.   *than*
    No *less* than twenty Persons.   *fewer*
    He has a *new Pair of* Shoes.   *Pair of new* (1796: 66, 67, 71, 74).[1]

---

[1] The grammar is not included in ECCO. For the fourth edition, used by Sundby et al. (1991), I am making use of a partial copy from Glasgow University Library.

In dealing with usage problems in this way, Knowles taught by example rather than by precept, contrary to the practice of the majority of the normative grammarians of the period. Rather than stating, for instance, with Lowth and Murray, that 'Two Negatives in English destroy one another, or are equivalent to an Affirmative' (Lowth 1763: 139; Murray 1795: 121), Knowles provided three examples of multiple negation, and corrected them into single negatives followed by *any* instead of *no*:

(2) I cannot by *no* Means allow it.   *any*
    Nor let *no* Intruder approach me.   *any*
    Nor is he now feared *no* more.   *any* (1796: 65).

The examples are short, made to fit the space of a single line, and appear to have been devised for the purpose instead of having been taken from the works of 'offending' literary authors, as in the case of Lowth's critical footnotes. Knowles's section 'Of verbal criticism' thus more closely approximates later usage guides, which became increasingly elaborate as time went by. Fowler's *Modern English Usage*, as its full title suggests, is a dictionary, which comprises individual words as well as brief linguistic articles on specific problem cases. Several of the longer articles, such as those on the placement of *only* and on the distinction between *moral* and *morale*, had originally appeared elsewhere, in the *Westminster Gazette*, the *Times Literary Supplement*, and, the majority of them, in the Tracts of the Society for Pure English (McMorris 2001: 164). Similarly consisting of what originated as a series of language columns which the author had been invited in 1976 to write for the American magazines *Esquire* and *More*, and in which he dealt with 'major and minor abuses of the English language' (1980: xvii), Simon's *Paradigms Lost* (1980) can be looked upon as a kind of unsystematically presented usage guide; but it deals with the same usage problems as those treated in regular usage guides.

The first usage guide proper, Baker's *Reflections on the English Language* (1770), consists of 127 rules on lexical and syntactic features (Vorlat 2001). It is as completely unordered as the *Five Hundred Mistakes*, and one can't help wondering how people seeking guidance on usage problems found their way about in it. It nevertheless appears to have been relatively popular, for in the preface to the second edition Baker wrote that the first edition 'had a tolerable sale' (1779: xxiii). Occasionally, there are some links between features, as between Rules XXVI and XXVII, the first of which concludes with the comment that 'many People write I'le' instead of *I'll*, which leads him into the next item, starting with the words 'The Mention of a double *L* puts me in Mind of a Mistake, that Writers often commit in speaking of a double Letter' (i.e. 'a DD, or *a double D...a double DD*'). The use of *Reflections* in the title – or *Remarks*: there are three copies in ECCO, somewhat differently arranged and with different titles – suggests that Baker had not intended his book to be used as an object of serious study. Baker, of whom we know nothing apart from what he informs us of in the preface to the *Reflections*, appears to have been a hack writer, who attempted to make money by publishing books for which he believed there was a market among the general public. An example is his *Witticisms and Strokes of Humour* (1766), which proved disappointing in its poor sales despite the fact that it was 'what I then thought and still think as diverting a Thing as ever appear'd' (1770: xlii). As suggested by its subtitle, Baker had been inspired in writing the *Reflections on the English Language* by Vaugelas's *Remarques sur la Langue françoise* (1647), which belonged to a genre that was very popular in seventeenth-century France (Ayres-Bennett 2002). Vaugelas's *Remarques* was frequently reprinted down to 1738 (Vorlat 1999: 2, drawing on Ayres-Bennett 1987), and Baker possibly stumbled upon a copy in the 'Circulating Library' to which he subscribed according to his own preface (1770: v). 'I have not [Vaugelas's] Book by me', he wrote in the opening paragraph of the preface, 'nor did I ever see more than one Copy of it; which Copy I had in my Posession [sic] for some Time' (1770: i). Writing from recollection, Baker decided to publish a similar book, as he appears to have entertained similar hopes for the English market. This is evident from his publication a year later of *Observations on the Pictures now in Exhibition at the Royal Academy, Spring Gardens and Mr. Christie's* (1771), by the same publisher as his *Reflections on the English Language*, John Bell. According to the preface to the *Reflections*, Baker even entertained plans for another book, consisting of 'a great Number of Remarks, that I had been making for four or five Years upon the several Performances of our Players; and which I had intended to digest and publish' (1770: xxiv–xxv). This book, which might have borne a title like *Remarks upon the several Performances of our Players*, never materialized: for some reason or other, Baker 'committed [it] to the Flames'. All this explains, I think, the random presentation of his linguistic reflections as well as the book's rambling style, even by his own admission: 'Having...rambled much,' he wrote in the preface, 'I shall continue to ramble on' (1770: xxvi). The book was meant as a form of entertainment rather than as a usage guide like Fowler's *Modern English Usage*. In this, the *Reflections* is not very different from Simon's *Paradigms Lost*, as is indeed reflected by that book's subtitle *Reflections on Literacy and its Decline*.

The intended audience of these usage guides is the same throughout their history: the linguistically insecure. As typical users Burchfield mentions in the preface to his revised edition of Fowler's *Modern English Usage*, 'a judge, a colonel, and a retired curator of Greek and Roman antiquities at the British Museum' (1996: ix), all of them, it seems, elderly, middle-class, fairly – but not too highly – educated (male?) professionals: 'all but professional linguistic scholars', as Burchfield put it, as indeed was confirmed by a small-scale survey I conducted among linguists (Tieken-Boon van Ostade 2008d) as well as by a wider survey reported on by Busse and Schröder (2008). This is not to say that linguists are not in need of linguistic guidance, but that as a rule they don't think highly of usage guides as such, and of Fowler in particular. This phenomenon calls for further explanation, and I will attempt to do this in Section 8.5. A well-known and fairly typical user of *Modern English Usage* was Sir Winston Churchill. When 'planning the invasion of Normandy,' McMorris writes on the final page of her book (2001: 217), he 'snapped at an aide to check a word in "Fowler"'. The *ODNB* described Churchill as someone who was believed to have been 'academically a bit of a dunce'; perhaps, too, he felt linguistically so insecure as to be in need of his Fowler, even in times of action. Whether apocryphal or not, of equal interest is the fact that Churchill is often cited as having produced the hypercorrect 'This is the sort of thing **up with which** I will not put!' (Crystal 1995: 194). The type of sentence he was allegedly trying to avoid here, however, is not a case of double preposition stranding but of a phrasal-prepositional verb which was fossilized to the extent that it doesn't allow for pied piping (**with which I will not put up*) (Quirk et al. 1985: 1160; Huddleston and Pullum 2002: 287).

In contrast to Vaugelas, who, according to Vorlat (1999: 3) 'wrote for courtiers in the first place, and for others whose use of good grammar helped further their careers', Baker's audience consisted of 'the average English speaker' (1999: 3). As Beal puts it, 'The Industrial Revolution brought prosperity for self-taught, self-made men, some of whom actually rose to peerage' (2004: 5), but the effects of this were already beginning to be felt during the second half of the eighteenth century. Mobility, social as well as geographical, of which there had been a lot all through the eighteenth century with London at first acting as a significant focus of attraction, entailed becoming acquainted with new norms of speaking and writing, and during the second half of the century, social mobility increasingly required 'a facility to speak well appropriately' (Fitzmaurice 1998: 309). Entrance into 'polite society' required access to its norms, linguistic and otherwise. By the early 1770s, Fitzmaurice writes, 'manners may be learned by those unfortunate enough not to have been born into polite society' (1998: 315). This also explains the success of cookery books like Hannah Glasse's *Art of Cookery, Made Plain and Easy,* first published in 1747 and many times reprinted, which offered the aspiring middle classes the means to entertain in style, and also of letter writing manuals like *The Compleat Letter Writer* (Anon. 1756, third edition, and frequently reprinted down to well into the nineteenth century). As far as access to new linguistic norms is concerned, Fitzmaurice (1998: 309) argues, grammars fulfilled a similar function. And indeed, while Lowth's immediate popularity can be explained along these same lines, it was the usage guide par excellence that assisted people in their upward social mobility, enabling them to avoid committing grammatical as well as lexical blunders that would betray their origins. Baker's audience, given his own background, may indeed have consisted of 'the average English speaker' as Vorlat puts it, but if Lowth's grammar catered for the middle classes with social aspirations, people like himself and his family, his grammar offered guidance to those slightly higher up the social scale, people who already had a certain amount of formal education, than Baker's intended audience.

From what little we know about him, Baker himself belonged to the same class: having, as he wrote in his preface, 'quitted the School at fifteen' (1770: ii), he was not very highly educated. He appears to have been largely self-taught in so far as his further education is concerned, mainly, it would seem, through his wide reading of literary books. These he borrowed from the circulating library of which he was a member. Circulating libraries were a new phenomenon in England at the time (Raven 1996), and they typically catered for men like Baker, who had no access to educational institutions like the universities. In this respect, he forms a complete contrast to Lowth, who had received his formal education at the best establishments available. Auer (2008: 69) describes 'the increasing interest of the bourgeoisie in books and reading [which] led to a greater demand in libraries' that were set up to comply with this interest; mostly, this interest concerned novels, but also poetry and belles-lettres. But Baker's interests reached further than what was often referred to as 'low' literature, for in the *Reflections* he quotes from a large collection of literary writers, among whom Vorlat (2001: 398) identified Addison, Shakespeare, Locke, Bolingbroke, Swift, Melmoth, Molyneux, and Richardson. But he read other writers as well, such as Warburton, Congreve, Harris, and Joseph Warton, criticizing their usage in strong terms. Melmoth in particular was singled out for criticism, which, however, seems merely due to the fact that Baker happened to be reading his translation of Cicero's letters, published in 1753, when collecting material for the *Reflections*. While in the case of Lowth's footnotes the writers criticized were all dead, this is not so with Baker: of the authors mentioned, Harris (d.1780), Melmoth (d.1799), Warburton (d.1779), and Warton (d.1800) were all still alive when the *Reflections* appeared. Baker was thus less concerned with the possibility of offending living authors, which might have led to a critical reception of his book and hence potential loss of sales. This suggests that, unlike in the case of Lowth's grammar, these authors did not belong to his target audience.

Baker claims to have been 'entirely ignorant of the Greek, and but indifferently skilled in the Latin' (1770: ii). Normally, skill in the classical languages would be the primary capacity needed for anyone wanting to write a grammar of English, so this would have disqualified him for the job in question (Chapman 2008). Baker's command of grammatical terminology, according to Vorlat (2001: 394), which he would have picked up as part of most boys' formal schooling, is indeed very patchy. For all that, he continues on the same page: 'why should this incapacitate a Man for writing his Mother-tongue with Propriety?' Reading his book in any case shows that he was well capable of using the subjunctive correctly, as in:

(3) Though *Every one* **be** a Noun of Number, it has no Grace as a Plural (1770: 96).

Like Lowth, he may have felt that this verbal form was appropriate to the style of a book on language. Lack of what seems at first sight the main credential for writing the book at hand is similarly discounted by Simon in his preface to *Paradigms Lost* when he writes: 'This book...must be recognized as the work of an amateur' (1980: xv), the reason being that, as the son of an immigrant, he had 'com[e] to English relatively late'. This, however, he turns to

a distinct advantage. One approaches that language with better credentials – linguistic (one's previous languages), cultural (one's awareness of language as the interpreter of a society), and emotional (one's ability to appreciate and love, which grows with the years). There is a sense in which one is both an insider and an outsider in that language, and the interplay between the two becomes creative play (Simon 1980: xiii).

Neither Baker nor Simon thus had the qualifications one would expect of a writer on language; both nevertheless knew that there was a market for what they wrote: they themselves, seems to be the implication in all this, would have benefited from having had access to books offering linguistic guidance.

Baker admits his own lack of qualifications by openly – even naively – claiming ignorance of the field:

It will undoubtedly be thought strange, when I declare that I have never yet seen the folio Edition of Mr. *Johnson's* Dictionary: but, knowing Nobody that has it, I have never been able to borrow it, and I have myself no Books; at least, not many more than what a Church-going old Woman may be supposed to have of devotional Ones upon her Mantle-piece; for, having always had a narrow Income, it has not been in my Power to make a Collection, without straitening myself. Nor did I ever see even the Abridgement of this Dictionary till a few Days ago, when, observing it inserted in the Catalogue of a Circulating Library where I subscribe, I sent for it (Baker 1770: iv–v).

Not only had he never heard of Johnson's dictionary, he also claims unfamiliarity with any grammars, so that 'Such as my Work is, it is entirely my own ... Not being acquainted with any Man of Letters, I have consulted Nobody' (1770: iv). I have found no reason to doubt what he wrote here, but it is peculiar that he had never heard of Lowth's grammar: by 1770, Lowth's grammar had already gone through at least six editions and .reprints (Alston 1965), and Auer (2008) discovered that Lowth's grammar was held by most of the lending libraries whose catalogues she analysed. Like Simon, Baker was an amateur at language, a complete outsider to the field. He admits to his own ignorance in the preface to the second edition of the *Reflections*:

I here declare, as in the Preface to the first edition, that the performance is entirely my own. I have had no assistance from any friend; nor have I borrowed from any work. I even did not know, till the late Dr. Salter shewed me the **Introduction to the English Grammar**, that any thing of the kind had ever appeared among us (1779: xxiii).

'Dr. Salter' was possibly the clergyman Samuel Salter (bap.1713, d.1778), who was evidently familiar with Lowth's grammar. Baker continues by commenting on the amazing correspondence between the grammar and his own work:

I then perceived that some (*not many*) of the observations I had made, had been already made by the author of that work. On the other hand, there are observations in a subsequent edition of the Introduction, which I had made in my first edition. But I have no suspicion that any of those observations were borrowed from *me*. Whoever will give himself the trouble to compare the two books will, indeed, be inclined to wonder that they do not oftener detect the same correctnesses than they actually do (1779: xxiii).

Baker rightly insists that the correspondence between his own work and Lowth's grammar is not due to plagiarism: both works are, though in different ways, typical of a new kind of text type, the usage guide, that, in offering guidance to its users, deals with the same features from the time of its inception down to the present day. It is all the more striking that, as early as the late 1770s, Baker had already noticed the extent to which such works, without being indebted to each other, were similar in content. This continues to be the case today.

For all his lack of credentials, Baker wrote in his preface that he 'paid no Regard to Authority' and that he 'censured even our best Penmen, where they have departed from what I conceive to be the Idiom of the Tongue, or where I have thought they violate Grammar without Necessity' (1770: iv). In this, he took a similar approach to Lowth in the footnotes to his grammar. According to Vorlat, Baker distinguished between different categories of writers: 'bad writers, incorrect ones, tolerable ones, not so good writers, though they may "pass for good Writers"...good writers and "our best authors", "our most judicious writers"' (Vorlat 2001: 397). Lowest on his scale of correctness were nurses and actors, preceded by 'journalists and people in trade' (2001: 397). His dislike of the language of journalists would later be shared by Fowler (Burchfield 1996: viii). Baker proposed the institution of an English Academy as a means to get rid of usage problems like the ones he discussed in his work. To this end, he dedicated the *Reflections* to the King, to whom he proposed to consider

whether it might not be proper to establish in *London* an Academy of the Nature of that of the *Belles Lettres* at *Paris*, and of several in *Italy*. This seems to be a Thing extremely wanted among us. Our Language, as has been often observed, is manly and expressive: but our Writers abound with Incorrectnesses and Barbarisms: for which such an Establishment might in a great Measure be a Cure (Baker 1770: i–ii).

Pleas for an Academy had, however, no longer been heard since the beginning of the eighteenth century, so the notion as such was already a thing of the past. The main aim of an English Academy would have been to codify the language by publishing an authoritative grammar and dictionary. Many such works had come out since the days when people like Dryden, Defoe, Addison, and Swift had made similar pleas in the early eighteenth century, of which Johnson (1755) and Lowth (1762) proved to be particularly authoritative, but this was something of which Baker was completely unaware. With the *Reflections*, he did not set out to codify English grammar but to deal with usage problems; as such, the book clearly belongs to the beginnings of the next stage in the standardization process, the prescription stage.

A typical example of Baker's treatment of a particular feature is Rule XXII, *Had retired for several Years past*. His comment reads:

We often find in our News-papers Paragraphs penn'd in the following Manner. *On such a Day died at ----- Mr. ----, who having aquired a good Fortune in Business, had retired for some Years past.*

This is an **improper** Expression. These Printers **ought to** say either, ... (1770: 20).

The language adopted in proscribing the feature in question, as illustrated by Baker's use of the words *improper* and *ought to*, is very similar to that found in Lowth's grammar. The words *improper/improperly* occur frequently in the *Reflections*, as do some of the other terms of condemnation used by Lowth (*confounded, mistakes, unintelligible*). Searching the *Reflections* in ECCO showed that the directive *ought to* occurs with very great frequency indeed. Another characteristic of normative writing that is similarly found in Fowler and in *Five Hundred Mistakes* is that Baker's approach is often quite humorous. In Rule xxx, for instance, criticizing *came* used as a past participle, he concluded: 'If these Writers persist in this Use of the Word *Came* [as in *He is Came*], I would advise them, not to be inconsistent with themselves, to employ the Word *Went* likewise with the Auxiliaries, and to say *He has went...*', observing, tongue-in-cheek, that 'if we should bring them all to conform to it, we should have a new Language' (1770: 30–1). On the forms *our'n, your'n, his'n*, which are used by 'infinite Numbers of the low People in the Country (and not a few in *London*)', he similarly wrote that he 'would advise [his readers] likewise, in Imitation of many of those low People, to say *Housen*, instead of *Houses*' (1770: 88).

Vorlat (2001: 392) suggests that Baker's *Reflections* was not very popular, but this is contradicted by Baker's preface to the second edition. The book was reviewed at least twice in 1771, in the *Monthly Review* and the *Critical Review* (Percy 2008), and one of the reviews was by Dr John Hawkesworth (bap.1720, d.1773), the editor of the official account of Captain James Cook's voyages around the world, published in 1773. Percy (1996) analysed the Hawkesworth corrections of Captain Cook's language, which reflect the type of linguistic strictures that filled Baker's *Reflections*. It is therefore no surprise that Hawkesworth felt called upon to review the book when it came out. Hawkesworth, according to Percy (1996: 549), appears to have been a stickler for grammatical correctness, and whether Baker's *Reflections* inspired Hawkesworth's linguistic corrections would be worth investigating. Baker's *Reflections* was popular enough to merit a second edition, which came out in 1779 and which included even more usage problems: by his own admission, Baker had 'now almost doubled the number of Remarks' (1779: xxiv). Furthermore, the title page of his *Observations on the Pictures now in Exhibition at the Royal Academy, Spring Gardens and Mr. Christie's* (1771) reads that the book was written 'by the author of the Remarks on the English Language', which confirms the popularity of the *Reflections*. While the book had originally been published anonymously, the second edition carried Baker's name on the title page. By this time, Baker had clearly made a name for himself. Vorlat (2001) discovered that 'quite a few of his rules and examples were ... copied (directly or indirectly) by such grammarians as James Wood (1777), John Hornsey (1793), Alexander Bicknell (1796), John Knowles (1796) and William Angus (1800)'. Knowles and Angus (with Brittain) occupy the top three in the league table of proscriptive comments in Figure 8.1, so it is interesting to see that this is partly due to their reliance on Baker. Of these grammars, only Hornsey is available in ECCO, but he doesn't appear to refer to Baker. He does mention Lowth quite frequently in his grammar, advising his readers to proceed to Lowth if they 'should wish to prosecute the study of *English grammar* any farther' (Hornsey 1793: 4).

8.4 LOWTH'S FOOTNOTES: A USAGE GUIDE IN EMBRYONIC FORM

Despite the many similarities between Lowth's grammar and Baker's *Reflections*, which even Baker himself was struck by, there seems to have been no indebtedness from one to the other or vice versa. For all that, their approach to the usage problems they deal with is remarkably similar. This is evident from their choice of usage labels and use of grammatical metalanguage, but also from the form of their strictures. Vorlat describes Baker's rules as being 'typically structured as follows: spoken or written English frequently has structure *a* (for the written examples the erroneous source is often mentioned explicitly). This is wrong, and ought to be replaced by structure *b*' (2001: 392), and this equally applies to Lowth. Compare the stricture from Baker discussed in Section 8.3 above with the following one from Lowth:

'*Did* he *not fear* the Lord, and *besought* the Lord, and the Lord *repented* him of the evil, which he had pronounced against them?' Jer. xxvi. 19. Here the Interrogative and Explicative forms are **confounded**. It **ought to** be, 'Did he not *fear* the Lord, and *beseech* the Lord? and *did not* the Lord *repent* him of the evil, – ? (Lowth 1762: 117).

The repudiation of the language of the best authors is likewise a common starting point in the two works. In this they both deviate from the contrary approach in this respect taken by Dr Johnson, but, as I have argued in Chapter 4, doing so had been a deliberate decision on Lowth's part. Baker, by contrast, had been completely unaware of the existence of Johnson's dictionary until he had practically finished his book. Baker's reason for shunning the example of the language of 'our best Penmen' must have been his own lack of education, which, rather than make him linguistically insecure, must have made him aware of the fact that a literary reputation alone doesn't warrant correctness in language use. As argued in Section 8.3, such a reaction seems typical of normative writers in his position. Though phrased with greater explicitness, Lowth had made this very point in his preface when advertising the need for his grammar: 'we have writers, who have enjoyed these advantages [i.e. "much practice in the polite world, and a general acquaintance with the best authors"] in their full extent, and yet cannot be recommended as models of an accurate style' (Lowth 1762: vii). It is interesting to see that, apart from the authors' presumed wide reading, Lowth refers to their social position here. Though Baker was in possession of the former, I have argued that he was probably lacking in the latter, hence the motivation for his book.

Lowth's model of linguistic correctness, as I have argued in Chapter 7, was not his own usage but that of the social class to which he, and many others like him, aspired. He never made this point in his preface as such,

but perhaps he did not need to. Baker, however, as someone who presented himself as lacking the necessary qualifications for the job in hand,
was in a different position, and in the preface he wrote: 'But don't let the
Reader imagine me vain enough to suppose my own Stile preferable upon
the whole, or at all equal to that of some of the Writers, whom I have thus
criticised' (1770: iv). (Baker here pre-empted the kind of criticism Lowth
actually received from Aitchison, who tacitly assumed that he based the
model of correctness in his grammar on his own usage.) What model of
correctness Baker did adopt for the strictures he presented in the *Reflections* can be arrived at only indirectly by considering the usage he disapproved of, that of people living away from London, particularly in the
northern counties, as well as of 'Nurses', actors, shopkeepers, and journalists (Vorlat 2001: 397). Lowth, by contrast, never made such sociolinguistic
comments in his grammar. Baker's model of correctness was that of the
social class above those whose language he criticized, the educated London
middle classes, which is also evident from the fact that he praised the
language of contemporary writers like Addison, Congreve, Johnson, and
Bolingbroke, authors whom, with the exception of Johnson as a living
writer, were all criticized by Lowth. Lowth, in turn, aimed at the linguistic
norm of the class above that.

Baker, as I have shown above, often took a humorous approach to the
linguistic mistakes he criticized in the *Reflections*, in the same way that
other writers of usage guides were to do after him. Though Lowth's
grammar is presented in a serious tone throughout, the unexpected and
unappreciated little joke he makes when observing on the use of preposition stranding that 'This is an Idiom which our language is strongly
inclined to' foreshadows the genre of the usage guide. This and the
many other similarities between his grammar, particularly the footnotes
to the syntax section, and Baker's *Reflections* as the first usage guide proper
suggests that this part of Lowth's grammar may be seen as a usage guide
in embryonic form. Lowth and Baker dealt with many identical usage
problems, such as *fly/flee*, *lie/lay*, the proper use of *who/whom*, double
negation, the pleonastic perfect infinitive, and other items. Baker deals
with many more features that became the stock-in-trade of later usage
guides, such as whether it should be *different to* or *from*, the differences
between *ago* and *since*, *set* and *sit*, and, surprisingly, the plural of the word
mussulman, but it is clear that Lowth's critical footnotes already anticipated
the rise of the new genre less than a decade later.

But in many instances Lowth wasn't the first to deal with these items either. In the case of the various strictures which carry his name he first found them elsewhere: Harris's *Hermes* (1751) for participial *wrote*, Dryden in that of preposition stranding, while double negation was such a general issue, raised even in Shakespeare's *Much Ado about Nothing*, that it could barely fail to be included in a grammar like his. Percy (2009), moreover, shows that many of the strictures found in Lowth's grammar were already commonly criticized in the *Monthly Review* and the *Critical Review* before they made their appearance in his or any other grammar, and she argues that these writings helped create the 'climate of linguistic anxiety' that led to a widespread interest in grammars and other works dealing with usage problems. All this helps explain the immediate popularity of Lowth's grammar: its focus on usage problems reflected general public interest, and it fuelled linguistic criticism by individuals enjoying the game of 'picking faults and finding Errors' in each other's writings, as illustrated by the letter from Thomas Fitzmaurice to Adam Smith quoted in Section 3.6. Though it had a more scholarly readership as well, the grammar's primary function came to be to serve the needs of those who felt insecure about their language, thus creating a distinct market for such works that was capitalized upon by Robert Dodsley and his associates.

The desire for linguistic correctness also operated at the level of the individual writer, as has already been discussed in relation to Walpole's criticism of Robert Dodsley's use of preposition stranding. Walpole had also complained in a private letter about the use of *between you and I*, a grammatical mistake he associated with the language of women (Tieken-Boon van Ostade 1994). We find similar attention to linguistic correctness in the correspondence between Edward Synge (1691–1762), Bishop of Elphin, County Roscommon in Ireland, and his daughter Alicia (1733–1807). As her sole surviving parent, and being away from home for long stretches of time in exercising his episcopal duties, Synge kept in close touch with Alicia by letter. Altogether, some two hundred letters have come down to us, written between 1746 and 1752, though, as in the case of Lowth's letters to his wife, only those written by Synge himself (Legg 1996). Ruberg (2008) argues that the letters functioned as a kind of 'pedagogical tool' for Synge, as a means to educate his daughter, even from a distance: 'they served to make her acquainted with current notions of politeness', but they did a lot more besides. 'Through these letters,' Ruberg writes, 'Bishop Synge taught his daughter how to spell and how to compose letters' (2008: 208), but he also tried to instil into her a notion of what constituted correct grammar, repeatedly pointing out that she had committed 'a defect in Grammar', a 'bad expression', an 'error in your English', and that she had produced various instances of 'bad' or 'false English'. Typical grammatical errors which Synge pointed out in the language of his daughter were the use of *who* for *whom* and *whom* for *who*, and of *between you and I*, the omission of the relative, the improper use of prepositions, and the omission of *but*, as in:

(4) I doubt not that half the town,

on which he commented:

I can't say I doubt, that this is not correct English. I am sure it is not. Consider it a little and you'll find it out your Self. There ought to be *but*, between not and that, or you might drop *that* to make it run smoother, tho' this is authoriz'd rather by Custom than Grammar (Legg 1996: 188).

Synge's approach to grammar was as normative as that of Lowth and Baker, and many of the features he dealt with in his letters later appeared in Lowth's grammar. Lowth's grammar would have suited Synge very well in the education of his daughter if it had been available to him, and girls like Alicia – she was thirteen at the time the correspondence began – would have made up the right kind of readership for the grammar. It is, moreover, of interest to see that both men, who were to have identical positions in society, shared similar concerns for the education of their children.

   Though foreshadowing the new text type, Lowth's grammar was not a usage guide. It may have been used as such, and its focus on grammatical correctness may have earned the grammar its popularity, but the book was first and foremost a grammar. This is how it was viewed by Lowth himself, as is evident from Lowth's refusal of having an 'index' or table of contents added to a reprint of the grammar in order to 'promote the Sale' (§3.7). The letter in which this suggestion was made has not come down to us, nor has the index, which had already been prepared by a certain Mr Holmes, but Lowth's reply suggests the purpose of such an index: 'A Grammar always is, or ought to be, ranged so exactly under its proper heads in so clear a method, y^t. **no one can be at a loss to find y^e. part on wch. it is to be consulted**' (Lowth to James Dodsley, 21 July 1778). Evidently, guidance in more easily finding the places in the grammar where particular usage problems were treated had been considered a possible asset to the grammar. By 1778, when the discussion took place and by which time Baker was about to be reprinted, the interest among the general audience in usage problems and a demand for works that dealt with them would have been very much apparent. Ten years earlier, in his second edition of 1768, Priestley had already collected the notes in his grammar to present them in a separate section called 'Notes *and* Observations, For the Use of those who have some Proficiency in the Language' (1768: 57) (Straaijer 2009). Lowth never did likewise, but the fifteen pages 'Of Verbal Criticism' in the fourth edition of Knowles's *Principles of English Grammar* (1796) similarly shows that grammars and usage guides were in the process of becoming distinct text types. Baker's *Reflections* is the first example of a publication that shows how this could be put into effect.

8.5 DIFFERENT COMMUNITIES OF PRACTICE

There are many differences between Lowth and Baker. To begin with, they had very different educational, and hence presumably also social, backgrounds: having attended Winchester College and having studied at New College, Oxford, from which university he also obtained a doctorate, Lowth was educated in the fullest possible form. Baker, by contrast, left school when he was only fifteen, and doesn't appear to have enjoyed any formal education since. He was primarily a self-taught man, profiting from his membership of the fairly new phenomenon of the circulating library, which was intended precisely for men of his social standing. Libraries have been called 'the poor man's university', and this is an apt qualification in Baker's case, too. He barely possessed any books, he wrote in his Preface, while Lowth owned a fairly extensive library at the time of his death, comprising well over two hundred titles. As a writer, and also no doubt due to his later high status, Lowth was able to acquire books not by paying for them but as presentation copies from fellow writers. He was even in the position of using the publication of one of his own books as a means to establish a coalition, which could serve him well in his new status as Bishop of London. Baker was in no such position: he could, it seems, barely afford to spend a great deal on presentation copies. That for him publishing was a means of making money for his own subsistence is evident from his complaint in the preface to the *Reflections* on the lack of interest in his earlier book called *Witticisms and Strokes of Humour* (1766), which had hardly any Sale. Thereupon I made presents of some Hundreds, and sold six hundred at a very low Price to an ignorant Bookseller; of which I soon repented; for I found the Booby had altered the Title-page, and had inserted a long Account of *Humbugs, Funny Jokes, Conundrums, Arch Waggeries,* &c. with my Name at the bottom of all this Nonsense (1770: xlii–xliii).

Baker ended the preface by telling a few 'witticisms' to advertise the book, adding that 'Some of the Copies are still remaining where these Remarks [i.e. the *Reflections*] are sold. The Price is but a poor *Shilling*' (1770: xliii).

Another difference between the two men is that Lowth was an established author when he published his grammar, while Baker was seeking to become one. Lowth's grammar continued to appear anonymously, but buyers of the grammar knew the author's name, and some of them added it on the title page in their own hand. The grammar was advertised in the public press along with Lowth's other publications, and his name acted as a selling device for the publishers who pirated his grammar. The Dodsleys similarly advertised the book as '**Dr. Lowth's** Introduction to English Grammar' in advertisements for other publications by him, despite the fact that his authorship was never referred to on the title page. The publication of the *Reflections* made Baker's name: one of his subsequent publications advertised on the title page as having been published 'by the author of the Remarks on the English Language', while the second edition of the *Reflections* carried his name. No later publications by Baker are included in ECCO, so he may no longer have been active as a writer – or even alive – after 1779.

A final difference between Lowth and Baker is the question of their expertise: by Chapman's list of explicit credentials for the ability to write a grammar, 'education, university degrees, occupation, publications and membership of professional societies' (2008: 23), Lowth scores highest of all those examined. Having obtained a doctorate from the University of Oxford, where he occupied a chair as Professor of Poetry for several years, he had published two important books before embarking on his grammar and became a Fellow of the Royal Societies of Göttingen and London – though after, not before, he had published his grammar. Baker scores extremely low on all these qualifications: his lack of a university education and having only one earlier publication, his *Witticisms and Strokes of Humour* (1766), barely qualifies him as an author for a usage guide. His membership of a circulating library, moreover, counts as no further qualification either, though this is how he acquired his wide reading as well as the material for his book. He may, however, have been a teacher of French. Evidence for this may be found on the one hand in his familiarity with Vaugelas's *Remarques sur la Langue françoise* (1647), and on the other hand in the fact that in the dedication of the *Reflections* to the King, Baker not only makes a plea for the institution of an English Academy comparable to those in France and Italy, but also presents an elaborate plan for the improvement of the teaching of languages and in particular for that of French (1770: viii). According to Chapman (2008: 31), 'It is not unusual to find claims from grammarians for their expertise in teaching'. Even though his experience was not with English as such, if Baker was indeed a teacher of French this would certainly count as a certain amount of qualification for his expertise in writing the *Reflections*. Lowth, however, had never been a teacher of English, and this is what may have caused his grammar to have been too difficult for young children, certainly in the eyes of Ellenor Fenn, who exploited this lack of expertise as a means to advertise her own grammar as one that would be particularly suitable for very young children (see §3.6).

Despite the many differences between them and despite the fact that there was no link between their respective publications, Lowth and Baker were very much doing the same thing: they were engaged in a similar battle, 'determin'd', as Lowth wrote to Merrick soon after the grammar was first published, 'to repell the invasions of y^e. enemy to the utmost of my power, & to give no quarter to any of their straglers that shall ^{fall} into my hands' (Lowth to Merrick, 4 May 1762), the 'enemy' being the example of bad grammar by authors of repute. To explain this phenomenon, it is helpful to consider Watts's discussion of the question of whether the eighteenth-century grammarians should be considered a community of practice or a discourse community. Citing Wenger's (1998) work on the subject, Watts defines a community of practice as 'displaying mutual engagement, a joint enterprise and a shared repertoire' (2008: 42). A discourse community, by contrast, is

a set of individuals who can be interpreted as constituting a community on the basis of the ways in which their oral or written discourse practices reveal common interests, goals and beliefs, i.e. on the degree of institutionalisation that their discourse displays. The members of the community may or may not be conscious of sharing those discourse practices (Watts 1999: 43).

Taking this approach explains what Priestley envisaged in the preface to the second edition. Acknowledging what he calls his 'obligation to *Dr. Lowth,* whose *short introduction to English grammar* was first published about a month after the former edition of mine' and from which he had 'taken a few of his examples (though generally for a purpose different from his) to make my own more complete', he wrote that Lowth 'is welcome to make the same use of' the material in his own grammar. In other words, he invited Lowth to establish a community of practice with him, explaining that 'it is from an amicable union of labours, together with a generous emulation in all the friends of science, that we may most reasonably expect the extension of all kinds of knowledge' (Priestley 1768: xxiii). Lowth, however, never responded to this invitation: as I have shown in Chapter 3, he never once referred to Priestley in his grammar, presumably because of their different religious backgrounds. Whether a similar opportunity ever occurred in relation to Johnson and his *Dictionary* I do not know. If it did, Lowth almost certainly would have refused, due to his radically and deliberately different opinion as to what constituted a model of grammatical correctness. My analysis of Lowth's social network has shown that Johnson was never more than a peripheral member of it, someone who happened to have published a dictionary with the same publisher and whose dictionary Lowth possessed a copy of, but with whom he felt no other more significant link.

Watts concludes that the eighteenth-century grammarians did not form a community of practice. Instead, he argues, they will 'have mutually engaged with publishers and booksellers' (2008: 51), thus forming communities of practice with them rather than with their fellow grammarians. This is indeed the case if we look at Dodsley and Johnson in connection with the *Dictionary,* which has been widely acknowledged to be a 'booksellers' project' (Reddick 1996). As for Dodsley and Lowth, it is not only with the publication of the grammar that the two men would similarly have formed a community of practice, as they were also mutually engaged in producing what, with the publication of Dodsley's fables in 1761, would result in a set of educational works (Chapter 2). Even the idea for the fables may have been initiated by Lowth. Several of the contributors to this joint project, in particular William Melmoth, Joseph Spence, and Robert Dodsley's brother James, contributed in their different ways to the grammar as well: Melmoth read a draft version of it, Spence was among those personally invited to submit comments and suggestions for the improvement of it – 'You do very well in laying in materials for the improvement of it,' Lowth had told him, and for all we know he did – and James Dodsley took over the publication of the grammar's later editions and reprints after his brother Robert had died.

If the eighteenth-century grammarians did not form a community of practice, a much better designation of them, Watts concludes, is that of a discourse community. They did indeed have 'common interests, goals and beliefs' (Watts 2008: 41) in their aim to codify the English language by means of the publication of grammars in which they presented a norm of grammatical correctness. In doing so they believed in the notion of a standardized language as subsequently defined by Milroy and Milroy (1991: 26), seeking to reduce 'optional variability in language'. Their common goals were '(1) to codify the principles of the language and reduce it to rule; (2) to settle disputed points and decide cases of divided usage; and (3) to point out common errors or what were supposed to be errors, and thus correct and improve the language' (Baugh and Cable 2002: 277), and they went about this by applying three major considerations, 'reason, etymology, and the example of Latin and Greek' (2002: 280). Examples of how these principles were applied can be found in their treatment of double negation (reason, or logic: two negatives make a positive), preposition stranding (etymology: a preposition should be pre-posed), and the split infinitive (the example of Latin, where infinitives are single words and cannot be split). Double negation and preposition stranding have already been dealt with extensively in the chapters above. As for the split infinitive, this is a stricture that is only first found in the 1830s (Bailey 1996: 248), but it is a good example of the operation of the example of Latin and Greek in the formulation of a grammatical stricture. Burchfield (1996: 736) provides the argument in his edition of *Modern English Usage*: 'In Latin such a construction could not arise because an infinitive (*amāre* 'to love', *crescere* 'to grow') is indivisible and is not preceded by a grammatical particle'. It is clear from the widespread and long-standing occurrence of the construction – Mittins et al. (1970: 70) mention Wycliffe, Tyndale, Donne, Goldsmith, Burns, Browning, Coleridge, and George Eliot as authors who used it – that actual usage did not play a role here. Lowth not only did not deal with the split infinitive in his grammar, he did not use the construction either. Being well versed in the classical languages, he may have proceeded in his own writing from the principle that infinitives cannot be split. As he swerved not even once in his most private letters, this suggests that the split infinitive in his own idiolect was not an issue of what Busse and Schröder (forthcoming) call 'disputed usage'. The split infinitive had not yet turned into a shibboleth.

The strictures with which the normative grammarians sought to eradicate optional variability, as I have demonstrated in Chapter 4, became increasingly prescriptive. Straaijer (2009) has shown that this is even evident in the metalanguage in Lowth's and Priestley's grammars, which barely differ in this respect despite these authors' reputations as icons of prescriptivism and descriptivism, respectively. But writers of usage guides likewise can be looked upon as forming a discourse community: they, too, are united by having 'common interests, goals and beliefs', which, moreover, overlap to a certain extent with those of the normative grammarians. Writers of usage guides similarly have as their main aim the reduction of optional variability in language by means of grammatical strictures, but also by lexical ones. This is true for Baker (1770), 43 of whose 127 strictures, according to Vorlat (2001: 392), deal with lexical issues – such as the difference between *eminent* and *imminent* and whether it should be *possessed of* or *by* – and the rest with grammatical ones, and also for Knowles (1796) and Burgess (1856). This, then, is a major distinction between normative grammarians and writers of usage guides, along with the fact that they produce different text types: grammars are divided into sections called Orthography, Etymology, Syntax, and Prosody or Letters, Syllables, Words, and Sentences (as in Lowth's case) and they deal with the system of parts of speech in a systematic way, while usage guides are collections of more or less haphazardly collected – and at first presented – usage problems that occur in the fields of grammar and lexis. Lowth's treatment of grammatical problems in his footnotes was an innovation at the time, and he therefore to some extent belongs to both types of discourse communities. By refusing an 'index' to his grammar that would have helped to make the two-pronged approach to grammar and usage more explicit, he himself at the time, 1778, clearly failed to recognize the ongoing development. Priestley was more up to date in this respect. That Baker's *Reflections* happened to become the first usage guide proper is due to the major difference between the two men and their works: Lowth was a scholar, whose grammar was in fact an accidental product resulting from his interest in the education of his own children, and the opportunities for which were rightly spotted by his publisher Robert Dodsley, while Baker was a man who sought to make a living by writing. Fairly accidentally it seems, he produced the kind of work for which there developed an ever-growing demand among the general public eager to improve themselves and their language. It is interesting to see that in drawing upon the example of the French, he produced the kind of work for English that had had its first impact in France well over a century earlier. It would also be interesting to speculate about whether Dodsley, whose eye for the market was unusually innovative (Tierney 1988: 29), would have been aware of the ongoing developments if he hadn't died so soon after Lowth's grammar had appeared.

8.6 THE LINGUISTS VERSUS THE PRESCRIPTIVISTS

Looking at eighteenth-century normative grammarians and writers of usage guides as forming distinct discourse communities helps explain the nature of the critical footnotes in Lowth's grammar. The contents of the footnotes differs completely from the grammar, and so does its metalanguage, as has been demonstrated by Straaijer (2009), who showed, both for the first and the second editions of the grammar, that the footnotes are considerably more prescriptive than the grammar proper. In thus anticipating the later development of the usage guide as a new text type, Lowth's grammar became enormously popular, a development that was fuelled by a widespread interest in the local press as well as in private communication between people interested in similar usage problems as the ones Lowth dealt with. This demonstrates that the next stage in the standardization process of the English language, the prescription stage, was imminent when Lowth's grammar was first published. Though first and foremost a grammar, the *Short Introduction* is therefore also part of the same phenomenon as that which produced writers like Baker, Burgess, Fowler, Gowers, Simon, Burchfield, Truss, and many others. As the precursor to the large-scale prescriptive movement that characterizes the nineteenth century, and a popular one at that, it is not surprising that Lowth came to bear the brunt of the attack on prescriptivism by twentieth-century linguists, the more so since he eventually occupied an important public position as Bishop of London. This is indeed primarily how he is remembered today. His critical footnotes were an innovation within the English grammatical tradition, so it is only natural that they drew attention to themselves as a new phenomenon. The footnotes were even commented upon, according to Percy (2008: 136), by a contemporary reviewer, who, as early as 1771, noted that 'Dr. Lowth was the first who struck out of the common road'. Today, Hussey (1995: 154) argues, these footnotes are largely responsible for Lowth's poor reputation among linguists.

Viewing writers of usage guides as a distinct discourse community also helps explain why writers like Lowth and Fowler are despised by linguists. Linguists similarly belong to a discourse community of their own, with different 'interests, goals and beliefs' from writers of usage guides or normative grammarians like Lowth. The first sentence in Milroy and Milroy (1991: 1) reads: 'In this book we attempt to look **dispassionately** at *prescription* in language and the effects of prescriptive attitudes on the daily lives of individuals.' It is their use of the word 'dispassionately' that strikes the eye, for it refers to the sensitive nature of the topic dealt with in their book, and in my own. Several pages further down they refer to *The Language Trap* (1983) by John Honey, who 'blame[d] the discipline of linguistics for [the] decline' of English language teaching (Milroy and Milroy 1991: 9). Nearly fifteen years later, Honey published *Language is Power. The Story of Standard English and its Enemies* (1997), which, together with Trudgill's review of the book published in 1997 and Honey's rejoinder of 2000, emphasizes the extent to which they represent two distinct camps within linguistics that are diametrically opposed in their interests and methodologies. The Honey–Trudgill controversy, with its fiercely personal attacks, demonstrates that members of either camp refuse to take the other side seriously, failing to recognize each other's different 'interests, goals and beliefs'. Another example of this is Stephen Pinker who, in *The Language Instinct* (1994), calls Simon, the author of *Paradigms Lost* (1980), a 'malicious know-nothing'. Pinker continues:

Simon has simply discovered the trick used with great effectiveness by certain comedians and talk-show hosts, and punk-rock musicians: people of modest talent can attract the attention of the media, at least for a while, by being unrelentingly offensive (1994: 385).

Trudgill similarly calls Honey 'a skilful self-publicist, [who] court[s] attention through his polemics', and he denies that Honey was a linguist:

His linguistic 'training', I believe, and I apologise if I am wrong, consisted merely of a one-year MA course at Newcastle University under Barbara Strang. Those of us who have taught such courses know that they do not necessarily succeed in converting students into linguists. In Honey's case, he seems, rather, to have been turned into an anti-linguist. Honey has never done any linguistic research. He is not sympathetic to the goals of linguistics ... (Trudgill 1997).

In the same review, Trudgill complains of the 'ad-hominem tone' of Honey's book, which he illustrates with the following passage:

Meanwhile it was chastening to watch the enemies of standard English prosper. Professor Trudgill went onwards and upwards through professorships at Reading and Essex to a chair in Switzerland, thus becoming one of the highest-paid professors of English linguistics in the world, and Jenny Cheshire achieved similar status at two other Swiss universities. Viv Edwards was given a professorship at Reading University... (Honey 1997: 221).

Trying to deal with the issue in hand, as Milroy and Milroy (1991) attempt to do in *Authority in Language*, calls for a 'dispassionate' approach indeed.

The issue, I think, would benefit from viewing the two so-called camps as distinct discourse communities, each with their respective 'common interests, goals and beliefs'. On the one hand there are the normative grammarians, including writers of usage guides, as they share with the grammarians their aims and approaches in trying to reduce optional variability in language, though doing so in a different form and by not limiting themselves to grammatical issues only; their roots can be found in the eighteenth-century attempts at linguistic codification and, subsequently, prescribing a model of grammatical correctness. On the other hand there are the structural linguists, whose origin as a scientific discipline goes back to the late nineteenth century. Hodson (2006: 60) refers to de Saussure's claim 'that the genesis of 20th-century linguistics lies in the rejection of 18th-century grammar'. This, she argues, has led to descriptivism being considered basic to the study of language, which at the same clouded the perspective with which structural linguists viewed the products of the eighteenth-century grammarians. The result is that Lowth is branded as an icon of prescriptivism while Priestley came to be designated 'as a lone prophet of descriptivist linguistics' (Hodson 2006: 63; Tieken-Boon van Ostade forthcoming). Pullum (1974) has shown that analysing Lowth from a modern, structuralist perspective produces a distorted view of his grammar and what it stood for, arguing that Lowth 'is more mentioned than read by the majority of grammarians today'. The same is true, Hodson shows, for Priestley. She demonstrates, moreover, that 'important aspects of Priestley's work have been overlooked because they do not fit comfortably with [the] schematic "prescriptivist versus descriptivist" account' advocated by twentieth-century linguists. By analysing the metalanguage used by Lowth and Priestley in their grammars, Straaijer (2009) arrived at the same conclusion. It is increasingly recognized that this dichotomy does not work for the eighteenth-century normative grammars, and this recognition has come about by studying the grammars in the context in which they were written and with the aims for which they were produced in mind (Tieken-Boon van Ostade 2000*c*).

In his review of Honey (1997), Trudgill lists a number of linguists who were regarded by Honey as enemies of the English language, thus neatly defining them as members of one of the two linguistic discourse communities discussed here: 'Jenny Cheshire, Jim Milroy, Lesley Milroy, Roy Harris, Sir John Lyons, David Crystal, Jean Aitchison, Frank Palmer, Michael Stubbs, Michael Halliday, William Labov, Stephen Pinker [sic: see below], Suzanne Romaine, Walt Wolfram, Donna Christian, Howard Giles – and Noam Chomsky' (Trudgill 1997). The other discourse community consists of those who claim to have the fate of Standard English at heart, and it is represented by writers like John Honey. Jean Aitchison's presence in the above list calls for little comment in the light of my discussion of her treatment of Lowth, but it is surprising to find James and Lesley Milroy included as well, as the publication of their book *Authority in Language* attempts to bridge the gap between the two discourse communities by analysing the phenomenon of prescription in language in the context of the standardization process. Another bridge-building publication, though at first without any noticeable impact perhaps because of its very topic, is Pullum (1974), which offers a 're-evaluation' of Lowth's grammar. It is time the article should be given the credit it deserves.

8.7 THE DOMAIN OF NORMATIVE LINGUISTICS

Lowth's critical footnotes may have been an innovation within the English grammatical tradition, their nature was not new as such. Percy (2009) shows that many similar comments appeared in the *Critical Review* and *Monthly Review* around the time the grammar was first published, while individuals like Sir Horace Walpole and Edward Synge complained privately about grammatical errors they encountered before Lowth's grammar was at their disposal. Lowth's grammar, however, was still a grammar and not a usage guide – this is how he viewed it himself – but the reception of the grammar shows that it was also consulted for the advice it offered on correct usage. Usage guides proper did not come into existence until about a decade later, with the publication of Robert Baker's *Reflections on the English Language*. Though Lowth's grammar offered no direct contribution to Baker's collection of linguistic criticisms, Baker's book may well owe its moderate popularity to Lowth's grammar, which fuelled current interest in linguistic criticism. Both Lowth's grammar and Baker's *Reflections* came at the right time in the history of English, when many people were in search of linguistic guidance in trying to acquire the linguistic norms that accompanied their social aspirations. It is interesting to see the many similarities – as well as the many differences – between Lowth and Baker. Apart from the ones discussed, it may be noted that both were in fact self-proclaimed experts at writing on linguistic correctness. Baker does so quite openly and perhaps naively in his preface. Lowth, however, never did so: it is only as a result of reading his private correspondence that we understand that his grammar came about as an accidental publication, due to the fact that as a parent he had the education of his elder son at heart and because he encountered another parent with the same interests in his immediate social circle. More copies could only be made available, he explained to his friend and fellow scholar James Merrick, by having the grammar printed. It took the efforts of a publisher like Robert Dodsley to realize the potential among a much wider reading public of the grammar Lowth had produced.

In their concern for linguistic correctness, Lowth and Baker, and along with them many others, then as well as now, form a distinct discourse community, whose members have the same interests at heart, share the same approach to linguistic correctness, and, in the end, largely deal with the same linguistic issues. Viewing them in this light explains their critical reception by modern linguists, who from the time when linguistics first developed as a discipline at the end of the nineteenth century had quite distinct aims and objectives when studying language, applying what were considered fundamentally different methodologies in doing so. But continuing to treat normative writers on language as a kind of pseudo-linguists does not greatly contribute to an understanding of the phenomenon of, for instance, the usage guide, or why the books by Honey should enjoy any popularity. Seeing them as a distinct discourse community does contribute towards a greater appreciation of what the eighteenth-century grammarians were doing at the time, and to what end, and it also helps explain today's interest in prescriptivism. If Trudgill and others are structural linguists, those engaged in studying the phenomenon of prescriptivism in linguistics can be called normative linguists. But it is striking that Trudgill also co-edited, with Laurie Bauer, a collection of short articles in a volume called *Language Myths* (Bauer and Trudgill 1998). The articles deal with so-called myths about language, or ideas common among the general public such as that 'the meanings of words should not be allowed to vary or change' (Trudgill), that 'the media are ruining English' (Aitchison), that 'some languages have no grammar' (Bauer), and that 'America is ruining the English language' (Algeo). The idea behind the book was to let linguists, rather than journalists (like Bill Bryson, author of *Mother Tongue*), editors (like Robert McCrum, co-author of the popular book and television series *The Story of English*), or psychologists (like Stephen Pinker, already discussed), 'inform the general public about language' (1998: xv), by tackling popular linguistic notions. Bauer and Trudgill end their introduction to the collection by making a plea for a 'dispassionate and objective' approach to language (1998: xviii). But what they do not attempt to try and explain is the origins of the linguistic myths as a phenomenon in its own right: proper attention to such issues is the domain of normative linguistics.

9

CONCLUSION

FOR the purpose of this study I have drawn upon two types of material, Lowth's grammar and its many editions and reprints, and Lowth's private documents – his letters, his Will and as many other documents that he produced as I was able to locate, such as his short Memoirs. Lowth's grammar and the many prejudices it gave rise to over the years, the most persistent one being that he wrote the *Short Introduction* as Bishop of London, are central to this book, as it seemed high time for a thorough reconsideration of its aims and origins, and to show that Lowth's status as an icon of prescriptivism is undeserved. Indeed, as Chapman (2008: 36) has argued, a better candidate for this would be Lindley Murray. Murray, as I have demonstrated here, made extensive use of Lowth's grammar, and in adopting the rules and strictures he found there, turned them into more strongly prescriptive pronouncements. In doing so, he was merely following the tide of his time, which was moving towards an increasing emphasis on prescriptivism in language use. To illustrate the persistence of the current view on Lowth, Yáñez-Bouza (2008, 2009), for instance, though arguing in favour of 'undemonising' Lowth, still interpreted his discussion of preposition stranding as a strong bias on his part in favour of the fronted position. Yet, as I argued above, what Lowth wrote on preposition stranding is neither prescriptive nor proscriptive but entirely descriptive. In carefully identifying a stylistic distinction between the use of the two variant constructions, observing that the former 'prevails in common conversation, and suits very well with the familiar style in writing' while the latter 'agrees much better with the solemn and elevated Style' (1762: 127–8), Lowth's discussion of the phenomenon is even strikingly modern. We find the same description in Milroy (1998), one of the brief articles in the volume edited by Bauer and Trudgill (1998) already referred to in

Chapter 8. The myth Lesley Milroy deals with is 'Bad grammar is slovenly', and in the article she discusses three linguistic strictures, the one against the use of preposition stranding, the use of *different to* instead of *from*, and the split infinitive, showing that all three are in general use and should even be considered appropriate, from a sociolinguistic perspective, to the context in which they occur. On preposition stranding she notes that:

'Who am I speaking to?' is normal in most contexts, while 'To whom am I speaking?' will generally be interpreted as marking social distance. Thus the real difference between these forms is stylistic; both are good English sentences in appropriate contexts (Milroy 1998: 95).

The 'Final verdict' which Burchfield pronounces on the subject in his revised edition of Fowler's *Modern English Usage* is virtually identical:

In most circumstances, esp. in formal writing, it is desirable to avoid placing a preposition at the end of a clause or sentence, where it has the appearance of being stranded. But there are many circumstances in which a preposition may or even must be placed late ... and others where the degree of formality required governs the placing (Burchfield 1996: 619).

It seems somewhat surprising that the same description occurs in the grammar of a man who is commonly blamed for being an arch-prescriptivist, the more so since Burchfield actually refers to Lowth's grammar in this section.

Analysing the language of Lowth's letters has demonstrated how accurate his description of the use of preposition stranding and pied piping was, at least with respect to his own idiolect: preposition stranding is indeed more frequent in his most informal usage, as represented by the letters to his wife, than in his more formal styles of writing. Sairio's analysis of preposition stranding in the language of the eighteenth-century bluestocking Elizabeth Montagu shows that Mrs Montagu's usage changed over the years, due to the influence of the then current climate that gave rise to the large-scale increase in normative grammars (Sairio 2008), but she also shows that Montagu's usage did not correlate with the addressee of her letters (Sairio 2009: 212). This, however, seems due to the fact that Montagu's relationship with the two different groups of addressees distinguished in Sairio's study, family and friends, did not call for any significant stylistic differences which would have involved making particular linguistic choices in the case of preposition stranding. My own analysis of Lowth's communicative competence in as much detail as possible, including not only letters to friends and family but also to more distantly related addressees, has enabled me to offer a fuller account of this particular individual's ability to vary his language in significant and effective ways. Analysis of other idiolects will have to demonstrate to what extent my findings for Lowth are exceptional or not. I very much doubt, however, that they are; after all, his description of preposition stranding is still, as Milroy (1998) suggests, very applicable to usage today. My findings that the amount of variation attested in Lowth's letters correlates with the relationship with his addressee are not limited to the occurrence of preposition stranding. In this, Lowth, as a speaker/writer living in the eighteenth century, is no different from speakers today. As a case study, my analysis confirms once again that, as Nevalainen and Raumolin-Brunberg (2003: 26) put it, 'there is no need in historical linguistics to overstress what Labov calls "bad data"'. Instead, they continue, they 'would rather place the emphasis on making the best use of the data available', to which end they recommend in particular a careful embedding of the data in their historical context. I want to add to this that a basic requirement for historical sociolinguistic analysis is to take the informants' communicative competence into account as well. As a result, I think that the data which I have had at my disposal have turned out to have been very good data indeed.

Analysing Lowth's letters has allowed me to study him as a person, as a language user like all the rest of us, but also as a member of a social network which provided him with emotional support during the long stretch of time while he was away from home, which enabled him to fulfil his ambitions with respect to social advancement, as well as to share his scholarship with like-minded individuals, and through which he tried to secure support when, as Bishop of London, he had reached his highest position in life. Crucially for this study, his social network also contributed in an important way to making his name as the most authoritative grammarian of the eighteenth century: when he needed more copies of his grammar, he turned to his publisher Robert Dodsley, and when in need for comments and suggestions for improvement of the grammar he turned to his friends James Merrick and Joseph Spence. Coupled with the way in which he phrased many of his pronouncements on grammar – e.g. '**Ought it not to be**, by *these means*, by *those means*?' (1762: 120n) – this is a far cry from Aitchison's assertion that 'he should have felt so confident about his prescriptions' or even that he would have been 'divinely inspired' about them (1981: 25). Studying his private documents has also shown that the grammar occupied no major part in his life, less so than the other books which he produced. In his preface he referred to his grammar as a 'short System' and as 'an Essay' (1762: xv). This was no expression of false modesty, for at that time Lowth could not have guessed the enormous impact his grammar would have. It is only when reviewing his life's work during the early 1780s that he realized the significance of this publication. In the meantime, he had acquired the status as an expert on grammar, and his expertise would occasionally be drawn upon by members of his social network.

For the world at large his status as a grammarian was evident from the start. The publication of the grammar was eagerly awaited, as were new editions announced in the press. His grammar soon gained the status of a standard textbook, and its rules were copied extensively, often without acknowledgement and frequently being adapted in the process. His fame as a grammarian reached outside his native country, as when the grammar was pirated, translated into German, and used as a basis for a contrastive English–Spanish grammar published in Madrid in 1784. Its fame also reached beyond Lowth's own time, though not within the linguistic community at large. There, particularly within what Milroy and Milroy (1991: 10) refer to as 'mainstream' linguists, it acquired a strongly negative prestige, as being responsible for many of the pronouncements that have come to make up the canon of prescriptivism. That this should have happened is due to the development from the late nineteenth century onwards of linguistics as a proper scholarly and scientific discipline. Consequently, and in fact surprisingly, modern linguists came to judge pre-scientific linguistic efforts with criteria derived from their own discipline. The fallacy of this approach, particularly with respect to what Lowth set out to do, was, as far as I know, first pointed out by Pullum (1974), and I hope to have contributed to correcting it further with the present study.

Lowth's grammar is a mixture of traditional and innovative elements in its approach to grammar. The former place it firmly in the context of the grammatical tradition of its age; the latter, in the form of the critical footnotes particularly in relation to errors in matters of syntax, gave it its status as a prescriptive grammar, even to the extent that pronouncements that were never phrased as such came to be interpreted as prescriptive statements. This is the common fate of all works on language that purport to offer relatively objective descriptions of usage, such as, to give just one example, the grammar by Quirk et al. (1985) (Léon 2009). Moreover, as Finegan (1998: 545) points out, 'scholars of diverse stripes sometimes experience difficulty writing pure descriptions of their own language'. But in its innovative nature, Lowth's critical footnotes anticipate the development of a new text type that would offer explicit guidance on matters of linguistic correctness, the usage guide. With Baker's *Reflections on the English Language* being identified by Leonard (1929) as the first usage guide proper, the new type of handbook was to become an unprecedented success, largely due to the fact that increasing numbers of people were in need of linguistic guidance. On the one hand this was due to the fact, put forward by Beal (2004: 123), that the eighteenth-century normative grammarians 'have left us a legacy of "linguistic insecurity"', on the other hand it is a direct consequence of the increased social (and geographical) mobility since the effects of the Industrial Revolution first made themselves felt. Increased mobility, whether social or geographical, produces the need for the acquisition of new linguistic norms, and usage guides came to have an important function as self-help manuals in this process. Understanding this phenomenon is made possible by looking at the standardization process from the perspective of the model presented by Milroy and Milroy (1991), which, in an improvement to the model usually resorted to, Haugen (1966), includes a prescription stage subsequent to the stage in which the language was first codified. This view also explains why a standardization process can never be completed when it concerns a language: a completely standardized language, characterized by absence of variability, would no longer be a living medium.

In 1712, Swift published his 'Proposal for Correcting, Improving and Ascertaining the English Tongue', in which he advocated the standardization of the English language in the strictest possible sense: having been corrected and improved, it would have to be fixed. Lowth, in his 'capacity of grammarian' as he put it himself in a letter to Merrick, felt called upon to correct and improve the language. Though recognizing that grammar was generally regarded as 'a Subject . . . of little esteem', yet, he wrote in his preface, it was 'of no small importance' (1762: xv). To bring this about he felt 'as in Duty bound to abide by these Principles' (Lowth to Merrick, 4 May 1762). For all that, it is very clear from the way in which he phrased many of the rules in his grammar that he did not believe in an invariable language: as was evident from his own usage in his letters, he was aware of the fact that there were different styles in language, ranging from 'common conversation' to 'the solemn and elevated Style'. Lowth, moreover, was well aware of the distinction between usage and the language system, as is evident from his recommendation, also in the preface to his grammar, that readers 'who would enter more deeply into this Subject' should turn to 'HERMES, by JAMES HARRIS Esq; the most beautiful and perfect example of Analysis that has been exhibited since the days of *Aristotle*' (1762: xiv–xv). These are enlightened perspectives by any standards, based as they are on his knowledge, acquired as a philologist, of how language is structured and how it operates at the level of the speaker. This is what, at last, he deserves full credit for.

APPENDIX 1

SOURCES OF LOWTH'S CORRESPONDENCE

For further biographical information on the letters' addressees and senders, see Appendix 2.

OUT-LETTERS

Addressee	Source
Shute Barrington	Bodleian Library MS Eng. Lett. C. 574, ff. 101–2
Philip Barton	Winchester College Archives, MS 20596
John Brown	Lowth (1765 [1766]: 137–1)
Thomas Brudenell Bruce	Wiltshire and Swindon Archives, MS 1300/4680–1884
Richard Burn	Lambeth Palace Library FP/Lowth/1, ff. 126, 105–6, FP/Lowth/2, ff. 215–16, FP/Lowth/3, ff. 93–4
Thomas Cadell	Beinecke Library, Osborn MS files 19015
William Cavendish	The Devonshire Collection, Chatsworth
Thomas Chapman	British Library Add. MS 4297, ff. 66–7
Sir David Dalrymple	Nat. Lib. Scotl. MS 25299, ff. 43, 45–7, 49, 51, 53–5, 57, 59, 61, 63, 65, 67, 70
Sir Francis Dashwood	Bodleian Library MS D.D. Dashwood C. 5, 11/7/13a–b, 14a–b; British Library Add. MS 32,954, f. 114
'M^r. Day'	Oxfordshire Record Office MS Oxf. Dioc. C. 654, f. 70
James Dodsley	British Library Add. MS 35,339, ff. 29–30, 33–9, 41, 45–47, 49; Bodleian Library MS Montagu D. 17, f. 184
Robert Dodsley	British Library Add. MS 35,339, ff. 1–28, 31–2
William Duncombe	Beinecke Library, Osborn Files 16979
John Eames	Winchester College Archives, MS 20597
Richard Eastman	Oxfordshire Record Office MS Oxf. Dioc. C. 654, f. 75
Mary Jackson	Bodleian Library MS Eng. Lett. C. 572, ff. 1–126
Charles Jenkinson	British Library Add. MSS 38,214, f. 31, 38,217, ff. 175–6
Samuel Johnson	Bodleian Library, MS Eng. Lett. d.83; Anon. 1941: 200–1
Thomas Henry Lowth	Bodleian Library MS Eng. Lett. C. 574, ff. 29–30
William Lowth	Private possession of the Lowth family
James Merrick	Bodleian Library MS Eng. Lett. C. 573, ff. 1–4, 9–10, 19, 36, 39–42, 58–59, 61, 98–109

Johann David Michaelis	Niedersächsische Staats- und Universitätsbibliothek Göttingen Cod. MS Michaelis 325, ff. 402–13, 416–29, 432–43; Bodleian Library MS Eng. Lett. C. 574, ff. 36–8
Philip Morant	British Library Add. MS 37,222, ff. 96, 204–5
John Nichols	Beinecke Library, Osborn MS files 17429
John Nourse	Edinburgh University Library, Special Collections Gen. 2127/9
Francis Osborne	British Library Add. MS 28,060, f. 15
Thomas Pelham-Holles	British Library Add. MSS 32,972, ff. 110–11, 358–9; 32,982, f. 83
Thomas Percy	British Library Add. MS 32,329, ff. 33–4, 91
'M'. de Precetes'	Bodleian Library MS Eng. Lett. C. 574, f. 14
Sir Joshua Reynolds	Bodleian Library MS Eng. Lett. C. 574, f. 47
Glocester Ridley	Joseph Spence Papers, OSB MSS 4, Box 1, Folder 20, letters 1–21; Beinecke Library, Osborn MS Files L. 9290
John Roberts	Bodleian Library MS Eng. Lett. C. 574, ff. 52–3, 56
John Rotheram	Pitts Theology Library, Collection Lowth MSS 105
Thomas Secker	Bodleian Library MS Eng. Lett. C. 574, ff. 69–70, 112
Samuel Speed	Winchester College Archives, MSS 20595, 20618, 20629; Bodleian Library MS Eng. Lett. C. 574, ff. 76–8
Joseph Spence	Bodleian Library MS Eng. Lett. C. 574, ff. 82–9; Beinecke Library, Joseph Spence papers, Osborn MS 4, 21
John Sturges	Bodleian Library MS Eng. Lett. C. 140. ff. 30–1
John Thomas Troy	Bodleian Library MS Eng. Lett. C. 574, f. 40
Robert Darley Waddilove	Bodleian Library MS Eng. Lett. C. 574, f. 90
'M'. Walter'	Bodleian Library MS Eng. Lett. C. 574, f. 93
William Warburton	Bodleian Library MS Eng. Lett. C. 572, ff. 128–31, 138–48, 151–2, 155–6, 161, 164, 166
Joseph Warton	Wooll (1806: 261–2, 385–6)
Thomas Warton	Wooll (1806: 249–52, 274, 351–5, 364, 368–9); British Library Add. MS 42560, f. 225
Charles Watson Wentworth	Sheffield Archives, WWM/R/194, 1–4
Charles Godfrey Woide	British Library Add. MSS 48707, ff. 64–8, 48708, f. 53
'Professeur Woog'	Bodleian Library MS Eng. Lett. C. 574, ff. 97–8
Philip Yorke	British Library Add. MS 35,618, f. 244
Unidentified	National Library of Wales, MS S.D. Ch/LET.1; Oxfordshire Record Office MS Oxf. Dioc. C. 654, f. 73, C. 2160, f. 84; Bodleian Library MS Eng. Lett. C. 574, f. 111; Bodleian Library MS. Eng. Lett. C. 574, ff. 103–6, 108

IN-LETTERS

Sender	Source
Sir George Baker	Bodleian Library MS Eng. Lett. C. 574, f. 1
Shute Barrington	Bodleian Library MS Eng. Lett. C. 574, ff. 3–5
James Beattie	National Library of Scotland, MS 2521, f. 11
John Burton	Bodleian Library MS Eng. Lett. C. 574, ff. 8, 10

John Cooke	Oxfordshire Record Office MS Oxf. Dioc. C. 654
Sir Alexander Dick	Bodleian Library MS Eng. Lett. C. 574, ff. 12–3
Robert Dodsley	Robert Dodsley Letter Book, Birmingham Public Libraries, ff. 65–7
Richard Eastman	Oxfordshire Record Office MS Oxf. Dioc. C. 654
William Gilpin	Bodleian Library MS Eng. misc. D. 583, ff. 75–7
Edward Gore	Oxfordshire Record Office MS Oxf. Dioc. C. 654
Samuel Hallifax	Bodleian Library MS Eng. Lett. C. 574, ff. 17–9, 21–2
John Hodgson	Oxfordshire Record Office MS Oxf. Dioc. C. 654
Charles Jenkinson	British Library Add. MS 38309, f. 10b
Samuel Johnson	Bodleian Library, MS Eng. Lett. D. 83
Samuel Kennan	Durham University Library Add. MSS 451, ff. 221–2
Benjamin Kennicott	Bodleian Library MS Eng. Lett. C. 574, ff. 23, 25, 27–8
John Lincoln	Oxfordshire Record Office MS Oxf. Dioc. C. 654
James Merrick	Bodleian Library MS Eng. Lett. C. 573, ff. 62, 64–6, 71, 75
Philip Morant	British Library Add. MS 37,222, ff. 96v, 205v
'Dᴿ Neve'	Oxfordshire Record Office MS Oxf. Dioc. C. 654
Thomas Nicolls	Oxfordshire Record Office MS Oxf. Dioc. C. 654
Edward Pearson	Durham University Library Add. MSS 451, ff. 208, 210–13, 215–19, 221–6
Thomas Pelham-Holles	British Library Add. MS 32,976, ff. 287–8, 32,982, f. 81
William Pitt	Bodleian Library MS Eng. Lett. C. 574, f. 42
Daniel Prince	Bodleian Library MS Eng. Lett. C. 574, f. 44–6
Sir Joshua Reynolds	Ingamells and Edgcumbe (2000: 77–9)
John Roberts	Bodleian Library MS Eng. Lett. C. 574, ff. 50, 54
Thomas Secker	Bodleian Library MS Eng. Lett. C. 574, ff. 67–8, 71, 73
Joseph Spence	Bodleian Library MS Eng. Lett. C. 574, f. 80
Paulo Tookie	Oxfordshire Record Office MS Oxf. Dioc. C. 654
John Trew	Durham University Library Add. MSS 451, f. 227
Andrew Walsh	Oxfordshire Record Office MS Oxf. Dioc. C. 654
William Warburton	Bodleian Library MS Eng. Lett. C. 572, ff. 132–6, 150, 153, 157–9, 162, 167; British Library Add. MS 4297, ff. 64–5
Joseph Warton	Bodleian Library MS Eng. Lett. C. 574, f. 95
Thomas Warton	British Library Add. MS 42560, f. 226
John Wesley	Telford (1931)
Charles Godfrey Woide	Beinecke Library, Osborn MS files W. 16335
Unidentified	Beinecke Library, Osborn MS Files L. 892, K. 8319; Sheffield Archives, WWM/R/194, 1–4; Bodleian Library MS Eng. Lett. C. 574, ff. 108–9

Appendix 2

LOWTH'S CORRESPONDENTS

The following list includes the names of people whose correspondence with Lowth has actually been attested. Dates for those people for whom no information is provided in reference works such as the *ODNB* are supplied on the basis of Lowth's correspondence. The identity of some people has, however, remained uncertain. Identifications within quotation marks derive from the *ODNB*.

Name	Identity	Relationship with Lowth	Source for relationship	Letter type
Sir George **Baker** (bap.1723, d.1809) (elevation 1776)	physician	acquaintance	correspondence	in
Shute **Barrington** (1734–1826)	'Bishop of Durham' (Bishop of Llandaff 1769–82)	(barely) acquainted	correspondence	out, in
Dr Philip **Barton** (fl.1755–61)	clergyman; prebendary of Winchester (1731–3)	acquaintance	correspondence; Cheyney's Will; Crook (1984)	out
James **Beattie** (1735–1803)	'poet and philosopher'	work-related (Church)	correspondence	in
John **Brown** (1715–66)	'author and moralist'	enemy (friend of Warburton)	correspondence	out
Thomas **Brudenell–Bruce** (1729–1814)	Earl of Ailesbury	barely acquainted	correspondence	out
Richard **Burn** Esqʳ (fl.1778–85)	attorney at law	work-related (Church)	correspondence	out
John **Burton** (fl.1759–71)	master at Winchester College	acquaintance	correspondence	in
Thomas **Cadell** (1742–1802)	'bookseller'	work-related (publishing)	correspondence; title-page editions Lowth's grammar	out

Dr Thomas Chapman (1717–60)	'prebendary of Durham' (1750)	close friend	correspondence ('Brother')	out
John Cooke (fl.1768)	one of Lowth's parishioners	work-related (Church)	correspondence	in
Sir David Dalrymple (1726–92)	'judge and historian'	fellow scholar	correspondence	out
Sir Francis Dashwood (1708–81)	'politician and rake'	close friend, until the early 1760s	Markham (1984); correspondence	out
'M'. Day' (fl.1770–71)	one of Lowth's parishioners	work-related (Church)	correspondence	out
Sir Alexander Dick (1703–85)	'physician'	friend	correspondence; Boswell's journal	in
James Dodsley (1724–97)	'bookseller'	work-related (publishing)	Tierney (1988); correspondence	out
Robert Dodsley (1704–64)	'bookseller and writer'	work-related (publishing) → friend	Tierney (1988); correspondence	out, in
William Duncombe (1690–1769)	'writer'	acquaintance	correspondence	out
John Eames (fl.1764)	Lowth: 'Council for the Heirs at Law'	acquaintance (Cheyney's inheritance)	correspondence	out
Richard Eastman (fl.1774)	one of Lowth's parishioners	work-related (Church)	correspondence	out, in
William Gilpin (1724–1804)	'writer on art and headmaster'	fellow scholar	correspondence	in
Edward Gore (fl.1770)	one of Lowth's parishioners	work-related (Church)	correspondence	in
Samuel Hallifax (1733–90)	fellow at Trinity Hall, Cambridge, 1760–75 (Bishop of St Asaph, 1789–90)	friend	correspondence	out, in
William Cavendish, Marquess of Hartington, Duke of Devonshire (bap.1720, d.1764)	'prime minister' (1756–7)	patron	Hepworth (1978: 44); correspondence	out
John Hodgson (fl.1769)	one of Lowth's parishioners	work-related (Church)	correspondence	in
Mary Jackson (1730–1803)	daughter of Lawrence Jackson and Charity Stevens	wife	correspondence; Cheyney's Will; Anthony Lowth's family tree	out
Charles Jenkinson, first Earl of Liverpool (1729–1808) (elevation 1796)	'politician'	work-related (Church)	correspondence	out, in

Samuel **Johnson** (1709–84)	'author and lexicographer'	barely acquainted	lack of record; correspondence	out, in
Samuel **Kennan** (fl.1766)	clergyman	work-related (Church)	correspondence	in
Benjamin **Kennicott** (1718–83)	'biblical scholar'	close friend	correspondence	in
John **Lincoln** (fl.1767)	one of Lowth's parishioners	work-related (Church)	correspondence	in
Thomas Henry **Lowth** (1753–78)	clergyman	son	correspondence; Anthony Lowth's family tree	out
William **Lowth** (1707–95)	clergyman	brother	correspondence; Anthony Lowth's family tree	out
James **Merrick** (1720–69)	'biblical and classical scholar and translator'	friend/fellow scholar	correspondence; Markham (1984)	out, in
Johann David **Michaelis** (1717–91)	Oriental scholar, Göttingen	fellow scholar	correspondence (Tierney 1988: 39)	out
Philip **Morant** (1700–70)	'historian and Church of England clergyman'	acquaintance	correspondence	out, in
'Dr **Neve**' (fl.1768)	one of Lowth's parishioners	work-related (Church)	correspondence	in
John **Nichols** (1745–1826)	'printer and writer'	work-related (publishing)	correspondence	out
Thomas **Nicolls** (fl.1768)	one of Lowth's parishioners	work-related (Church)	correspondence	in
John **Nourse** (bap.1705, d.1780)	'bookseller'	work-related (publishing)	correspondence	out
Francis **Osborne**, Duke of Leeds, Marquess of Carmarthen (1751–99)	'politician'	barely acquainted	correspondence	out
Edward **Pearson** Esq. (fl.1766)	church official	Lowth's secretary	correspondence	in
Thomas **Pelham-Holles**, Duke of Newcastle (1693–1768)	'prime minister' (1754–6, 1757–62)	patron	correspondence	out, in
Thomas **Percy** (1729–1811)	Dean of Carlisle, Bishop of Dromore (1782)	acquaintance → friend	correspondence	out

William Pitt (1759–1806)	prime minister (1783–1801, 1804–6)	work-related (Church)	correspondence	in
'M^r. de Precetes'	Chaplain to Lord Grantham, English ambassador in Madrid	barely acquainted	correspondence	out
Daniel Prince (d.1796)	Oxford bookseller (Tierney 1988)	work-related (publishing)	correspondence	in
Sir Joshua Reynolds (1723–92) (elevation 1769)	portrait and history painter and art theorist; from 1768 president of the Royal Academy	acquaintance	correspondence	out, in
Glocester Ridley (1702–74)	'writer'	friend; co-executor of Spence's Will	correspondence; Wright (1950)	out
John Roberts (fl.1775)	?	work-related (Church)	correspondence	out, in
John Rotheram (1725–89)	'theologian'	work-related (Church)	correspondence	out
Thomas Secker (1693–1768)	'Archbishop of Canterbury'	patron	correspondence	out, in
Samuel Speed (1705–75)	usher Winchester College, rector of Martyr Worthy (1755)	friend	Markham (1984: 611); correspondence	out, in
Joseph Spence (1699–1768)	'literary scholar and anecdotist'	close friend	correspondence ('Brother'); Wright (1950)	out, in
John Sturges (1735–1807)	clergyman	nephew	correspondence; Anthony Lowth's family tree	out
Paulo Tookie (fl.1771)	clergyman	work-related (Church)	letter	in
John Trew (fl.1766)	clergyman	work-related (Church)	letter	in
John Thomas Troy (1739–1823)	Bishop of Ossory (1776); 'Roman Catholic Archbishop of Dublin'	friend	correspondence	out
Robert Darley Waddilove (1736–1828)	chaplain to ambassador of Spain; 'Dean of Ripon'	acquaintance	correspondence	out
Andrew Walsh (fl.1769)	one of Lowth's parishioners	work-related (Church)	correspondence	in
Mr. Walter (fl.1777)	clergyman	work-related (Church)	correspondence	out

William **Warburton** (1698–1779)	'Bishop of Gloucester [1760] and religious controversialist'	enemy	Hepworth (1978: out, in 99–105); correspondence
Joseph **Warton** (bap.1722, d.1800)	'poet and literary critic'	close friend	correspondence out, in
Thomas **Warton** (1728–90)	'poet and historian'	work-related (publishing)	correspondence out, in
Charles Watson **Wentworth**, second Marquess of Rockingham (1730–82)	'prime minister' (1765–6, 1782); coin collector	acquaintance	correspondence out
John **Wesley** (1703–91)	'Church of England clergyman and a founder of Methodism'	work-related (Church)	correspondence in
Charles Godfrey **Woide** (1725–90)	'oriental scholar and librarian'	fellow scholar	correspondence; out, in Hepworth (1978: 144–5)
'Professeur **Woog**'	theologian at Leipzig	fellow scholar	correspondence out
Philip **Yorke**, second Earl of Hardwicke (1720–90)	'politician and writer'	work-related (Church)	correspondence out

APPENDIX 3

PRESENTATION COPIES OF *ISAIAH*

The longer list: Bodleian Library MS Eng. Lett. C. 574, ff. 115–16 (first edition)
The shorter list: Bodleian Library MS Eng. Lett. C. 574, ff. 113–14 (second edition)

First edition

Royal Family	5.
Cavendish	8̶7̶.
Arch B^p. Cant.	
— York	
Duke of Montague.	
Earl of Ailesbury.	
Marquis of Rockingham.	
Lady Hillsborough.	
L^d. North.	
L^d. Dartmouth.	
L^d. Suffolk	
D. Marlborough L^d. Dacre.	
Winchester.	
Warden	
D^r. Warton	
M^r. Collins	
M^r. Huntingford	
M^r. Sturges	8̶.̶9̶.
M^r. Garnier	
Coll Library	
Ch. Library	
M^{rs}. Covey.	
Oxford	
Vice Can. [?]	
Dean of X^{ch}.	
President of Corpus.	
D^r. Wealer	8. + 2
D^r. Kennicott	
M^r. Burns.	Warden N. C.
New Coll. Library	M̶^{rs}̶.̶L̶.̶.̶.̶.̶
Bodleian Library.	M^{rs}. Sc … th … [?]

Bp. Winchester
  Durham
  Chichester
  Bristol.
  Landaff.
  Bangor
  Chester.
L^d. Primate Ireland
  Bp. of Ossory.
  Bp. of Oxford.
M^r. Lowth[?], M^r. Blackwell.
M^r. Eaton
D^r. Horsely
D^r. Stevens
M^r. Harris
M^r. Woide
M^r. Begant [?]
M^r. Salisbury
M^r. Whitehead
~~M^r. Darley~~
M^r. Farmer
D^r. Addington   D^r. Wealer.
D^r. Baker   D^r. Owen.
D^r. Heberden   D^r. Hallifax.
M^r. Loveday   D^r. Bell
D^r. Jubb.   Dean of Christ . . .
L^d. Sandys   M^r. Harmer
M^rs. Molyneux   Burgh Esqr. York.
M^r. Webb.   M^r. Townson
D^r. Frampton   D^r. Percy
M^r. Rolle   S^r. Josh. Reynolds
~~Gr . . . Sharp.~~
D^r. Morton
S^r. John Pringle
R. Soc. Library   Sion. Coll. L.
M^r. Michaelis   D^r. Michaelis.
M^r. Heyne
M^r. Velthusen   M^r. Best.
M^r. Jones, Temple
D^r. Chandler, ~~MD^r.~~ Jughis.
M^r. Page   D^r. Cowper
D^r. Dickens   Govr. Hutchinson
Durham Ch. Library.   Douglas Sharp
                        ~~Rothman~~

M^r. Ph. Burton. Chr. Quicke.
M^{rs}. Smythe
M^r. Schutz
Gr. & I. Sharpe 166.
M^{rs}. Cowper
Misc. [?]
British Museum
D^r. Gabriel
8. Ma...
  Be...
D^r. Duncan
S. Warnb. [?]
M^r. Maseres [?].
    Temple
S^r. Dav. Dalrymple
M^{rs}. Lucas.
M^r. Koppe.
M^r. Hunter.
M^{rs}. Kennicott
D^r. Jubb.

Second edition

Royal Family 5.
Arch B^{ps}. & B^{ps}. in Town.
Duke of Devonshire
L^d. George Cavendish
    Frederick
    John   Cavendish.
    Richard   Gr. Marlb, Street
    George Henry
    Charles
L^d. North
Earl of Guilford
Marquis of Rockingham
Duke of Marlborough
L^d. Dartmouth
L^d. Suffolk
L^d. Ailesbury
Countess of Hillsborough.
L^d. Dacre   L^d. Sandys
L^d. Chancellor
L^d. Mayor
Speaker of ye H. of Commons

                              to be sent
Duke of Montagu   to me wth.
Marquis of Carmarthen   those for
Dr. Bell   y^e. R. Fam.
L^d. Primate of Ireland. Conduit Street

Dean of Bristol
      Exeter
      Windsor
      Peterborough
      Rochester
      Salisbury
      Winchester.   Winch^r. House
      Carlisle   Chelsea
D^r. Hamilton, S^t. Martins
D^r. Waller, Kensington.
D^r. Wilson, S^t. Pauls
D^r. Douglas, ditto
D^r. Parker, S^t. James's West.
D^r. Weales, S^t. Sepulchre
M^r. Gibson S^t. Magnus Lond. Bridge
D^r. Owen, S^t. Olave Hart St.
D^r. Stinton $^{Esq.}$ George St. West
D^r. Markham, White Chapel
M^r. Sellon, Clerkenwell
M^r. Fitzherbert, S^t. Pauls
D^r. Finch, S^t. Michael Cornhill
M^r. Morrice, Allhallows Bread Street   Hatton Quad.
M^r. Hand S^t. Giles's Cripple[g]
D^r. Conybeare S^t. Botolph Bishop G.
D^r. Richardson S^t. Ann's Soho.
Bp. of L...ley
M^r. Heslop, S^t. Peter le poor, ...
D^r. Bailey Sub-dean of Ch. R.
S^r. George Baker
D^r. Addington
D^r. Heberden
D^r. Jubb, Sackville St.
S^r. John Pringle
D^r. Morton Mins...
M^r. Bryant.
M^r. Harris
M^r. Whitehead.
W^m. Jones Esqr., Temple.
D^r. Chandler, $^{no.\ 10}$ John St Oxford Road.
Governor Hutchinson, Sackvil St.
Granville Sharp Esqr. Old Jewry.
Governor Pownal
F^r. Page Esqr. Pall Mall.
S^r. John Hawkins.
      Oxford
Vice Can. [?]
D^n. Christchurch

P. of C.C.C.
Warden of New Coll.
D^r. Kennicott
M^r. Burns.
D^r. Whealer
M^r. White
M^r. Holmes New Coll. 12.
Master of Baliol
Winchester, To Rev^d. M^r. Lowth 8.
Cambridge,
Dean of Ely.
D^r. Hallifax. 2.

~~Warden of Merton~~
Rector of Exeter
Provost of Queens

References

PRIMARY SOURCES

Unless otherwise indicated, eighteenth-century works have been consulted through ECCO.

ALDERSON, JAMES (1795). *English Grammatical Exercises*. London.

ANGUS, WILLIAM (1800). *An Epitome of English Grammar*. Glasgow.

ANON. (1756). *The Compleat Letter Writer*. (Third edition.) London.

ASH, JOHN (1760). *Grammatical Institutes: or Grammar, Adapted to the Genius of the English Tongue*. Worcester.

BAKER, ROBERT (1770). *Reflections on the English Language, In the Nature of Vaugelas's Reflections on the French*. London. (Second edition, 1779, London.)

—— (1771). *Observations on the Pictures now in Exhibition at the Royal Academy, Spring Gardens and Mr. Christie's*. London.

—— (1766). *Witticisms and Strokes of Humour*. London.

BARKER, ISAAC (1733). *An English Grammar Shewing the Nature and Grounds of the English Language, in its Present State*. York.

BAYLY, ANSELM (1758). *An Introduction to Languages, Literary and Philosophical*. London.

BEATTIE, JAMES (1783). *The Theory of Language*, in *Dissertations Moral and Critical*. London.

BELL, JOHN (1769). *A Concise and Comprehensive System of English Grammar*. Glasgow.

BRIGHTLAND, JOHN, and GILDON, CHARLES (1711). *A Grammar of the English Tongue*. London.

BRITTAIN, LEWIS (1788). *Rudiments of English Grammar*. Louvain.

BRYSON, BILL (1990). *Mother Tongue*. London: Hamish Hamilton.

BUCHANAN, JAMES (1762). *The British Grammar*. London.

BURGESS, WALTON (1856). *Five Hundred Mistakes of Daily Occurrence in Speaking, Pronouncing, and Writing*. New York.

BURN, JOHN (1766). *A Practical Grammar of the English Language*. (Fourth edition, 1786.) Glasgow.

BURR, JONATHAN (1797). *A Compendium of English Grammar, for the Use of Schools and Private Instructers*. Boston.

CAREY, MATHEW (1799). *A Plumb Pudding for the Humane, Chaste, Valiant, Enlightened Peter Porcupine*. (Second edition.) Philadelphia.

CARPENTER, THOMAS (1796). *The Scholar's Spelling Assistant*. London.

CARTER, JOHN (1773). *A Practical English Grammar*. Leeds.

CHAPMAN, GEORGE (1792). *A Treatise on Education*. (Fifth edition.) London.

CLARKE, JOHN (1733). *A New Grammar of the Latin Tongue*. London.

COBBETT, WILLIAM (1818). *A Grammar of the English Language*. New York.

COLLYER, JOHN (1735). *The General Principles of Grammar*. Nottingham.

COOTE, CHARLES (1788). *Elements of the Grammar of the English Language*. London.

DARWIN, ERASMUS (1797). *A Plan for the Conduct of Female Education, in Boarding Schools*. Derby.

DEVIS, ELLIN (1775). *The Accidence; or First Rudiments of English Grammar*. London.

DUNCAN, DANIEL (1731). *A New English Grammar*. London.

FELL, JOHN (1784). *An Essay towards an English Grammar*. London.

FENN, ELLENOR (1798?). *The Mother's Grammar*. London.

—— (1799). *The Child's Grammar*. Dublin.

FISHER, ANN (1745). *A New Grammar*. (Second edition, 1750; fifth edition, 1757.) Newcastle upon Tyne.

FOGG, PETER WALKDEN (1792–6). *Elementa Anglicana*. (Two volumes.) Stockport.

FOWLER, H. W. (1926). *A Dictionary of Modern English Usage*. Oxford: Oxford University Press.

GLASSE, HANNAH (1747). *The Art of Cookery, made Plain and Easy*. London.

GOUGH, JAMES (1754). *A Practical Grammar of the English Tongue*. (Second edition, 1760.) Dublin.

GREENWOOD, JAMES (1711). *An Essay towards a Practical English Grammar*. London.

—— (1737). *The Royal English Grammar*. London.

HARRIS, JAMES (1751). *Hermes, or, A Philosophical Inquiry Concerning Language and Universal Grammar*. London.

HENSON, JOHN (1760?). *A Compendium of English Grammar*. Nottingham.

HORNSEY, JOHN (1793). *A Short English Grammar*. York.

JOHNSON, SAMUEL (1747). *The Plan of a Dictionary of the English Language*. London.

—— (1755). *A Dictionary of the English Language*. (Two volumes.) London. (Reprinted in facsimile, 1868. Hildesheim: Georg Olms Verlagsbuchhandlung.)

JONES, HUGH (1724). *An Accidence to the English Tongue*. London.

JONSON, BENJAMIN (1640). *The English Grammar*. London.

KIRKBY, JOHN (1746). *A New English Grammar*. London. *English Linguistics* (Alston 1974).

KNOWLES, JOHN (1796). *Principles of English Grammar.* (Fourth edition.) Liverpool.

KNOX, VICESIMUS (1781). *Liberal Education: or, a Practical Treatise on the Methods of Acquiring Useful and Polite Learning.* London.

LAWRENCE, JOHN (1796–8). *A Philosophical and Practical Treatise on Horses, and on the Moral Duties of Man towards the Brute Creation.* London.

LILY, WILLIAM (1549). *A Short Introduction of Grammar.* London. (Dublin edition, 1702.)

LOUGHTON, WILLIAM (1734). *A Practical Grammar of the English Tongue.* (Eighth edition, 1755.) London.

[LOWTH, ROBERT] (1743). *The Judgment of Hercules.* Glasgow.

LOWTH, ROBERT (1753). *De Sacra Poesi Hebræorum Praelectiones.* Oxford.

—— (1758). *The Life of William of Wykeham.* London.

—— (1762). *A Short Introduction to English Grammar.* (Second edition, 1763.) London.

—— (1765). *A Letter to the Right Reverend Author of the Divine Legation of Moses Demonstrated.* (Fourth edition, 1766.) Oxford.

—— (1778). *Isaiah, A New Translation.* London.

MACKINTOSH, DUNCAN (1797). *A Plain, Rational Essay on English Grammar.* Boston. *English Linguistics* (Alston 1974).

MARTIN, BENJAMIN (1748). *Institutions of Language.* London. *English Linguistics* (Alston 1974).

—— (1754). *An Introduction to the English Language and Learning.* (Second edition, 1756.) London.

MURRAY, ALEXANDER (1787). *An Easy English Grammar.* (Second edition.) London.

MURRAY, LINDLEY (1795). *English Grammar.* (Fourth edition, 1798; sixth edition, 1800; thirtieth edition, 1818.) York.

NEWBERY, JOHN (1745). *An Easy Introduction to the English Language.* (Third edition, 1755.) London.

PARTRIDGE, ERIC (1965). *Usage and Abusage. A Guide to Good English.* (Sixth edition, reprint, 1971.) London: Hamish Hamilton.

POOLE, JOSHUA (1657). *The English Parnassus.* London.

POSTLETHWAITE, RICHARD (1795). *The Grammatical Art Improved: In which the Errors of Grammarians and Lexicographers are Exposed.* London.

PRIESTLEY, JOSEPH (1761). *The Rudiments of English Grammar.* (Second edition, 1768.) London.

SAXON, SAMUEL (1737). *The English Scholar's Assistant.* (Second edition.) Reading.

SEALLY, JOHN (1788). *The Lady's Encyclopedia.* (Volume 2.) London.

SHENSTONE, WILLIAM (1769). *The Works, in Verse and Prose, of William Shenstone, Esq.* (Volume III.) London.

SIMON, JOHN (1980). *Paradigms Lost. Reflections on Literacy and its Decline.* London: Penguin.

SMITH, ADAM (1759). *The Theory of Moral Sentiments.* London.

SMITH, JOHN (1755). *The Printer's Grammar.* London.

STORY, JOSHUA (1793). *An Introduction to English Grammar.* (Fifth edition.) Newcastle upon Tyne.

STRUNK, WILLIAM, and WHITE, E. B. (1918/1959). *The Elements of Style.* New York: Macmillan.

TRUSS, LYNNE (2003). *Eats, Shoots and Leaves. The Zero Tolerance Approach to Punctuation.* London: Profile Books.

WALLIS, JOHN (1653). *Grammatica Linguae Anglicanae.* (Fourth edition, 1674; sixth edition, 1765.) Oxford. EEBO.

WARBURTON, WILLIAM (1766?). *The Second Part of a Literary Correspondence, between the Bishop of Gloucester and a Late Professor of Oxford.* [Oxford?]

WARD, JOHN (1758). *Four Essays upon the English Language.* London.

WARD, WILLIAM (1765). *An Essay on Grammar.* London.

WELLS, SAMUEL (1760). *The Construction of the English Language.* [Cheltenham?]

WESLEY, JOHN (1748). *A Short English Grammar.* Bristol.

—— (1768). *A Short Account of the School, in Kingswood, near Bristol.* Bristol.

WHITE, BENJAMIN ([1769]). *A Catalogue of the Entire Libraries of the Rev. Mr. Joseph Spence, . . . Of William Duncombe, . . . and of Several Other Valuable Collections.* London.

WHITE, JAMES (1761). *The English Verb.* London.

WOOD, JAMES (1777). *Grammatical Institutions, or a Practical English Grammar.* Newcastle upon Tyne.

SECONDARY SOURCES

AARTS, F. G. A. M. (1986). 'William Cobbett: Radical, Reactionary and Poor Man's Grammarian'. *Neophilologus*, 70: 603–14.

—— (1994). 'William Cobbett's *Grammar of the English Language*'. *Neuphilologische Mitteilungen*, XCV: 319–32.

AITCHISON, JEAN (1981). *Language Change: Progress or Decay?* (Reprint, 1984; second edition, 1991; third edition, 2001.) Bungay: Richard Clay (The Chaucer Press) Ltd.

ALSTON, R. C. (1965). *A Bibliography of the English Language from the Invention of Printing to the Year 1800.* (Volume 1.) Leeds: Arnold and Son.

—— (ed.) (1974). *English Linguistics 1500–1800. A Collection of Facsimile Reprints.* Menston: Scolar Press.

ANDERSON, HOWARD, and EHRENRPREIS, IRVIN (1966). 'The Familiar Letter in the Eighteenth Century: Some Generalizations', in Howard Anderson, Philip

B. Daghlian, and Irvin Ehrenpreis (eds.), *The Familiar Letter in the Eighteenth Century*. Lawrence: University of Kansas Press, 269–82.

ANON. (1941). 'Dr. Johnson Bows to a Bishop'. *The Bodleian Library Record*, 1939–1941, 199–201.

AUER, ANITA (2006). 'Precept and Practice: The Influence of Prescriptivism on the English Subjunctive', in Christiane Dalton-Puffer, Dieter Kastovsky, Nikolaus Ritt, and Herbert Schendl (eds.), *Syntax, Style and Grammatical Norms: English from 1500–2000*. Bern: Peter Lang, 33–53.

—— (2008). 'Eighteenth-Century Grammars and Book Catalogues', in Tieken-Boon van Ostade (ed.) (2008*e*), 57–100.

—— and TIEKEN-BOON VAN OSTADE, INGRID (2007). 'Robert Lowth and the Use of the Inflectional Subjunctive in Eighteenth-Century English', in Ute Smit, Stefan Dollinger, Julia Hüttner, Ursula Lutzky, and Gunther Kaltenböck (eds.), *Tracing English through Time: Explorations in Language Variation*. Vienna: Braumüller, 1–18.

AUSTIN, FRANCES (1994). 'The Effect of Exposure to Standard English: The Language of William Clift', in Stein and Tieken-Boon van Ostade (eds.), 285–313.

AYRES-BENNETT, WENDY (1987). *Vaugelas and the Development of the French Language*. London: Modern Humanities Research Association.

—— (2002). 'An Evolving Genre: Seventeenth-Century *Remarques* and *Observations* on the French Language', in Rodney Sampson and Wendy Ayres-Bennett (eds.), *Interpreting the History of French. A Festschrift for Peter Rickard on the Occasion of his Eightieth Birthday*. Amsterdam/New York: Rodopi, 353–68.

AZAD, YUSEF (1989). 'The Government of Tongues: Common Usage and the "Prescriptive" Tradition 1650–1800.' Unpublished doctoral dissertation, Oxford University.

BAILEY, RICHARD W. (1996). *Nineteenth-Century English*. Ann Arbor: University of Michigan Press.

BAKER, FRANK (1980). *The Works of John Wesley*. (Volume 25, *Letters* I, 1721–1739.) Oxford: Clarendon Press.

BAKER, PAUL (2006). '"The Question is, How Cruel is It?" Keywords, Foxhunting and the House of Commons'. Paper presented at the AHRC ICT Methods Network Expert Seminar on Linguistics, 'Word Frequency and Keyword Extraction', Lancaster University, UK <www.methodsnetwork.ac.uk/redist/pdf/es1_07baker.pdf> (consulted summer 2009).

BARBER, GILES (1960). 'J. J. Tourneisen of Basle and the Publication of English Books on the Continent *c*. 1800'. *The Library* s5–XV: 193–200.

BATELY, JANET M. (1964). 'Dryden's Revisions in the *Essay of Dramatic Poesy*: The Preposition at the End of the Sentence and the Expression of the Relative'. *The Review of English Studies*, 15/59: 268–82.

BATTESTIN, MARTIN C., and PROBYN, CHARLES T. (eds.) (1993). *The Correspondence of Henry and Sarah Fielding.* Oxford: Clarendon Press.

BAUER, LAURIE and TRUDGILL, Peter (eds.) (1998). *Language Myths.* London: Penguin.

BAUGH, ALBERT C., and CABLE, THOMAS (2002 [1951]). *A History of the English Language.* (Fifth edition.) London: Routledge.

BEAL, JOAN C. (2003). 'John Walker: Prescriptivist or Linguistic Innovator?', in Dossena and Jones (eds.), 83–105.

—— (2004). *English in Modern Times 1700–1945.* London: Arnold.

—— (2008). '"Shamed by your English?" The Market Value of a Good Pronunciation', in Beal, Nocera, and Sturiale (eds.), 21–40.

—— (2009). 'Three Hundred Years of Prescriptivism (and Counting)', in Tieken-Boon van Ostade and van der Wurff (eds.), 35–55.

——, NOCERA, CARMELA, and STURIALE, MASSIMO (eds.) (2008). *Perspectives on Prescriptivism.* Bern: Peter Lang.

BIBER, DOUGLAS, CONRAD, SUSAN, and REPPEN, RANDI (eds.) (1998). *Corpus Linguistics. Investigating Language Structure and Use.* Cambridge: Cambridge University Press.

BIJKERK, ANNEMIEKE (2004). '*Yours sincerely* and *Yours affectionately*: On the Origin and Development of two Positive Politeness Markers', in Nevalainen and Tanskanen (eds.), 297–311.

Biographisch-Bibliographisches Kirchenlexikon. <www.bautz.de/bbkl/> (consulted summer 2009).

BLOOM, EDWARD A., and BLOOM, LILLIAN D. (eds.) (1989–2002). *The Piozzi Letters. Correspondence of Hester Lynch Piozzi, 1784–1821 (formerly Mrs. Thrale).* Newark: University of Delaware Press.

BREWER, CHARLOTTE (2007). *Treasure-House of the Language. The Living OED.* New Haven/London: Yale University Press.

BROWN, PENELOPE, and LEVINSON, STEPHEN C. (1987). *Politeness: Some Universals in Language Usage.* Cambridge: Cambridge University Press.

BURCHFIELD, R. W. (1996). *Fowler's Modern English Usage.* (Third edition.) Oxford: Oxford University Press.

The 17ᵗʰ–18ᵗʰ Century Burney Collection Newspapers. <www.gale.cengage.com/> (consulted summer 2009).

BUSCHMANN-GÖBELS, ASTRID (2008). 'Bellum Grammaticale (1712) – A Battle of Books and a Battle for the Market?' in Tieken-Boon van Ostade (ed.) (2008e), 81–100.

BUSSE, ULRICH, and SCHRÖDER, ANNE (2008). 'How Fowler Became "The Fowler": An Anatomy of a Success Story'. Paper presented at the workshop Normative Linguistics, ISLE-1, Freiburg, October 2008.

—— (forthcoming). 'Problem Areas of English Grammar between Usage, Norm and Variation', in Alexandra Lenz and Albrecht Plewnia (eds.), *Grammar between Norm and Variation.* Amsterdam: Benjamins.

CAJKA, KAREN (2008). 'Eighteenth-Century Teacher-Grammarians and the Education of "Proper" Women', in Tieken-Boon van Ostade (ed.) (2008*e*), 191–221.

CANNON, GARLAND (ed.) (1970). *The Letters of Sir William Jones.* (Two volumes.) Oxford: Clarendon Press.

CASH, DEREK (2002). *Access to Museum Culture: The British Museum from 1753 to 1836.* <www.britishmuseum.org/research/research_publications/online_publications/access_to_museum_culture.aspx> (consulted summer 2009).

CHAFE, WALLACE L. (1985). 'Linguistic Differences Produced by Differences between Speaking and Writing', in David R. Olson, Nancy Torrance, and Angela Hildyard (eds.) *Literacy, Language, and Learning. The Nature and Consequences of Reading and Writing.* Cambridge: Cambridge University Press. 105–23.

CHAPMAN, DON (2008). 'The Eighteenth-Century Grammarians as Language Experts', in Tieken-Boon van Ostade (ed.) (2008*e*), 21–36.

CHESHIRE, JENNY (1994). 'Standardization and the English Irregular Verbs', in Stein and Tieken-Boon van Ostade (eds.), 115–33.

CHRISTIE, IAN R. (1954). 'Horace Walpole: The Gossip as Historian'. *History Today,* 4: 291–300.

CLARKE, NORMA (2000). *Dr. Johnson's Women.* London/New York: Hambledon and London.

COOK, J. H. (1879). *Bishop Lowth: His Life and Writings.* Leipzig: Ackerman and Glaser.

CRYSTAL, DAVID (1995). *The Cambridge Encyclopedia of the English Language.* Cambridge: Cambridge University Press.

CUSACK, BRIDGET (1998). *Everyday English 1500–1700. A Reader.* Edinburgh: Edinburgh University Press.

DOSSENA, MARINA, and JONES, CHARLES (eds.) (2003), *Insights into Late Modern English.* Bern: Peter Lang.

—— and TIEKEN-BOON VAN OSTADE, INGRID (eds.) (2008), *Studies in Late Modern English Correspondence: Methodology and Data.* Bern: Peter Lang.

DURY, RICHARD (2006). 'A Corpus of Nineteenth-Century Business Correspondence: Methodology of Transcription', in Marina Dossena and Susan M. Fitzmaurice (eds.), *Business and Official Correspondence: Historical Investigations.* Frankfurt and Bern: Peter Lang, 193–205.

ECCO: Eighteenth Century Collections Online. Thomson Gale. www.gale.com/EighteenthCentury/.

EEBO: Early English Books Online. Chadwyck Healey. http://eebo.chadwyck.com/home.

FACCHINETTI, ROBERT (2000). 'The Modal Verb *Shall* between Grammar and Usage in the Nineteenth Century', in Kastovsky and Mettinger (eds.), 115–33.

FAIRMAN, TONY (2006). 'Words in English Record Office Documents of the Early 1800s', in Merja Kytö, Mats Rydén, and Erik Smitterberg (eds.) (2006), *Nineteenth-Century English. Stability and Change*. Cambridge: Cambridge University Press, 56–88.

FEATHER, JOHN (1988). *A History of British Publishing*. (Reprint, 1991.) London/New York/Sydney: Helm.

FENS-DE ZEEUW, LYDA (2008). 'The Letter-Writing Manual in the Eighteenth and Nineteenth Centuries: From Polite to Practical', in Dossena and Tieken-Boon van Ostade (eds.), 163–92.

FINEGAN, EDWARD (1992). 'Style and Standardization in England: 1700–1900', in Tim William Machan and Charles T. Scott (eds.), *English in its Social Contexts*. New/York: Oxford University Press, 103–30.

—— (1998). 'English Grammar and Usage', in Suzanne Romaine (ed.), *The Cambridge History of the English Language*. (Volume 4.) Cambridge: Cambridge University Press, 536–88.

FITZMAURICE, SUSAN (1998). 'The Commerce of Language in the Pursuit of Politeness in Eighteenth-Century England'. *English Studies*, 79: 309–28.

—— (2000a). 'The Spectator, the Politics of Social Networks, and Language Standardisation in Eighteenth Century England', in Laura Wright (ed.), *The Development of Standard English 1300–1800: Theories, Descriptions, Conflicts*. Cambridge: Cambridge University Press, 195–218.

—— (2000b). 'Coalitions and the Investigation of Social Influence in Linguistic History', in Ingrid Tieken-Boon van Ostade, Terttu Nevalainen, and Luisella Caon (eds.), *Social Network Analysis and the History of English*. Special issue of *European Journal of English Studies*, 4/3: 265–76.

—— (2002). *The Familiar Letter in Early Modern English*. Amsterdam/Philadelphia: John Benjamins.

—— (2008). 'Epistolary Identity: Convention and Idiosyncrasy in Late Modern English Letters', in Dossena and Tieken-Boon van Ostade (eds.), 77–112.

FRIES, CHARLES C. (1925). 'The Periphrastic Future with *Shall* and *Will* in Modern English'. *Publications of the Modern Language Association of America*, 40: 963–1024.

GARSIDE, P. D. (2003). 'Subscribing Fiction in Britain, 1780–1829'. *Cardiff Corvey: Reading the Romantic Text* 11. <www.cardiff.ac.uk/encap/journals/romtext/reports/cc11_no3.pdf> (consulted summer 2009).

GASKELL, PHILIP (1972). *The New Introduction to Bibliography*. Oxford: Clarendon Press.

GONZÁLEZ-DÍAZ, VICTORINA (2008). 'On Normative Grammarians and the Double Marking of Degree', in Tieken-Boon van Ostade (ed.) (2008e), 288–310.

GÖRLACH, MANFRED (1997). '...A Construction than which None is More Difficult', in Nevalainen and Kahlas-Tarkka (eds.), 277–301.

GÖRLACH, MANFRED (1998). *An Annotated Bibliography of Nineteenth-Century Grammars of English.* Amsterdam/Philadelphia: John Benjamins.

—— (1999). *English in Nineteenth-Century England. An Introduction.* Cambridge: Cambridge University Press.

—— (2001). *Eighteenth-Century English.* Heidelberg: Universitätsverlag C. Winter.

GUILLE, JOHN, and BUXTON, RICHARD (2003). *A Millennium of Archdeacons. The Archdeacons of Winchester from the 11th to the 20th Centuries.* Winchester: George Mann Publications.

GUZMÁN-GONZÁLEZ, TRINIDAD (1989). 'El Género Atribuido en Lengua Inglesa: Textos Poéticos de los Siglos XVIII, XIX y XX'. Unpublished PhD thesis, University of León.

HAUGEN, EINAR (1966). 'Dialect, Language, Nation'. *American Anthropologist,* 68: 922–35. (Reprinted in J. B. Pride and Janet Holmes (eds.) (1972), *Sociolinguistics.* London: Penguin, 97–111.)

HENSTRA, FROUKJE (2009). 'The Problem of Small Numbers: Methodological Issues in Social Network Analysis', in Tieken-Boon van Ostade and van der Wurff (eds.), 361–90.

—— (in preparation). 'The Language of Horace Walpole and his Correspondents: A Case Study'. PhD dissertation, University of Leiden.

HEPWORTH, BRIAN (1978). *Robert Lowth.* Boston: Twayne Publishers.

HODSON, JANE (2006). 'The Problem of Joseph Priestley's (1733–1804) Descriptivism'. *Historiographia Linguistica,* 33: 57–84.

—— (2008). 'Joseph Priestley's two *Rudiments of English Grammar:* 1761 and 1768', in Tieken-Boon van Ostade (ed.) (2008e), 177–89.

HOGG, RICHARD (1988). 'Snuck: The Development of Irregular Preterite Forms', in Graham Nixon and John Honey (eds.), *An Historic Tongue: Studies in English Linguistics in Memory of Barbara Strang.* London: Routledge, 31–40.

HONEY, JOHN (1997). *Language is Power. The Story of Standard English and its Enemies.* London: Faber and Faber.

—— (2000). 'A Response to Peter Trudgill's Review of *Language is Power'. Journal of Sociolinguistics,* 4/2: 316–19.

HUDDLESTON, RODNEY, and PULLUM, GEOFFREY K. (2002). *The Cambridge Grammar of the English Language.* Cambridge: Cambridge University Press.

HUGHES, ARTHUR, and TRUDGILL, PETER (2005). *English Accents and Dialects: An Introduction to Social and Regional Varieties of English in the British Isles.* (Fourth edition.) London: Edward Arnold.

HUSSEY, STANLEY (1995). *The English Language. Structure and Development.* London/New York: Longman.

INGAMELLS, JOHN, and EDGCUMBE, JOHN (eds.) (2000). *The Letters of Sir Joshua Reynolds.* New Haven: Yale University Press.

JANSOHN, CHRISTA, and MEHL, DIETER (2007). '*Venus and Adonis* und *The Rape of Lucrece* in der Übersetzung von Heinrich Christoph Albrecht', in Roger Paulin (ed.), *Shakespeare im 18. Jahrhundert*. Göttingen: Wallstein Verlag, 49–62.

JONES, BERNARD (1983). 'William Barnes on Lindley Murray's English Grammar'. *English Studies*, 64: 30–5.

—— (1996). 'The Reception of Lindley Murray's *English Grammar*', in Tieken-Boon van Ostade (ed.) (1996*d*), 63–80.

KASTOVSKY, DIETER, and METTINGER, ARTHUR (eds.) (2000). *The History of English in a Social Context*. Berlin/New York: Mouton de Gruyter.

KEAST, WILLIAM R. (1957). 'The two Clarissas in Johnson's *Dictionary*'. *Studies in Philology*, 54: 429–39.

VAN KEMENADE, ANS (2000). 'Ontkenning Ontkend'. Inaugural lecture, Katholieke Universiteit Nijmegen.

KEMP, BETTY, (1967). *Sir Francis Dashwood. An Eighteenth-Century Independent*. London: Macmillan/New York: St Martin's Press.

KEMP, J. A. (ed.) (1972). *John Wallis's Grammar of the English Language*. London: Longman.

KLIPPEL, FRIEDERIKE (1994). *Englischlernen im 18. und 19. Jahrhundert*. Münster: Nodus.

KYTÖ, MERJA, and ROMAINE, SUZANNE (2005). '"We had Like to have Been killed by Thunder & Lightning". The Semantic and Pragmatic History of a Construction that Like to Disappeared'. *Journal of Historical Pragmatics*, 6/1, 1–35.

LABOV, WILLIAM (1994). *Principles of Linguistic Change*. (Volume 1. Internal Factors.) Oxford: Wiley-Blackwell Publishing.

LASS, ROGER (1994). 'Proliferation and Option-Cutting: The Strong Verb in the Fifteenth to Eighteenth Centuries', in Stein and Tieken-Boon van Ostade (eds.), 81–113.

—— (2004). '"Ut Custodiant Litteras": Editions, Corpora and Witnesshood', in Marina Dossena and Roger Lass (eds.), *Methods and Data in English Historical Dialectology*. Frankfurt am Main: Peter Lang, 21–50.

LEFANU, WILLIAM (ed.) (1960). *Betsy Sheridan's Journal. Letters from Sheridan's Sister*. (Reprinted 1986.) Oxford: Oxford University Press.

LEGG, MARIE-LOUISE (ed.) (1996). *The Synge Letters. Bishop Edward Synge to his Daughter Alicia. Roscommon to Dublin. 1746–1752*. Dublin: The Lilliput Press.

LEHNERT, MARTIN (1937/38). 'Die Abhängigkeit frühneuenglischer Grammatiken'. *Englische Studien*, 72: 192–206.

LÉON, JACQUELINE (2009). 'When Usage and Prescription are Based on the Systematic Description of Use: Randolph Quirk and the *Survey of English Usage*'. Paper presented at the colloquium 'Bon Usage', Cambridge, 16–18 July 2009.

LEONARD, S. A. (1929). *The Doctrine of Correctness in English Usage, 1700–1800*. Madison: University of Wisconsin.

LEWIS, W. S. et al. (1937–83). *The Yale Edition of Horace Walpole's Correspondence.* (48 Volumes.) New Haven: Yale University Press.

LUSTIG, IRMA S., and POTTLE, FREDERICK A. (eds.) (1982). *Boswell: The Applause of the Jury. 1782–1785.* London: Heinemann.

LYONS, JOHN (1968). *Introduction to Theoretical Linguistics.* Cambridge: Cambridge University Press.

MARKHAM, SARAH (1984). *John Loveday of Caversham, 1711–1789. The Life and Tours of an Eighteenth-Century Onlooker.* Salisbury: Michael Russell.

MCARTHUR, TOM (1992). *Oxford Companion to the English Language.* Oxford/New York: Oxford University Press.

MCFADDEN, TOM (2007). 'Auxiliary "Selection" and Restrictions on Perfect Semantics: An Early English/Modern Scandinavian Parallel'. Paper presented at the 6th York–Newcastle–Holland Symposium on the History of English Syntax, Leiden, 2007.

MCINTOSH, CAREY (1986). *Common and Courtly Language. The Stylistics of Social Class in 18th-Century English Literature.* Philadelphia: University of Pennsylvania Press.

MCKNIGHT, GEORGE H., and Emsley, B. (1928). *Modern English in the Making.* New York/London: D. Appleton & Co.

MCMORRIS, JENNY (2001). *The Warden of English. The Life of H. W. Fowler.* Oxford: Oxford University Press.

MENCKEN, H. L. (1919). *The American Language.* (Reprint, 1977.) New York: Alfred A. Knopf.

MICHAEL, IAN (1970). *English Grammatical Categories and the Tradition to 1800.* Cambridge: Cambridge University Press.

—— (1987). *The Teaching of English from the Sixteenth Century to 1870.* Cambridge: Cambridge University Press.

—— (1991). 'More than Enough English Grammars', in G. Leitner (ed.), *English Traditional Grammars.* Amsterdam: John Benjamins, 11–26.

—— (1997). 'The Hyperactive Production of English Grammars in the Nineteenth Century: A Speculative Bibliography'. *Publishing History,* 41: 23–61.

MILROY, JAMES, and MILROY, LESLEY (1991). *Authority in Language. Investigating Language Prescription and Standardisation.* (Second edition.) London: Routledge and Kegan Paul.

MILROY, LESLEY (1987). *Language and Social Networks.* (Second edition.) Oxford: Blackwell.

—— (1998). 'Bad Grammar is Slovenly', in Laurie Bauer and Peter Trudgill (eds.), *Language Myths.* London: Penguin, 94–102.

MITTINS, W. H., SALU, MARY, EDMINSON, MARY, and COYNE, SHEILA (1970). *Attitudes to English Usage.* (Reprint, 1975.) London: Oxford University Press.

MIZUNO, KAZUHO (1991). 'Variations in Boswell's English'. *Hiroshima University Studies*, 50: 150–74.

MOLENCKI, RAFAŁ (2003). 'Proscriptive Prescriptivists: On the Loss of the "Pleonastic" Perfect Infinitive in Counterfactual Constructions in Late Modern English', in Dossena and Jones (eds.), 175–96.

MOSSNER, E. C., and ROSS, I. S. (eds.) (1987). *Correspondence of Adam Smith*. (Volume VI of the *Glasgow Edition of the Works and Correspondence of Adam Smith*.) Indianapolis: Liberty Fund.

MUGGLESTONE, LYNDA (2003). '*Talking Proper*'. *The Rise of Accent as Social Symbol*. (Second edition.) Oxford: Oxford University Press.

MYHILL, JOHN (1995). 'Change and Continuity in the Functions of the American English Modals'. *Linguistics*, 33/2: 157–211.

NAGASHIMA, DAISUKE (1968). 'Mutual Debt between Johnson and Lowth: A Contribution to the History of English Grammar'. *Studies in English Literature* (Japan), 44: 221–32.

NANGLE, BENJAMIN CHRISTIE (1934). *The Monthly Review: First Series 1749–1789: Indexes of Contributors and Articles*. Oxford: Clarendon Press.

NATIONAL LIBRARY OF AUSTRALIA <http://catalogue.nla.gov.au/> (consulted summer 2009).

NAVEST, KARLIJN (2007). 'Marginalia as Evidence: The Unidentified Hands in Lowth's *Short Introduction to English Grammar* (1762)'. *Historiographia Linguistica*, 34/1: 1–18.

—— (2006). 'An Index of Names to Lowth's *Short Introduction to English Grammar* (1762), (1763), (1764)'. *Historical Sociolinguistics and Sociohistorical Linguistics*, 6. <www.let.leidenuniv.nl/hsl_shl/> (accessed May 2007).

—— (2008). '"Borrowing a Few Passages": Lady Ellenor Fenn and her use of sources', in Tieken-Boon van Ostade (ed.) (2008e), 223–43.

—— (2009). 'Reading Lessons for "Baby Grammarians": Lady Ellenor Fenn and the Teaching of English Grammar', in Morag Styles and Evelyn Arizpe (eds.), *Acts of Reading: Teachers, Text, and Childhood*. Stoke-on-Trent: Trentham, 73–86.

—— (in preparation). 'John Ash and the Rise of the Children's Grammar'. PhD thesis, University of Leiden.

NEVALAINEN, TERTTU, and RAUMOLIN-BRUNBERG, HELENA (2003). *Historical Sociolinguistics*. London: Longman.

—— and TANSKANEN, SANNA-KAISA (eds.) (2004). *Letter Writing*. Special Issue of *Journal of Historical Pragmatics*, 5/2.

—— and TIEKEN-BOON VAN OSTADE, INGRID (2006). 'Standardisation', in Richard Hogg and David Denison (eds.), *A History of the English Language*. Cambridge: Cambridge University Press, 271–311.

NEVALAINEN, TERTTU, and KAHLAS-TARKKA, LEENA (eds.) (1997). *To Explain the Present: Studies in the Changing English Language in Honour of Matti Rissanen.* Helsinki: Société Néophilologique.

NURMI, ARJA, and PALANDER-COLLIN, MINNA (2008). 'Letters as a Text Type: Interaction in Writing,' in Dossena and Tieken-Boon van Ostade (eds.), 21–49.

ODNB: The Oxford Dictionary of National Biography. Online edition, <www. oxforddnb.com/>.

OED Online: The Oxford English Dictionary. Online edition, <www.oed.com>.

Old Bailey Online: <www.oldbaileyonline.org/>.

OLDIREVA, LARISA (1999). '*Catched* or *Caught*: Towards the Standard Use of Irregular Verbs', in Irma Taavitsainen, Gunnel Melchers, and Päivi Pahta (eds.), *Writing in Nonstandard English*. Amsterdam/Philadelphia: John Benjamins. 263–84.

OLDIREVA GUSTAFSSON, LARISA (2002*a*). *Preterite and Past Participle Forms in English 1680–1790.* Uppsala: University of Uppsala.

—— (2002*b*). 'Variation in Usage and Grammars: The Past Participle Forms of *Write* in English 1680–1790'. *Historical Sociolinguistics and Sociohistorical Linguistics*, 2. <www.let.leidenuniv.nl/hsl_shl/index.html>.

OSSELTON, N. E. (1963). 'Formal and Informal Spelling in the 18th Century: *Errour, Honor*, and Related Words'. *English Studies*, 44: 267–75.

—— (1984). 'Informal Spelling Systems in Early Modern English: 1500–1800', in N. F. Blake and Charles Jones (eds.), *English Historical Linguistics: Studies in Development*. Sheffield: CECTAL, 123–36.

Oxford Advanced Learner's Encyclopedic Dictionary (1992). (Reprint, 1993.) Oxford: Oxford University Press.

PERCY, CAROL (1996). 'In the Margins: Dr Hawkesworth's Editorial Emendations to the Language of Captain Cook's *Voyages*'. *English Studies*, 6: 549–78.

—— (1997). 'Paradigms Lost: Bishop Lowth and the "Poetic Dialect" in his English Grammar'. *Neophilologus*, 81: 129–44.

—— (2008). 'Mid-Century Grammars and their Reception in the *Monthly Review* and the *Critical Review*', in Tieken-Boon van Ostade (ed.) (2008*e*), 125–42.

—— (2009). 'Periodical Reviews and the Rise of Prescriptivism: The *Monthly* (1749–1844) and *Critical Review* (1756–1817) in the Eighteenth Century', in Tieken-Boon van Ostade and van der Wurff (eds.), 117–50.

—— 'Database of Linguistic and Stylistic Criticism in Eighteenth-Century Periodical Reviews'. <www.chass.utoronto.ca/reviews/>.

PHILLIPPS, K. C. (1970). *Jane Austen's English.* London: André Deutsch.

PINKER, STEVEN (1994). *The Language Instinct: The New Science of Language and Mind.* London: Penguin.

POLDAUF, IAN (1948). *On the History of some Problems of English Grammar before 1800.* Prague: University Karlovy.

POTTLE, FREDERICK A., and BENNETT, CHARLES H. (1963). *Boswell's Journal of a Tour to the Hebrides with Samuel Johnson, LL.D., 1773*. Melbourne: Heinemann, with Yale University.

PULLUM, GEOFFREY (1974). 'Lowth's Grammar: A Re-Evaluation'. *Linguistics*, 137: 63–78.

—— (2008). 'Prescriptive Grammar in America: The Land of the Free and The Elements of Style'. Paper presented at the workshop Normative Linguistics, ISLE-1, Freiburg, October 2008.

QUIRK, RANDOLPH, GREENBAUM, SIDNEY, LEECH, GEOFFREY, and SVARTVIK, JAN (1985). *A Comprehensive Grammar of the English Language*. New York: Longman.

RAVEN, JAMES (1996). 'From Promotion to Proscription: Arrangements for Reading and Eighteenth-Century Libraries', in James Raven, Helen Small, and Naomi Tadmor (eds.), *The Practice and Representation of Reading in England*. Cambridge: Cambridge University Press, 175–201.

REDDICK, ALLEN (1996). *The Making of Johnson's Dictionary 1746–1773*. (Revised edition.) Cambridge: Cambridge University Press.

REIBEL, DAVID (ed.) (1995). *Robert Lowth. The Major Works*. London: Routledge/Thoemmes Press.

REID, S. W. (1977). 'An Index to Robert Lowth's Short Introduction to English Grammar'. *Studia Neophilologica*, 49: 135–7.

RODRÍGUEZ-GIL, MARÍA E. (2003). 'Ann Fisher, Descriptive or Prescriptive Grammarian?'. *Linguistica e Filologia*, 17: 183–203.

RUBERG, WILLEMIJN (2008). 'Epistolary and Emotional Education. The Letters of an Irish Father to his Daughter, 1747–1752'. *Paedagogica Historica*, 44: 207–18.

RYDÉN, MATS, and BRORSTRÖM, SVERKER (1987). *The Be/Have Variation with Intransitives in English*. Stockholm: Almqvist & Wiksell International.

SAIRIO, ANNI (2005). '"Sam of Streatham Park": A Linguistic Study of Dr. Johnson's Membership in the Thrale Family'. *European Journal of English Studies*, 9/1: 21–35.

—— (2008). 'Bluestocking Letters and the Influence of Eighteenth-Century Grammars', in Dossena and Tieken-Boon van Ostade (eds.), 137–62.

—— (2009). *Language and Letters of the Bluestocking Network. Sociolinguistic Issues in Eighteenth-Century Epistolary English*. Helsinki: Société Néophilologique.

SCHLAUCH, MARGARET (1959). *The English Language in Modern Times (since 1400)*. Warszawa: Państwowe Wydawnictwo Naukowe.

SCHOFELD, ROBERT E. (1997). *The Enlightenment of Joseph Priestley. A Study of his Life and Work from 1733 to 1773*. University Park, PA: The Pennsylvania State University Press.

SHER, RICHARD B. (2006). *The Enlightenment and the Book. Scottish Authors & their Publishers in Eighteenth-Century Britain, Ireland & America.* Chicago: University of Chicago Press.

SLEDD, JAMES H., and KOLB, GWIN J. (1955). *Dr. Johnson's Dictionary.* Chicago: University of Chicago Press.

SMEND, RUDOLF (2004). 'Lowth in Deutschland', in *Bibel und Wissenschaft. Historische Aufsätze.* Tübingen: Mohr Siebeck, 51–70.

SMITH, ROBIN D. (1998). 'Eighteenth-Century Linguistics and Authorship: The cases of Dyche, Priestley, and Buchanan', in Jacek Fisiak and Marcin Krygier (eds.), *Advances in English Historical Linguistics (1996).* Berlin and New York: Mouton de Gruyter, 435–41.

SOLOMON, HARRY M. (1996). *The Rise of Robert Dodsley. Creating the New Age of Print.* Carbondale and Edwardsville: Southern Illinois University Press.

SØRENSEN, KNUD (1984). 'Charles Dickens: Linguistic Innovator'. *English Studies,* 65: 237–47.

SPECK, W. A. (1982). 'Politicians, Peers, and Publication by Subscription 1700–50', in Isabel Rivers (ed.), *Books and their Readers in Eighteenth-century England.* New York: St Martin's Press, 47–68.

STAMMERJOHANN, HARRO (gen. ed.) (1996). *Lexicon Grammaticorum: Who's Who in the History of World Linguistics.* Tübingen: Niemeyer.

STAVES, SUSAN (2003). 'Church of England Clergy and Women Writers', in Nicole Pohl and Betty A. Schellenberg (eds.), *Reconsidering the Bluestockings.* San Marino: Huntington Library Press, 81–103.

STEIN, DIETER, and TIEKEN-BOON VAN OSTADE, INGRID (eds.) (1994). *Towards a Standard English 1600–1800.* Berlin/New York: Mouton de Gruyter.

STEVICK, PHILIP (ed.) (1971). Samuel Richardson, *Clarissa.* San Francisco: Rinehart Press.

STONE, LAWRENCE (1990). *The Family, Sex and Marriage in England, 1500–1800.* London: Penguin.

STRAAIJER, ROBIN (2009). 'Deontic and Epistemic Modals as Indicators of Prescriptive and Descriptive Language in the Grammars by Joseph Priestley and Robert Lowth', in Tieken-Boon van Ostade and van der Wurff (eds.), 57–87.

SUAREZ, MICHAEL F. (2000). 'The Business of Literature: The Book Trade in England from Milton to Blake', in David Womersley (ed.), *A Companion to Literature from Milton to Blake.* Oxford: Blackwell, 131–47.

SUBBIONDO, JOSEPH (1992). 'John Wallis' *Grammatica Linguae Anglicanae* (1653): The New Science and English Grammar', in Anders Ahlqvist (ed.), *Diversions of Galway. Papers on the History of Linguistics.* Amsterdam/Philadelphia: John Benjamins, 183–90.

SUNDBY, BERTIL, BJØRGE, ANNE KARI, and HAUGLAND, KARI E. (1991). *A Dictionary of English Normative Grammar 1700–1800*. Amsterdam: John Benjamins.

TANSKANEN, SANNA-KAISA (2004). 'Intertextual Networks in the Correspondence of Lady Katherine Paston', in Nevalainen and Tanskanen (eds.), 255–69.

TELFORD, JOHN (1931). *The Letters of John Wesley*. London: Epworth Press. <http://wesley.nnu.edu/john_wesley/letters/index.htm> (consulted summer 2009).

TIEKEN-BOON VAN OSTADE, INGRID (1982). 'Double Negation and Eighteenth-Century English Grammars'. *Neophilologus*, 66: 278–85.

—— (1985). '"I Will be Drowned and No Man Shall Save Me": The Conventional Rules for *Shall* and *Will* in Eighteenth-Century English Grammars'. *English Studies*, 66: 123–42.

—— (1987). *The Auxiliary Do in Eighteenth-Century English: A Sociohistorical Linguistic Approach*. Dordrecht: Foris.

—— (1988). 'Dr. Johnson and the Auxiliary *Do*'. *Hiroshima Studies in English Language and Literature*, 33: 22–39. (Also published in 1991 in *Folia Linguistica Historica* X/1: 145–62.)

—— (1990). 'Drydens versies van *The Tempest* en *Troilus and Cressida*: De bewerker als purist', in J. B. den Besten et al. (eds.), *Traditie & Progressie. Handelingen van het 40ste Nederlands Filologencongres*. 's Gravenhage: SDU Uitgeverij, 161–9.

—— (1991). 'Samuel Richardson's Role as Linguistic Innovator: A Sociolinguistic Analysis', in Ingrid Tieken-Boon van Ostade and John Frankis (eds.), *Language, Usage and Description*. Amsterdam/Atlanta, GA: Rodopi, 47–57.

—— (1992). 'John Kirkby and *The Practice of Speaking and Writing English*: Identification of a Manuscript'. *Leeds Studies in English*, 23: 157–79.

—— (1994). 'Standard and Non-Standard Pronominal Usage in English, with Special Reference to the Eighteenth Century', in Stein and Tieken-Boon van Ostade (eds.), 217–42.

—— (1996a). 'Two Hundred Years of Lindley Murray: An Introduction', in Tieken-Boon van Ostade (ed.) (1996d), 9–25.

—— (1996b). 'Lindley Murray and the Concept of Plagiarism', in Tieken-Boon van Ostade (ed.) (1996d), 81–96.

—— (1996c). 'Social Network Theory and Eighteenth-Century English: The Case of Boswell', in Derek Britton (ed.), *English Historical Linguistics 1994*. Amsterdam/Philadelphia: John Benjamins, 327–37.

—— (ed.) (1996d). *Two Hundred Years of Lindley Murray*. Münster: Nodus Publikationen.

—— (1997). 'Lowth's Corpus of Prescriptivism', in Nevalainen and Kahlas-Tarkka (eds.), 451–63.

TIEKEN-BOON VAN OSTADE (1999). 'Of Formulas and Friends: Expressions of Politeness in John Gay's Letters', in Guy A. J. Tops, Betty Devriendt, and Steven Geukens (eds.), *Thinking English Grammar. To Honour Xavier Dekeyser, Professor Emeritus*. Leuven/Paris: Peeters, 99–112.

—— (2000*a*). 'Normative Studies in England', in Sylvain Auroux, E. F. K. Koerner, Hans-Josef Niederehe, and Kees Versteegh (eds.), *History of the Language Sciences/Geschichte der Sprachwissenschaften/Histoire des Sciences du Langage*. (Volume 1.) Berlin/New York: Walter de Gruyter, 876–87.

—— (2000*b*). 'Sociohistorical Linguistics and the Observer's Paradox', in Kastovsky and Mettinger (eds.), 441–61.

—— (2000*c*). 'Of Norms and Networks'. Plenary Paper Presented at the 11th International Conference for Historical Linguistics, Santiago de Compostela, September 2000.

—— (2001). 'Lowth's *Short Introduction to English Grammar* Reprinted'. *Publishing History*, 49: 83–95.

—— (2002*a*). 'Robert Lowth and the Strong Verb System'. *Language Sciences*, 24: 459–69.

—— (2002*b*). '*You Was* and Eighteenth-Century Normative Grammar', in Katja Lenz and Ruth Möhlig (eds.), *Of Dyuersite & Chaunge of Langage: Essays Presented to Manfred Görlach on the Occasion of his 65th Birthday*. Heidelberg: C. Winter Universitätsverlag, 88–102.

—— (2002*c*). 'Robert Lowth and the Corpus of Early English Correspondence', in Helena Raumolin-Brunberg, Minna Nevala, Arja Nurmi, and Matti Rissanen (eds.), *Variation Past and Present. VARIENG Studies on English for Terttu Nevalainen*. Helsinki: Société Néophilologique, 161–72.

—— (2005). 'Eighteenth-Century English Letters: In Search of the Vernacular'. *Linguistica e Filologia*, 21: 113–46.

—— (2006*a*). 'Eighteenth-Century Prescriptivism and the Norm of Correctness', in Ans van Kemenade and Bettelou Los (eds.), *The Handbook of the History of English*. Oxford: Blackwell, 539–57.

—— (2006*b*). '"Disrespectful and too Familiar"? Abbreviations as an Index of Politeness in Eighteenth-Century Letters', in Christiane Dalton-Puffer, Nikolaus Ritt, Herbert Schendl, and Dieter Kastovsky (eds.), *Syntax, Style and Grammatical Norms: English from 1500–2000*. Frankfurt and Bern: Peter Lang, 229–47.

—— (2008*a*). 'The 1760s: Grammars, Grammarians and the Booksellers', in Tieken-Boon van Ostade (ed.) (2008*e*), 101–24.

—— (2008*b*). 'The Codifiers and the History of Multiple Negation in English, or, Why were 18th-Century Grammarians so Obsessed with Double Negation?', in Beal, Nocera, and Sturiale (eds.), 197–214.

—— (2008c). 'Grammars, Grammarians and Grammar Writing: An Introduction', in Tieken-Boon van Ostade (ed.) (2008e), 1–14.

—— (2008d). 'Henry Fowler and his Eighteenth-Century Predecessors'. *Bulletin of the Henry Sweet Society of the History of Linguistic Ideas*, 51: 5–24.

—— (ed.) (2008e). *Grammars, Grammarians and Grammar Writing in Eighteenth-Century England*. Berlin/New York: Mouton de Gruyter.

—— (2010). 'Lowth as an Icon of Prescriptivism', in Raymond Hickey (ed.), *Ideology and Change in Late Modern English*. Cambridge: Cambridge University Press. 73–88.

—— (forthcoming). 'Age and the Codification of the English Language', in Anna Ouszak and Urszula Okulska (eds.), *Language, Culture and the Dynamics of Age*. Berlin/New York: Mouton de Gruyter.

—— and BAX, RANDY (2002). 'Of Dodsley's Projects and Linguistic Influence: The Language of Johnson and Lowth'. *Historical Sociolinguistics and Sociohistorical Linguistics*, 2. <www.let.leidenuniv.nl/hsl_shl/index.html>

—— and NAVEST, KARLIJN (2006). 'Introduction' to Karlijn Navest (2006), 'An Index of Names to Lowth's *Short Introduction to English Grammar* (1762), (1763), (1764)'. *Historical Sociolinguistics and Sociohistorical Linguistics*. <www.let.leidenuniv.nl/hsl_shl/>.

—— and VAN DER WURFF, WIM (eds.) (2009). *Current Issues and Late Modern English*. Bern: Peter Lang.

—— (forthcoming). 'Age and the Codification of the English Language', in Anna Duszak and Urszula Okulska (eds), *Language, Culture and the Dynamics of Age*. Berlin/New York: Mouton de Gruyter.

TIERNEY, JAMES E. (1988). *The Correspondence of Robert Dodsley 1733–1764*. Cambridge: Cambridge University Press.

TRAUGOTT, ELIZABETH CLOSS, and ROMAINE, SUZANNE (1985). 'Some Questions for the Definition of "Style" in Socio-Historical Linguistics'. *Folia Linguistica Historica*, VI/1: 7–39.

TRUDGILL, PETER (1997). 'Review of John Honey, *Language is power*'. *Journal of Sociolinguistics*, 2/3: 457–61.

—— (2003). *A Glossary of Sociolinguistics*. Oxford: Oxford University Press.

TUCKER, SUSIE (1967). *Protean Shape. A Study in Eighteenth-Century Vocabulary and Usage*. London: The Athlone Press.

UHRSTRÖM, WILHELM (1907). *Studies on the Language of Samuel Richardson*. Uppsala: Almqvist & Wiksell.

VALLINS, G. H. (1957). *The Wesleys and the English Language*. London: The Epworth Press.

VICKERY, AMANDA (1998). *The Gentleman's Daughter. Women's Lives in Georgian England*. New Haven and London: Yale University Press.

VIÑA ROUCO, MAR (2005). 'Metodología Inductiva y Deductiva en la Enseñanza de las Lenguas Vivas en España en el Siglo XIX'. *Porta Linguarum*, 4: 185–200.

VISSER, F. Th. (1963–73). *An Historical Syntax of the English Language.* (Four volumes.) Leiden: E. J. Brill.

VORLAT, EMMA (1959). 'The Sources of Lindley Murray's "The English Grammar"'. *Leuvense Bijdragen,* 48: 108–125.

—— (1975). *The Development of English Grammatical Theory, 1586–1737, with Special Reference to the Theory of Parts of Speech.* Leuven: Leuven University Press.

—— (1979). 'Criteria of Grammaticalness in 16th and 17th Century English Grammar'. *Leuvense Bijdragen,* 68/2: 129–40.

—— (1996). 'Lindley Murray's Prescriptive Canon', in Tieken-Boon van Ostade (ed.) (1996*d*), 163–82.

—— (1999). 'Robert Baker's Dependance on Vaugelas'. *Beiträge zur Geschichte der Sprachwissenschaft,* 9/1: 1–19.

—— (2001). 'Lexical Rules in Robert Baker's "Reflections on the English Language"'. *Leuvense Bijdragen.* 90/4: 391–401.

—— (2007), 'On the History of English Teaching Grammars', in Peter Schmitter (ed.), *Sprachtheorien der Neuzeit III/2.* Tübingen: Gunter Narr Verlag, 500–25.

WATTS, RICHARD (1999). 'The Social Construction of Standard English: Grammar Writers as a "Discourse Community"', in Tony Bex and Richard Watts (eds.), *Standard English. The Widening Debate.* London: Routledge, 40–68.

—— (2008). 'Grammar-Writers in Eighteenth-Century Britain: A Community of Practice or a Discourse Community?', in Tieken-Boon van Ostade (ed.) (2008*e*), 37–56.

WEIS, CHARLES MC., and POTTLE, FREDERICK A. (eds.) (1971). *Boswell in Extremes, 1776–1778.* London: Heinemann.

WENGER, ETIENNE (1998). *Communities of Practice.* Cambridge: Cambridge University Press.

WILHELM, F. A. (2005). *English in the Netherlands. A History of Foreign Language Teaching 1800–1920.* Utrecht: Gopher Publishers.

WIMSATT, WILLIAM K., and POTTLE, FREDERICK A. (eds.) (1960). *Boswell for the Defence: 1769–1774.* Melbourne: Heinemann.

WOOLL, JOHN (1806). *Biographical Memoirs of the late Rev^d. Joseph Warton, D.D..* London: T. and W. Davies. (Facsimile reprint, Farnborough: Gregg, 1969.)

WRIGHT, AUSTIN (1950). *Joseph Spence. A Critical Biography.* Chicago: University of Chicago Press.

WRIGHT, SUSAN (1994). 'The Critic and the Grammarians: Joseph Addison and the Prescriptivists', in Stein and Tieken-Boon van Ostade (eds.), 243–84.

YÁÑEZ-BOUZA, NURIA (2008). 'Preposition Stranding in the Eighteenth Century: *Something to Talk About*', in Tieken-Boon van Ostade (ed.) (2008*e*), 251–77.

—— (2009). 'If Scotsmen and Irishmen were to "Fix a Standard" … Attitudes to "Correct" English in 18th-Century Grammar-Writers'. Paper presented at the conference 'Prescriptivism(e) & Patriotism(e)', August 2009, Toronto.

INDEX